# ABELARD AND HELOISE

# THE LETTERS
## AND OTHER WRITINGS

# ABELARD AND HELOISE

# THE LETTERS
# AND OTHER WRITINGS

Translated
with Introduction and Notes, by

## WILLIAM LEVITAN

## SELECTED SONGS AND POEMS

Translated by Stanley Lombardo
and by Barbara Thorburn

Hackett Publishing Company, Inc.
Indianapolis/Cambridge

For further information, please address:

Hackett Publishing Company, Inc.
P.O. Box 44937
Indianapolis, IN 46244-0937

www.hackettpublishing.com

Cover design by William Levitan and Abigail Coyle
Composition by William Hartman

Library of Congress Cataloging-in-Publication Data

Abelard, Peter, 1079–1142.
    [Selections. English. 2007]
    The letters and other writings / Abelard and Heloise;  translated,
with introduction and notes, by William Levitan ; selected songs and
poems translated by Stanley Lombardo and by Barbara Thorburn.
      p. cm.
    Includes bibliographical references and index.
    ISBN 978-0-87220-876-6 — ISBN 978-0-87220-875-9 (pbk.)
    1. Abelard, Peter, 1079–1142—Correspondence.   2. Heloïse,
1101–1164—Correspondence.   3. Abbesses, Christian—France—
Correspondence.   4. Theologians—France—Correspondence.
5. Love-letters.   6. Hymns.   7. Poetry.   I. Héloïse, 1101–1164.
II. Levitan, William.   III. Title.
B765.A21L48 2007
189'.4--dc22
[B]
                 2006034700

FOR

DEBRA

*Mellificas enim tu, sed non soli tibi.*

# CONTENTS

# Acknowledgments

Like every student of Abelard and Heloise, I am indebted to a large number of critics and scholars, many of whose names appear in the select bibliography at the end of this volume. There is a smaller group, however, whose work I have found especially useful and continually stimulating throughout the course of this project: Michael Clanchy, Peter Dronke, David Luscombe, John Marenbon, the late Mary Martin McLaughlin, T. P. McLaughlin, and J. T. Muckle. In the absence of standard commentaries, I have freely consulted earlier translations for a community of opinion on many specific points; even when our interpretations and approaches differ, I have learned a great deal as a reader and translator from, in particular, the clarity of J. T. Muckle, the learned grace of Betty Radice, the wry idiosyncrasy of C. K. Scott Moncrieff (if the verb "perpend" has never been restored to common English usage, it was not for the lack of his example), and the vivacity of Jean de Meun.

I count it as my privilege to have carried on this work in the company of collaborators, students, and colleagues, so many of whom are also friends. I am especially grateful to Stanley Lombardo and Barbara Thorburn not only for their brilliant translations of Abelard's poetry but also for their encouragement and perceptive criticism of my own translations of Abelard and Heloise's prose. Roger Gilles, Sue Stauffacher, Adam Thorburn, and David Thorburn read large sections of the book in draft with empathy and careful discrimination. Bruce O'Brien discussed problems of translation with me and provided essential guidance on many historical points. Lloyd Gerson kindly lent his advice and suggestions on questions of medieval dialectic. Ben Lockerd and Micheline Lockerd were crucially helpful on matters of Church liturgy. They have my deepest thanks. I also thank many others whose interest, insight, and support proved invaluable at various junctures throughout the work, in particular, Kathleen Blumreich, Patricia Clark, Coeli Fitzpatrick, Asli Gocer, Ginny Klingenberg, Herb Levitan, Jim Muehlemann, Kathy Muehlemann, Mark Pestana, Soula Proxenos, Jerilyn Perrine, and Lois Tyson.

Audiences at Grand Valley State University, Michigan State University, and the University of Kansas provided important sounding boards for much of the material in the book. For their suggestions and stimulating discussion, I particularly thank the members of the MSU seminar on women and the problem of agency in the pre-modern era, especially Katie Dubois, Julia Holderness, Emily Klockenkemper, and Katharyn Lowerre. My friends at Middlebury College provided both a warm welcome and a congenial nest for the incubation of the earliest parts of the book; Grand Valley State University provided support in the form of a sabbatical leave, during which the latter parts were completed. I am grateful, too, for the friendship and conversation of Stephen Donadio, editor of *New England Review,* where earlier versions of the *Calamities* and the First and Third Letters have appeared.

From its first conception, this book has been for Debra Nails, who has also played a profound role in its development. Sometime collaborator, assiduous reader, trenchant critic, and constant inspiration, she has left marks of her judgment and example on nearly every page. If the tones of authentic moral passion and devotion ring true at any point in these translations, it is because I heard them in her voice. For all of this, the dedication of a volume can be only the merest shadow of my thanks.

WL

# INTRODUCTION

The story of Abelard and Heloise is, in the first instance, a story of tragic love, one so firmly established in the canon of such stories that its contours are familiar even to those who may not recognize the names. The stormy, charismatic instructor; his brilliant, unconventional student; the explosion of sexual passion and the radical act of violence that alters their lives forever; the decades of separation and inconsolable longing—who does not know that story in some form? Yet like every story of actual individuals, theirs has more than one dimension. It is also a story of fierce *intellectual* passion, of the commitment to reason and to the ideals of the philosophical life; a story of the conflicting logics of celebrity and solitude, of the tensions between the public and private person and between public and private ambitions. It is a story, too, of identity formation, of a struggle for a certain kind of self-definition and of the limits beyond which self-definition cannot go. It becomes a story also of making-do, of carrying-on, of the determination to fashion a useful life for oneself under trying and disappointing circumstances; a story of absence and remarkable endurance. To no small degree, it is a story of complex ego projection—of each of the pair onto the other, of both of them onto themselves, and of nearly 900 years of readers and scholars onto Abelard and Heloise together. For some, it is a story of sin and redemption.

To any version of the story, the writings of Abelard and Heloise must be central, and in particular their famous correspondence. More than raw data for the story, these writings are part of the story themselves. Abelard and Heloise were both renowned as creatures of the written word well before they ever met, Abelard as a teacher and philosopher, Heloise as the most learned woman in the France of her time, versed in Hebrew and Greek as well as the Latin classics. The habits of high literacy were woven into the fabric of their lives. A good part of their earliest relationship, they both tell us, revolved around their reading and their writing, and by the time they came to write their extant letters, their writing had assumed an even more urgent role than it had before. The defining events of their lives—their tumultuous love affair and marriage, his brutal castration at the hands of her kinsmen, and their subsequent entrance into religious orders—had taken place perhaps as long as fifteen years earlier; Heloise was now abbess of the convent of the Paraclete on the banks of the Ardusson River in the countryside near Troyes, while Abelard was some 350 miles away, the reformist head of a rebellious monastery in Brittany and, ever the magnet for calamity, under constant threat of assassination. Under the conditions of this complex separation—in space, time, and circumstance—only one way remained open to them as a recompense for other absences: their entire relationship, the obligations each had to the other, to the past they had in common, and to a future each hoped very differently to define, all now had to be matters for the written word. The letters became events in a continuing story, intentional acts of serious consequence with a public as well as a private function. Abelard and Heloise wrote from the justified conviction that their writing mattered, and to more than themselves alone; Heloise in particular often wrote as if the world depended on each sentence. Few works in Latin literature approach the urgency of these letters, their poignancy, or sense of personal drama. Few project more vivid, complex voices. Few works are more scandalous and frank, yet remain as strictly disciplined by a hard intellectual rigor. None was written as part of a more compelling story.

## ABELARD IN THE *CALAMITIES*

Abelard tells his own story in the *Calamities*. It is in fact the chief source for the events of his life throughout the early 1130s, a vivid memoir of his rise to prominence as the foremost European philosopher of the twelfth century and the most charismatic teacher since the end of the ancient world, and also of the appalling set of adversities he faced.[1] The traditional Latin title of the work, *Historia Calamitatum*, was not assigned by Abelard himself but dates from the fourteenth century, deriving from the phrase "history of my calamities" in the last section as an apt description of its contents. In form, the *Calamities* is couched as a letter of consolation to an unnamed and almost certainly fictitious friend, who provides a rhetorical pretext for an account of Abelard's life. Its truer purpose and intended audience, however, may be surmised from the circumstances surrounding its composition. The *Calamities* was written

---

[1] Clanchy 1997 provides a fine, full biography of Abelard; Marenbon 1997, 7–35, an excellent biographical sketch.

around 1132 or 1133—the earliest possible date is provided by its reference to the papal charter granted to the nuns of the Paraclete in November, 1131—while Abelard was living in Brittany as abbot of the monastery of St. Gildas of Rhuys under the dangerous conditions the memoir describes. By 1136 at the latest, however, he was reestablished as a teacher in Paris. It is reasonable to see the *Calamities*, then, as part of a successful campaign of public rehabilitation, with different segments of Abelard's audience needing assurance on different points of his extremely checkered past. This at least explains much of what may seem inconsistent in the letter, the remarkable range of distinct tones and poses Abelard assumes throughout the work—now repentant and reformed, now unreconstructed and gleefully defiant, now defensive, now triumphant, now maudlin and self-pitying, now just trying to set the record straight—as well as the shifting causes he posits for events, and the shifting moral lessons he would have the reader draw from the example of his life.

The letter presents both an offense and a defense. On the one hand, it offers continual reminders of Abelard's well-known intellectual powers, his success with students, and the support he could expect to receive in certain secular and ecclesiastical quarters. On the other hand, it rebuts specific charges that had been laid against him. The charge of habitual womanizing in his earlier life Abelard flatly denies; the charge of taking up teaching under possibly inappropriate circumstances as a monk he answers on the simple grounds that he was forced to it, by the insistence of others in one case and by dire poverty in another. For the rest, he defends himself by pointing to the misunderstanding, ignorance, incompetence, or envy and malice of others. The *Calamities* proceeds episodically, then, from Abelard's first entrance into the field of philosophy. It recounts his difficult relations with his teachers, William of Champeaux and Anselm of Laon; his establishment as a teacher himself at the cathedral school in Paris; his affair with Heloise, their marriage, and his castration; his troubles at the abbey of St. Denis and his first resumption of teaching as a monk; his condemnation at the Council of Soissons; his further troubles at St. Denis, foundation of the hermitage of the Paraclete, and second resumption of teaching; the continual attacks by "a pair of new apostles," Norbert of Xanten and Bernard of Clairvaux; his subsequent retreat to St. Gildas; his refoundation of the Paraclete as a convent of nuns under Heloise's direction and the further attacks on him that it occasioned. By the end of the story, Abelard is in desperate straits, "a vagabond and fugitive on the earth, . . . tormented without end," and in constant fear for his life, but nonetheless resigned to the will of God. Throughout all the cycles of these disasters, only in his early relationship with Heloise does Abelard depict himself as significantly at fault.

As a memoir and a narrative that seeks to reveal some order in a life, the *Calamities* is certainly a rich, compelling work. Some of its undoubted power stems from the very narrowness of its focus. Great social, political, and intellectual movements—even those in which Abelard himself played considerable roles—exist only as dim background or at most emerge in the form of personal encounters with individual antagonists or supporters, most of whom remain unnamed. The focus stays on Abelard himself and the particular pattern of his interaction with the world, what he calls "the string of my calamities, which has continued unbroken until the present day." Yet, for all its personal focus and straightforward narrative vigor, the *Calamities* has little of the penetrating self-analysis or confidence in life's direction found in other memoirs—most notably the *Confessions* of Augustine—which Abelard could have taken up as models if he had wished. Only rarely does he show much critical self-awareness, and readers may be struck by the unattractive figure he often cuts in his own pages. To a certain extent, I think, this is deliberate and in places even overdone, as perhaps it is in his account of the affair with Heloise, where he, Heloise, and Fulbert are temporarily cast as stock characters in a farce: the cunning, cold seducer; the young innocent; and the poor, deluded cuckold, butt of jokes. Here, the motive is in part protective, I suspect—for Abelard to take all the moral burden on himself and shield, to the extent he can, the now widely respected abbess of the Paraclete—and also in part justificatory—to magnify the crime to the proportions of its punishment. But in general it is hard to account for Abelard's repeated assertions of his brilliance and repeated displays of his supreme self-confidence as anything but ingrained parts of Abelard himself and integral to the fabric of his story.

Vanity and its comeuppance are surely not adequate terms for the pattern Abelard describes. There are gifted individuals in every field who are notoriously aware of their own gifts, individuals of enormous originality, talent, and achievement whose high opinion of themselves is well deserved. They also may be charismatic individuals, who easily inspire fierce loyalty among a following and as fierce an enmity among others. The enmity in fact can be essential to the way such people exist in the world—a way that is not always of their choosing—part of a dynamic of self-realization, in which scenes of confrontation are repeatedly enacted as means by which the self is then repeatedly enforced. The great tragic paradigms of Prometheus or Socrates come to mind, but there is no need to invoke them in order to understand the company Peter Abelard is in; scores of memoirs point to the same dynamic. Arrogance and one-upmanship are endemic human diseases, and so, too, are envy and resentment; and any may be played out against a background of larger, though still shadowy, forces. When the dynamic of self-realization spins out of control, when its stakes become critical, how can one distinguish among these factors and point to one as the single cause? The question is as pertinent to Abelard's *Calamities* as it was in the matter of J. Robert Oppenheimer, the great atomic physicist whose fall from public grace became a *cause célèbre* in the depths of the Cold War.

The *Calamities* does not work progressively to a single narrative goal but rather in cycles through series of repetitions, small and large. Any resolution the narrative seems to establish quickly proves illusory. "At last I reached Paris," Abelard says with an air of finality early in the work, but he is forced to leave the city and in fact leaves several times. Later, and again with an air of finality: "So after a few days, I returned to Paris, back to the school which had long been destined for me, which had once been offered to me, and from which I had at first been expelled." Much of the motion of the first part of the *Calamities* consists of such inconclusive repetitions—to and from Paris, to and from Brittany, the shuffling of positions in the schools and in the town, virtually identical encounters with teachers and fellow students, the pattern of obstruction and overcoming, of others' hostility and his own greatness—all driven by envy, ambition, and political machination. The explanations themselves become a kind of mantra: "As my reputation grew, so other men's envy was kindled against me"; "His naked envy in fact won me wide support"; "But the more openly that man's malice hounded me, the more it confirmed my own stature"; "Persecution only added to my fame." Such a series could well go on indefinitely, or at least there is nothing in the nature of events or in the dynamic of self-realization itself to preclude such an extension.

All this appears to change, however, as Abelard approaches the affair with Heloise and the catastrophic event in his life that was, by its nature, irreversible and therefore unrepeatable—his castration. Just at what seems the culmination of his triumph, the narrative focus shifts to include a more general view and a different moral basis for events; at the same time, there is suddenly a new structure and a new meaning posited for the story:

> But success always puffs up the fool; worldly ease saps the strength of the mind and soon destroys it through the lures of the flesh. Now I thought I was the only philosopher in the world and had nothing to fear from anyone, and now I began to give free rein to my lust. . . . As I was weighed down by lechery and pride, the grace of God brought me relief from both . . . : first from my lechery, by cutting from me the means I used to practice it, and then from the pride born of my learning . . . by humbling me with the burning of the book of which I was most proud. . . . I had no dealings with common whores. . . . So fickle Fortune, as she's called, found a better way to seduce me and knock me down from my lofty perch—or perhaps it is better to say, for all my pride and blindness to the grace held out before me, God's mercy brought me low and claimed me for his own.

Abelard's castration, understandably enough, becomes a crisis, a point around which all of his life can be more neatly organized into a *before* and *after*, presented here in the traditional formulas of pride and fall, sin and grace. It also becomes a constant standard of reference throughout the rest of the *Calamities,* but in an unusual way. The castration is a unique event—in its violence, in its irreversibility, in Abelard's accepting at least some moral responsibility for it—but set against the calamities to come, it is consistently downplayed, as if negated or denied. Each new calamity, Abelard insists, was certainly far worse: "I set what I had suffered in my body against what I was suffering now. . . . That other betrayal seemed nothing next to this, far less painful that wound to my body than this to my reputation"; "My earlier troubles seemed nothing to me now"; "I suffer more from the cost to my reputation than the loss to my body." Even the pain from a fall from his horse, he says, "was far greater and more debilitating."

As the castration—at least in this one way—fades from sight, so too does the moral mechanism of divine punishment and, along with it, the narrative shape it temporarily imposes on the work. Abelard was to be punished for two things, as he saw it, his lechery and his pride, the latter by the burning of his book at the Council of Soissons. By the time he comes to describe the council, though, this perspective has entirely disappeared. He is forced to burn his book in a symbolic repetition of the literally unrepeatable castration, the formidable philosopher unmanned, cut down to the status of a pre-pubescent child, "the merest schoolboy," as he says. And behind this rank injustice, he insists, again lay the connivance of political ambition and the envy and incompetence of others. Immediately after the account of his castration, in fact, the whole earlier dynamic of repeated confrontation, repressed for an instant, returns with greater, even accelerating, force. Each new confrontation becomes more charged, each new iteration of calamity more perilous and insidious than the last. The return of such a structure of obsessive repetition means, among other things, that the true narrative crisis of the *Calamities* is always *impending*, never past, that no single episode will ever be definitive, but that, whatever conditions prevail at the start of any episode, they will remain recoverable in the next.

In his letters to Heloise written after the *Calamities*, Abelard insists that his situation at St. Gildas was at a point of crisis, the greatest he had faced. It became another crisis he was able to survive. He returned to Paris, resumed his teaching, and became a fountainhead of logic for yet another generation of students. But the pattern he describes in the *Calamities* survived as well. Within a few years, some new antagonists arose—"twisted men who twist all things," he calls them in his *Confession of Faith*—who were to bring about a new calamity. This time, however, there would be no further episode; Abelard died before he could recover.

In 1140, Abelard was charged with heresy by a no less formidable opponent than Bernard of Clairvaux. Although the charges were to be debated openly at a Church council scheduled for the town of Sens, Bernard met privately with the assembled bishops the evening before the council convened, read out the supposed heresies one by one, and had the bishops condemn them by reciting in unison, "*Damnamus*—We condemn it"—after each: when Abelard appeared before the council the next day, he would be faced—as he had been nineteen years earlier at Soissons—with a fait accompli. A bitter account of the proceedings by Berengar of Poitiers, one of Abelard's most partisan adherents, describes the evening meeting as a drunken affair, in which the sodden bishops could only mumble, "*'Namus*—We're aswim"—over their cups.[2] In

---

[2] For the plausibility of Berengar's account, despite its satiric intent, see Clanchy 1997, 309.

the morning, Abelard maneuvered to avoid Bernard's trap: rather than debate propositions that had already been privately condemned, he abruptly announced an appeal to the pope and left the assembly for Rome.

He got no further south than Burgundy, however, where the abbot of the great monastery of Cluny, Peter the Venerable, persuaded him to stay. An appeal to the pope was no longer possible: Innocent II had condemned Abelard's teaching within six weeks of the council's close, excommunicating him and ordering his books to be burned "wherever they might be found." Peter's diplomacy arranged for the excommunication to be lifted—the ban on Abelard's books was never rescinded, though it was widely ignored—and for Abelard to remain under the protection of Cluny. In an exchange of letters with Heloise after Abelard's death, Peter describes—perhaps with more tact than strict truth—the philosopher's final years as a model of Christian fortitude. Abelard died on April 21, 1142, and was buried at the Cluniac priory of St. Marcellus near Chalon-sur-Saône. In a striking act of humanity and homage, Peter had the body disinterred and escorted it himself to Heloise at the Paraclete, where Abelard had long desired to rest.

## HELOISE

Heloise has no analogous story, offered either by herself or anyone else. Evidence for the details of her external life is in fact so scarce that it is very difficult to imagine a narrative biography that is not merely a pendant to Abelard's *Calamities,* subordinating her existence to his in memory as strictly as she herself ever sought to do in life.[3] No wonder that even her most fervent admirers have tended to treat her as an emblem of some sort, perhaps an exalted but still a simplified device whose meaning resides elsewhere. To Jean de Meun and François Villon, she was *la belle Héloïse, la bonne Héloïse, la très sage Héloïse.* To the anonymous poet of the twelfth-century "Metamorphosis of Bishop Golias," she figured as the bride Philology.[4] On bumper stickers of the 1960s, she took on the whole burden of beleaguered womankind—ABELARD NEVER REALLY

[3] McLeod 1971 does what she can with limited material, and her account remains the fullest biography of Heloise to date.

[4] For the representation of Heloise in this poem, see Dronke 1976, 16–18.

LOVED HELOISE. Perhaps most notorious—because so perversely well-intentioned—is Henry Adams' characterization of her in his chapter on Abelard in *Mont Saint Michel and Chartres*:

> The twelfth century, with all its sparkle, would be dull without Abélard and Héloïse. With infinite regret, Héloïse must be left out of the story, because she was not a philosopher or a poet or an artist, but only a Frenchwoman to the last millimetre of her shadow.[5]

Even in the *Calamities* her name is mentioned only twice, and with such near-perfect symmetry in the narrative that a reader may suspect a symbolic purpose.[6] Both times, she seems merely called into the story to resolve some external impasse to Abelard's desires and to become the passive object of his interest—his lust in one instance, his charity in the other. But this is not how she remains. When, against all expectations, she opposes Abelard's wishes and argues vehemently and cogently against his proposal of marriage, the independence she always possessed becomes unmistakable.

When Heloise became Abelard's student, she was already a mature and formidable woman, in her mid- or late twenties at the time and famous throughout France for her learning.[7] This is what first brought her to Abelard's attention and to the notice of Peter the Venerable as far away as Burgundy. Learning was her most salient and stable characteristic and, I think, reveals more of Heloise as an intellectual, moral, and social being than even her love for Abelard can—a scholar "to the last millimetre of her shadow." To judge from her quotations and allusions, she was especially well versed in the works of Jerome, Augustine, Ovid, Virgil, and the Stoic writers Seneca, Lucan, Persius, and Cicero, though it is unlikely that Heloise would have identified a separate Stoic current in the stream of ancient thought—to her, as to others of her time, they were "philosophers"—but this only makes the Stoic exemplum more potent and

---

[5] Adams 1986, 270.

[6] That is, *Heloisa* 2,031 words from the beginning of the work and 2,231 from the end; elsewhere she is "she," "the girl," or something similar.

[7] For her birth around 1090 or slightly before, see Clanchy 1997, 173–74, in preference to the traditional date of 1100 or 1101 accepted by McLeod 1971, 8; Marenbon 1997, 14; and many others.

pervasive.[8] From her reading in general, she derived, as all readers must, a reservoir of precedents and possibilities with which to conceive and represent the world and a notion of a large intellectual culture of which she could see herself a part. From the Stoics in particular, she developed a more specific set of attitudes and ideas and a certain cast of mind that remained with her, at least as far as anyone can see, throughout her life.

There is, first a distinctive style of behavior, or a style at least of the verbal behavior recoverable in the record. Throughout her writing, Heloise tended to cast herself in a series of roles originated by the heroines of her classical reading—Lucan's Cornelia, Virgil's Eurydice and Dido, the abandoned women of myth in Ovid's *Heroides*, and even Jerome's Paula—taking their words and gestures for herself.[9] It is less learned imitation, though, than performance. From the Stoics of her reading, Heloise took up an appreciation for a kind of self-dramatization, a self displayed in a public theater through physical or verbal gestures that irresistibly command attention. What may strike some as stagey or operatic is in fact a mode endorsed by Stoic writers as an appropriate and effective means of moral communication, the establishment of a paradigmatic self. When Heloise takes the veil as a nun at Argenteuil, it is with a solemn theatrical grandeur, underscored by her quotation of Pompey's wife in Lucan's *Pharsalia*, as Abelard reports it in the *Calamities:*

> I remember many people tried to stop her . . . but they could not. Through her tears and sobs the best she could, she broke into Cornelia's great lament:
>
> > O my husband,
> > Too great for such a wife, had Fortune power
> > Even over you? The guilt was mine
> > For this disastrous marriage. Now claim your due,
> > And I will freely pay.

---

[8] Ebbesen 2004, 125, says of the Stoic strain in medieval thought, "Stoicism was nowhere and everywhere in the Middle Ages—but it was everywhere in a more important sense than the one in which it was nowhere."

[9] A point well stressed by Newman 1992, 150–51.

And with these words, she rushed to the altar, snatched up the veil which the bishop had just blessed, and bound herself to the convent in the presence of all.

When she offers her argument against marriage, her theatrical posture comes across even in the indirect speech of Abelard's report, as she begins:

And, she asked, is *this* how she would be remembered, as the woman who brought my name to ruin and shamed us both? What toll should the world exact from her if she robbed it of its great light? Could I even imagine what would follow this marriage—the censure and abuse, the tears of the philosophers, and the loss to the Church? What a pity it would be for me, whom nature had created for all mankind, now to become the property of a single woman— could I ever submit to this indignity? She rejected this marriage without qualification: it would be infamous and odious to me in every way.

And then, in direct speech:

she brought her case to a close in tears and sighs. "There is only one thing left for us," she said, "that in our utter ruin the pain to come will be no less than the love that has gone before."

This, of course, is Abelard's report some fifteen years after the event. But the tones and rhythms of speech—even the words—are so consistent with the Heloise of the later letters as to make it likely that he is quoting from a letter written at the time, despite his claim that he heard these words from Heloise's own mouth. In her later letters, Heloise's performance of a paradigmatic self only reaches greater heights. Listen to part of her own great lament, composed for the Third Letter:

I am the most unhappy of all women,
I am the most unlucky of all women,
to be raised as high above them all because of you
as I am cast down low because of you,
and because of myself as well. . . .
Has there ever been a Fortune of such extremes,

who knows no moderation in good or ill?
She made me blessed beyond others
to leave me broken beyond others,
so when I considered how much I have lost,
the grief that consumed me would be no less
than the loss that had crushed me,
and the pain that was to come would be no less
than the love that had gone before,
and the deepest of all pleasures would now end
in the deepest of all sorrows.

In the tradition of the Latin literary epistle, a letter entails a double addressee, the individual specifically named and the larger audience that will overhear. With Heloise—as with Abelard—the public side of the audience is always in mind, even when she reports what we may think would be her most intimate and private emotions: it is not some shamelessness that drives her to this language, but the controlled theatrical thrust of Stoic self-presentation. In this furious lament, it is not the self-indulgence of a Queen of the Night displayed for all to see, but the virtuosity of a Lucia Popp—but here it is Heloise performing the role of Heloise.

More significant is what Heloise derived about philosophy, for the Roman Stoics less a set of doctrines than a call to a way of life, one to which virtue was central. Heloise speaks of the philosophical life with nearly rapturous enthusiasm: the devotion to virtue, the devotion to reason—*here* is her passion—that she would share with Abelard. Note the thrilling tones of her words in the *Calamities*, again consistent with her later letters, as she tries to recall Abelard to what she sees as his mission in life:

If you care nothing for the privilege of a cleric, if you hold God's reverence in low esteem—if nothing else, at least defend the dignity of a philosopher and control this shamelessness with self-respect.

Heloise had what in her time was a rare sense of the ancient philosophers as imitable paradigms of virtue and proper exemplars of conduct. Their *lives* are consistently referenced, their virtue, the rigor of their devotion, which make them proper models even for Christian monastics. This was not the notion of philosophy as conceived and conducted in the schools, the aggressive dialectical combat in which Abelard excelled and which he describes early in the *Calamities*. When he came to found his school at the Paraclete, however, it was on the model of the primitive philosophical community whose outlines Heloise had already sketched. But this notion of philosophy has other implications that Heloise did not hesitate to embrace. In the First Letter, she recounts an argument once put forward by Aspasia, sexual partner—or what the letter elsewhere calls "concubine or whore"—of the ancient Athenian leader Pericles, pointedly calling her "philosopher" twice in two consecutive sentences, using the rare feminine form of the noun. It was unnecessary even to bring Aspasia into the discussion, since in Heloise's source the argument is introduced by Socrates, who in turn reports Aspasia's words; but Heloise ignores the middleman and insists on Aspasia as the origin. A woman can be a philosopher, as we see. And a concubine or whore can be a philosopher if she devotes herself to virtue. What kind of virtue can this be?

Heloise developed from her reading an idea of the quality of the virtue that must be central to the philosophical life: it is an inner disposition divorced from outer circumstance. Throughout her writing, she consistently emphasizes the distinction between the external realm of happenings and the inner realm of intentions and motives that alone constitute an ethical condition and merit reward or punishment. The idea is not only Stoic, of course, but Heloise puts a distinct Stoic cast on all her considerations of ethical issues, and especially on the principle that ethical character does not inhere in actions but intentions, not on external circumstances but on internal disposition. Thinking of what responsibility she might have had for Abelard's castration, she says:

> I am entirely guilty; as you know,
> I am entirely innocent.
> For blame does not reside in the action itself
> but in the disposition of the agent,
> and justice does not weigh what is done
> but what is in the heart

—that is, distinguishing between responsibility as a cause in the event and guilt through one's consent to the outcome. This distinction becomes a central element in Abelard's own ethical writings, in which he develops the doctrine of consent at length and with considerable philosophical rigor, apparently in response to Heloise's concerns.[10] And she also speaks with nothing but disdain for "those outward deeds that hypocrites do with greater zeal than any of the righteous."

Her contempt for hypocrisy and regard only for an inner disposition seem to present a problem in the Third Letter, in which Heloise accuses herself of hypocrisy, outwardly a dutiful nun but inwardly devoted not to God but to Abelard, outwardly following the strictures of sexual restraint but inwardly only too aware of her intense sexual longings, unable to repent of what she cannot regret. But insofar as her letters are *public* acts, *outward* declarations of her inner disposition, she is no hypocrite. Heloise never retracted what she wrote in any of her letters. There is no hint of a conversion of her devotion from Abelard to God. If she remained silent about her suffering after the Third Letter, it was because it was Abelard's order. She continued at the Paraclete doing her work for the reason she had first become a nun: because it was Abelard's order. For over twenty years after Abelard's death until her own death in 1163 or 1164, she remained faithful to her true vocation, the abbess of Abelard's foundation, leading and helping others to lead the philosophical life.

## THE LETTER COLLECTION

The *Calamities* and seven letters exchanged between Abelard and Heloise constitute a letter collection, compiled most probably at the Paraclete or at one of its daughter houses.[11] The collection does not

---

[10] Abelard's ethical writings were composed in the mid- or late 1130s and so postdate the letters of Heloise by a few years, but the questions they address had plainly been a subject of discussion between them for some time: "*as you know*, I am entirely innocent," Heloise writes in the First Letter. Ultimately, however, the issue of priority is of less moment than the fact that Heloise was an active participant in the ongoing philosophical endeavors of her time.

[11] Some versions of the collection do not recognize all of the long Seventh Letter, sometimes called "The Rule for Religious Women," which is preserved in several manuscripts as the last of the letters. In scholarly editions of Abelard's correspondence, the *Calamities* is labeled Epistle I, so that what is presented in this volume as the First Letter is there labeled Epistle II, and so on. I have followed the numbering of the latest complete editions of the letters by J. T. Muckle and T. P. McLaughlin, which also seems both the most sensible and the clearest for a reader. For the genesis of the collection, see Luscombe 1988a.

The entire collection was first translated into English by Joseph Berington in 1787 and again by C. K. Scott Moncrieff in 1926. The well-known translation by Betty Radice (1974; revised by Michael Clanchy 2003) redacts and summarizes much of the

include all their correspondence, even all their correspondence with each other, but follows a specific sequence, opening with the *Calamities*, which both triggers the subsequent exchange and, in retrospect, provides its narrative context. In some ways, the long Seventh Letter, in which Abelard suggests a formal rule for the Paraclete, appears to form a logical end to the sequence, although there are signs at the end of the letter that an editor or compiler intended a connection with a further letter preserved only apart from the collection. The Sixth and Seventh Letters were written as a complementary pair, but there is no indication that any other letter was composed with any putative purpose of the collection as a whole in mind: the letters are what they appear to be, the sequential written responses of Abelard and Heloise to each other.

Still, the collection has an overall shape. After the *Calamities*, the first four letters are relatively short, relatively personal, and have an integral drama of their own, in which Abelard and Heloise reflect on their relationship, read their common history in very different ways, and seek to define two very different futures. Abelard's castration and their entrance into monastic life had marked a new dispensation for them both, but while Abelard identified the new dispensation with divine grace and consistently pressed Heloise to be reconciled to it, Heloise saw in it little more than the exhausting prospect of a world turned upside down, of justice outraged and certainty denied, where every proper pattern might be broken, every normal sequence painfully reversed. By the beginning of the Fifth Letter, they are at an impasse, and the character of the correspondence changes. The longer Fifth, Sixth, and Seventh Letters may better be described as *letter-treatises* in which their personal concerns are displaced onto the institutional structures of their collaborative work at the Paraclete, and which seek in theoretical and practical terms to reconfigure the role of women in religious life.

While the authenticity of the letters has been challenged in different quarters, there remain no solid grounds for doubting that the letters are essentially the writings of Abelard and Heloise, as they appear to be.[12] There are signs, however, that the texts have been retouched, either by the compiler of the collection or by reader-

---

difficult Sixth Letter. Several English translations of the *Calamities* alone have been published under various titles, most recently by Muckle 1964.

[12] For a concise history of the question and a fair assessment of the arguments, see Marenbon 1997, 82–93.

copyists of unknown date, who have left comments and additions that have been incorporated into the common text. In the *Calamities* and the earlier letters, the signs are few and very minor; in the letter-treatises, however, which engage controversial issues of wide concern to monastic life, the interpolation of later material becomes significantly more frequent and extensive. I have suggested in the translation passages that are most likely to have been added by later hands than those of Abelard and Heloise. For this, I have used continuity of argument and rhetorical structure as a criterion throughout: passages that are demonstrably out of place have been bracketed as suspect.

## THE PROSE OF ABELARD AND HELOISE

Neither Abelard nor Heloise was a conversational writer, though Abelard could mimic the rhythms of conversation when he wished. Both were trained in the sophisticated modes of the learned Latin of the time and proficient in meeting its most literate expectations. Their prose has a distinctly oratorical cast, sharply conscious of the audience, large or small, for whom they were fashioning their appeals. We can see this most readily in the casual ease with which Abelard assumes the posture of a lectern speaker in, for example, the polished speech he puts into the mouth of the bishop of Chartres at the Council of Soissons in his *Calamities,* in his sudden address in the Sixth Letter to a male audience that cannot actually have been present—"Let me ask my brothers and my fellow monks, who every day gape after meat . . ."—or in a dozen other moments in the Sixth and Seventh Letters when he exhorts, admonishes, and instructs the nuns of the Paraclete. But this same oratorical cast and awareness of a public is present throughout the letters, even when they seem most private and most intimately reflective.

Speech like this must depend on the dynamics of the living voice, its energies, stress, rhythm, pace, and pauses, but here those dynamics can only be intimated by what is on the page. The prose of both Abelard and Heloise, however, is conspicuous for a tendency toward certain patterns, favored forms of repetition—of sounds, words, or concepts—that help define what is called their style and can help make their voices vivid. Chief among these, for Abelard and Heloise both, is the tendency toward formal balance, which operates in the conceptual, syntactic, and sensory dimensions of their language. In the first paragraph of the *Calamities,* the conceptual balance of opposing terms is most evident:

The force of example often does more than words to stir our human passions or to still them. With this in mind, I have decided to follow up the words of consolation I offered you while we were together and write an account of my own experience of calamities to console you while we are apart. I expect you will see that your trials are only slight next to mine, or even nothing at all, and then you will find them easier to bear.

"Example" is opposed to "words," "stirring passions" opposed to "stilling" them, and further oppositions follow: together/apart, your trials/mine, slight/nothing at all—the regular pulse of these oppositions creates the basic rhythm of the lines. In other places, syntactic balance, especially the use of correlative clauses (*tam . . . quam* and *tanto . . . quanto* clauses in Latin), often forms the primary structure of a sentence; there is an example early in the *Calamities*— "the more progress I made in my studies, the more passionately I devoted myself to them"—and it becomes very common throughout the letters, rising in frequency with the formality of the prose. The tendency toward balanced repetition extends also to the sensory aspects of language. Both Abelard and Heloise wrote highly rhythmical prose, marked with formalized stress cadences and phrases paired for a balanced syllable count; both also could be free with anaphora, alliteration, assonance, and even rhyme in the medieval tradition of rhymed prose. The full use of these sonic resources can create patterns of a very striking kind.

For Abelard in the *Calamities*, the full application is reserved for moments of special intensity. We need look only at the first sentences of his castration lament to get a sense of the possibilities; it will be best to set out the Latin in a form that highlights its verbal structure:

> Mane autem facto, tota ad me civitas congregata,
> quanta stuperet admiratione,
> quanta se affligeret lamentatione,
> quanto me clamore vexarent,
> quanto planctu perturbarent,
>     difficile immo impossibile exprimi.

By the next morning, the entire city had converged outside my door, shocked and appalled, moaning and howling and wailing such earsplitting cries that it is hard—no, impossible—to describe it.

After the light alliteration of *civitas congregata* there follow four
syntactically parallel phrases marked with anaphora of *quanta* and
*quanto;* with the full and unstressed rhymes of *stuperet* and *afflig-
eret, admiratione* and *lamentatione,* and *vexarent* and *perturbarent;*
and with the paired number of syllables in the parallel phrases
*clamore vexarent* and *planctu perturbarent.* The sentence ends by
moving away from this block of parallels, but not before it asserts
another set of opposing terms, *difficile* and *impossibile,* "hard" and
"impossible." Abelard, however, is just warming up; unfazed by
what he has just called the impossibility of verbal description, he
continues with more rhymes, part-rhymes, and paired phrases and
words:

> Maxime vero clerici
> ac precipue scholares nostri
>     intolerabilibus  me lamentis
>     et eiulatibus      cruciabant
> ut multo amplius ex eorum compassione
>   quam ex vulneris lederer passione
> et plus erubescentiam quam plagam   sentirem
> et pudore magis quam dolore       affligerer.

The clerics were the worst and my students worst among them,
crucifying me with their screams and laments until I suffered more
from their pity than my pain, more from chagrin than the injury
itself, and more from the scandal than the scar.

His third sentence is a grand flourish of anaphora, alliteration, assonance, and rhyme:

> Occurrebat animo
> quanta modo gloria pollebam;
> quam facili et turpi casu hec humiliata
>     immo penitus esset extincta;
> quam iusto Dei iudicio in illa corporis mei portione plectere
>       in qua deliqueram;
> quam iusta proditione is quem antea prodideram
>       vicem mihi retulisset;
> quanta laude mei emuli tam manifestam equitatem efferent;
> quantam perpetui doloris contritionem plaga hec
>        parentibus meis et amicis    esset collatura;
> quanta dilatione hec singularis infamia
>        universum mundum      esset occupatura;
> qua mihi ulterius via pateret,

<u>qua</u> fronte in publicum *prodi*rem

<u>omnium</u> <u>digitis</u> <u>demonstrandus,</u><br>
<u>omnium</u> <u>linguis</u> <u>corrodendus,</u><br>
<u>omnibus</u> monstruosum spectaculum <u>futurus</u>.

I thought of the glory I once enjoyed and the simple, vicious act
that brought it low, the judgment of a God who struck where I
most had sinned, the vindication by broken faith when I had broken faith, the exultation of my enemies over this so fitting reward,
the lasting grief this wound would bring to my parents and my
friends, the way my particular shame would spread throughout
the universe of men. No road was now left open to me, no face I
could show to the world, when every finger would point, every
tongue would mock the monstrous spectacle I would become.

This sort and degree of artifice, particularly in the set of circumstances it describes, has chilled many readers for both aesthetic and
psychological reasons. The novelist George Moore—no conversational writer himself—dismissed the whole passage as an interpolation in "the strained, rhetorical style of a student in rhetoric bidden
to write a theme on the feelings of a man gelt in the dead of night by
ruffians that a bribed servant let into the house,"[13] and others have
had similar reactions to what they see as its emotional inauthentic-
ity. But the passage, we remember, was written more than a dozen
years after the event, time enough for even such a powerful irrita-
tion to have developed a thick protective coating of pearl: the same
artifice that signals strong emotion also signals a conscious attempt
to regulate that emotion.

For Heloise, the techniques of sentence balance are similar but
more concentrated and consistent, and with a much stronger tendency to shape phrases and sentences according to their rhythms
and their sounds as well as their syntax. This patterning becomes
basic to her prose. Some of her most famous utterances are in fact
formed around rhymes, as this from the First Letter:

... si me Augustus universo presidens mundo
matrimonii honore <u>dignaretur</u>
totumque mihi orbem confirmaret in perpetuo possidendum,
<u>carius</u> mihi et <u>dignius</u> <u>videretur</u>
tua dici <u>meretrix</u>
quam illius <u>imperatrix</u>.

---

[13] Moore 1926, xv.

If great Augustus, ruler of the world, ever thought to honor me by making me his wife and granted me dominion over the earth, it would be dearer to me and more honorable to be called not his royal consort but your whore.

But she does not wait for the highest moments; the principle of sonic balance is evident even in her lists, as it is in the Third Letter:

feminam videlicet viro,
uxorem            marito,
ancillam          domino,
monialem          monacho,
et sacerdoti      diaconissam,
abbati            abbatissam.

[There I see] a woman before a man, a wife before a husband, a handmaid before her lord, a nun before a monk, a humble deaconess before a priest, and an abbess before an abbot.

In a shorter sentence or phrase, she often borrows word placement strategies from Latin hexameter poetry, as she does in this simple statement from the First Letter:

Solent etenim dolenti nonnullam afferre consolationem qui condolent.

A community of grief can bring some comfort to one in need of it.

*Solent* is first echoed in *dolenti*, and then both are echoed in *consolationem* and *condolent* and also amplified as if by the prefix *con-*. (There is an etymological relationship between *dolenti* and *condolent* but only a sonic one between *solent* and *consolationem:* Heloise does not shrink from a pun.) The sound play here reinforces another symmetry: the two finite (and rhyming) verbs *solent* and *condolent* frame the phrase with the infinitive verb *afferre* set between them and also between the noun *consolationem* and its adjective *nonnullam*.

In longer sequences, she uses anaphora and rhyme freely and often employs them to extend a pattern beyond a single sentence, building at times to rhetorical crescendo. From the First Letter:

Huius quippe loci tu post Deum   solus es fundator,
                                 solus huius oratorii constructor,
                                 solus huius congregationis edificator.

You alone, after God, are the founder of this place, you alone the builder of this oratory, you alone the architect of this congregation.

From the Third:

Noli, obsecro, de me tanta presumere,   ne cesses orando subvenire.
Noli estimare sanam                      ne medicaminis subtrahas gratiam.
Noli non egentem credere                 ne differas in necessitate subvenire.
Noli valitudinem putare                  ne prius corruam quam sustentes
                                             labentem.

Do not presume so much, I beg of you: you may forget to help me
with your prayers. Do not ever suppose that I am healed: you may
withdraw the grace of your healing. Do not believe that I am not in
need: you may put off your help when I most need it. Do not imagine that I am strong: I may collapse before you stop my fall.

And again from the First:

Quas videlicet tuas diligenter commemorans
cum eius intenderes consolationi,
nostre plurimum addidisti desolationi,
et dum eius mederi vulneribus cuperes,
nova quedam nobis vulnera doloris inflixisti
                       et priora auxisti.
Sana, obsecro, ipsa que fecisti
           qui que alii fecerunt curare sat agis.
Morem quidem amico et socio gessisti
        et tam amicitie
           quam societatis debitum persolvisti,
        sed maiore te debito nobis astrinxisti,
           quas non tam amicas
                 quam amicissimas,
              non tam socias
                 quam filias convenit nominari,
           vel si quod dulcius
              et sanctius vocabulum potest excogitari.

But as you told of them in such detail, while your mind was on his
consolation, you have worsened our own desolation; while you
were treating his wounds, you have inflicted new wounds upon us
and have made our old wounds bleed. I beg of you, heal these
wounds you have made, who are so careful to tend the wounds
made by others. You have done what you ought for a friend and
comrade and have paid your debt to friendship and comradeship.
But you are bound to us by a greater debt, for we are not your
friends but your most loving friends, not your comrades but your
daughters—yes, it is right to call us that, or even use a name more
sacred and more sweet if one can be imagined.

The rhythm of verbal correspondences becomes perhaps most spectacular in her most formal address, the rhymed prose of her letter to Peter the Venerable:

Visitante nos Dei misericordia,       dignationis vestre nos visitavit gratia.
Gratulamur, pater benignissime,
    et quod ad parvitatem nostram
    magnitudo vestra descenderit,  gloriamur.
Est si quidem vestra visitatio
magna magnis quibuslibet gloriatio.
Norunt alii quantum eis utilitatis
vestre contulerit presentia sublimitatis.
Ego certe non dicam enarrare dictu,
sed nec ipso valeo comprehendere cogitatu,
quam utilis, quam iocundus
vester mihi fuerit adventus.
    Abbas noster, dominus noster,
    apud nos . . . missam celebrastis
    in qua Spiritui Sancto nos commendastis.
    In capitulo . . . nos . . . cibastis.
    Corpus magistri nobis dedistis
    ac beneficium Cluniacense concessistis.

To us, the coming of your worthiness was the coming of God's mercy. We are grateful, kindest father, and we glory that your greatness has descended upon us, for we are small. Indeed, your coming would be cause for glory to anyone, however great. Others know what good they may derive from the good of your high presence. I myself do not have the words to say, or even the intellect to comprehend, all the good your visit brought to us, all the personal pleasure to me. My abbot and my lord: You celebrated Mass in our presence. . . . You commended us to the Holy Spirit in that Mass. You feasted us in our chapter. . . . You restored to us the body of our master and extended to us the kindness of Cluny.

But it is in the short salutation to the First Letter that the rhythms are used to their greatest and most concentrated effect:

| | |
|---|---|
| Domino suo | immo patri |
| coniugi suo | immo fratri |
| ancilla sua | immo filia |
| ipsius uxor | immo soror |
| Abaëlardo | Heloïsa. |

To her lord, no, her father; to her husband, no, her brother. From his handmaid, no, his daughter; his wife, no, his sister. To Abelard from Heloise.

The apparently simple task of a salutation, to identify the sender and recipient, is revealed as a complex problem in this case: what *are* these two to one another? With extraordinary compression, Heloise recapitulates the categories of her history with Abelard—lovers, spouses, nun and monk, communicant and priest—alternating between the terms of their personal and ecclesiastical relationships. But as the terms proliferate, each becomes inadequate and the aggregate itself collapses of its own weight: what remains as adequate is what also remains beyond types: their proper names, individual and unique. Along with the dense, implicit argument is an equally dense set of verbal repetitions and recurring sounds, shifting patterns of rhyme and part-rhyme, carefully controlled emphasis and acceleration through the sequence of terms, with a necessary catch or pause before the final pair of words, all held in place by a near-perfect syllabic alternation of five beats to four.

William Gass, one of our finest writers and theorists of prose, once noted:

> Language without rhythm, without physicality, without the undertow of that sea which once covered everything and from which the land first arose like a cautious toe—levelless language, in short, voiceless type, pissless prose—can never be artistically complete. Sentences which run on without a body have no soul. They will be felt, however conceptually well connected, however well designed by the higher bureaus of the mind, to go through our understanding like the sharp cold blade of a skate over ice.[14]

His point was to stress the irrational, the subliminal emotional force of such writing, and the force of such prose as Heloise wrote cannot easily be denied. But there is another, and for the moment a more important, consideration—the intellectual discipline, the emotional measure, the sheer psychological poise required to *do* such writing in the face of its shattering subject. For Heloise as well as Abelard, the cost of this poise, no doubt, was enormous, but it is a cost that must be borne by all those who, as Abelard and Heloise certainly did, elect to continue living their lives.

---

[14] Gass 1985, 122.

One of the fundamental aims of this translation is to respond as far as possible to the voices of Abelard and Heloise (and the other named and unnamed writers in this volume) as they shift from author to author and from circumstance to circumstance. For this, it uses a relatively formal and rhythmical English prose, although both the formality and the rhythms become lighter when the Latin text demands it. Any attempt at rhymed prose in English would of course be disastrous here, but I have tried to reflect some local effects through less assertive means—assonance, alliteration, and, very often, rhythmical correspondence. When the degree of verbal patterning in the Latin becomes especially intense—at strategic passages for Abelard but more commonly for Heloise—I have adopted the additional measure of setting out the translation in patterns perceptible to the eye, using line breaks and indentations to accommodate the pace, relative emphasis, recurring rhythms, and fabrics of verbal correspondence established in the Latin text. The introduction of these patterns in the English, of course, reflects no change in the visual arrangement of the Latin, which retains the familiar format of ordinary prose. The prose of Abelard and Heloise, however, was of an extraordinary character, and in our time it still may exert extraordinary force.

## NOTE ON THE TEXTS

The translations are based on the following Latin texts and editions, except where indicated in the notes.

*The Calamities of Peter Abelard:* J. T. Muckle, "Abelard's Letter of Consolation to a Friend (*Historia Calamitatum*)," *Mediaeval Studies* 12 (1950), 163–213.

The First–Fourth Letters: J. T. Muckle, "The Personal Letters Between Abelard and Heloise," *Mediaeval Studies* 15 (1953), 47–94.

The Fifth–Sixth Letters: J. T. Muckle, "The Letter of Heloise on Religious Life and Abelard's First Reply," *Mediaeval Studies* 17 (1955), 240–81.

The Seventh Letter: T. P. McLaughlin, "Abelard's Rule for Religious Women," *Mediaeval Studies* 18 (1956), 241–92.

*The Questions of Heloise:* Introductory Letter: J.-P. Migne, *Patrologia Latina*, vol. 178, 677–78.

*Abelard's Confession of Faith:* J.-P. Migne, *Patrologia Latina*, vol. 178, 375.

The Letters of Heloise and Peter the Venerable: Giles Constable, *The Letters of Peter the Venerable* (Cambridge, MA, 1967), Letters 115, 167, and 168.

"Lament of the Virgins of Israel for the Daughter of Jephtha": J.-P. Migne, *Patrologia Latina*, vol. 178, 1819–20.

"Lament of David for Saul and Jonathan": *Oxford Book of Medieval Latin Verse*, ed. F. J. E. Raby (Oxford, 1959), 246–50.

"How Great the Sabbath: Hymn for Saturday Vespers": *Oxford Book of Medieval Latin Verse*, ed. F. J. E. Raby (Oxford, 1959), 243–44.

"Adorn the Chamber, Zion: Hymn for the Feast of the Presentation": *Oxford Book of Medieval Latin Verse*, ed. F. J. E. Raby (Oxford, 1959), 244–45.

"After the Virgin's Highest Honor: Hymn for the Night Office and Vespers": J.-P. Migne, *Patrologia Latina*, vol. 178, 1812.

"Open Wide Your Eyes": Ulrich Ernst, "Ein unbeachteres 'Carmen figuratum' des Petrus Abelardus," *Mittellateinishes Jahrbuch* 21 (1986), 125–46.

"To Astralabe, My Son": J. M. A. Rubingh-Bosscher, *Peter Abelard, Carmen ad Astralabium: A Critical Edition* (Groningen, 1987).

*The Letters of Two Lovers:* Ewald Könsgen, *Epistolae duorum amantium. Briefe Abaelards und Heloises? Mittellateinisches Studien und Texte* 8 (Leiden, 1974).


All biblical passages are quoted in, or adapted from, the Douay-Rheims translation, as revised by Richard Challoner (1749–1752), and their citation corresponds to that version.

# SUGGESTIONS FOR FURTHER RESOURCES

These suggestions are put forward with the interests of students and other first-time readers of Abelard and Heloise in mind. For a fuller list, see the Works Cited and Select Bibliography.

Adams, Henry. 1986 (c. 1905). *Mont Saint Michel and Chartres*. Harmondsworth and New York: Penguin, chapter 14.

Brower, Jeffrey E., and Kevin Guilfoy, eds. 2004. *The Cambridge Companion to Abelard*. Cambridge: Cambridge University Press.

Clanchy, Michael T. 1997. *Abelard: A Medieval Life*. Oxford and Malden, MA: Blackwell.

Dronke, Peter. 1976. *Abelard and Heloise in Medieval Testimony*. Glasgow: University of Glasgow. Reprinted in Dronke 1992, 247–94.

———. 1984b. *Women Writers of the Middle Ages: A Critical Study of Texts from Perpetua (†203) to Marguerite Porete (†1310)*. Cambridge: Cambridge University Press, 107–43.

———. 1992. *Intellectuals and Poets in Medieval Europe*. Rome: Edizioni di storia e letteratura.

Gilson, Étienne. 1960 (c. 1938). *Heloise and Abelard*. Trans. L. K. Shook. Ann Arbor: University of Michigan Press.

Kauffman, Linda S. 1986. *Discourses of Desire: Gender, Genre, and Epistolary Fictions*. Ithaca, NY: Cornell University Press, 63–89.

Luscombe, David E., ed. and trans. 1971. *Peter Abelard's Ethics*. Oxford: Clarendon Press.

———. 1988a. "From Paris to the Paraclete: The Correspondence of Abelard and Heloise." *Proceedings of the British Academy* 74, 247–83.

———. 1988b. "Peter Abelard." In Dronke 1988b, 279–307.

Marenbon, J. 1997. *The Philosophy of Peter Abelard*. Cambridge: Cambridge University Press.

McLaughlin, Mary Martin. 1967. "Abelard as Autobiographer: The Motives and Meaning of His 'Story of Calamities.'" *Speculum* 42, 463–88.

————. 1975. "Abelard and the Dignity of Women." In Louis, Jolivet, and Châtillon 1975, 287–334.

McLeod, Enid. 1971. *Héloïse: A Biography*. 2nd ed. London: Chatto and Windus.

Mews, Constant J. 1999. *The Lost Love Letters of Heloise and Abelard: Perceptions of Dialogue in Twelfth-Century France*. Trans. with N. Chiavaroli. New York: St. Martin's.

*Monastic Song: 12th Century Monophonic Chant*. Performed by the Theatre of Voices, Paul Hillier, director. Harmonium Mundi, HMU 907209.

Newman, Barbara. 1992. "Authority, Authenticity, and the Repression of Heloise." *Journal of Medieval and Renaissance Studies* 22, 121–57. Reprinted in *From Virile Woman to WomanChrist: Studies in Medieval Religion and Literature*. Philadelphia: University of Pennsylvania Press, 1995.

Pernoud, Régine. 1973. *Heloise and Abelard*. Trans. P. Wiles. New York: Stein and Day.

Spade, Paul Vincent, trans. 1995. *Peter Abelard: Ethical Writings*. Indianapolis and Cambridge, MA: Hackett Publishing.

Wheeler, Bonnie, ed. 2000. *Listening to Heloise: The Voice of a Twelfth-Century Woman*. London: Macmillan.

## SOME NOTABLE RECREATIONS:

Audouard, Antoine. 2004. *Farewell, My Only One*. Trans. Euan Cameron. New York: Houghton Mifflin.

Brenton, Howard. 2006. *In Extremis: The Story of Abelard and Heloise*. London: Nick Hern Books.

Carson, Anne. 2005. "H & A Screenplay." In *Decreation*, 127–45. New York: Knopf.

Meade, Marion. 1979. *Stealing Heaven*. New York: William Morrow. See also the 1988 film of the same name directed by Clive Donner.

Millar, Ronald. 1970. *Abelard and Heloise: A Play*. London: Samuel French.

Moore, George. 1921. *Héloïse and Abélard*. New York: Horace Liveright.

Newman, Sharan. 1963. *Death Comes as Epiphany*. New York: Tom Doherty Associates. See also Newman's other mystery novels in the Catherine LeVendeur series.

Pope, Alexander. 1717. "Eloïsa to Abelard." Frequently reprinted.

Rinser, Luise. 1998. *Abelard's Love*. Trans. Jean M. Snook. Lincoln, NE, and London: University of Nebraska Press.

Twain, Mark. 1869. *The Innocents Abroad*. Hartford, CT: American Publishing Co., chapter 15. Frequently reprinted.

Waddell, Helen. 1933. *Peter Abelard—A Novel*. New York: Henry Holt. Frequently reprinted.

Whitman, Cedric. 1965. *Abelard*. Cambridge, MA: Harvard University Press.

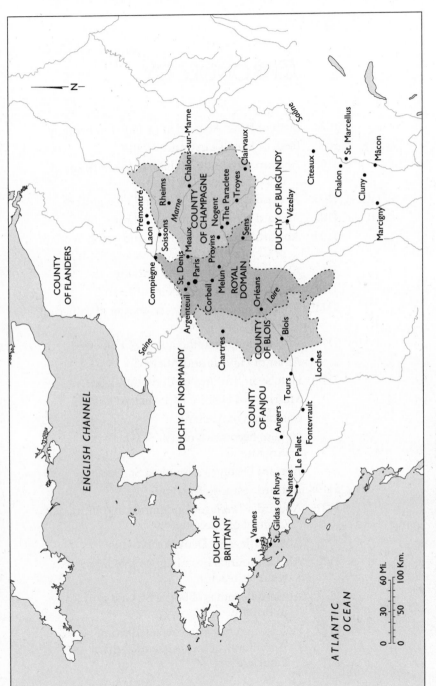

Northern France in the Time of Abelard and Heloise

# CHRONOLOGY

1079: Birth of Peter Abelard at Le Pallet in Brittany

c. 1090: Birth of Heloise in or near Paris

c. 1100: Abelard taught by William of Champeaux at cathedral school in Paris

c. 1102–c. 1105: Abelard master at Melun and then at Corbeil

c. 1105–c. 1108: Abelard returns home to Brittany

c. 1108: Abelard returns to Paris to study with William of Champeaux at St. Victor

c. 1112: Abelard again returns to Brittany

1113: Abelard taught by Anselm of Laon

c. 1114: Abelard returns to Paris as master at cathedral school

c. 1116: Abelard lodges in the house of Fulbert

Affair of Heloise and Abelard

c. 1117: Heloise in Brittany, birth of Astralabe

Marriage of Heloise and Abelard in Paris

Castration of Abelard

Heloise becomes a nun at St. Marie in Argenteuil

Abelard becomes a monk at St. Denis

c. 1119: Abelard resumes teaching

1121: Abelard's *Theology* condemned and burned at Council of Soissons

Abelard flees St. Denis for Provins

c. 1122: Abelard founds hermitage of the Paraclete, resumes teaching

c. 1127: Abelard becomes abbot of St. Gildas of Rhuys in Brittany

1129: Heloise and her nuns expelled from Argenteuil, accept Abelard's gift of Paraclete

1131 (Nov. 28): Charter of Innocent II takes Heloise and her
nuns under papal protection

c. 1132: Composition of the Calamities

Beginning of correspondence of Heloise and
Abelard

c. 1135: Abelard returns to Paris as master of school at
church of St. Geneviève

1140: Abelard accused of heresy by Bernard of
Clairvaux at Council of Sens, sentenced to
perpetual silence as a heretic by Innocent II,
taken under the protection of Peter the
Venerable at Cluny

1142 (April 21): Abelard dies at Cluniac priory of St. Marcellus
near Chalon-sur-Saône

1144? (Nov. 16): Abelard buried at the Paraclete

1163/64? (May 16): Death of Heloise, burial next to Abelard

c. 1285: French translation of letters of Heloise and
Abelard by Jean de Meun

1497: Reburial of Heloise and Abelard in new church
at Paraclete

1616: First printed edition of Latin texts of Heloise
and Abelard

1675: Beginning of vogue for "imposter texts";
French versions of the letters of Heloise and
Abelard circulating from 1687; others
published in 1693, 1695, 1697, 1703, 1711,
etc.

1713: English translation of "imposter texts" by John
Hughes, very often reprinted through the
1940s, inspiring many imitations

1792: Reburial of Heloise and Abelard in church of
St. Laurent at Nogent

Dissolution of Paraclete and sale of its
properties

1800: Transfer of remains of Heloise and Abelard to a
museum in Paris; some remains distributed
as relics to devotees

1817: Transfer of remains of Heloise and Abelard to
Père-Lachaise cemetery in Paris

# THE CALAMITIES

# OF

# PETER ABELARD

## A LETTER OF CONSOLATION TO A FRIEND

The force of example often does more than words to stir our human passions or to still them. With this in mind, I have decided to follow up the words of consolation I offered you while we were together and write an account of my own experience of calamities to console you while we are apart. I expect you will see that your trials are only slight next to mine, or even nothing at all, and then you will find them easier to bear.

To begin, then—

I was born on the edge of Brittany, about eight miles I think east of Nantes, in a town called Palatium, or Le Pallet.[1] Because of the nature of the land—or perhaps of my own origins—I was always quick in spirit with superior intelligence and a great aptitude for learning. But in addition, my father had had a little education before he became a knight and took to it with such enthusiasm that he decided to have all his sons trained in letters before they were trained in arms.[2] It turned out as he intended. Since I was his firstborn, he

---

[1] The town still stands, about twelve miles southeast of Nantes on the road to Poitiers. Its name gave Abelard the epithet "Palatinus," meaning both "man of Le Pallet" and "man of the palace," or, as its meaning developed in the twelfth century, "knight-courtier," pointing to Abelard's known elegance of manners and even his later image as a courtly lover, as well as his success in intellectual jousts; see Clanchy 1997, 145–47.

[2] Abelard's father, Berengar, was a minor member of the Breton nobility, probably of Poitevin birth. Somewhat unusually, he had gained some knowledge of "letters," as indicated here, meaning some facility in Latin and some familiarity with the Latin

saw to my education with all the care his special love for me could provide; and for my part, the more progress I made in my studies, the more passionately I devoted myself to them. In the end I fell so deeply in love with learning that I renounced the pomp of knighthood, turned over to my brothers my inheritance and other rights of the eldest, and quit the court of Mars to be raised at the bosom of Minerva. Of all the areas of philosophy, my primary interest lay in the weapons of dialectical reasoning, so I traded all my arms for these and gave up the trophies of war for the noisy clash of argument. Then I went out into the world, arguing my way through the provinces from one place to another, wherever I heard that the study of the art was most active, and became like one of the peripatetic philosophers of old.[3]

At last I reached Paris, which had long been the center of dialectical studies, and came to the school of William of Champeaux, then the leading figure in the field both in reputation and in fact.[4] I stayed with him for some time. At first I was made welcome but

---

classics. "Letters" in this sense was the substance of twelfth-century education, and it has been translated as "letters," "education," or "learning" as the context demands. The names of four of Abelard's siblings are known: brothers Dagobert, Porcarius, and Radulf, and sister Dionysia, or Denise.

[3] There were several schools in Brittany and its neighboring provinces that Abelard could have attended, but he omits all details of his early education. He is known, however, to have spent some years (probably after 1093 but before c. 1100, when he arrived in Paris) at Loches and Tours as student of Roscelin of Compiègne, one of the most famous and controversial teachers of dialectic of the time. Roscelin's theories about the nature of the Trinity led to charges of heresy against him at the Council of Soissons in 1092, and his "nominalist" theories about the logical status of universals provoked similar suspicions long afterward. Abelard was later to join in the attacks against his old master, and by c. 1120, their relationship had degenerated into unmixed acrimony. A vicious letter to Abelard remains Roscelin's only extant work.

The peripatetic philosophers were the ancient followers of Aristotle, probably so-named because of Aristotle's habit of "strolling around" as he taught. In later centuries, the adjective was reinterpreted as "traveling around," somewhat in the manner of a knight-errant, as Abelard describes himself here.

[4] This was the cathedral school of Notre Dame. Its master, William of Champeaux (c. 1070–1121), was a renowned teacher of rhetoric, grammar, and theology as well as dialectic, in which he held a "realist" position on the status of universals. He was also archdeacon of Paris and canon of the cathedral, a royal counselor, and an early supporter of Bernard of Clairvaux. Abelard mentions or alludes to other details of William's life: that he had been a student of Anselm of Laon, that he founded a community of canons regular and a school at the abbey of St. Victor (c. 1105), and that he became bishop of Châlons-sur-Marne (1113).

soon became nothing but a problem to him, doing what I could to refute his conclusions, often arguing against him in class, and more than once coming out the winner in debate. The so-called leaders among my fellow students resented this, of course, especially since I was so much their junior both in age and length of study. And so began the string of my calamities, which has continued unbroken until the present day, and as my reputation grew, so other men's envy was kindled against me.

It came to the point where, presuming on an intelligence beyond my years—I was still very young—I began to set my sights on directing a school of my own. I looked for a place where I could do this and settled on Melun, then a town of some importance and a residence of the king. My master anticipated this and, to put as much distance as possible between my school and his, schemed behind my back to block my plans and deny me the place I had settled on. But he had some enemies among the most powerful men of the country there, and with their help I got what I wanted. His naked envy in fact won me wide support.

From this first tour of duty at a school of my own, my reputation in dialectic began to spread until, slowly but surely, it eclipsed the fame of all my old schoolmates and even my master himself. This made me presume even further. I moved my school to the town of Corbeil, which was closer to Paris and allowed for more of those bold assaults of argument I would launch against him. Not long afterward, though, my health broke down under the strain of too much study and I had to return home to Brittany. I was away from France for several years, bitterly missed by everyone who cared about dialectic.

A few years later, after I had long recovered, William, who had been archdeacon of Paris, entered an order of canons regular,[5] with the idea, everyone said, of winning a greater reputation for piety and, hence, a greater chance of promotion within the Church, as in fact happened soon afterward when he was made bishop of Châlons. Even with his new status, though, he did not give up his normal practice of philosophy or even withdraw from the city;

---

[5] That is, priests bound by religious vows, living communally under the Rule (*regula*) of Augustine. William was founding abbot of the community of canons at the abbey of St. Victor, where he established a school that became one of the most important and influential of its time.

rather, he kept on with public teaching in his usual way, only now inside the walls of the monastery to which he supposedly had retired to pursue the religious life. I went back to him then for his lectures on rhetoric. In the course of all our philosophical wrangles, I once came at him with such clear logic that I forced him to mod-ify—or I should say, abandon—his long-held position on the com-monality of universals.[6] He had maintained that the same undivided nature exists essentially in all the particular members of

---

[6] The question is how universals (species or genera) are related to particulars (indi-vidual things, members of the species or genus), as Aristotle formulated it in his *Cat-egories*. In his own textbook, the *Logica "Ingredientibus,"* probably composed c. 1120, Abelard set out the argument against William's position without taking a final stand on the question himself. Originally, the position had been that, for example, Socrates and Plato are *essentially* the same because *human* is the essence of both, and that this single essence is wholly present in both of them at the same time. They are differenti-ated from one another in accidental (nonessential, contingent) ways: e.g., Socrates is snub-nosed and Plato has a cauliflower ear. Abelard points out, however, that Socrates and Plato also would have to be *essentially* the same in being *animals* and *liv-ing things*, and that Abelard's ass Brunellus, "Brownie," is also a living thing and an animal—but asinine, not human. Does this mean that Socrates, essentially human, also shares an essence with an ass, that an essentially rational creature is also an essentially irrational creature? Or does it prove that there *is* diversity in essence among Brownie, Socrates, and Plato, and that variety arises from what is essential as well as what is accidental? Moreover, if we consider the universal all three have in common, *animal*, it is unclear how many *animal natures* there are (if Socrates has an animal nature and Brownie has an animal nature, does that make two animal natures?), and also unclear whether Socrates' animal nature is different from Brownie's. A position Abelard calls "closer to the truth" holds that nothing shares an essence with anything else. William's new formulation prevents his having to say that Socrates and Brownie share an *essential* animal nature, but only by invoking a new category: Socrates and Brownie share a *non-different* animal nature. Such *non-difference* was explained in various ways, but to Abelard all these ways were objec-tionable since they all ultimately identified the species with the individual and led to the absurd collapse of any distinction between the particular and the universal. See further King 2004, esp. 66–72.

The entire question is part of an old controversy about the status of universals themselves, as Abelard indicates, which in the twelfth century took the form of a division especially between those who held that universals have a *real* existence and those who held that they have a purely *nominal* existence, that is, that they exist only in language. The controversy became particularly intense when it was thought to impinge on discussions of the nature of the Trinity, that is, the relationship between the single God and the individual divine persons of which he was considered to be composed. Some of the so-called nominalists found themselves charged with the her-esy of tritheism, or the belief in the existence of three separate Gods. Something of the sort happened to Abelard's old teacher, Roscelin, at the Council of Soissons in 1092, and to Abelard himself at Soissons in 1121.

a species, and that there is no distinctness in essence among them, but only a variety arising from the number of accidental properties. But now he changed his mind and said that the same nature exists in particulars not in *essence* but in *non-difference*. For dialecticians, of course, this has always been the fundamental question about universals: even Porphyry did not presume to settle it in the *Isagoge*, saying only, "It is a very profound matter."[7] So, when William shifted his position—or when I forced him to surrender it—his lectures disintegrated into such a muddle that he lost almost all credibility on every other issue of dialectic, as if this one position on universals comprised the whole subject.

From that point on, my own teaching gained so much in stature and substance that those who had been William's strongest supporters—and my own greatest enemies—now came to my school in flocks. Even the man who succeeded him at the school in Paris offered me his own post to become one of my students himself and join the rest of them there in the same spot where his master and mine had once had his day. Now, I had been in charge of dialectic at the school only a few days at most when my old master started carrying on, seething with such envy, boiling with such pain that words cannot do it justice. And once he started, he could not bear it long before he found a scheme to get rid of me even then. Because there was nothing he could do in the open against me, he began to work against the man who had given me his post, smearing him with the ugliest of charges until he wrested the school from his control and put one of my enemies in his place. I went back to Melun and set up my school as before, but the more openly that man's malice hounded me, the more it confirmed my own stature. As Ovid says, "Winds sweep the summits, envy seeks the heights."[8]

Shortly after, though—in fact, as soon as he became aware of all the gossip flying around about his newfound piety: almost no one took his religious retirement seriously since he had hardly withdrawn from the city at all—he gathered up a small community of brothers of his order and, along with his students, went off to some village far from town. Expecting no more trouble from that quarter, I came back to Paris right away. But since, as I said, he had installed

---

[7] Porphyry was a third-century Neoplatonic philosopher, whose introduction (*Isagoge*) to Aristotle's *Categories* remained an authoritative text in dialectic for centuries in its Latin translation by Boethius.

[8] *De Remedio Amoris* 1.369.

one of my enemies in the post that rightly belonged to me, I took my students to the hill of Saint Geneviève just outside the city and pitched camp there as if to lay siege to the occupying force.[9] No sooner had William heard about this than *he* came back to Paris right away—no sense of shame at all—and marched himself and his little community and whatever he could salvage of his school back inside their old monastery, thinking, I suppose, to break the siege and rescue the poor soldier he had left behind to hold the fort. He imagined he would do the man some good by this, but it only made things worse. Before this, he still had a handful of students of one sort or another, mostly because of his lectures on Priscian, which was supposed to be his specialty;[10] but after William's return to the city, he lost nearly every one of them and had to stop teaching altogether. Soon, in fact, he too retired to monastic life, as if he had finally given up any notion of worldly fame. Everything that happened after William's return—the jousts of argument my students had with him and his followers, the triumphs fortune gave us in our wars (myself not least among us)—is now an old story which certainly you know. To put it mildly, I can boast along with Ajax:

> And if you ask me how
> The fighting ended, he did not beat me down.[11]

But even if I said nothing, the facts speak for themselves and the end of the tale tells all.

While all this was going on, my beloved mother Lucia called for me to return home; my father Berengar had entered monastic life and she was making arrangements to do the same.[12] After everything was settled, I came back to France, where I wanted especially to take up the study of divinity. My master William was now in his

---

[9] Abelard's school was established at the church of St. Geneviève on the left bank of the Seine, south of the Île de la Cité and, hence, outside what then constituted the city of Paris proper.

[10] Priscian, sixth-century grammarian, author of *Institutiones Grammaticae*, a standard text on grammar at the time.

[11] Ovid, *Metamorphoses* 13.89–90.

[12] Such monastic retirement was not an unusual practice since monastic life provided its more elderly entrants with a modicum of medical care and the opportunity to supervise the distribution of their property while they were still alive, as well as a setting to prepare themselves spiritually for death.

glory as bishop of Châlons, but his old master was then considered to be the greatest authority on the subject from time immemorial. This was Anselm of Laon.[13]

So I went to the old man, who, I found, had bought himself a reputation more by long practice than by any capacity for learning or thought. Anyone who knocked on his door with a question went away more puzzled than before. Holding forth, he was a marvel to see; answering questions, he was nothing. The man had a marvelous way with words, but they were devoid of logic and abysmal in sense. He was like a fire which fills the house with smoke but gives no light, or a tree in full leaf if you see it from far off, but come up closer and look again, and it turns out to be barren. I came to this tree to gather fruit, but I saw it was the fig tree which the Lord cursed[14] or the ancient oak in Lucan's simile for Pompey:

> There stands the shadow of a once-great name,
> Like a towering oak in a fruitful field:
> Laden with the trophies of a nation,
> Clinging to earth with roots no longer strong,
> It stands fixed by its own weight; naked branches spread
> Leafless across the sky; only its trunk
> Casts a shadow, and though it totters, doomed
> To fall with the first wind, and all around it
> Many trees with healthy timber rise,
> Yet it alone is worshipped.[15]

---

[13] Anselm of Laon (c. 1055–c. 1117), student of St. Anselm and a well-known master of scriptural exegesis.

[14] See Mark 11:13–14:

> And when he had seen afar off a fig tree having leaves, he came if perhaps he might find any thing on it. And when he was come to it, he found nothing but leaves. For it was not the time for figs. And answering he said to it: May no man hereafter eat fruit of thee any more forever,

and Matt. 21:19.

[15] Lucan, *Pharsalia* 1.135–43. The manuscripts quote only the first two of these lines, though most of them add "etc." inviting consideration of the lines that follow, which are the ones that make Abelard's point. Directly after this passage, Lucan goes on to write of the younger warrior who ultimately defeated Pompey in Rome's civil wars, to whom Abelard may, at least in this context, wish implicitly to compare himself:

> But Caesar
> Had no such name or reputation, only
> A virtue that could not rest. . . .

Once I found this out, I did not lie lazing in his shadow for long. I started skipping his lectures more and more, which annoyed some of his favorite students, who somehow imagined that I had no respect for this great master of ours. With their secret plots and snide insinuations they succeeded in turning him too against me. Then one day, when I was joking with some of the other students after class,[16] one of them had the idea to challenge me by asking what I could possibly make of scriptural study when I had had no training at all outside philosophy. I answered that it certainly seemed very useful so far as the salvation of the soul was concerned, but that I was frankly amazed that educated men would find the writings or glosses of the Fathers insufficient by themselves to help them understand their commentaries without some extra instruction. They sniggered at this and asked if I thought *I* could do it or even presumed to try. I said, if that's what they wanted, I would, and they sniggered even more. "All right," they said, "we'll find you a commentary on some little-known text and see what you come up with," and they settled on an extremely obscure prophecy of Ezekiel. I took the commentary and invited them to a lecture on it the next day. No, they said, I couldn't hurry something as important as this; I should take my time to pore over the commentary and make sure of every point, especially with my total lack of practice. But I had no interest in their advice and told them in my most indignant tone that it was not my way to rely on practice but solely on the intelligence I was born with, and that either they would come to a lecture when and where I chose or else I would give the whole thing up.

Only a few people came, of course—everyone thought it was absurd that a complete novice in scriptural studies would charge straight into this—but they all thought the lecture was superb and

---

16 Abelard is more specific about the nature of the session, calling it *sententiarum collationes* (literally, "assemblage of conclusions"), which was both a type of class and an educational method. The traditional mode of scriptural education involved the exegesis of a biblical text through a verse-by-verse explanation, or gloss, by one of the Church Fathers. At this time, however—and to no small extent through the work of Anselm himself—another method was evolving, in which a teacher would lay out a set of conclusions (*sententiae*), arrived at by himself or another recognized authority, on a sequence of theological themes and then proceed to expand, elaborate, or, if necessary, defend them in a setting that could allow for more discussion than a lecture. Abelard's objection to it, as he goes on to explain, is that an educated man should not need a teacher for this kind of work: the writings and glosses of the Fathers ought to be enough by themselves to allow him to understand their commentaries without intermediary. See further Clanchy 1997, 85 ff., and Muckle 1964, 22 n. 22.

insisted that I prepare a gloss on the text along the same lines. When word got out, everyone who had not been to my first lecture came crowding to my second and my third, all of them frantic to copy out the glosses I had begun on the first day.

The old man was beside himself with envy. Certain individuals at the school, as I've mentioned, had already turned him against me, and now they egged him on to persecute me in scriptural study as William had done earlier in philosophy. There were two of the old man's students in particular—some considered them better than the rest—Alberic of Rheims and Lotulf the Lombard, two whose hatred of me was matched only by their self-infatuation[17]—it was largely due to their connivance, as it later came out, that the old man had the gall to forbid me from continuing my work on the gloss in a place where *he* was the master. He had a pretext, of course—to make sure that the mistakes I would make through my raw ignorance would not be attributed to him—but when the students heard about it, they exploded with outrage at this unprecedented attack of open spite. But the more open it was, the more honor it brought me: persecution only added to my fame.[18]

So after a few days, I returned to Paris, back to the school which had long been destined for me, which had once been offered to me, and from which I had at first been expelled. I had a peaceful tenure there for several years. My first aim was to complete the glosses on Ezekiel I had begun in Laon, and they were so well received that I won the same prestige in scripture as I already had in philosophy.[19] My school then grew by leaps and bounds, as students of both subjects swelled its ranks. The wealth and fame this brought me I'm sure you already know.

---

[17] Alberic of Rheims (c. 1085–1141) and Lotulf of Novara in Lombardy appear again as Abelard's prosecutors at the Council of Soissons in 1121 when Alberic was archdeacon of Rheims and both were masters at the school there. Alberic finished his career as archbishop of Bourges; little else is known of Lotulf.

[18] Anselm's actions may not have been as unreasonable as Abelard paints them, especially in this era of intense politicization of religious thought, neither his objection to an untrained student assuming the position of teacher in his school nor his insistence on maintaining a supervisory role for himself. At least his actions were not unique to Abelard's case. A book of Gilbert de la Porrée—a student of Anselm's, who may have been at Laon at the same time as Abelard—concludes: "Here ends the gloss of Master Gilbert de la Porrée, which he read out in the presence of his master, Anselm, so that he might correct it." See Clanchy 1997, 90.

[19] No trace of the glosses exists, and it is doubtful that Abelard ever finished them, despite the implication here that he did.

But success always puffs up the fool; worldly ease saps the strength of the mind and soon destroys it through the lures of the flesh. Now I thought I was the only philosopher in the world and had nothing to fear from anyone, and now I began to give free rein to my lust. I had lived with complete self-restraint up till now, but the more progress I made in philosophy and scripture, the more I fell short of philosophers and scholars of scripture in the foulness of my life. For we know that philosophers, and no less scholars of scripture—the ones, that is, who actually want to learn what scripture teaches—have grown strong through their self-restraint. As I was weighed down by lechery and pride, the grace of God brought me relief from both, though not in the ways I would have it: first from my lechery, by cutting from me the means I used to practice it, and then from the pride born of my learning—"Knowledge puffeth up," the apostle Paul says[20]—by humbling me with the burning of the book of which I was most proud.

Now, I want you to learn the truth of these events in all their proper order, and I want you to learn it not from hearsay but from the facts. I had no dealings with common whores—their foulness always disgusted me—and the demands of my scholarly life kept me from mixing often with high-born women, or women of the people for that matter. So fickle Fortune, as she's called, found a better way to seduce me and knock me down from my lofty perch—or perhaps it is better to say, for all my pride and blindness to the grace held out before me, God's mercy brought me low and claimed me for his own.

This is how it happened—

There was in Paris a young woman by the name of Heloise.[21] She was niece of one of the canons there called Fulbert, who doted on

---

[20] 1 Cor. 8:1.

[21] Heloise's birth date, and hence her age at this time (c. 1116), is not known. The tradition that she was sixty-three when she died (in 1163 or 1164) rests on no firm evidence but may well be derived from an imagined symmetry with Abelard, who died at that age. From Peter the Venerable's first letter to Heloise, it can be deduced that she was born c. 1090 and therefore was in her mid- or late twenties when she and Abelard met and not, as she has often been imagined, in her teens; see Clanchy 1997, 173–74. The most complete account of Heloise's life and what little can be known about her family is McLeod 1971, although a new biography by the late Mary Martin McLaughlin has been scheduled for publication for some years.

her and did everything he could to further her education. In her looks she was not the least of women, but in her learning she was supreme. As a gift for learning is so rare in a woman, it added all the more to her appeal and had already made her famous throughout the whole kingdom of France. Now, having carefully considered all the things that usually serve to attract a lover, I concluded that she was the best one to bring to my bed. I was sure it would be easy: I was famous myself at the time, young, and exceptionally good-looking, and could not imagine that any woman I thought worthy of my love would turn me down. But I thought that this particular girl would be even more likely to give in because of her knowledge and love of letters. Through the written messages we could send one another we could be together even when we were apart. We also could write some things to each other more boldly than we could ever speak them and so could always be carrying on some very pleasant dialogues.[22]

I was all on fire for the girl and needed a way I could get to know her on a private and daily basis to win her over. So I approached her uncle through some of his friends and arranged for him to take me as a lodger in his house, which was right next to the school; I would pay whatever he asked. I told him that the burdens of my own household kept me from concentrating properly on my academic work and that, besides, it had been costing me too much. The man had two weaknesses, his love of money and his ambitions for his niece's education. Working on both, I easily got what I wanted, while he stood there gaping after my cash and imagining how much she would learn from my instruction. On top of this, he begged me—actually begged—and it was beyond anything my love could have dared to hope—to take complete charge over the girl, to spend all the time I had free from school teaching her, night and day, and not only that, but to beat her severely if I found her slacking off. The simplicity of the man just staggered me, as if he had set a ravening wolf to watch over a lamb. When he put her in my hands not only to teach but to discipline as well, what else was he doing but giving me complete freedom, even if I never took advantage of it, to convince her by force if more gentle inducements did not prevail? But two things kept him from any suspicion, his love for his niece and my solid reputation for self-restraint.

---

[22] Some scholars have identified the remnants of these early letters in the fragmentary text known as *The Letters of Two Lovers*; see Appendix B to this volume.

What more do I need to say? First we were joined in one house, then in one heart. Under the pretext of study, we had all our time free for love, and in our classroom all the seclusion love could ever want. With our books open before us, we exchanged more words of love than of lessons, more kisses than concepts. My hands wandered more to her breasts than our books, and love turned our eyes to each other more than reading kept them on the page. To avert suspicion, there were some beatings, yes, but the hand that struck the blows belonged to love, not anger, to pleasure, not rage—and they surpassed the sweetness of any perfume. We left no stage of love untried in our passion, and if love could find something novel or strange, we tried that too. New at the game, we went at it with heat, and it never grew old for us.

But the more I was taken up with these pleasures, the less time I had for philosophy or teaching. It was torture to drag myself over to the school and utterly exhausting to stay there, since I was spending all my days in study and all my nights in love. My lectures became lukewarm and slack, relying now on my past practice and not on my intelligence at all. I did everything by rote, repeating only what had been new years before. All my new work, such as it was, now went into writing love songs and not the mysteries of philosophy. Many of these songs are still popular, as you know, and are sung throughout the country, especially by those who like the sort of life I myself was living then.[23] But what of my students? It is hard even to imagine their misery, their sorrow, their wails of lamentation when they understood what was preoccupying, or I should say, what was deranging my mind. It was all so plain that few could have been taken in, and no one was, I think, except the man whose honor was most at stake, that is, her uncle. People would give him hints from time to time, but he could not believe them because, as I said before, he doted on his niece and trusted in my well-known self-restraint. It never is easy to think ill of those we love: suspicion cannot exist where there is great affection. As Jerome says in his letter to Castrician, "We are the last to learn the evils of our own house or the faults of our wives and children, and the first to turn a deaf ear to what all the neighbors are saying."[24] But what is learned last is still learned eventually, and what all people know is hard to hide from one. After a few months, this is just what happened with us.

---

[23] See "Dull Is the Star" in this volume for the probable text of one of these songs.

[24] *Epistulae* 147.10. Abelard is in error here, however: the letter is to Sabinian.

How could I describe her uncle's grief when he found out, or our own grief when we were parted? What can I say about my shame and remorse, how I suffered at what she suffered, or the waves of anguish she endured at the thought of my disgrace? All our concern was for what could hurt the other, all our pain was for each other, not ourselves. But this same separation was the fusion of our hearts: love denied made us burn the more. The old shame we had felt now made us shameless, and we felt shame the less with each new chance to act. And then, what once happened in myth to Venus and Mars now happened to us: we were caught.[25] Soon after, though, the girl discovered she was pregnant and wrote me in a delirium of joy asking what I thought we should do. And so, one night, when her uncle was away, I took her secretly from his house and brought her to Brittany, as we had agreed. She stayed there with my sister until she gave birth to a boy, whom she called Astralabe.[26]

When her uncle came back, he went almost insane, boiling with such pain and writhing with such mortification that no one would believe it who had not seen it for himself. What should he do to me? How should he get me back? He had no idea. Have me killed or maimed somehow? But then his niece might have to pay for it among my people back in Brittany. No good to kidnap me and lock me up somewhere—I would be watching out for this, sure that's exactly what he'd try as soon as he could or dared. Finally, I took pity on the man. I met with him and, denouncing myself for this lover's trick as if it had been some supreme betrayal, threw myself on my knees and promised to do anything he asked to make this right. I pleaded the great power of love and what women had done from the beginning of the human race to bring even the greatest men to ruin. And I went further, offering him a satisfaction he never

---

[25] Mars and Venus were discovered together in bed by her husband, Vulcan. See Ovid, *Ars Amatoria* 2.561 ff. and *Metamorphoses* 4.169 ff.

[26] An extraordinary name, to say the least, bringing to mind some celebrity tot of the tabloids. An astrolabe is a scientific instrument used to measure the height of celestial bodies, though the word was also (falsely) etymologized as *astris lapsus*, "fallen from the stars." Few details of the life of Petrus Astralabius are available. That he grew to manhood, maintained at least some contact with his parents, and took up a career in the Church is indicated by the long poem Abelard addressed to him sometime after 1133 (see p. 295) and by the request Heloise makes of Peter the Venerable for a prebend for "your Astralabe" in her letter to him after Abelard's death. There is an "Astralabe" recorded as a canon of the cathedral of Nantes c. 1150, and this is almost certainly he, although there is more doubt about someone of that name who appears as abbot of the monastery of Hauterive in Fribourg in 1162–1165.

could have hoped: I undertook to marry the girl I had wronged, so long as it was all done in secret in order to keep my standing intact.[27] He agreed to every point, pledged his own faith and the faith of his relations, and then, to seal our compact, he kissed me— all the easier to betray me later on.

I went straight to Brittany to bring back my lover and make her my wife. But far from falling in with the idea, she vigorously argued against it on two fundamental grounds: it was dangerous, she said, and it would mean my disgrace.[28] She swore that her uncle could never be appeased by this or anything else, as later proved to be true. And, she asked, is *this* how she would be remembered, as the woman who brought my name to ruin and shamed us both? What toll should the world exact from her if she robbed it of its great light? Could I even imagine what would follow this marriage—the censure and abuse, the tears of the philosophers, and the loss to the Church? What a pity it would be for me, whom nature had created for all mankind, now to become the property of one woman—could I ever submit to this indignity? She rejected this marriage without qualification: it would be infamous and odious to me in every way.

Along with the disgrace, she brought up the problems of marriage the Apostle warns us against when he says:

> Art thou loosed from a wife? Then seek not a wife. But if thou take a wife, thou hast not sinned. And if a virgin marry, she hath not sinned: nevertheless, such shall have tribulation of the flesh. But I spare you. . . . I would have you be without solicitude. He that is without a wife is solicitous for the things that belong to the Lord, how he may

---

[27] Though somewhat fatuous under the circumstances, Abelard's desire for secrecy was not unwarranted. While it was permitted and not uncommon for clerics up through the rank of priest to be married, marriage for a cleric entailed the loss of Church benefices. It was also seen as morally incompatible with the position of a teacher, especially for one of Abelard's eminence and ambition: not only was Abelard's "standing" at stake but his career was at stake as well. For applicable canon law at the time, see McLaughlin 1941. For a more general discussion, see Brooke 1989 and, more briefly, Clanchy 1997, 187–91.

[28] Heloise's arguments against marriage, set out here and expanded in the First Letter, became well known in medieval literature, paraphrased by Jean de Meun (who also translated the *Calamities* and the letters into French) in *The Romance of the Rose*, lines 8745 ff., and thence taken up by Chaucer in the Wife of Bath's Prologue in *The Canterbury Tales*, and by others as well.

please God. But he that is with a wife is solicitous for the things of the world, how he may please his wife, and he is divided.[29]

But if I wouldn't take Saint Paul's advice or listen to the Fathers about the heavy yoke of matrimony, then at least, she insisted, I should turn to the philosophers for what they said on the subject and what was said about them. The Fathers themselves would often do the same—as Jerome does in his first book against Jovinian when he turns to Theophrastus for details of the stress of married life and his argument that the wise man should never marry; he then caps the philosopher's proof with his own conclusion, "When Theophrastus argues like this, can any Christian hear him and not blush?" and continues on to say:

> After Cicero divorced Terentia, Hirtius asked him to marry his sister, but Cicero refused, explaining that he could not give equal attention both to philosophy and to a wife. He did not say just "attention" but "*equal* attention" since he did not want to do anything to compete with his study of philosophy.[30]

"But to leave aside for the moment this obstacle to philosophy, think of the real conditions of that respectable way of life.[31] Scholars and nursemaids, writing desks and cradles, a book and a distaff, a pen and a spindle—what harmony can there be in *that*?[32] What husband could ever concentrate on philosophy or scripture and still put up with babies howling, nurses mumbling their lullabies, and a riotous gang of servants tramping all throughout the house? What wife could stand the endless mess of children? Certainly the rich ones can, you'll say, who have room enough in their mansions and

---

[29] 1 Cor. 7:27–28, 32–33. The manuscripts do not include the final two sentences of this passage, relying on an added "etc." to invoke the extended context on which Heloise's point in fact depends.

[30] *Contra Jovinianum* 1.47–48.

[31] In the next two paragraphs, the grammatical first person shifts to Heloise, as if Abelard is reporting her actual words, although Heloise would later complain that he has omitted many of her arguments (see her First Letter). The narrative here slips easily into Heloise's voice just as her argument begins to take on relevance for the future of her own intellectual life as well as Abelard's.

[32] Cf. 2 Cor. 6:14–16 and its extension in Jerome, *Epistulae* 22.29 for the rhetorical form.

money enough to ignore the expense and the torment of worrying every day. But I say to you, this is not the way it is with philosophers, for the rich or anyone else concerned with worldly occupations will have no time for what philosophers must do. That is why the great philosophers of the past put so little value on the world—not merely turning their backs on it but actively striving to escape it—and why they denied themselves all pleasures, that they might rest in the arms of philosophy alone. The greatest of them, Seneca, wrote to Lucilius:

> Philosophy is not something for just a little spare time. We have to ignore everything else, work only at this, for which no time is ever enough. . . . It does not matter if you leave off for a moment or leave off forever, for once put aside, philosophy does not last. . . . Give up all other business: do not simply put it in order—eliminate it.[33]

"How the true monastics of our time live in their devotion to God is how the pagan philosophers lived in their pursuit of philosophy.[34] There have always been individuals among every people—pagan as well as Jewish or Christian—who were exceptional in their faith or ethical conduct and who cut themselves off from the mass of others out of some rare austerity or self-restraint. Among the ancient Jews there were the Nazirites, who consecrated themselves to the Lord according to the law;[35] the sons of the prophets, whom Jerome refers to as monks;[36] and later, the Pharisees, Sadducees, and Essenes Josephus speaks about in his *Antiquities*.[37] Among us there are monastics, the true ones, that is, who live the communal life of the apostles or the solitary life of John. But among the pagans, as I say, there were the philosophers; for the term 'philosophy' or 'wisdom' did not then refer to extensive knowledge but to a conscientious way of life, as we know from the word's origin as well as from the Fathers. Saint Augustine tells us:

---

[33] *Epistulae ad Lucilium* 72.3.

[34] These "true monastics" are *monachi* in the original, literal sense, that is, those who live their lives "alone" (*monos* in Greek), withdrawn from the world in austerity and self-denial.

[35] See, e.g., Num. 6:21; Judg. 16:17; and Amos 2:11.

[36] See 4 Kings 6:1 and Jerome, *Epistulae* 125.7.

[37] *Antiquitates* 18.1.11.

Pythagoras of Samos, founder of philosophy in Italy, was said to be the first to use the term. Before him men who seemed especially worthy in some mode of life were called simply *wise men*. But when someone asked him his profession, he replied that he was a *philosopher*—that is, a lover of wisdom—since it seemed the height of arrogance to call himself wise.[38]

Note the words 'especially worthy in some mode of life': the wise men among the pagans—the *philosophers*—were so named not because of their knowledge but because of the character of their lives. To give examples of their sobriety and self-restraint would be teaching wisdom to Minerva, but I will ask you this: If pagans and laymen could lead such lives as these while bound by no religious calling, what should *you* do—you, a cleric and a canon—to hold your sacred duties above your pleasures, to keep yourself from plunging headlong into this Charybdis and sinking irrevocably into sensuality and shame?[39] If you care nothing for the privilege of a cleric, if you hold God's reverence in low esteem—if nothing else, at least defend the dignity of a philosopher and control this shamelessness with self-respect. Remember that Socrates was married and what an ugly penance he had to undergo to purge this stain to philosophy before he could become a caution to others. Jerome speaks of this as well in his first book against Jovinian:

> One day, after enduring a long stream of abuse from Xanthippe in a window overhead, he was suddenly doused with slops from above. All he did was wipe his head and say, 'Just as I expected—first the thunder, then the rain.'"[40]

She went on to point out that it would be dangerous for me to bring her back, and added in the end that it would be dearer to her—and more honorable to me—for her to be called my lover than my wife. I would be hers through a love freely offered, not forced and constrained by some marital tie, and the time we spent apart could only increase the sweetness of our reunion, our joys together as precious as they were rare. But when she saw that she could not

---

[38] *De Civitate Dei* 8.2.

[39] Charybdis is the whirlpool from which Ulysses escaped. It is also used as an image of sensuality in the Fourth Letter.

[40] *Contra Jovinianum* 1.48.

prevail against my adamant stupidity nor bear the thought of committing an offense against me, she brought her case to a close in tears and sighs. "There is only one thing left for us," she said, "that in our utter ruin the pain to come will be no less than the love that has gone before." And in this too, the spirit of prophecy did not fail her, as all the world has learned.

And so, we entrusted our little boy to my sister and returned to Paris in secret. In secret, too, a few days later, we spent a night of prayer in a church I will not name, and at dawn in that same church, in the presence of her uncle and some friends, we were joined by the blessing of marriage. Soon after, and again in secret, we took our separate ways and later saw each other only rarely and when we could be unobserved, careful to keep hidden what we had done. But soon her uncle and his household, looking for some way to restore his public honor, began to spread word of the marriage, breaking every pledge he had given me. She responded by cursing him and swearing it was a bare-faced lie, and he exploded with fury and fits of abuse.

As soon as I heard what was happening, I took her away to an abbey of nuns in a town near Paris called Argenteuil, where she had been brought up as a small girl, and had her fitted and dressed in the garments of monastic life, except for the veil.[41] But when her uncle heard about it, he, his kinsmen, and connections thought I had come up with an easy trick to disentangle myself by making her a nun. Then their anger reached its peak and they plotted their revenge. One night, as I slept peacefully in an inner room of my lodgings, they bribed one of my servants to let them enter and proceeded to wreak the savage vengeance that has made the whole world shudder—they cut off the parts of my body with which I committed the wrong they complained of—and then they fled. The only two who could be caught were blinded and had their genitals cut away, including the man who, while still in my service, was led by greed to betray me.

---

[41] Abelard's action would ordinarily have signified an intention to dissolve the marriage, though Heloise's formal consent would have been required for such a step. Neither Abelard nor Heloise, however, seems to have understood it this way, and his insistence on the absence of the veil seems designed to underscore a different intent.

The convent of St. Marie in Argenteuil—now an industrial suburb just north of Paris—was a royal foundation dating to the seventh century and, at the time of Abelard and Heloise, one of the wealthiest and most prestigious religious houses for women in the area of Paris.

By the next morning, the entire city had converged outside my door, shocked and appalled, moaning and howling and wailing such earsplitting cries that it is hard—no, impossible—to describe it.

The clerics were the worst and my students worst among them,
crucifying me with their screams and laments
until I suffered more from their pity than my pain,
more from chagrin than the injury itself,
and more from the scandal than the scar.
I thought of the glory I once enjoyed
and the simple, vicious act that brought it low,
the judgment of a God who struck where I most had sinned,
the vindication by broken faith when I had broken faith,
the exultation of my enemies over this so fitting reward,
the lasting grief this wound would bring
to my parents and my friends,
the way my particular shame would spread
throughout the universe of men.
No road was now left open to me,
no face I could show to the world,
when every finger would point,
every tongue would mock
the monstrous spectacle I would become.
An abomination before God,
according to the deadly letter of the law,
forbidden to enter a church, as if stinking and unclean—
that is what a eunuch is,
his testicles broken or cut away.
Even such an animal is despised for sacrifice.[42]

---

[42] Inspired by Abelard's biblical reminiscences, Deut. 23:1 and Lev. 22:24 (Num. 72 in an earlier system of biblical citation), the extant manuscripts continue with the full supporting passages and references:

> Book of Numbers, Chapter 72—"You shall not offer to the Lord any beast that hath the testicles bruised, or crushed, or cut and taken away." Deuteronomy, Chapter 23—"A eunuch, whose testicles are broken or cut away, or organ cut off, shall not enter into the church of the Lord."

Their redundancy within the paragraph and the uncharacteristic baldness of their presentation indicate that the quotations are most likely a later interpolation in the text. The suggestion of an interpolation here was made by Orlandi 1980, in the context of a debate on Abelard's authorship of the entire *Calamities*.

It was my shame, I will admit, my guilt and my confusion rather than my commitment to the religious life that brought me to the refuge of the cloister. In the meantime, she had taken the veil freely at my command. We both, then, put on the habit at the same time, I in the abbey of Saint Denis,[43] she in the convent at Argenteuil, which I mentioned before. I remember that many people tried to stop her, concerned that for someone of her age the yoke of monastic rule would be a penance too hard to bear, but they could not. Through her tears and sobs the best she could, she broke into Cornelia's great lament:

> O my husband,
> Too great for such a wife, had Fortune power
> Even over you? The guilt was mine
> For this disastrous marriage. Now claim your due,
> And I will freely pay.[44]

And with these words, she rushed to the altar, snatched up the veil which the bishop had just blessed, and bound herself to the convent in the presence of all.

My wounds were still healing when my students started at me, rivers of them, flooding me and my abbot with their never-ending demands: I must take up my studies again, not for wealth or fame as before, but out of a love of God. I must understand that the great sum the Lord had lent me now must be paid back with interest, that while I was used to tending to the rich, now I must be teacher to the poor. I must realize that I was touched by the hand of the Lord, and now that I was freed from the lures of the flesh and the stresses of secular life, I would have the leisure for study to become, not the philosopher of the world, but in truth the philosopher of God.

Yes. But the abbey of my retirement was still part of this secular life and in the most corrupt way, and the abbot, great prelate that he

---

[43] The abbey of St. Denis was a prestigious royal foundation just north of Paris, dedicated to the patron saint of France. The rebuilding program that was to transform its church into one of the splendors of medieval architecture was only a few years in the future.

[44] Lucan, *Pharsalia* 8.94–98. Cornelia, the wife of Pompey, speaks these words to him shortly after his catastrophic defeat at the battle of Pharsalus. Contrast Abelard's earlier citation of Lucan, in which it is Anselm of Laon who is likened to Pompey. Abelard will return to Lucan's Pompey and Cornelia again in the Fourth Letter.

was, was as great in degeneracy and scandal.[45] Certainly I brought
this to my brother monks' attention, loudly and often, both in public
and in private, denouncing their intolerable filth and making myself
very well detested by them all. They would be happy to use the
opportunity of my students' daily rounds as a means of getting rid
of me. And so, as time passed and the students persisted, my abbot
and the monks stepped in, and I withdrew to a priory somewhere to
take up my teaching in my usual way.[46] My students followed in
such a stream that the place could not provide enough lodging for
them, or the land provide enough food.

I concentrated on scripture while I was there, since it was more
appropriate to my new position, but my main expertise was in the
secular arts and that is what the students called for. So I used these
arts as a kind of hook, offering them a taste of philosophy—as the
History of the Church tells us Origen, the greatest Christian philosopher, also did[47]—to draw them in to the true philosophy. When it
became clear that God had given me a gift for scripture no less than
for secular learning, the number of my students increased dramati-
cally in both subjects while all the other schools saw steep declines.
Because of this, the other masters became jealous and resentful and
worked to undermine me in every possible way, constantly sniping
behind my back with their charges, on the one hand, that my interest in secular studies was contrary to the profession of a monk and,
on the other, that my interest in scripture was presumptuous since I
was setting myself up as a master without having had a master in
the subject myself. Their aim, of course, was to bar me from any sort
of teaching whatsoever, and to that end they constantly went
around pressuring bishops, archbishops, abbots, and anyone else in
the Church hierarchy they could find.

My first set of lectures expounded on the fundamentals of our faith
by analogy with human reason, and I wrote a treatise of theology

---

[45] Abbot Adam, whose subsequent history with Abelard remained contentious until
his sudden death in 1122, as Abelard recounts later.

[46] Abelard does not say where this was, though it was most likely in or near Nogent-
sur-Seine in Champagne, where St. Denis held considerable property (including a
priory) and where Abelard would later found the Paraclete.

[47] The Historia Ecclesiae of Eusebius, 6.8 ff. Origen, the third-century writer and
teacher of Alexandria, provides a model for Abelard in another way as well: he was a
eunuch, having castrated himself to avoid any gossip or suspicion when he began to
take on women students, as Abelard will later note.

*On the Unity and Trinity of God* for the use of my students who kept asking for rational arguments, demanding things that could be understood instead of just mouthed.[48] In fact, they said that words were pointless if understanding did not follow, that nothing can be believed if it is not first understood, and that for someone to preach to others what neither he nor they could understand was a ludicrous example of what Christ condemned as the blind leading the blind.[49] When the treatise was circulated, it met with wide acceptance, appearing to answer every question on the subject in a thoroughly satisfactory way, the subtlety of my solutions seeming all the more impressive in light of the importance of the problems they addressed.

This only infuriated my enemies and they convened a council against me, those two old plotters in particular, Alberic and Lotulf, who, with the deaths of our masters William and Anselm, were determined to succeed them as their heirs and rule alone in their place. They directed the school in Rheims together and, with their constant prods and innuendoes, were able to bring their archbishop Radulf to their side. He and Cardinal Cono of Palestrina, papal legate in Gaul at the time,[50] organized in the town of Soissons a little meeting which they grandly styled a council. They invited me to

---

[48] This treatise, condemned at the Council of Soissons in 1121 as Abelard explains later, evolved through many versions throughout the rest of Abelard's life. The first version, known in manuscripts as *De Trinitate* (*On the Trinity*) or *Theologia "Summi Boni"* (named from its opening phrase), was expanded into the *Theologia Christiana* (*Christian Theology*) and again reworked in the 1130s into the *Theologia "Scholarium,"* which was the text condemned following the Council of Sens in 1140. This last version explicitly returns to the intentions of the first, beginning with the phrase that supplies its title, "*Scholarium nostrorum petitioni*—At the request of my students." See Buytaert and Mews 1987.

Although Abelard was not the first to introduce the term theology (in the sense of "rational discourse about God") in place of the more conventional divinity, it seems to have been a catchword for him and both novel enough and provocative enough for Bernard of Clairvaux to mock Abelard's work as *stultologia,* or "stupidology," in his Letter 190.

[49] See Matt. 15:14. Abelard's students here are also specifically and significantly reversing a widely cited version of Isa. 7:9, "Unless you believe, you will not understand," thereby offering a new understanding of the relationship between reason and faith.

[50] Cono, bishop of Palestrina, was the most senior Church diplomat and powerful enough to have twice excommunicated Emperor Henry V on his own initiative; reportedly he had been the chosen successor of Pope Gelasius II in 1119, two years before the Council of Soissons.

come and bring a copy of my treatise on the Trinity, and so I did. By this time, though, Alberic and Lotulf had already so worked up the clerics and the people against me that, as soon as I arrived in town with a few of my students, the mob nearly stoned us, claiming I had written and preached that there were three Gods, for that in fact is what they had been told.[51]

I went straight to the legate, presented the book for his examination and judgment, and announced myself ready to receive correction and make amends if I had said or written anything contrary to the Catholic faith. But he simply told me to take it to the archbishop and the prosecutors since they were the ones who had brought the charge—it seemed that the words, "Our enemies themselves are judges" were to be fulfilled in my case.[52] They took their time inspecting it and reading it over and over again, but they found nothing they could bring up against me in open session, so they postponed the condemnation they were panting for until the council's closing day.

In the meantime, every day before the council sat, I gave a set of public lectures, open to all, expounding the Catholic faith according to the arguments in my book. Everyone who heard them was deeply impressed by both my explanation and interpretation. This made the clerics and the people start to wonder, and they asked each other, "'Behold, he speaketh openly, and they say nothing to him.'[53] He was supposed to be the target of the council, but it looks like it is going to end soon. Have the judges learned that the mistake was not his but theirs?" And so, every day, my enemies became more and more enraged.

One day while all this was going on, Alberic came to me, a few of his students in tow, with the idea of challenging me. After some

---

51 There is no reason to think that Abelard either imagined or exaggerated the threat against him. Charges of heresy were occasions for public theater as much as for juridical proceedings, and mob violence against suspected heretics often had official sanction. Just seven years before in Soissons, two accused heretics were dragged from their cells and burned by the mob; and in 1092, also in Soissons, Abelard's former master, Roscelin, was attacked by the mob, stripped, and robbed, although he already had been acquitted of the heresy of tritheism, precisely the popular charge against Abelard here. In both cases, the violence was subsequently endorsed by ecclesiastical authorities. See Clanchy 1997, 289–92.

52 Deut. 32:31.

53 John 7:26.

polite small talk, he said that something he had noticed in my book was puzzling him, that is, while God begat God, and there is only one God, nonetheless I said that God did not beget himself.

"Oh," I said easily, "I'll go through the rational argument for you if you like."

"We don't care about the rational argument," he said, "or any interpretation *you* might have. The only thing that matters is the word of authority."

"Then turn the page," I said, "and you'll find it." I quickly leafed through the copy of the book he had with him to a passage I knew was there, though he had not seen it or else only bothered to notice what he thought could be used against me. By God's will I found it right away—the passage clearly headed "Augustine, *On the Trinity*, Book I":

> Whoever thinks that God has the power to beget himself is wrong. God does not have this power, any more than any spiritual or corporeal creature. There is no being whatsoever that can beget itself.[54]

His students stood there with their mouths wide open, turning a brilliant red, while he tried to cover himself, blustering, "But of course this must be understood in the correct way."

Yes, I said, of course; there was nothing new in that, but it also had nothing to do with the present circumstances: he was looking for words, not interpretation. But if he wanted interpretation *and* a rational argument, I was perfectly ready to give him both and prove by his own pronouncement that he had fallen into the heresy of believing the Father to be his own Son. At this he exploded and resorted to threats, swearing that none of my arguments or authorities would help me now. Then he stormed off.

On the last day of the council, before the official session was set to take up again, the papal legate and the archbishop held a long conference with Alberic, Lotulf, and some others to decide what to do about me and my book, which was the main reason the council had been convened in the first place. Since nothing I had said or written gave them any grounds for action, they all were silent for a while— or at least somewhat less open in their hostility—until Geoffrey,

---

[54] *De Trinitate* 1.1.

bishop of Chartres, who was first among the bishops there in piety and the dignity of his see, began to speak.[55]

"My lords," he said, "all of you here know the quality of this man's teaching and you know his intelligence. In whatever studies he has taken up, he has won so many followers that he has eclipsed the fame of his own masters as well as ours, and his vine, as it were, has spread its branches from sea to sea.[56] If you act against him without a hearing—as I am sure you will not—even if your action is correct, you must know it will outrage many people, and many will readily come to his defense—all the more so since we see nothing in the book before us to justify its public condemnation. Now, since 'open courage will always have its enemies,' as Jerome tells us, 'and "Lightning always strikes the highest peaks,"'[57] make sure no act of violence on your part will add to his reputation or do more harm to us through the envy of our charge than we can ever do to him through its justice. 'A false rumor is soon crushed,' the learned Jerome also remarks, 'and a man's later life pronounces judgment on his past.'[58]

"If, on the other hand, you would act according to rule, then bring his teaching or his writing here before us, and let him be free to answer our questions. Then, if he is convicted or confesses his error, he can be silenced once and for all. Remember the words of Saint Nicodemus when our Lord himself stood accused: 'Doth our law judge any man unless it first hear him and know what he doth?'"[59]

My enemies broke into an uproar. "Oh, this is really brilliant advice," they said, "to have us wrangle with this silver-tongued sophist whose arguments confound the whole world!"

"Surely, though," the bishop replied, "it was harder to wrangle with Christ, but Nicodemus still demanded that *he* be heard."[60]

When he saw he could not persuade them, he tried another way to keep their envy from running wild. There were too few people present for a matter of this weight, he said, and the case needed

---

[55] Geoffrey of Lèves, bishop of Chartres, 1116–1149.

[56] Cf. Ps. 79:12.

[57] *Quaestiones Hebraicae in Genesim, Praefatio;* the internal quotation is from Horace, *Odes* 2.10.11–12.

[58] *Epistulae* 54.13.

[59] John 7:51.

[60] The manuscripts omit any indication of direct speech or attribution of speaker here. Without it, however, the sentence remains a very uncharacteristic aside of Abelard's own.

more time for examination; and so, he recommended that my abbot take me back to Saint Denis, where a larger number of more learned men could be brought together to examine my case more thoroughly and determine what should be done. The legate accepted this plan, as did everyone else. Then, rising to celebrate Mass before the council session formally began, he sent word through Bishop Geoffrey of his permission for me to return to my monastery and await a decision there.

My enemies knew they would have accomplished nothing if the matter were moved to another diocese, where, with no case in law, they could have no recourse to violence. So they persuaded their archbishop that it would be both an affront to have the case heard somewhere else and a serious risk to let me slip away. They all went running to the legate, made him change his mind, and convinced him against his better judgment to condemn the book without a hearing, burn it in the sight of all, and sentence me to perpetual confinement in another monastery. It should be enough to condemn the book, they told him, that I had read it in public and had it transcribed without sanction of pope or Church; the Christian faith would only be stronger if such presumption were crushed by the force of my example. Because the legate was less educated than he should have been, he fell back on the archbishop's advice, as the archbishop fell back on theirs.

As soon as the bishop of Chartres saw what was coming, he came and told me of the whole dirty scheme. He urged me not to take it too hard—their violence was clear enough to everyone, and violence like this, he said, driven so plainly by envy, was bound to work against them and in my favor. As for the confinement, he knew the legate felt pressured into it and would release me a day or two after the council ended and he left town. We were both in tears as he gave me what consolation he could.

I was called before the council and, without any question or discussion, was forced to throw the book into the fire with my own hands and burn it. To make it seem as if they had at least *something* to say, one of my enemies mumbled that he had heard the book claimed that only God the Father was almighty.[61] The legate caught a little of this and said that he was shocked; he couldn't believe even

---

[61] Abelard's argument, reiterated and refined throughout his life, is that the divine property of power is expressed in the Father, as wisdom is in the Son, and goodness is in the Holy Spirit.

a child would make a mistake like this since our faith clearly holds and professes that there are three Almighties. A man named Thierry, who was master of a school of his own,[62] snorted in derision and intoned the words of the Athanasian Creed, "And yet they are not three Almighties, but one Almighty." His bishop started to rebuke him as though he were guilty of high treason, but he held his ground and continued on in the words of Daniel, "'Are ye so foolish, ye children of Israel, that without examination or knowledge of the truth, you have condemned a son of Israel? Return to judgment,'[63] and judge the judge himself, the same one you have established for instruction in the faith and correction of error. Yet when he ought to pass judgment, he has condemned himself out of his own mouth, while God in his mercy today delivers this innocent man, as he once delivered Susanna, from the hands of false accusers."

The archbishop stood up to confirm the legate's opinion, tactfully changing its wording somewhat, as certainly was called for: "Yes, my lord, the Father is almighty, the Son is almighty, the Holy Spirit is almighty, and whoever dissents from this is clearly in error and should not be heard. And now, if it is your pleasure, it is fitting that this our brother should profess his faith in the presence of all, for us either to approve or to censure and correct, as may be appropriate."

But just as I was rising to profess my faith and explain it in my own words, my enemies stopped me, demanding that I do nothing more or less than recite the Athanasian Creed, a thing the merest schoolboy could just as easily do. And to prevent, as they said, a plea of ignorance—as if I were some dunce who did not know those words by heart—they handed me the text and made me read. I was choked with tears and sobs, but I read the best I could. Then, as if I were truly guilty and had been lawfully condemned, I was remanded to the abbot of Saint Médard and dragged off to his cloister as if to prison. The council was immediately dissolved.

The abbot and monks of Saint Médard welcomed me with open arms, glad to think I would be with them indefinitely.[64] Though they did what they could to comfort me, it was little use.

---

62 Generally taken to be Thierry, chancellor of Chartres from 1141.

63 Dan. 13:48–49, which, however, speaks of a "daughter of Israel," referring to Susanna.

64 A different perspective on Abelard's reception at St. Médard is revealed by the medieval biographer of St. Godwin, prior of the monastery at the time and a former student of Abelard's who had fallen out with him at his school on Mont Ste. Geneviève. According to him, St. Médard functioned as a kind of monastic reformatory

God, who are the judge of equity,
with what gall and bitterness of mind did I reproach you,
accuse you in my wild madness,
repeating over and over the lament of Saint Anthony,
"Good Jesus, where were you?"
I could feel then but cannot describe now
the storm of my grief, the tumult of my shame,
and the anguish of my despair.
I set what I had suffered in my body
against what I was suffering now
and thought I was the unhappiest of men.
That other betrayal seemed nothing next to this,
far less painful that wound to my body than this to my reputation,
for I had brought that other wound on myself
but was brought to this open violence
by the pure intention and love of our faith
which compelled me to write.

Soon enough, however, the council's cruel and reckless act found the universal condemnation it deserved. The individuals involved began to shift the blame onto others, even my enemies denied responsibility, and the legate made a public statement deploring the envy of the French in this affair. Regretting now that he had complied with their envy under pressure, he released me from this new monastery after a few days and sent me back to Saint Denis. But there, at Saint Denis, things were still as I described them. Nearly every monk who had been there before detested me; their vile way of life and shameless practices made them hate a man whose censure they could not endure. Only a few months passed before luck gave them their chance to destroy me.

By accident one day, I came across a passage in Bede's commentary on the Acts of the Apostles, in which he records that Dionysius the Areopagite was not the bishop of Athens but of Corinth.[65] Now,

---

where "ignorant monks were sent to be educated, dissolute ones to be corrected, and headstrong ones to be tamed," and Abelard was threatened with corporal punishment for his sarcastic retorts.

[65] This odd episode, beginning with an accident and a joke, would have remained purely comic if its consequences had not turned so serious, threatening Abelard with a charge of treason against the French crown and significantly changing the course of his career yet again. Behind it lay the confusion—both by Bede and, in a different pattern,

this seemed directly to contradict the boasts of those who take their own Saint Denis—whose history shows he was indeed bishop of Athens—to be the famous Areopagite converted by Saint Paul. There were a few monks standing around at the time and I showed them the passage as a kind of joke—Bede's testimony against our abbey. They were outraged, called Bede a liar, and said that their own abbot Hilduin was a far better witness to the truth, having traveled throughout Greece for years looking into just this question and finally dispelling any possible doubt in the life of the saint he had written. One of them demanded to know right then and there where *I* stood on the matter—with Hilduin or with Bede? I answered that I thought the authority of Bede, whose writings after all were known throughout the Latin Church, did seem to carry a little bit more weight.

They became incensed and started shouting that finally I had shown myself to be the enemy of the monastery I had always been and, what's more, a traitor to the entire country, a thief of that honor that was uniquely its own, to deny as I'd done that their patron was the Areopagite. I said I hadn't denied that he was the Areopagite, and besides, it didn't seem to matter very much whether he was the Areopagite or someone else from somewhere else, so long as he was worthy of such a great crown in the eyes of God. But they went running off to the abbot to tell on me and what they had made me say. The abbot—who feared me more than the others, being much more corrupt than the others—grinned at the news, relishing any chance he could get to destroy me. He summoned his council and the chapter of brethren and threatened to send me to the king for punishment as a would-be thief of the country's honor and even the king's own crown. In the meantime, I would be kept under close guard. I offered to submit myself to the discipline of the monastic rule if in fact I had done anything wrong, but he would not listen.

---

by the abbey's official account—of several distinct individuals: (a) Dionysius the Areopagite, converted by Paul in the first century (Acts 17:34) and traditionally considered to have been the first bishop of Athens; (b) a second-century bishop of Corinth also called Dionysius; and (c) the third-century St. Dionysius (St. Denis) venerated by the abbey and regarded as the patron of France, who, having been beheaded on the elevation in Paris now known as Montmartre ("Martyrs' Hill") was said to have carried his own severed head to his place of burial at the site of the abbey church. Bede confuses (a) and (b). The abbey's official life of St. Denis, composed by its abbot Hilduin in the ninth century, dates (c) to the first century and identifies him as a bishop of Athens and, therefore, as (a). Somewhat later in the controversy, Abelard would write a conciliatory letter to Abbot Adam and the monks of St. Denis at least partly retracting his support for Bede's claim.

I was horrified to think what they would stoop to, and, with everything else that had happened, I lost all hope, convinced that the whole world had conspired against me. Yet there were still some monks who pitied me and some of my students who would help me, so I slipped out of the monastery one night and made for the lands of Count Theobald not far away, where I had stayed in a priory some time before.[66] I already had a slight acquaintance with the count and knew that he felt deeply for what I had suffered. I then took up residence in the town of Provins within a house of monks from Troyes, whose prior was an old, dear friend of mine.[67] He was naturally very happy I had come and looked after me with every consideration.

One day not long thereafter, the abbot of Saint Denis came to Provins on some business with the count. The prior and I asked the count to intercede with him on my behalf, requesting his absolution and his permission for me to live as a monk wherever I could find a suitable place. The abbot and his party took the question under advisement and promised an answer before they left later in the day. In the course of their discussions, they decided my intention was to transfer to another abbey, and that, they felt, would be a great dishonor to Saint Denis. They took it as their abbey's special pride that I had come to them when I first became a monk, as if I had deliberately rejected all the rest, and now it would be a pointed affront if I rejected them and transferred somewhere else. They would hear nothing of our requests but instead laid down an ultimatum: I must soon return to Saint Denis or face excommunication, and the prior, too, who was sheltering me must henceforth cease or become a partner in my fate. We both, of course, were appalled when we heard this.

The abbot left town clinging stubbornly to his position but died a few days later. When his successor was chosen, I went with the bishop of Meaux to meet with him and repeat my request.[68] At first, he too refused, but I appealed to the king through the interest of

---

[66] Most likely when Abelard withdrew from St. Denis earlier to take up his teaching. The powerful Theobald II was count of Champagne, Provins, and Meaux; count of Blois and Chartres from 1107; and count of Troyes from 1125 until his death in 1152.

[67] Radulf, prior of St. Ayoul, a house belonging to the monastery of St. Peter.

[68] The successor was the famous Abbot Suger (c. 1081–1151), adviser to Kings Louis VI and VII and rebuilder of the great abbey church of St. Denis.

some friends and soon got what I wanted. Stephen de Garlande,[69] king's high steward at the time, summoned the abbot and his advisers to a meeting and demanded to know why they would keep me at the abbey against my will when it was clear that their way of life and mine were not compatible; there could be no good in this situation, he said, only a scandal in the making. I was also aware of the sentiment among the royal council that an abbey without rule should be subject to the king as a useful source of revenue, so I was sure I would win their support. It turned out as I thought it would. Our two sides, then, came to an agreement, which was confirmed in the presence of king and council. To maintain the honor Saint Denis derived from my membership there, I undertook not to place myself under obedience to another abbot. Otherwise, I was free to go to whatever place of solitude I liked.

I went to a place of solitude I knew, a certain wilderness in the countryside near Troyes.[70] The land was given to me and, with permission of the local bishop, I built a kind of oratory there out of thatch and reeds, which I dedicated to the Holy Trinity. In this seclusion, with only one of my clerics for company, I could cry out to the Lord in truth, "Lo, I have gone off flying away and I abode in the wilderness."[71]

As soon as they discovered where I was, however, my students started flocking from all over, leaving the towns and cities to come and live in this wilderness, giving up mansions to build themselves huts, fine foods to eat greens and coarse bread, soft couches to lie on mats of reed and straw, and tables to heap up mounds of turf instead. In all, you would have thought they were taking up the ways of the early philosophers Saint Jerome describes. He explains their rationale:

> Vice enters the soul through the windows of the senses, and
> the fortress of the mind cannot fall unless the enemy rush its

---

69 Stephen de Garlande (c. 1070–c. 1148), most powerful member of a powerful political family and holder of numerous royal and ecclesiastical posts under the reigns of Philip I and Louis VI. The sequence of these posts, their timing, and the vicissitudes of his long career correspond so well with the stages of Abelard's own career that it is reasonable to conclude that Abelard enjoyed the active sponsorship of the de Garlandes over many decades and not on this occasion alone. See Bautier 1981, 21–77.

70 On the banks of the Ardusson River, about four miles southeast of Nogent-sur-Seine and roughly thirty miles northwest of Troyes.

71 Ps. 54:8.

gates. . . . If someone finds pleasure in the spectacle of games, the contest of athletes, the agility of mimes, the beauty of women, or the shimmer of gems, silks, and the like, then the freedom of his soul is taken through the windows of the eyes, and the words of the prophet are fulfilled: "For death is come up through our windows."[72] When the armies of distraction have broken through these gates into the fortress of the mind, where is its freedom then, or its strength, or its thoughts of God—especially when sensation can leave traces of past pleasure and, through memories of vice, enlist the mind to rehearse, as it were, what it does not actually do?

That is why many philosophers left the crowds of the city and the gardens beneath the city walls—with their ponds and trees and birdsongs, reflecting pools and babbling brooks and every lure for eye or ear—to keep luxury and wealth from ever weakening the strength of the soul or compromising its purity. Why get used to sights that someday may enslave you, or even taste what someday you may miss? Even the Pythagoreans shunned the life of the city and made their homes in the wilderness and desert wastes. And Plato himself, though certainly rich—Diogenes would wipe his muddy feet on Plato's couch[73]—still set his Academy far from the city to safeguard the leisure he needed for philosophy, and he even chose a site that was unhealthy in order to break the assaults of lust by constant illness and focus his students' pleasure on their studies alone.[74]

It was just such a life that the sons of the prophets also led, the followers of Elisha whom Jerome calls the monks of their time in a letter he wrote to the monk Rusticus:

> The sons of the prophets, the monks we read of in the Old Testament, built huts for themselves on the banks of the Jordan, living on barley-meal and greens far from the throngs of the city[75]

---

[72] Jer. 9:21.

[73] In his life of Diogenes the Cynic, Diogenes Laertius reports this gesture of contempt for Plato's supposed pride; see *Lives of the Philosophers* 6.26.

[74] *Contra Jovinianum* 2.8 ff.

[75] *Epistulae* 125.7; see 4 Kings 6:1.

—as my students now built their huts on the banks of the Ardusson, looking more like hermits than the scholars they were.

But as more students came and put up with more hardships all for the sake of my teaching, the more my enemies felt my renown and their own humiliation. Everything they had done to hurt me had turned to my good, and it stung them. And so, in the words of Jerome, "Far from the cities, the courts, and the crowds, as Quintilian says, envy found me in my seclusion."[76] Now they would sulk in silence or mutter to each other, "'Behold, the whole world is gone after him.'[77] Our persecution has only added to his glory. We tried to eclipse his fame but it just shines the brighter. Here are the students in the city with everything they need at hand, and look how they despise its luxuries and flood to the wilderness, actually choosing misery and want on their own."

This time it was poverty more than anything that drove me back into teaching. Since "to dig I was unable and to beg I was ashamed,"[78] I returned to the art I knew, working with my tongue instead of my hands. My students happily provided for all my basic needs—food and clothing, work on the land or help with the cost of building—to keep these practical matters from distracting me from my studies. Since my oratory could not hold even a fraction of their number, they had to enlarge it and build a solid new construction of stone and wood. The building had been founded and first dedicated in honor of the Holy Trinity, but since I had taken refuge there in my despair and found some consolation by the grace of God, I renamed it for the Paraclete in memory of the gift I was given.

This new name struck many as odd, and some even attacked me for it with considerable violence, charging that by ancient custom a church must not be named for the Holy Spirit alone, any more than for the Father alone, but only for the Son or for the Trinity as a whole. What lay behind these charges, no doubt, was their belief that *Paraclete* can refer only to the Holy Spirit Paraclete, but this is an error. Just as the Trinity or any of its members may be called *God* and *Sustainer,* so it is correct to address each or all of them as *Paraclete,* or *Consoler.* As the Apostle said, "Blessed be the God and Father of our Lord Jesus Christ, the Father of mercies, and the God

---

76 *Quaestiones Hebraicae in Genesim,* quoting Quintilian, *Declamationes* 13.2.

77 John 12:19.

78 Luke 16:3.

of all consolation, who consoleth us in all our tribulation"; and the Truth said, "And he shall give you another Paraclete."[79]

Moreover, when the entire Church is consecrated in the name of the Father, Son, and Holy Spirit and belongs to them all without distinction, why should a house of the Lord not be named for the Father or the Holy Spirit as well as for the Son? Who would dare erase the owner's name from the door of his own house? And when the Son has sacrificed himself to the Father, and prayers at Mass are addressed to the Father and the Host is offered specifically to him, why should the altar not belong to the Father, to whom appeals and sacrifice are made? Is it really more proper that the altar be named for the Son, who makes the sacrifice, than for the Father, who receives it? Or better to name an altar for the Lord's Cross or the Sepulcher, for Saint Michael, Saint John, Saint Peter, or any other saint who makes or receives no sacrifice there and has no prayers addressed to him? Surely even among the heathen, temples and altars belonged to those who received sacrifice and worship there.

I can imagine the claim that there should be no church or altar dedicated to the Father on the grounds that there is no deed of the Father that warrants a feast day dedicated specifically to him. But while this argument detracts from the Trinity as a whole, it does not detract from the Holy Spirit. For the Holy Spirit has the Feast of Pentecost to commemorate his coming, as the Son has the Nativity to commemorate his birth: as the Son was sent into the world, so the Holy Spirit was sent among the disciples, and this justifies his feast. In fact, it seems more reasonable to dedicate a temple to the Holy Spirit than to any other member of the Trinity, especially when we consider both the authority of Saint Paul and the operation of the Holy Spirit himself. To none of the three does Paul ascribe a spiritual temple except to the Holy Spirit. He does not speak of a temple to the Father or to the Son in his first letter to the Corinthians, but of a temple to the Holy Spirit: "He that is joined to the Lord is one Spirit," and "Know you not that your body is the temple of the Holy Spirit who is in you, whom you have of God, and you are not your own?"[80] And it is well known that the sacraments of the Church are ascribed specifically to the operation of divine grace, which means the Holy Spirit. We are baptized by

---

[79] 2 Cor. 1:3–4; John 14:16.
[80] 1 Cor. 6:17, 19.

water and the Holy Spirit and are reborn as a special temple for God. We are confirmed in the sevenfold grace of the Spirit, and this temple is adorned and dedicated. Is it at all strange then to name a material temple for the member of the Trinity to whom Saint Paul has specifically ascribed a spiritual one? Is there anyone else to whom a church more properly belongs than the one to whose operation all the sacraments administered in the Church are ascribed?

At any rate, it was not my intention to honor only one member of the Trinity when I named my oratory for the Paraclete. It was, as I mentioned before, simply in memory of the consolation I found there. But if it *had been* my intention, as was widely believed, it would not have been against the dictates of reason, though it was perhaps against the ways of custom.

Now, all the while my body lay hidden in this seclusion, my fame roamed free through the universe of men, ringing like Echo in the myth, whose voice was everywhere and substance nowhere.[81] My old enemies now were too feeble for any action on their own, so they raised up against me a pair of new apostles, whose boasts were winning credit in the world—one that he had reformed the life of canons regular, the other that he had reformed the life of monks.[82] These two now went scurrying through the world, preaching up and down, and gnawing away at me with all their impudent might. For a while they convinced some Church and secular powers that I was hateful, and spread such twisted lies about my faith and way of life that even my strongest supporters turned from me, and if any still retained a part of their old love, they had to keep it hidden out of fear. As God is my witness, whenever I heard that a group of churchmen was meeting somewhere, I was sure that they met to condemn me. Stunned, I sat waiting for their lightning to strike, expecting any moment to be dragged off to their councils or their synagogues as a heretic or profaner. Though some may think the comparison unfair—an elephant to an ant or a lion to a flea—never did the heretics of old pursue Saint Athanasius with more cruelty

---

81 See Ovid, *Metamorphoses* 3.359.

82 The standard view identifies this pair with Norbert of Xanten, founder of the Order of Premonstratensian Canons, and the powerful Bernard, founder of the Cistercian abbey at Clairvaux and Abelard's dedicated antagonist at the Council of Sens in 1140. Though this view has been challenged, it remains the most probable. For a concise discussion, see Marenbon 1997, 10, and his references there.

and spite than my enemies now came after me.[83] Often, God knows, my despair reached such depths that I thought of leaving the Christian world entirely to go off among the pagans and live quietly there, whatever the tribute I would have to pay, a Christian life among the enemies of Christ. I was convinced that they would treat me well. With these charges against me, they would hardly believe I was a Christian at all, but instead a likely convert to their sect.[84]

While I was pondering this desperate step—taking refuge with Christ among the enemies of Christ—the chance came, as I thought, to escape the plots against me, and I took it; but I fell into hands far more savage than pagans', and this among Christians and monks. The abbey of Saint Gildas of Rhuys in the diocese of Vannes in Brittany had been without a head since the death of its last abbot.[85] I was invited there as the unanimous choice of its monks, the local lord approved, and my own abbot and monks quickly gave their consent. And so, as Jerome was driven east by the envy of the Romans, I was driven west by the envy of the French. Except for the attacks I was continually under, I would never have accepted such an offer, God knows. The country there was barbarous, I did not know the language, the monks were all notoriously corrupt beyond control, and even the people were uncivilized brutes. But I was like a man who plunges off a cliff in fear of the sword above his head, exchanging in an instant one death for another. I went from danger to danger with eyes wide open, and there, by the waves of the dread-sounding ocean where no spit of land now could offer me flight, I called out in my prayers again and again, "To thee have I cried from the ends of the earth when my heart was in anguish."[86]

The whole world, I think, knows the anguish I suffered and how that rabble of monks I had promised to direct tortured my heart night and day as I had to weigh the dangers to my body and my soul. If I tried to force them to the life of rule they professed, I was

---

[83] Athanasius (295–373), patriarch of Alexandria and Doctor of the Church. For his staunch defense of orthodox teaching on the Trinity against the Arian heresy, he was exiled five times. It was also believed that he was the author of the creed that bears his name.

[84] Most probably Abelard is imagining the Muslims of Spain, who were known to tolerate Christian communities.

[85] Dedicated to a Celtic saint who fled his native Britain in the sixth century, the abbey faced the Atlantic by the rugged Pointe de Grand Mont, about 100 miles northwest of Abelard's birthplace at Le Pallet.

[86] Ps. 60:3.

sure I would be murdered; if I did not do what I could, I was sure I would be damned. But there was more: the abbey itself had long been in the power of a despot, a tyrant in the area who took advantage of the disorder in the monastery to appropriate all its adjacent land for his own use and extort from the monks a heavier tribute than even Jews have to pay. The monks kept pressing me for their daily needs even though there was no common fund I could distribute—they had all been supporting their concubines and children from their own purses—and they gleefully tormented me over this. And they kept stealing, too, making off with everything they could get their hands on to force me to let up on my discipline when I finally came up empty, or else to get out altogether. Since the people of the country were all barbarians and every bit as lawless as the monks, there was no one I could turn to for help. I found all their behavior equally repugnant. Outside our walls, the tyrant and his minions would never stop harassing me; inside, the monks would never stop their plots. "Combat without, terror within," the apostle Paul once said,[87] and his words now seemed aimed straight at me.

It was a useless, wretched life that I was living—
I thought this often and I wept—
pointless and barren for myself as well as others.
I had students once and once had done them good,
but I threw them aside for these monks.
And now for those students, for these monks, it is waste:
all I began, all I undertook, everything I tried, all waste.
Above all men it can be said of me,
"This man began to build but could not finish."[88]
And when I remembered what I had fled
and saw where I had come, I would despair.
My earlier troubles seemed nothing to me now,
and I would groan, saying over and over,
"All this have I deserved.
Forsaking the Paraclete and my consolation there,
I have plunged into real desolation;
anxious to avoid the dangers that were threatened,
I escaped into dangers that are real."

---

[87] 2 Cor. 7:5.
[88] Luke 14:30.

Above all else, what tormented me most was this—that when I left my oratory behind, I was not able to provide for the proper celebration of the Divine Office there since the area was so poor it could barely supply the needs of even one man. But now, once again, the true Paraclete brought me true consolation as I lay there desolate and lost. He saw to the oratory himself, as was only fitting, for it was indeed his own.

I have spoken of the convent of Argenteuil, where Heloise, my wife—now more, my sister in Christ—had taken the veil as a nun. By some means or other, my abbot at Saint Denis took possession of it, alleging that it was originally part of his monastery's domain, and he forcibly expelled its community of nuns, of which she, my companion, was now prioress.[89] They now were scattered through the world like exiles. I saw this as an opportunity from God for the future of my oratory. So I returned to the Paraclete and invited her to come, bringing any of the women who wished to stay with her. Then, when I had gathered them together, I turned the oratory over to them with all its properties and land by deed of gift. With the consent and the help of our bishop, my donation was later confirmed by Pope Innocent II through a charter to the nuns and their successors forever.[90]

Their life at first was hard, for a time they were desolate, but the God whom they served with devotion soon brought them solace and showed himself their true Paraclete. He opened the hearts of the local people to pity and kindness toward them and, God knows, their worldly goods grew more in a year than mine could have grown in a hundred. As women are the weaker sex, their need more moves our human passions and their virtue finds more favor with God as well as men. And on her, my sister, who had direction of the nuns, God bestowed such favor in men's sight that bishops loved her as a daughter, abbots as a sister, the people as a mother, and all alike marveled at her wisdom and dedication, her unmatched gentleness

---

[89] Abbot Suger claimed to have seen documents proving the ownership of the convent by St. Denis and also seems to have laid charges of immorality against its nuns. The claims were endorsed by the papal legate, local bishops, and the king, and St. Denis gained control of the convent in 1129. See the discussion of McLeod 1971, 93–104.

[90] The original charter, dated November 28, 1131, is preserved at Châlons-sur-Marne. The Paraclete remained a convent, honoring Abelard as its founder and Heloise as its first abbess, for over 600 years until its dissolution and the sale of its property on November 14, 1792, during the French Revolution.

and patience in all things. If she appeared in public only rarely—to devote more time to prayer and meditation in the cloister of her room—the world outside was only the more eager for her presence and her spiritual counsel.[91]

Now, the people in the neighborhood started taking me to task for not doing as much for the women as I should or could, even by the preaching which would be easy to do.[92] So I began to visit them more often and provide for them with any means in my power. But even in *this* I met slander and spite, and this blameless act of charity was now twisted—as they twisted everything in their foul, perverted way—into a lust they said still enslaved me to the woman I once loved and could never bear to be without. I often thought of Saint Jerome's complaint in his letter to Asella about false friends:

> My only crime is my sex, and even that is not an issue except when Paula comes to Jerusalem. . . . Before I knew the house of that saintly woman, all of Rome sang my praises and thought I was worthy of the highest priestly office. . . . But I know the road to heaven runs through fair report and foul.[93]

Remembering the malice directed against this great man gave me no small comfort, and I thought, What if my enemies had *those* grounds to suspect me—imagine the malice they would aim at me then! But now that God's mercy has freed me from that suspicion and my power to commit those acts is gone, how could there be suspicion left at all? What can this latest accusation mean? The

---

[91] Abelard could have been speaking only of the first year or two of Heloise's tenure, but the material institutional growth of the Paraclete under her leadership was in fact phenomenal; by the time of her death, no less than six daughter houses had been founded. For an excellent brief survey of the expansion of the Paraclete in its first thirty years, see McLaughlin 2000.

[92] Abelard's involvement with the Paraclete was in fact intense. In time he came to write a collection of thirty-four sermons for use at the Paraclete (of which Sermon 30 was designed specifically for fund-raising), several sequences, and over ninety hymns for its liturgy. He also contributed to its educational program through a letter on the study of literature, a commentary on the Hexameron of Genesis, his answers to *The Questions of Heloise* (see excerpt), and the Sixth Letter. In the Seventh Letter he set out the terms of an extensive monastic rule for the convent to follow.

[93] *Epistulae* 45.2.

nature of eunuchs removes them so clearly from suspicion that women are entrusted to them for protection and care, as the Bible tells us about Esther and the other maidens of King Ahasuerus.[94] We read, too, of the eunuch of Queen Candace, a powerful man who had charge over her treasure and whom an angel sent the apostle Philip to convert and baptize.[95] Men like these have always had honor and trust in the households of virtuous women precisely to the extent that they are beyond suspicion of this kind. In fact, it was to remove this suspicion at the root that Origen, the greatest Christian philosopher, laid violent hands on himself when he first undertook the religious education of women.[96] When God set me free for a similar work, he was kinder to me than to Origen, though; for what Origen did himself—without reflection, it is thought, and in that he incurred no small blame—was done to me by others with no responsibility of my own and with only brief and sudden pain since I was asleep when they attacked me and felt almost nothing.

But if perhaps there was little pain from the wound at the time, there is more now from this protracted slander, and I suffer more from the cost to my reputation than the loss to my body. As it is written in Proverbs, "A good name is better than great riches,"[97] and as Saint Augustine reminds us in his sermon on the life and morals of clerics, "It is a cruel man who thinks only of his conscience and neglects his reputation," because, as he says earlier:

> "We look toward what may be good not only before God but also before men," the Apostle says. For the sake of ourselves, our conscience is sufficient, but for the sake of others, our reputation should be strong, not scorned. . . . Conscience and reputation are two separate things: your conscience exists for yourself alone while your reputation exists for your neighbor.[98]

What would they have said about Christ if they had been living at the time—about Christ himself or his followers, the prophets, apostles, or other Fathers of the Church? Imagine their malice toward

---

[94] See Est. 2:3.

[95] See Acts 8:26 ff.

[96] Eusebius, *Historia Ecclesiae* 6.8.

[97] Prov. 22:1.

[98] Augustine, Sermon 355; the internal quotation is from 2 Cor. 8:21.

*them* when they saw them in such close association with women, and they with their bodies intact. As Augustine shows, women were inseparable companions of the Lord Christ and his apostles, even traveling with them when they preached:

> Faithful women of means would go with them and provide for them from their substance so that they would lack none of the necessities of life. . . . If anyone doubts that women of holy life traveled with the apostles wherever they preached the Gospel . . . , let him but read the Gospel itself and learn that in this they had the example of the Lord. . . . In the Gospel of Luke it is written: "And it came to pass afterwards that he traveled through the cities and towns, preaching and evangelizing the kingdom of God, and the twelve with him and certain women who had been healed of evil spirits and infirmities: Mary who is called Magdalene . . . , and Joanna the wife of Chusa, Herod's steward, and Susanna, and many others who provided for him from their substance."[99]

And Pope Leo IX says in his treatise against the epistle of Parmenianus of the monastery of Studius:

> We declare that no bishop, priest, deacon, or subdeacon may give up the care of his wife in the name of religion or fail to provide for her food and clothing, though he may not lie with her carnally. For this was the practice of the holy apostles, as we read in Saint Paul: "Have we not power to carry about a woman, a sister, as well as the rest of the apostles and the brethren of the Lord and Cephas?" See now, you fool, he does not say, "embrace a woman" but "carry about," meaning that they should support their wives on the income from their preaching, not that there should be any carnal intercourse between them.[100]

---

[99] Augustine, *De Opere Monachorum* 4.5 and 5.6; the internal quotation is from Luke 8:1 ff.

[100] Abelard's elaborate citation is confused. The passage is from the response of Cardinal Humbertus to a tract written by the monk Niceta of the monastery of Studius in Constantinople, though a version contained in the *Decree of Gratian* attributes it to Leo IX while Humbertus was his legate. Augustine wrote a treatise "against the epistle of Parmenianus," which is, however, otherwise unconnected with this passage; see Muckle 1950, 207–08. The internal quotation is from 1 Cor. 9:5.

Certainly the Pharisee who spoke within himself, "This man, if he were a prophet, would know surely who and what manner of woman this is that toucheth him, that she is a sinner,"[101] could more easily imagine—so far as human judgment ever could—a charge of vice against the Lord than *they* could imagine against me. Whoever saw the mother of the Lord entrusted to the care of a young man or the prophets conversing with the widows who took them in would have far firmer grounds for suspicion.[102] And what would they have said, those slanderers of mine, if they saw Malchus, the captive monk Jerome describes living in the same cottage as his wife? A great crime to them, surely, but to Jerome, an occasion for praise:

> There was an old man there named Malchus . . . a native of the place, living in his cottage with an old woman . . . both of them devout and both ever wearing down the threshold of the church. You would have thought they were Zachariah and Elizabeth in the Gospel, except that there was no John between them.[103]

Finally, how can they justify *not* slandering the Fathers, whom we often read about or see founding convents for women and providing for their needs, after the example of the seven deacons the apostles appointed to wait at table and look after the women?[104] The weaker sex so needs the help of the stronger that Saint Paul requires that the man always be over the woman as her head, and that in token of this she must keep her own head veiled.[105] I am more than surprised, then, at the long-standing practice in convents of giving abbesses the same authority over women as abbots have over men, and of binding women to the profession of the same rule as men when there is so much in the rule that no woman, either abbess or nun, can possibly fulfill. There even are places where the natural order is overturned, and we see abbesses and nuns ruling over clerics, the same clerics whom the people must

---

[101] Luke 7:39.

[102] See John 19:27 and 3 Kings 17:10.

[103] According to Jerome's *Vita Malchi*, quoted here, Malchus was captured by the Saracens and forced to marry, though he and his wife were pledged to celibacy.

[104] See Acts 6:1–3.

[105] See 1 Cor. 11:3–6.

obey.[106] Can they not, then, lead men more easily to improper desires when they have this authority over them and keep them underneath this heavy yoke? Why else does Juvenal say, "The worst of things is a woman who is rich"?[107]

After long consideration, I decided I would do everything I could to provide for the sisters and look after their affairs. And to win their greater respect, I would be with them in person, keeping watch and tending to their needs. My persecution from the monks at Saint Gildas was greater now, more persistent and severe, than it ever had been from the monks at Saint Denis, so I hoped I could turn to the nuns as a haven of peace in this storm, escaping its seething violence to find some rest. At least with the nuns I could do some good, which was impossible with the monks, and as urgent as this was for them, it would be as welcome to me and as good for the health of my soul.

Now Satan has blocked my path. Wherever I turn, wherever I go, I find no place to rest, no place to live. A vagabond and fugitive on the earth, I am hounded everywhere like the accursed Cain, tormented without end by this "combat without and terror within," as I said before, only now it is combat and terror without *and* within.[108] The persecution from my monks rages on, more dangerous by far than from my enemies and more constant, for they are always with me and I face their treachery without cease. If I leave the cloister, I see the violence of my enemies threatening my person, and within the cloister I face the never-ending violence and deceit of my own sons—those monks, that is, entrusted to my paternal care as abbot. How often have they tried to poison me, as happened to Saint Benedict himself.[109] If I ever thought of following the example he once set of a loving father abandoning his depraved sons, it was because I would not tempt God rather than love him or become my own destruction by exposing myself to certain death. Although

---

[106] Abelard is careful to distance himself from the type of double monastery subject to the control of an abbess, such as existed at Frontevrault under the abbess Petronilla. In the Seventh Letter he endorses a model of a double monastery with an abbot, however, in overall charge.

[107] *Satires* 6.10.

[108] 2 Cor. 8:5. For the reference to Cain, see Gen. 4:14.

[109] Benedict was called from his hermitage at Subiaco to become abbot of a monastery at Vicovaro, where the monks tried to poison him. He subsequently left the monks and returned to his hermitage.

I guarded myself as well as I could against their ordinary plots by preparing my own food and drink, they once tried to murder me in the very act of sacrament by poisoning the chalice I used. Another time, when I had gone to Nantes to visit the sickbed of the count and was staying in the home of my brother, they tried to poison me by working through one of my servants, imagining, I suppose, that I would be less alert to a stratagem of this kind. Through the providence of God, I did not touch the food set out for me, but a monk I had brought with me from the monastery took a taste without knowing it was poisoned and died on the spot, and the servant who had dared do this deed fled in terror, driven by his guilt and the plain facts of the case.

From that point on, it was all out in the open, both their evil and the measures I took to counter their conspiracies. I started living outside the monastery in small rooms with only a few men around me, but whenever they found out I would be on the road, they would hire assassins and station them there to kill me. Beside everything else I had to contend with, I was struck by the hand of the Lord one day and fell from my horse, breaking a bone in my neck; the pain from the fracture was far greater and more debilitating than my earlier injury. There were times when I tried to control the insurgency by excommunication or by forcing the more dangerous ones to swear a public oath that they would leave the abbey forever and never trouble me again. But just as publicly, they kept breaking their oaths until they were forced to swear them again and promise other things as well, this time by the authority of Pope Innocent himself through a special legate he sent us for this purpose, and in the presence of the bishops and the count.[110]

Even still they have not stopped. I returned to the abbey only recently, having gotten rid of the ones I was talking about, to come back among the monks I thought I could trust. But these turned out to be much worse than the others. It was not poison now but a knife at my throat, and only with the protection of a local nobleman did I manage to escape with my life. I am contending with this danger even now. Every day I see a sword above my head, and I hardly dare to take a breath at meals. I remember the man we read about who thought the tyrant Dionysius sublimely happy with all his wealth and power until he looked up and saw the sword that hung

---

[110] The papal legate was the same Geoffrey of Lèves, bishop of Chartres, who defended Abelard at the Council of Soissons.

above him by a thread, and *then* he knew the happiness that comes with earthly power.[111] This is my experience every moment, a poor monk elevated to be an abbot, who grows more wretched as he grows in wealth. Let the force of my example curb the ambition of those who seek this course of their own will.

**M**y most beloved brother in Christ and closest companion of all these years, this is the history of my calamities, which have weighed down upon me almost since the cradle. Let it now serve you in the wrongs you have suffered and in your own desolation. As I said at the beginning, you will see that your trials are only slight next to mine, or even nothing, and you will bear them more easily the smaller you consider them to be. Always take comfort from what the Lord told his followers about the followers of the devil: "If they have persecuted me, they will also persecute you. If the world hate you, know that it hath hated me before you. If you had been of the world, the world would love its own." And the Apostle said, "All that will live godly in Christ shall suffer persecution," and "Do I seek to please men? If I yet pleased men, I should not be the servant of Christ." And the Psalmist said, "They have been confounded that please men because God hath despised them."[112]

Jerome, whose heir in slander and detraction I see I am, knew these words well when he wrote to Nepotianus, "The Apostle tells us, 'If I yet pleased men, I should not be the servant of Christ.' He ceased pleasing men and became the servant of Christ"; and to Asella, "Thank God that I am worthy of the hatred of the world"; and to the monk Heliodorus:

> You are wrong, my brother, wrong if you think that a Christian never suffers persecution. . . . Our adversary "goeth about as a roaring lion seeking someone he may devour," and you think of peace? "He sitteth in ambush with the rich in private places that he may kill the innocent."[113]

We must take heart from these precepts and examples and bear our burdens with the more composure the more we know that they

---

[111] See Cicero's *Tusculan Disputations* 5.20–21 for the story of the sword of Damocles.

[112] John 15:18–20, out of order; 2 Tim. 3:2; Gal. 1:10; and cf. Ps. 52:6.

[113] *Epistulae* 52.13, 45.6, and 14.4, in which the internal quotations are from 1 Pet. 5:8 and Ps. 10:8.

are without justice. And if they do not serve our merit, we should not doubt that they serve to cleanse our souls. All things happen by the ordinance of God, and every faithful soul in every affliction should at least find consolation in this: that his supreme goodness allows nothing to be done outside his plan, and that all things that are wrong or twisted or perverse he himself will bring to their best end. And so, in all things it is right to say to him, "Thy will be done."[114] What great consolation to learn from the Apostle, "For we know that to them that love God all things work together unto good."[115] Solomon, the wisest of the wise, knew this well, for in Proverbs he said, "Whatsoever shall befall the just man, it shall not make him sad."[116] All who are angered, then, by some physical distress, though they know it was done by God's plan, leave the path of justice to be led, not by the will of God, but by their own, and when they set their own will before God's, they are struggling in their hearts against the words, "Thy will be done."

Farewell.

---

[114] Matt. 6:10.
[115] Rom. 8:28.
[116] Prov. 12:21.

# LETTERS OF ABELARD AND HELOISE

# FIRST LETTER

## HELOISE TO ABELARD

*To her lord, no, her father*
*To her husband, no, her brother*
*From his handmaid, no, his daughter*
*His wife, no, his sister—*

*To Abelard from Heloise.*

The other day, my most beloved,
one of your men brought me a copy
of the letter you wrote as consolation
for your friend.[1]
From what was written at its head I knew at once
that it was yours, and I began to read it
with a warmth as great as the love
with which I hold its writer in my heart.
I hoped that at least by its words
I could be restored to life,
as if by some image
of the one whose real substance I have lost.
Almost every line, I noticed,
was filled with vinegar and gall,
as it told the sad story
of our entrance into monastic life
and the unending crosses which you,

---

[1] I have followed Peter Dronke's restoration of Heloise's original text, reading *vestrum* for the manuscripts' *vestram* and omitting *forte*. Dronke relies on the thirteenth-century French translation of Jean de Meun, which in turn relies on a text predating any extant manuscript of the letter. See Dronke 1984b, 304.

49

my only one,
have always had to bear.

The letter well fulfilled the promise you made
your friend at its beginning, that he would think
his own troubles small or nothing next to yours.
You wrote of your persecution
at the hands of your teachers,
the supreme betrayal
of the mutilation of your body,
and the enmity and hateful malice
of Alberic and Lotulf, who were once
your fellow students.
You wrote of what happened, through their intrigue,
to the glorious book of your *Theology*
and to you yourself
when you were condemned as if to prison.
You wrote of the plots of your abbot and false brothers,
the attacks of those spurious apostles
which the same enemies instigated against you,
and the scandal which arose when you gave
the Paraclete its uncustomary name.
And then, when you came to those unbearable assaults
which still are launched against you by that tyrant
and by the worst of all monks you call your sons,
you brought the sad story to an end.

No one, I am sure, could read or hear it without tears,
and my own grief became fresh with every detail,
and it grows greater still as the danger to you
even now is increasing.
We are all driven to despair of your life,
and every day our hearts beat in fear
of some final word of your death.
So, by that Christ who keeps you for his own even now,
we beg of you,
as we are his handmaids and yours,
write to us,
tell us of those storms
in which you find yourself tossed.
We are all you have left: let us share
your grief or your joy.

A community of grief can bring some comfort
to one in need of it, since many shoulders
lighten any burden or even make it
seem to disappear.
If, on the other hand, this storm abates
even just a little, you must write to us quickly
when your letters will bring us more joy.
But whatever it is you write to us about,
it will be no small relief, for in this way
at least you will show you are thinking of us.
Seneca teaches us by his own example
how much joy there is in letters from absent friends,
as he writes to his friend Lucilius:

"I am grateful that you write to me often,
for you show yourself to me in the one way you can.
When I receive a letter from you, we are suddenly together.
If images of absent friends bring joy,
if they refresh our memory and soothe the ache
of absence even with their false and empty solace,
how much more joy is there in a letter,
which carries the true signature of an absent friend?"[2]

And I am grateful to God that here at least
is a way you can grant us your presence,
one which no malice will hinder,
no obstacle impede,
and no negligence—I beg of you—delay.

You have written your friend a long letter of consolation,
addressing his adversities but recounting
your own.
But as you told of them in such detail,
while your mind was on his consolation,
you have worsened our own desolation;
while you were treating his wounds,
you have inflicted new wounds upon us
and have made our old wounds bleed.
I beg of you,

---

[2] *Epistulae ad Lucilium* 40.1.

heal these wounds you have made, who are so careful
to tend the wounds made by others.
You have done what you ought
for a friend and comrade
and have paid your debt to friendship and comradeship.
But you are bound to us by a greater debt,
for we are not your friends but your most loving friends,
not your comrades but your daughters—yes,
it is right to call us that, or even use
a name more sacred and more sweet
if one can be imagined.

We need no arguments or testimony
to prove the obligation you have toward us:
if men will keep their silence, the facts will speak
for themselves.
You alone, after God, are the founder of this place,
you alone the builder of this oratory,
you alone the architect of this congregation.
Nothing you have built
is on the foundation of another:[3]
it is all your creation, everything here.
Before you, this was a wilderness,
an empty range for wild beasts and outlaws;
it knew no human settlement and not a house stood.
Among these lairs of beasts, these dens of outlaws,
where the name of God was never pronounced,
you raised a tabernacle of the Lord
and dedicated a temple of the Holy Spirit
for him to call his own.
Nothing you brought to the task
was from the wealth of kings and princes,
though you could have had so much at your disposal:
it was all to be yours, whatever was done here,
yours alone.
The clerics and students who came flooding here
to learn from you provided all that was needed;
and suddenly, those who were used to living
on the benefices of the Church,

---

[3] Cf. Rom. 15:20.

who had learned how to receive offerings
but not how to make them,
who had opened their hands to take
but not to give,
now became prodigal in their gifts
and even pressed them upon you.

Yes, it is yours,
truly yours, this newly planted garden,
whose living shoots are young, still delicate,
and need watering to thrive.[4]
From the nature of women alone the garden is tender
and would not be hardy even if it were not new.
Its cultivation, then, must be more careful,
in the way Saint Paul intended when he wrote:

"I have planted, Apollos has watered,
and God has given the increase."[5]

He had planted the Corinthians in the faith
by the doctrine he had preached, and his student Apollos
had watered them with his encouragement,
and the grace of God bestowed on them
the increase of their virtues.
But you are tending another's vine
in a vineyard you have not planted,
and it has turned to bitterness for you,
all your words wasted and vain.[6]
While you lavish your care on another's vine,
remember what you owe your own.

You try to teach rebels and do not succeed;
you are casting pearls of God's word before swine.[7]
While you lavish so much on those who defy you,
consider what you owe those who obey.

---

[4] Abelard uses similar terms to speak of the Paraclete in his Sermon 30, which seeks
to raise funds for the new convent.

[5] 1 Cor. 3:6.

[6] Cf. Jer. 2:21.

[7] Cf. Matt. 7:6.

While you squander so much on your enemies,
think what you owe your daughters.
But leave aside these others for a moment—
remember what you owe *me*,
and all you owe
this whole community of devoted women
you may repay at once to her who is,
with more devotion, your only one.

The wealth of your learning
knows better than the poverty of my own
how many treatises the Fathers have composed—
long, weighty, careful treatises—to teach,
encourage, and, yes, console women in religious orders.
That is why, in the tender early time
of my convent life long ago,
your oblivion came as no small surprise to me
when, unpersuaded by any reverence for God,
or any love for me, or any example
set by these same Fathers,
you did not try to console me as I foundered,
overwhelmed in sorrow day after day—
never once, neither by a word when we were together
nor a letter when we were apart—
and yet you would know
that you are bound to me by a greater debt,
obliged to me by the sacrament of marriage,
and beholden to me further by what is plain
to everyone:
that I have always held you in my heart
with a love that has no measure.

You know, my dearest,
all world knows, how much I have lost in you,
how that supreme, that notorious betrayal
robbed me of my very self
when it robbed me of you,
and how incomparably worse than the loss itself
is the pain from the way it happened.
This greater pain must have a greater solace,
and it can come only from you, not from another.
As you alone are the source of my grief,

you alone can grant the grace of consolation.
You alone have the power to make me sad,
to make me happy or to console me,
and you alone owe me this debt,
now above all,
when I have so completely fulfilled your commands
in every particular
that, rather than commit a single offense
against you,
I threw myself away at your command.
And the greater irony is that my love
then turned to such insanity
that the one thing it desired above all else
was the one thing it put irrevocably beyond its reach
in that one instant when, at your command,
I changed my habit along with my heart
to show that my body along with my heart
belonged only to you.

I never wanted anything in you
but you alone,
nothing of what you have
but you yourself,
never a marriage, never a dowry,
never any pleasure, any purpose of my own—
as you well know—
but only yours.[8]
The name of wife may have the advantages
of sanctity and safety, but to me
the sweeter name will always be *lover*
or, if your dignity can bear it,
*concubine* or *whore*.

Do you imagine
I debased myself to earn your gratitude
and preserve your glorious distinction in the world?
You were not so entirely oblivious

---

[8] In the margin of his own manuscript copy of the letter, the poet Petrarch wrote at this point, "You are acting throughout with gentleness and perfect sweetness, Heloise."

when it suited your own purposes in that letter
to your friend,
and did not think it beneath your dignity
to set out at least some of the arguments
I used when I tried to dissuade you
from this marriage of ours and its disastrous bed.
You kept your silence, though, about most of the reasons
why I preferred love over marriage,
freedom over a chain.
So I call my God to witness now:
If great Augustus, ruler of the world,
ever thought to honor me by making me his wife
and granted me dominion over the earth,
it would be dearer to me
and more honorable to be called
not his royal consort but your whore.

No man's real worth is measured by his property or power:
fortune belongs to one category of things
and virtue to another.[9]
And no woman should think herself any the less for sale
if she prefers a rich man to a poor one
in marriage and wants what she would get
in a husband more than the husband himself.
Reward such greed with cash and not devotion,
for she is after property alone
and is prepared to prostitute herself
to an even richer man given the chance.
This is the argument the philosopher
Aspasia used with Xenophon and his wife
in the dialogue of Aeschines the Socratic.
After she set out her argument
aimed at reconciling the pair,
the philosopher capped her proof with this conclusion:

---

[9] This argument will find its way into Abelard's *Ethics* (Luscombe 1971, 48): "If this were true [that merit depends on external circumstances], then great wealth could make someone better or more worthy (that is, if wealth in itself could bring about merit or the increase of merit), and the richer men are, the better they could become because out of their abundance of riches they could add more in deeds to their devotion. But to think that wealth can add to real happiness or the worthiness of the soul, or to think that its lack can detract from the merits of the poor is utterly insane."

"Therefore, if you two are not convinced
that no worthier man exists and no finer woman exists
anywhere on earth, then above all else
you will always be seeking that one thing
you think is best—
to have the best of all possible husbands
or the best of all possible wives."[10]

This notion goes beyond philosophy
and should not be called the pursuit of wisdom
but wisdom itself.
There is a blessed delusion among the married,
a happy fantasy that perfect love
keeps their marital ties intact less through the restraint
of their bodies than through the chastity
of their hearts.
But what is a delusion for other women,
for me is the manifest truth.
What other women only think about their husbands,
I—and the entire world—not only believe
but *know* to be true about you,
and in this way my love is far from any delusion.

Has there been a philosopher or even a king
whose renown could equal yours?[11]
Has there been any region of the country,
any city, any town that did not boil
with excitement just to see you?
Has there been a single person
who did not come running
to catch a glimpse as you came into sight,
who did not stretch his neck and strain his eyes
to follow you as you left?
Has there been a woman, married or unmarried,

---

[10] Cicero, *De Inventione* 1.31.52. Aspasia was the companion (the "concubine or whore," as it were) of the Athenian leader Pericles, widely respected for her character and intellect. In Cicero, Aspasia's words are reported by Socrates, but Heloise has bypassed the middleman and gone straight to the source, the original philosopher herself.

[11] Petrarch wrote in the margin of his manuscript copy at this point, "About Peter's fame—if love doesn't make her testimony suspect."

who did not long for you when you were gone
or lust for you when you were present?
Has there been a great lady or even a queen
who did not envy me the pleasures of my bed?

And two things that belonged to you alone
would win the heart of any woman—
your beautiful voice and your gift for writing songs.
These are not common among philosophers, I know,
but for you they were amusements, a diversion
from your philosophical work.
You left countless songs,
both in the classical meter of love
and in the rhythms of love as well,
that kept your name on everyone's lips;
and they were of such surpassing sweetness
that their melodies alone would not allow
even the unlettered to forget you.[12]
For this above all, women sighed with love for you.
And since most of the songs told of your love and mine,
in what then seemed an instant my name was sung
in every corner of the country,
and the envy of women was kindled against me.[13]

---

[12] The indications here are that these songs were in Latin. The distinction between "meter" and "rhythm" is between verse forms based on syllable quantity (as in classical Latin) and syllable quality or stress accent (as in the accented verse of much medieval Latin poetry). The "classical meter of love," then, is the elegiac couplet, the standard form of classical Latin love poetry. The "unlettered" are those who did not know Latin but who nonetheless found it easy to memorize Abelard's songs because of the qualities Heloise notes. Outside what may be preserved in *The Letters of Two Lovers* (see Appendix B), little of Abelard's elegiac poetry addressed to Heloise survives; see, however, the end of the Second Letter. For a likely example of his "rhythmic" poetry to Heloise, see "Dull Is the Star."

[13] Petrarch commented in the margin at this point, "*Muliebriter*—Just like a woman." Far from descending into vanity, however, Heloise is adapting Abelard's own remarks about the role of fame and envy in his life to help confirm a parallel between their experiences. In the next sections, she proceeds to apply to herself the specific language Abelard used about his castration, the examination of his book at the Council of Soissons, and his isolation at St. Gildas of Rhuys, and refers to her own "*calamitas*—calamity."

Has there been a grace of mind or body
that you did not possess when you were young?
And is there now, of all the women then
who envied me,
a single one who does not feel compassion
when my own calamity has cut me
from those joys?
Is there any man or woman, even among
our ancient enemies, who is not softened now
by the pity owed to me?

I am entirely guilty; as you know,
I am entirely innocent.
For blame does not reside in the action itself
but in the disposition of the agent,
and justice does not weigh what is done
but what is in the heart.[14]
And what my heart has always been toward you,
you alone can judge, who have put me to the test.
I submit it all for your examination,
and rest my case on your testimony alone.

Now answer me one question if you can:
why, after our entrance into religious life—
which you alone decided, you alone—
why I have fallen into such neglect
and oblivion with you that I am neither
restored to life with a word when we are together
nor comforted with a letter when we are apart.
Yes, tell me if you can,
and I will tell you
what I, no, what everyone suspects—
that it was appetite and not affection
that connected you to me, your lust and not your love;
and that when what you desired suddenly became

---

[14] What evidently has been an issue of mutual concern between them will become
central to the doctrine of Abelard's *Ethics*, that intentions alone, not actions in themselves, are subject to moral judgment; see, e.g., *Ethics* (Luscombe 1971, 52): "Indeed,
we call an intention good, that is, right in itself; we do not say of an action, however,
that it takes on any good in itself but rather that it proceeds from a good intention."

impossible,
everything you put on for its sake
also disappeared.
My most beloved,
this is not my inference alone but everyone's,
not private and particular to me
but public and universal.
I wish it were just mine alone,
for then your love could find
someone to defend it, someone I could turn to
to relieve the pain I am suffering now.
I wish there were
some plausible excuse I could invent,
for then I could find, in defending you,
some way of covering my own cheapness.

Remember what I ask, I beg of you—
you will find it is small and easy to do:
so long as I am cheated of your presence,
present me with an image of yourself
at least in words,
of which you have an exceptional supply.
I cannot expect your generosity in substance
if I find you miserly in words.
Up to now
I had thought I deserved so much from you
since everything I have done was for your sake
and even now I continue in your service.
It was not any commitment to the religious life
that forced me to the rigors of the convent
when I was the young woman I once was:
it was your command alone.
If even in this
I deserve nothing from you, then you may judge
how all my work here has been wasted.
I can expect no reward from God since it is clear
I have yet done nothing out of love for him.
I followed *you* as you went striding off
to God and to his monastery—
No,
I did not follow: I went first.
Were you haunted by the image of Lot's wife

turning back[15]
when you delivered me up to these vows and holy vestments
even before you delivered yourself to God?
That you doubted me in this one thing, my love,
overwhelmed me with grief and shame.
But, as God knows,
I would have followed you
to Vulcan's flames if you commanded it,
and without a moment's hesitation
I would have gone first.

My heart was never my own but was always
with you,
and now even more, if it is not with you
it is nowhere:
without you it cannot exist at all.[16]
Let it be at peace with you, I beg of you.
And it will be at peace with you if you are kind,
if you return grace for grace,[17] small things for large,
words for real substance.
My love, I wish your love
had less confidence in me,
so that it would be more careful and concerned.
But now it seems the more secure of me
I have made you feel, the more negligent
you have become.

Recall what I have done, I beg of you.
Remember what you owe me.
In the days
when we shared the pleasures of the flesh,
no one was sure if I acted out of love or lust.
Now the end confirms the beginning.
I have denied myself all pleasure to follow your will:
I kept nothing for myself but to become yours.
If you now give me less when I deserve

---

15 See Gen. 19:26.

16 Petrarch's marginal comment is "*Amicissime et eleganter*—Written with elegance
and the greatest love."

17 Cf. John 1:16.

so much more,
if you now give me nothing at all,
think what your injustice will be then.
And it is so small a thing I ask and so easy
for you to do.
So, by that God who claims your dedication,
I beg of you,
grant me your presence in the one way you can—
by writing me some word of comfort,
so that at least in this one way
I may be restored to life,
readier and fit for my own service to God.
In the days
when you sought me out for pleasures long ago,
you showered me with letter after letter,
and with your songs you set your Heloise
on the lips of everyone, and every home
and every street re-echoed
*Heloise.*
Is it not better now to summon me to God
than it once was to call me to your bed?

Think what you owe me, remember what I ask,
I beg of you,
and I will end my long letter
with these brief words—

Farewell, my only one.

# SECOND LETTER

## ABELARD TO HELOISE

*To Heloise, his most beloved sister in Christ*
*From Abelard, her brother in Christ.*

**I**f I have written you no consolation or encouragement in the time since we turned our lives toward God, it was not because of negligence on my part but because of your own wisdom, in which I have always had implicit trust. I did not believe you needed these things from me when the grace of God has given you all you need to instruct the wayward, console the weak, and hearten the lukewarm through word and example. This you have long been used to do since your first days as prioress under your abbess. So, if you show your daughters now the thoughtful care you showed your sisters then, I am sure that it is ample and that anything further from me could only be superfluous. But if in your humility you think otherwise and believe you need my writings or my guidance in any matter that pertains to God, then write and tell me what you wish, and I will write back so far as the Lord allows me.

For the present, though, I must thank God that he has filled your hearts with anxiety for me in the constant and terrible dangers I face, and has allowed you all to share in my affliction. With the support of your prayers, I hope his mercy will protect me and quickly crush Satan beneath our feet. To this end above all, my sister—once dear to me in the world, now dearest to me in Christ—I have been quick to send you the psalter you requested,[1] with which you may

---

[1] It is not precisely certain what this psalter may be or when or how Heloise may have made her request. The convent is most likely to have had a book of psalms already, but Abelard may be referring to a text of the Psalms properly translated and corrected, such as he mentions in the prefatory letter to the first book of hymns he

63

offer perpetual prayer to the Lord for our many great sins and for the dangers I confront every day.

There is certainly evidence enough to show how high a place the prayers of the faithful have with God and his righteous, especially the prayers of women for their loved ones and wives for their husbands. The apostle Paul then tells us to "pray without ceasing."[2] We read that the Lord said to Moses, "Let me alone that my wrath may be kindled," and to Jeremiah, "Do not thou pray for this people . . . and do not withstand me,"[3] and see that he himself bears witness that the prayers of the righteous put a bridle on his wrath, holding it back from raging against sinners as they deserve. When justice leads him to the vengeance he would take, the appeals of his friends can turn him aside and, almost by some force, restrain him, as it were, against his will. This is why before or during prayer a man will hear, "Let me alone and do not withstand me." The Lord forbids our prayers for the unrighteous, but the just man prays despite the Lord's injunction, and he gains what he requests and alters the sentence of the angry judge. And this is why later in the passage about Moses we read, "The Lord was appeased from doing the evil which he had spoken against his people."[4] Elsewhere it is written about the works of God in general, "He spoke and it was so";[5] but here, though God said that the people deserved their affliction, still he did not do what he first said that he would do, prevented by the power of prayer. If Moses gained by prayer what was forbidden to his prayer and could turn God from what he had spoken, then surely you must see how great the power of prayer will be if we should simply pray as we are told.

The prophet Habakkuk once said to God, "When thou art angry, thou wilt remember mercy."[6] I only wish the princes of the earth would hear this and take note when they are headstrong more than just in carrying out a sentence they have pronounced, ashamed to seem weak if they are merciful or to seem false if they go back on a

---

composed for the Paraclete, where he also cites a request from Heloise. Heloise does not ask for a psalter in any extant letter but may easily have done so orally or in a written communication we do not have.

[2] 1 Thess. 5:17.

[3] Exod. 32:10; Jer. 7:16.

[4] Exod. 32:14.

[5] The words are Ps. 32:9, though the thought is widespread.

[6] Hab. 3:2.

word they spoke in haste, even though they can now correct it with their actions. Such men remind me most of Jephtha, who had made a foolish vow and then more foolishly fulfilled it when he sacrificed his only one, his daughter.[7] But those who would belong to the community of God will say along with the Psalmist, "Mercy and judgment I will sing to thee, O Lord."[8] It is written that mercy is exalted above judgment, and that judgment is without mercy to him that hath not done mercy.[9] So, taking this to heart, the psalmist David granted the appeal of Abigail, Nabal's wife, and though he had sworn in justice to destroy the man along with his entire house, he showed her mercy and broke the oath that he had sworn.[10] In this way he set prayer above justice, and what the husband had done wrong the wife wiped clean.

There is an example in this for you, my sister, and an assurance that if this woman's prayers achieved so much from a mere man, your prayers for me can claim much more from God. For surely God our Father loves his children more than David loved the woman who entreated him, and while David was known as merciful and pious, God is mercy and piety itself. Besides, the woman Abigail was only secular and lay, not joined to God by a religious calling. So, even if your prayers perhaps should not be enough in themselves, the holy convent of virgins and widows you have with you certainly will gain what you cannot gain alone. Christ tells his disciples, "Where there are two or three gathered in my name, there am I in the midst of them," and "If two of you shall consent concerning anything they ask, it shall be done by my Father in heaven."[11] Who, then, can be blind to the power before God of an entire congregation at constant prayer? If, as the apostle James said, "the continual

---

[7] See Judg. 11:30–40. As an offering of thanks for victory, Jephtha had vowed to sacrifice whoever of his house first greeted him on his return from battle. When this turned out to be his only child (the Vulgate's term is *unigenita filia*, "only-begotten daughter"; Abelard writes *unicam*, "only one"), Jephtha regretted his vow but fulfilled it nonetheless. The annual ritual that arose from this event among the daughters of Israel is mentioned in the Sixth Letter and was reflected in Abelard's "Lament for the Daughter of Jephtha," one of a series of laments he composed for use at the Paraclete; see p. 284.

[8] Ps. 100:1.

[9] Jas. 2:13.

[10] See 1 Kings 25 for the story of Nabal the Carmelite. When Nabal died soon after, David married the widowed Abigail.

[11] Matt. 18:19–20.

prayer of a just man availeth much,"[12] think what we can hope from your whole sacred congregation. You know, my dearest sister, from the thirty-eighth homily of Saint Gregory, what help the prayers of an entire monastery brought to a single monk even when he doggedly refused it; how even at the point of death, when his soul was laboring in misery and fear, still in his stark despair and in his weariness of life he would try to call his brothers from their prayers.[13] Yes, your wisdom surely knows what is written there.

I hope all this will call you to your prayers—you and your sisters of the convent—with greater confidence that God will keep me alive for you, the God through whom, Paul tells us, "women received even their dead raised to life again."[14] Throughout the pages of the Old Testament and Gospel, you will find that the greatest miracles recorded there, the miracles of raising the dead, all were performed especially for women, either at their request or on their bodies. The Old Testament speaks of two men raised from death by Elijah and Elisha, his disciple, and both were raised at the entreaty of their mothers.[15] And the Gospel contains just three instances of resurrection which the Lord himself performed, each time again especially for women. At the gates of Nain, he restored a son to his widowed mother because he was moved to pity for her; his friend Lazarus, too, he brought to life at the prayers of his sisters, Mary and Martha; and when on her father's request he bestowed the same grace on the daughter of the ruler of the synagogue, then as well "women received their dead raised to life again," since on her return to life she took back the body she had, as those women took back the bodies of their dead.[16]

These dead were raised at the prayers of just a few. Your prayers, then, for the preservation of my life—the prayers of so many, so devout—these I know will easily prevail. God loves the abstinence and self-restraint you all have consecrated to him, and in his love he will be more inclined to hear your prayers with favor. For all we

---

[12] Jas. 5:16.

[13] *Homiliae in Evangelia* 2.38.16.

[14] Heb. 11:35. Abelard departs very slightly from the Vulgate's wording here, though he returns to it in his citation later in the paragraph.

[15] See 3 Kings 17:17–24 and 4 Kings 4:32–35.

[16] See Luke 7:12–16 for the widow at the gates of Nain; John 11:17–44 for Lazarus; and Luke 8:40–56, Mark 5:21–43, and Matt. 9:18–26 for the daughter of the ruler of the synagogue.

know, many of those for whom these miracles were performed were not even among the faithful—we read nothing at all of the widow's faith whose son the Lord restored without her asking—but in *our* case, an intact faith binds us together and the same religious calling unites us all.

Now let me leave aside your whole community for a moment, where virgins and widows in their number offer continual devotion to the Lord, and turn to you alone. I have no doubt your sanctity has power before God, and with that power you owe me this debt—now above all, when I am laboring at the point of crisis. Always remember in your prayers the one who is specially yours, and pray with greater confidence knowing it is right for you to do so, and hence it is acceptable to God. I beg of you, listen with the ear of your heart to what your body's ear has often heard. In Proverbs it is written, "A diligent woman is a crown to her husband," and "He that hath found a good wife hath found a good thing and shall receive a pleasure from the Lord," and again "House and riches are given by parents, but a prudent wife is from the Lord." And in Ecclesiasticus, "Happy is the husband of a good wife," and "A good wife is a good portion." And on the authority of Paul, "The unbelieving husband is sanctified by the believing wife."[17]

We have special, God-given proof of this here in our kingdom of France. When Clovis was turned to the faith of Christ—less because of the preaching of holy men than because of the prayers of his wife[18]—his whole kingdom submitted to God's laws so that the lesser men among them would be challenged by the greater and called by their example to insistent prayer. We too are called to this insistent prayer by the urgent invitation of the Lord. His parable tells us:

> If he shall continue knocking, I say to you, although he will not rise and give him because he is his friend, yet because of his importunity he will rise and give him what he needeth. And I say to you, Ask and it shall be given you: seek and you shall find: knock and it shall be opened. For everyone

---

[17] Prov. 12:4, 18:22, 19:14; Ecclus. 26:1, 26:4; 1 Cor. 7:14.

[18] Clovis (c. 466–511), founder of the Frankish monarchy, was baptized as a Catholic in 496 at the urging of his wife, the Burgundian princess Clotilda, revered as a saint in France.

that asketh receiveth; and he that seeketh findeth; and to
him that knocketh it shall be opened.[19]

It was by the same importunity of prayer, if I may call it that, that
Moses softened the harshness of God's justice and altered his sentence, as I said before.

You know, my most beloved, the heartfelt charity your convent
used to show me in its prayers when I was there among you, how
every day at the close of every canonical Hour, it would offer to the
Lord a special prayer on my behalf. After the proper response and
versicle were read, a prayer and collect were added, which went like
this:

*Response:* Do not forsake me nor be far from me, O Lord.

*Versicle:* Always come to my assistance, O Lord.[20]

*Prayer:* Save your servant, O my God, whose hope is in you.
Hear my prayer, O Lord, and let my cry rise up to you.[21]

*Let us pray:* O God, who through your servant has seen fit
to gather together your handmaids in your name,
we ask you to grant both to him and to us
steady perseverance in your will.
Through our Lord Jesus Christ, your Son,
who lives and reigns with you
in the unity of the Holy Spirit, one God.
Forever and ever. Amen.[22]

But now that I am apart from you, I have all the more need for
your prayers, as this greater danger holds me in its grip. So, I
implore and beg you, I beg and I implore: let me know in my
absence how your charity extends to someone who is gone, by your
adding at the close of every canonical Hour the following as a form
of proper prayer:

---

[19] Luke 11:8–10. The manuscripts include only the first sentence of this passage, indicating the extended context with "etc."

[20] Cf. Ps. 38:22 and 69:2.

[21] Ps. 101:2.

[22] The manuscripts include only the first words of this section, "Through our Lord . . . ,"
indicating what follows with "etc."

*Response:* Do not forsake me, O Lord,
my Father and the Governor of my life.
Do not let me fall before my adversaries
or let my enemy rejoice over me.[23]

*Versicle:* Take hold of arms and shield, and rise up to help me[24]
that my enemy not rejoice over me.

*Prayer:* Save your servant, O my God, whose hope is in you.
O Lord, send him aid from your holy place
and watch over him from Zion.
Be his tower of strength, O Lord, in the face of his enemy.
Hear, O Lord, my prayer, and let my cry rise up to you.

*Let us pray:* O God, who through your servant has seen fit
to gather together your handmaids in your name,
we ask you to protect him in all adversity
and restore him safely to your handmaids.
Through our Lord Jesus Christ, your Son,
who lives and reigns with you
in the unity of the Holy Spirit, one God.
Forever and ever. Amen.

And if the Lord should deliver me into the hands of my enemies
that they prevail over me and slay me, or if by some other chance I
go the way of all flesh while I am not there with you, I beg of you,
take my body wherever it may lie, buried or unburied, and bring it
to your convent cemetery.[25] There every day my daughters—but I
should now say, my sisters in Christ—may look on my grave and
then pour out more fully to the Lord their prayers for me. There is
no place more welcome and secure for a soul grieving in desolation
for its sins than the place of the Consoler, the true Paraclete, consecrated to him and marked specifically with his name. There is no fit-
ter place for Christian burial among any of the faithful than among

---

[23] Cf. Ecclus. 23:3.

[24] Ps. 34:2.

[25] After Abelard's death at the priory of St. Marcellus in 1142, his body was transferred to the Paraclete through the personal intervention of Peter the Venerable and
buried in the oratory there (see Heloise's letter to Peter). Heloise was later buried at
Abelard's side. Although their bodies were moved several times in the following centuries, they were reinterred in 1817 in the cemetery of Père-Lachaise in Paris in the
neo-Gothic tomb where they lie today.

women devoted to Christ. With precious oils they tended to the burial of the Lord Jesus Christ, coming before and following after, keeping watch around his grave and bewailing the Bridegroom with tears and sighs, as it is written: "Women sat at the tomb, weeping and lamenting the Lord." There they first took comfort in the fact that he had risen when an angel came and announced the news to them, and soon they understood the joys there were in his resurrection when he twice appeared to them and found them worthy to touch his risen body with their hands.[26]

Above all else, I make this last request of you: that all of you who now are so concerned for the safety of my body will later remain concerned for the salvation of my soul, and that the love you showed the living man you will later show to me when I am dead through the special prayers you offer in my name.

Farewell, live long, yourself and all your sisters—
Live long and well, but in Christ remember me.

---

[26] Various details from Matt. 26; Luke 23:55–56; and Mark 14:3–8 and 16:1 are woven into this account. The quotation itself is from the antiphon to the *Benedictus* in the Roman Breviary for Holy Saturday.

# THIRD LETTER

## HELOISE TO ABELARD

*To her only one after Christ*
*From his only one in Christ.*

**I** find it strange, my only one,
that you have gone so far outside
the well-known rules of writing letters—
I should say, against the order of nature itself—
that you have put my name ahead of yours
in the greeting of the letter you wrote to me.
There I see a woman before a man,
a wife before a husband, a handmaid
before her lord, a nun before a monk,
a humble deaconess before a priest,
and an abbess before an abbot.
Surely it is the right and proper order
to put the other's name first
when writing to an equal or superior,
but to follow the normal precedence of rank
when writing to someone whose importance is less.[1]

I also found it not a little strange
that where you owed some comfort
you have only brought more sorrow,
and when you should have dried our tears
you have made them flow the faster.
Not one of us could listen without tears

---

[1] Heloise refers to the precepts of the *ars dictaminis,* "art of composition," the rhetoric
of epistolary practice, codified in several handbooks available at the time.

to what you wrote toward the end of your letter:

"And if the Lord should deliver me into the hands of my enemies
that they prevail over me and slay me. . . ."

What were you thinking, dearest,
that you could say a thing like that?
May God never be so oblivious to his handmaids
as to let us live on without you.
May he never grant us a life
that would be worse than any death.
No, you must celebrate *our* funeral rites,
you must commend *our* souls to God,
you must send ahead of you to God
those whom you have gathered in his name—
*this* is what is proper—
so that then you may rest easy about us
and follow us to God with greater joy,
more certain in the knowledge of our salvation.
Spare us this, I beg of you, my lord,
spare us any more words of this kind.
Do not heap misery on our misery
and take from us before our death
the only thing in which we live.
"Sufficient unto the day is the evil thereof,"[2]
and that day, dark with every bitterness,
will bring sorrow enough to everyone it finds.
"What need is there," says Seneca, "to conjure future evils
and throw away your life before your death?"[3]

You say, my only one, that if somehow
you lose your life while you are not here with us,
we are to bring your body to the convent cemetery,
where our memory of you, forever fresh,
could bear you a richer harvest of our prayers.
But how could you imagine that our memory would fail,
or that *that* will be a fitting time for prayer—
         that day on which the deepest agitation

---

[2] Matt. 6:34.
[3] Cf. *Epistulae ad Lucilium* 24.1.

will shatter all our calm,
when the soul will lose its reason
and the tongue will lose its speech,
and the mind in its madness,
then more outraged against God
than ever at peace with him,
will never appease him with its prayers so much
as enrage him with its protests and complaints?
Yes, then there will be time enough for tears,
but not for prayers.
Yes, then it will be time for us to follow you in death,
readier to be buried at your side
than to see you in the earth—
that day on which we will have lost our lives in you
and can no longer live when you are gone.
Far better that we die before that day.
Even the thought of your death is a death to us—
then what will be its stark reality
if that day finds us living after you?
May God never allow us to repay
the debt we owe you and live on.
May we never render you the service you owe us.
In *this* we should go first, not follow you.

Spare us then, I beg of you—
spare your only one, at least—
any more words of this kind.
They pierce our souls like swords of death
and make what comes before our death
much worse than death itself.
The heart cannot be still when it is overwhelmed in sorrow;
the mind can never free itself for God
when it is occupied with such a deep unrest.
I beg of you, do not impede that service to God
to which, above all, you have bound us.
If a sorrow must come, we must hope it will come quickly
and not torture us beforehand with a long and vain foreboding
that no knowledge of the future can allay.
This was the poet Lucan's prayer to God:

"Let it be sudden, whatever it is you plan,
And let the mind of man be blind to fate:

Allow our fear some hope."[4]

But *is* there hope for me if you are gone?
Or any reason to linger on this pilgrimage of life
when I have no other answer but you,
and nothing else *in* you but the fact that you are living,
when every other joy from you has been forbidden,
and even your presence is denied me,
which could restore me to myself from time to time?

> O, the ungodly savagery of God, if I may say it!
> The mercilessness of his mercy!
> The vast misfortune of that Fortune
> who besets me in her universal war!
> She has launched all her arrows against me,
> keeping none for her rage against others.
> See—her quiver now is empty,
> no one else should fear attack.
> And if she had a single arrow more,
> she could find no place in me
> that does not already have its wound.
> Among so many wounds there is just one
> that gives her pause,
> the one that ends my torment with my death.
> Never does she rest in my destruction,
> but while she rushes to destroy me,
> she would not have me destroyed.

> I am the most unhappy of all women,
> I am the most unlucky of all women,
> to be raised as high above them all because of you
> as I am cast down low because of you,
> and because of myself as well:
> the steeper my ascent, the worse my fall.

> Has there ever been a woman of power and birth
> whom Fortune preferred to me,
> who was then so overthrown and overwhelmed in grief?
> Has there been glory like the glory that was mine

---

4 *Pharsalia* 2.14–15.

because of you?
Or ruin like the ruin that is mine
because of you?
Has there ever been a Fortune of such extremes,
who knows no moderation in good or ill?
She made me blessed beyond others
to leave me broken beyond others,
so when I considered how much I have lost,
the grief that consumed me would be no less
than the loss that had crushed me,
and the pain that was to come would be no less
than the love that had gone before,
and the deepest of all pleasures would now end
in the deepest of all sorrows.

And every law of justice was reversed
to spite us further.
When we were still pursuing the joys of love
and—to use an ugly but a more expressive phrase—
abandoning ourselves to fornication,
God spared us his hard judgment.
But when we took steps to correct what we had done,
to cover the illicit with the licit
and repair our fornication with the proper rites of marriage,
the Lord raised up an angry hand against us
and struck our now-chaste bed when he had winked
at our unchaste bed for so long before.
The punishment you suffered would be fit
for men taken in adultery,
but it was for no adultery that you suffered,
but for a proper marriage with which you thought
you had made good any wrong you might have done:
what faithless women bring their partners in adultery,
your lawful wife brought you, her lawful husband.
We had even given up our former pleasures at the time
and were living in abstinence and apart,
you at the school in Paris
and I with the nuns at Argenteuil, at your command.
And when in this seclusion you became
more diligent in your work and I became
more free for study of the scriptures and for prayer—
at just the time when both of us

were living lives of greater piety as well as abstinence,
then you alone paid the price in your body
for what we two had done.
One alone was punished while the two of us were at fault.
You took the entire payment on yourself
although you owed no debt;
for inasmuch as you had made full restitution
by humbling yourself for me
and had elevated me and all my family alike,
then in the eyes of God as in the eyes
of those men who betrayed you,
you were not liable to further penalty.

But *me*—
Was it my sorry birthright to become the cause of evil,
the well-known curse of womankind
to lead the greatest men to greatest ruin?[5]
Is *this* why the Book of Proverbs has this warning against woman—

"Now, therefore, my son, hear me
and attend to the words of my mouth.
Let not thy mind be drawn away in her ways,
neither be thou deceived with her paths.
For she has cast down many wounded,
and the strongest have been slain by her.
Her house is the way to hell,
reaching even to the inner chambers of death"[6]—

and the Book of Ecclesiastes this—

---

[5] Here and in the following section, Heloise expands on a long-lived misogynist canard. Compare Abelard's plea to Fulbert in the *Calamities* on the basis of "what women had done from the beginning of the human race to bring even the greatest men to ruin" and Heloise's corresponding fear of falling victim to the pernicious cliché: "Is *this* how she would be remembered, as the woman who brought [Abelard's] name to ruin and shamed [them] both?" The passage here contrasts pointedly with Abelard's praise of women's piety at the end of the Second Letter, but by the passage's end Heloise will have shifted primary blame from womankind itself and will also have distanced herself from the group of evil female exemplars she mentions: by the ethical doctrine developed in the First Letter and later in Abelard's *Ethics*, she cannot be held morally responsible for Abelard's downfall since she did not consent to it.

[6] Prov. 7:24–27.

"I have surveyed all things with my mind
and I found more bitter than death
a woman who is the hunter's snare:
her heart is a net and her hands are bands.
He that pleaseth God shall escape from her,
but he that is a sinner shall be caught."[7]

The first action by a woman lured man from paradise,
becoming his undoing when the Lord
created her to be his helpmeet.
Then Samson, the mightiest Nazirite of the Lord,
whose conception even an angel had announced,
was vanquished by Dalila single-handed;
betrayed to his enemies and his eyes put out,
his grief at last compelled him to destroy
himself along with them in general ruin.[8]
The wisest man of all, King Solomon,
lost his wits through the workings of one woman
he had taken to his bed;
she drove him to such insanity that that great man,
whom the Lord himself had chosen to build his Temple,
when even his righteous father had been rejected for the task,
foundered to the end of his days in the worshipping of idols,
abandoning the worship of the Lord,
which he had taught and preached in all his words.[9]
And Job, whose sanctity was matchless,
endured his last and heaviest blow
from his wife, who urged him to curse God.[10]
Oh yes,
the great Seducer in his cunning
knew one thing well, and that from long experience:
the easiest path to ruin for men
is always through their wives.
So, when he would extend his well-known malice
to our own time and found a man
he could not bring down through fornication,

---

[7] Eccles. 7:26–27.
[8] See Judg. 13:3 and 16:4–31.
[9] See 3 Kings 11.
[10] See Job 2:9.

he tempted him with marriage instead,
using good to work his evil,
now that evil was denied him for the purpose.

At least I can thank God for this—that the Seducer
never drew me into guilt with my consent,
as he did these other women,
though he did make me a cause in the event.
My heart, however, is clear of guilt,
no blame through my consent.
There were many earlier sins, I know,
for which I bear responsibility—
my devotion to the pleasures of the flesh,
whose consequences have become
a fitting punishment for me—
and to that bad beginning do I owe this twisted outcome.
I only wish it lay within my power
to do a penance worthy of the wrong
done against *you*,
that at least by long contrition I could offer
some recompense for the wound that you sustained
and take upon my mind throughout a lifetime of remorse
what your body suffered in that hour.
This is but just, and in this way
I may make some fit amends—
to you at least, that is, if not to God.

There is no penance I could undergo
that can appease God—
not if I should open my most wretched heart completely
and confess all its weaknesses to him—
since I charge him forever with the savagery of that act
and, forever unreconciled to his will,
offend him more with my outrage
than I can soothe him with any fitting penance.
How can it be called repentance of sins,
whatever affliction the body undergoes,
if the mind retains the will to sin
and seethes with its old desires?
Easy to announce that one is guilty
and easy to confess one's sins,
or even to afflict the body in some outward act of penance—

but it remains the hardest thing of all
to wrench the heart away from its desires
for the greatest pleasures it has ever known.
So it was with every reason that Job began,
"I will let go my speech against myself"—
    meaning, "I will open my mouth in confession
    to accuse myself of my sins"—
and then immediately went on,
"I will speak in the bitterness of my soul."[11]
As Saint Gregory explains:

"Some confess their sins aloud
but cannot groan when they confess them:
they announce their remorse with joy in their hearts.
So, if someone speaks with genuine displeasure for his sins,
he then must speak 'in the bitterness of his soul,'
since it is this very bitterness that punishes
whatever the tongue confesses
through the judgment of the mind."[12]

But just how rare the bitterness of true repentance is
Saint Ambrose tells us:

"I have always thought it easier to find
someone who has kept his innocence intact
than someone who has actually repented."[13]

For me,
the pleasures we shared in love were sweet,
so sweet
they cannot displease me now,
and rarely are they ever out of mind.
Wherever I turn, they are there before my eyes
with all their old desires.
I see their images even in my sleep.
During Holy Mass itself,
when prayer should be its purest,
unholy fantasies of pleasure so enslave my wretched soul
that my devotion is to *them* and not my prayers:

---

[11] Job 10:1.

[12] *Moralia* 9.43.

[13] *De Poenitentia* 2.10.

when I ought to groan for what I have done,
I sigh for what I have lost.
Not only what we did but when and where—
these are so fixed within my heart
that I live through them again with you
in all those times and places.
I have no rest from them even in sleep.
At times my thoughts betray themselves
in a movement of my body
or even in involuntary words.
In my unhappiness,
the lament of that despondent soul is mine:
"Wretch that I am, who shall deliver me
from the body of this death?"
I wish I could continue as he did,
"The grace of God through Jesus Christ our Lord."[14]

It seems, my dearest, that this grace came earlier to you,
when the injury to your body freed your soul
from all such torments,
and the God who seemed your enemy proved your friend,
at least in this,
a staunch physician, surely, not to spare his patient pain
if he believed it would bring about a cure.
But this is not the way it is with *me*.
I am still young, and the passions of youth
and my experience of those sweet pleasures
exacerbate the torments of the flesh,
and their assaults against me are more fierce,
the weaker the nature is that they assault.

Men call me chaste who do not see the hypocrite I am.
They count purity of the flesh among the virtues
though the virtue belongs to the heart and not the body.[15]

---

[14] Rom. 7:24–25, following a sentence that reads (7:22–23):

For I am delighted with the law of God according to the inner man: but I see
another law in my members, fighting against the law of my mind and captivating
me in the law of sin that is in my members.

[15] Paraphrasing Augustine, *De Bono Coniugali* 21, which Heloise cites directly in the
Fifth Letter.

Men give me praise, but I deserve no praise from God,
who searches heart and mind and sees in all the secret places.[16]
They judge me a woman of religion at a time
when little in religious life is *not* hypocrisy,
when the highest praise flows to the one
who does not offend man's judgment.
Perhaps it *is* worth praise to some extent
and acceptable enough to God
if I do *not* become a scandal to the Church by overt deed,
regardless of my inward disposition,
if I do *not* blaspheme the name of God for infidels to hear
or shame my professed orders before laymen.
I know it is no trivial gift of grace,
not only to do good but to keep from evil.
In vain, though, does one come first
if the other does not follow—"Decline from evil
*and* do good," it is written[17]—and both are vain
if not done for the love of God.

But in every circumstance throughout my life,
as God knows well,
I have feared an offense against you
more than any offense against him,
and I have sought to please you more than him.
It was your command, not love for him, that brought
me to put on this habit of religion.
Consider *then* the life that I am living—
how unhappy, how much more miserable than others'—
if I must bear my burdens here in vain
with no hope of compensation in the future.
You too were taken in by my charade
like all the rest,
mistaking my hypocrisy for religion.
And now you commend yourself to my prayers—
to *my* prayers above all—
and ask from me what I expect from you.

---

[16] Cf. Prov. 24:12; Ps. 7.10; Jer. 11:20, 17:10, 20:12; etc. See also the Fifth Letter, and Abelard's *Ethics* (Luscombe 1971, 42) along with the discussion there.

[17] Ps. 36:27. Cf. also Abelard's *Ethics* (Luscombe 1971, 128).

Do not presume so much, I beg of you:
    you may forget to help me with your prayers.
Do not ever suppose that I am healed:
    you may withdraw the grace of your healing.
Do not believe that I am not in need:
    you may put off your help when I most need it.
Do not imagine that I am strong:
    I may collapse before you stop my fall.

False praise has done great injury before,
destroying the security we need.
As the Lord cries out through the mouth of Isaiah,
"They that call thee blessed deceive thee
and destroy the way of thy steps,"[18]
and through the mouth of Ezekiel,
"Woe to them that sew cushions for each elbow
and pillows for the heads of every age
to deceive men's souls."[19]
But, then, through Solomon we learn,
"The words of the wise are like goads
and as nails deeply fastened,"[20]
and nails like these are never gentle with a wound
but can only pierce it through.

Then stop this praise of me, I beg of you,
or you will win yourself a name for flattery
and risk the charge of lying,
and vanity like a puff of air
will blow away any good you have found to praise.
No one skilled in healing ever judges
the sickness within from outward signs alone.
God finds no merit in what is common
to his chosen and his rejected alike,
those outward deeds that hypocrites do

---

[18] Isa. 3:12.

[19] Ezek. 13:18. Whatever the original meaning of this obscure passage, it is taken here as a warning against those who offer deceptive comfort. Abelard offers a similar interpretation of the passage in his Sermon 33 on John the Baptist.

[20] Eccles. 12:11.

with greater zeal than any of the righteous.[21]
"The heart of man is perverse and unsearchable:
who can know it?"[22]
"There are ways that seem just to a man,
but their ends lead to death"[23]
Yes, the judgment of man is reckless and unstable
in what is reserved for the scrutiny of God,
and that is why it is also written,
"Praise no man in his lifetime,"[24]
that is, while praise
still has the power to make him unworthy of praise.
Your praise of me brings danger, and all the more
because I want to hear it;
I am the more caught up in it and charmed,
the more I strive to please you in all things.

You must put no trust in me, I beg of you,
but instead you must be constantly afraid:
only your fear can help me.
And now you have most cause to be afraid—
now above all,
when you have no answer in you for my lack of self-restraint.
Do not talk to me of strength or of fighting the good fight.
Do not tell me that power is made perfect by weakness,
and that no one is crowned who does not strive.[25]
I seek no crown of victory—
enough that I keep from risk,
far safer to keep from risk
than to keep struggling in these wars.
Whatever corner of heaven God may grant
will fit me well enough:
no one will envy another's state

---

[21] Cf. Abelard's *Ethics* (Luscombe 1971, 4, 28, and 44).

[22] Jer. 17:9.

[23] Cf. Prov. 16:25 and 14:12.

[24] Ecclus. 11:30.

[25] See 2 Cor. 12:9 and 2 Tim. 2:5. Both were favorite passages of Abelard's, the first quoted in Sermons 26 and 30, the second in Sermon 1 and in his *Ethics* (Luscombe 1971, 4). He will respond to Heloise by citing these passages again in the Fourth and Sixth Letters.

when what each has will always be enough.
If there must be authority to confirm what I resolve,
then let it be authority strong as oak—
yes,
let us hear the words of Saint Jerome:

"I confess my utter weakness:
I will not fight in the hope of victory,
or else some day I may lose the victory. . . .
What need is there to hazard what is certain
by flitting after things that are uncertain?"[26]

---

[26] *Adversus Vigilantium* 16.

# FOURTH LETTER

## ABELARD TO HELOISE

*To the bride of Christ*
*From his servant.*

There are four points, by my count, in your last letter on which you base your sense of injury; I see nothing in the letter more than that. First, you complain that, "outside the well-known rules of writing letters" and even "against the order of nature itself," my letter to you put your name ahead of mine in its greeting. Second, that I brought you sorrow when I owed you comfort and made your tears flow faster when I should have dried them—this, it seems, by my writing in my letter, "And if the Lord should deliver me up to my enemies," and so on. Third is your old and continual complaint against God about the manner in which we came to the religious life and the savagery of the act of betrayal committed against me. Finally, you countered my praise of you with an accusation against yourself, along with a not-inconsiderable appeal that I refrain from praising you again.

I will answer each of these points in turn. My purpose is not to make excuses for myself but rather to instruct you and to urge you, first, to accede to my requests when you understand that they are grounded in reason; then, to hear me out when I speak of your requests, once you see I am not blameworthy in my own; and last, to be somewhat more reluctant to condemn me when you realize I do not deserve your reproach.

First, then, in the matter of my greeting, whose order you say I have reversed—You will note it was consistent with what you yourself have claimed. It is certainly common knowledge, as you say, that in letters to superiors their names should be placed first. But you must understand that you *are* my superior and have been so from the time you became my lady, that is, on your becoming the bride of my Lord. As Saint Jerome wrote to Eustochium, "I write to you as 'My lady Eustochium' because, surely, I ought to call my Lord's own bride 'my lady.'"[1] A happy exchange of marriage ties for you, then—the wife, first, of the least of men, now raised to wedlock with the greatest of all kings. As a consequence of this honor, you have been lifted not only above the man who was once your husband but above all the other servants of that King. It should not seem strange to you, then, if I commend myself, living or dead, to the prayers of the women of your convent, since by a widely accepted right brides have power of intercession with their lords beyond that of any member of their households, as befits the relative status of ladies and servants. In fact, the *type* of these brides[2] is the queen and bride of that great King himself, carefully presented in the psalm which says, "The queen stood on thy right hand, in gilded clothing, surrounded with splendor. Hearken, O daughter, and see. . . . The daughters of Tyre and the rich among the people shall entreat thy favor with gifts."[3] In other words, she stands next to her husband, clinging closely to his side, and walks at a pace with him while all the others, as it were, follow behind or stand a long way off.

In the Canticles the bride rejoices over her distinction, the Ethiopian woman whom, in a certain sense, Moses took to wife.[4] "I am black but beautiful, O ye daughters of Jerusalem," she says; "therefore, the king hath loved me and hath led me into his chamber." And just after, "Do not consider me that I am brown, because the sun hath altered my color."[5] She represents in *genus* the contemplative soul, which in *species* is called the bride of Christ; but in a more particular way the terms pertain to all of you, as your outer habit

---

[1] *Epistulae* 22.2.

[2] That is, the prototype or model, which may be presented in symbolic or allegorical terms. For the concept and its use in medieval exegesis, see the classic essay by Auerbach 1959.

[3] Ps. 44:10–13. The manuscripts cite the passage up to "on thy right hand," indicating the extended context with "etc."

[4] That is, applying a typological understanding to Moses' marriage to an Ethiopian in Num. 12:1, so that Moses' wife and the bride of the Canticles are expressions of the same type. Abelard will assimilate this kind of reading with the categories of his dialectic just below.

[5] Cant. 1:4–5 in a pre-Vulgate version.

also indicates.[6] The garb of coarse black cloth you wear—so much like the mourning dress of worthy widows who lament the deaths of the husbands they loved—shows that you are, as the Apostle says, truly widowed in this world and desolate, deserving of the assistance of the Church.[7] Scripture also remembers the widows' grief for their Bridegroom who was slain, saying, "Women sat at the tomb, weeping and lamenting the Lord."[8]

Now, the Ethiopian woman also has a black exterior—in her skin—and appears less beautiful than other women with respect to outward things. She is not different, though, in inward things, and in some of these she may even be whiter and more beautiful, as in, for example, her bones and teeth. [The whiteness of teeth, in fact, is praised even in a bridegroom, as in the phrase, "And his teeth are whiter than milk."][9] She is black, then, in outward things but beautiful in inward things, as if because she is outwardly blackened in her flesh by her affliction in this life with tribulations of the flesh—as Saint Paul says, "All that live godly in Christ shall suffer persecution,"[10] and, just as prosperity is signified by white, so adversity is appropriately signified by black. She is white within, though—as in her bones—as if because her soul remains strong in virtue, as it is written, "All the glory of the daughter of the king is within."[11] For the bones within, which are covered by the flesh, are the strength of the flesh they sustain; they then well represent the soul which is within the flesh, and gives life to the flesh, and sustains and moves and governs the flesh, and supplies all its well-being. And its whiteness, or its beauty, lies in the virtues which adorn it.

She is also black in outward things because, so long as she remains an exile on her pilgrimage in this life, her condition is degraded and low so that she may be exalted in the life to come—

---

[6] Abelard is using the terms of formal dialectic, speaking of the contemplative soul as the *genus*, or large category, of which the nun, or bride of Christ, is a *species*, or smaller category, of which the nuns of the Paraclete are particular examples.

[7] See 1 Tim. 5:3, 16.

[8] From the antiphon to the *Benedictus* in the Roman Breviary for Holy Saturday. See the Second Letter.

[9] A parenthetical remark included in the manuscripts, which most likely represents a scribal interpolation. The quotation is from Gen. 49:12.

[10] 2 Tim. 3:12.

[11] Ps. 44:14.

the life which is hidden with Christ in God[12]—when she will have gained her home country at last. The true sun alters her color because the love of her Bridegroom in heaven humbles her or torments her with trials so that prosperity can never make her proud. He alters her color and, in that, distinguishes her from the rest of women who fix their eyes on earthly things and seek the glory of the world. She becomes a lily-of-the-valley in her humility,[13] not a lily-of-the-mountain-peaks like those foolish virgins who swell themselves with pride at their purity of the flesh—their abstinence in outward things—only to wither in the heat of temptation. She is right to address the *daughters* of Jerusalem—that is, the more imperfect among the faithful who do not deserve the name of *sons*—and say to them, "Do not consider me that I am brown, because the sun hath altered my color," or in other words, "If I bear my adversities in humility like a man, it is not through my own virtue but through the grace of him I serve." Hypocrites and heretics will act otherwise, of course, who, always with their eyes on the eyes of other men, affect the most abject humility in the hope of earthly glory and endure their many trials to no avail. We can only wonder at their self-abasement and self-imposed austerity, for they are by far the wretchedest of men, with no share in the good things of this life or of the life to come. [Thinking about this carefully, then, the bride says, "Do not consider it strange why I do this." But we can only wonder about *them* when, seething with a desire for earthly praise, they deprive themselves of earthly goods to no avail, remaining wretched both now and in the future.][14] Such, in fact, is the self-restraint of the foolish virgins of the parable who were shut outside the door.[15]

She is also right to say that, because she is black and beautiful, the king loved her and led her into his chamber—that is, into the seclusion and repose of contemplation—and to his bed, about which she says, "In my bed by night I sought him whom my soul loveth."[16] Her color itself is not beautiful and prefers the hidden to the open, the private to the public; and a wife like this desires the

---

[12] Cf. Col. 3:4.

[13] Cf. Cant. 2:1.

[14] A partial doublet of the sentences preceding, apparently deriving from an alternate version of the paragraph only imperfectly reconciled with what else of the letter we have.

[15] See the parable of the wise and foolish virgins in Matt. 25:1–13.

[16] Cant. 3:1.

private pleasures of her husband more than the open ones, would rather, for example, be touched in bed than seen at table. Though less appealing to the eye, the flesh of black women is often softer to the touch, and so the pleasure derived from them is greater and more suitably enjoyed in private than in public, and their husbands then take pleasure in their wives by leading them into their chambers rather than out in public view. Continuing with the figure, then, the spiritual bride is right to say, "I am black but beautiful," and to add immediately, "therefore the king hath loved me and hath led me into his chamber," aligning each particular with particular—that is, *because she is beautiful*, the king loved her, and *because she is black*, he led her into his chamber. As I said earlier, she is beautiful within, that is, with the virtues that the bridegroom loves; and she is black without, that is, with the adversity of the body's tribulations.

This blackness—that is, of the body's tribulations—can easily turn the minds of the faithful away from a love of earthly things toward a longing for eternal life, and it sometimes also draws them from the tumult of the world toward private contemplation, as Saint Jerome said happened in the case of Paul at the inception of our monastic way of life.[17] This low, coarse clothing, too, indicates seclusion more than public life, in keeping with the humble retirement most appropriate to our calling. There is nothing that more calls for public display than the expensive clothes no one wants or needs for any other purpose than the empty pomp and glory of the world, as Saint Gregory has shown: "No one adorns himself like this in private, but only where he can be seen."[18] Moreover, the chamber of the bride I spoke of earlier is the one to which the Bridegroom in the Gospel invites anyone who prays: "When thou shalt pray," he says, "enter into thy chamber and, having shut the door, pray to thy Father in secret," not in the streets or in public places like the hypocrites.[19] He calls this chamber a place apart, secluded from the sight and tumult of the world, a place where prayer can be more quiet and more pure. The seclusion of monastic solitude is very much like this, a place where we are told to close the door and shut out anything that could disturb the purity of prayer or allow the eye to distract the unhappy soul.

---

[17] See Jerome's *Vita Pauli Primi Eremitae* 5.

[18] *Homilia in Lucam* 40.16.

[19] Matt. 6:6 and cf. 6:5.

I take it hard, then, that many members of my order choose to flout God's teaching about this, as if it were a mere suggestion and no mandate—opening up their cloisters and their choirs when they celebrate the Divine Offices, carrying on without a scruple or a blush in full view of women as well as men, and polluting themselves with their high-priced trinkets above all during Mass, as worldly as the audience that watches their display. For them our rites are celebrated best when their outward show is richest and the offerings of their tables are overflowing. I know it is better to keep silent about this—disgraceful enough just to speak about their miserable blindness, so thoroughly opposed to the Christian faith, which should be concerned with the poor. They are more like the scribes and Pharisees of the Jews,[20] as they follow their own custom, not the rule, and void the commandment of God for the sake of their traditions, not doing what they must but what they are most used to—as if Augustine never reminded us that the Lord said, "I am truth," not "I am tradition."[21] If someone wants to commend himself to the prayers of men like these—those prayers of the open door—let him go and do as he likes. I turn instead to *you*, to all of you who are led by heaven's King into his chamber to rest in his embrace behind doors forever closed. There you are given wholly to him, and as the Apostle has said, "Whoever is joined with the Lord is one with him in spirit."[22] The more you cling to his side, the more I place my trust in the purity and power of your prayers, and the more I call upon their aid. I believe they will be offered on my behalf with all the devotion due our bond of mutual charity and love.

Now, if I have given you cause for disturbance by mentioning the dangers I face or the death I have reason to fear, let me remind you that this too was done at your request, or I should say, at your most strenuous insistence. In your first letter to me, you wrote:

> So, by that Christ who keeps you for his own even now, we beg of you, as we are his handmaids and yours, write to us, tell us of those storms in which you find yourself tossed. We are all you have left: let us share your grief or your joy. A

---

[20] The sentence draws heavily from the language and thought of Jesus' condemnation of the scribes and Pharisees in Matt. 15:1–6.

[21] *De Baptismo Contra Donatistas* 3.6.9, with reference to John 14:6.

[22] 1 Cor. 6:17.

community of grief can bring some comfort to one in need of it, since many shoulders will lighten any burden or even make it seem to disappear.[23]

Then why do you object that I let you share my fear when in fact it was you who insisted on it? When I am in despair for my life, is it better for you to feel *glad*? Or would you want to be partners only in joy but not in grief, to "rejoice with them that rejoice" but never "weep with them that weep"?[24] There is no greater difference between a false and true friend than that one would share in prosperity alone, the other in adversity as well.

Then, stop your complaints on this subject, I beg of you: they are far from the heart of charitable love. You still may resent it, but I am at such a point of danger and despair for my life that I must take thought for the welfare of my soul and act to secure it while there is time. If you truly care for me, you will not object to this—no, I will go further: if you have any hope that God will show me mercy, you will *want* me to be freed from the troubles of this life when you see they are unbearable to me. Whoever frees me from this life, you can be sure, will rescue me from terrible suffering. No one can know what pains I will face hereafter, but what pains I will escape no one can doubt. The end of every wretched life is welcome, and those who truly feel compassion for the suffering of others and grieve when others grieve will want that suffering to end, even at some cost to themselves: if they truly care for those whom they see suffer, they will look to the others' interests, not their own. This is how it is with a mother whose child has long been ill: she wants his illness to end even if it means his death, because the illness itself is unendurable to her, and she can more easily bear to lose her child than to keep him with her to share her agony. And someone who takes pleasure in the presence of a friend would rather that the friend be happy, although absent, than unhappy and present, because he cannot bear to see suffering unrelieved. But as it is, even my unhappy presence is denied you. So, unless you are acting to secure something in your interest, I cannot see why you want me to live on in this abject misery rather than to die in relative happiness. If it *is* to

---

[23] Abelard's reference to this as the "first letter" indicates either that there indeed had been no earlier letter from Heloise or that the compiler of the letter collection has harmonized at least some of its elements.

[24] Rom. 12:15.

gain some interest, though, that you want my suffering prolonged, you have proved yourself my enemy, not my friend. But if this is not how you would like to appear, then, as I said, you must stop these complaints.

I do approve of your rejection of praise, however, since it shows you are even worthier of praise. "The just is first accuser of himself," it is written, and "He that humbleth himself shall be exalted."[25] I only hope you take to heart what you have written. If you do, then yours is the true humility which will not vanish merely because of something I might say. I beg of you, though, take care that you are not looking for praise by seeming to avoid it or rejecting in your words what you long for in your heart. Jerome wrote to Eustochium about this, saying among other things:

> We are led along by an evil in our nature. We listen happily to those who flatter us, and though we may say we are not worthy and a coy little blush may come over our cheeks, still the soul within us is very glad to hear the praise.[26]

Virgil describes the same coyness in the nymph Galatea, who sought what she wanted by running away and stirred her lover even more by the pretense of refusing him, "Fleeing to the willows, wanting to be seen."[27] That is, before she could hide, she wanted to be seen in the act of flight, by which she both gained and yet seemed to reject the company of the young man in love with her. It is the same with the praise of men: so long as we seem to shun it, we only increase it, and when we affect a wish to hide so that no one can find the good in us to praise, we lead our shameless flatterers on to praise us even more because we then seem to deserve it even more. Now, I am saying this because it often is the case and not because I suspect you of any coyness—about your humility I have no doubts—but I want you to refrain from this subject as well. Not everyone knows you as I do, and I would not want you to seem to be "chasing glory by running away," in Jerome's phrase.[28] I know my praise will never puff you up but will only challenge you to

---

[25] Prov. 18:17; Luke 18:14.

[26] *Epistulae* 22.24.

[27] *Eclogues* 3.65.

[28] Cf. *Epistulae* 22.27.

higher things; and if you strive to please me, as you say, you will embrace the things I will have praised. And my praise does not pay tribute to your piety in a way that can feed your pride: we should put no more stock in the approval of our friends than we put in the censure of our enemies.

I come now to the last remaining point—what I called your old, continual complaint, in which you dare lay charges against God for how we came to the religious life when in justice you ought to glorify his name. I had thought that your bitterness of heart at such a clear example of God's mercy had vanished long ago—as dangerous as it is to you, eating away at your body and soul, it is as sad and disturbing to me. If, as you claim, you strive to please me in all things, then to please me most—or at least in this one thing to keep from torturing me further—you will put this bitterness aside. You cannot please me with it or attain the state of blessedness at my side. Could you bear it that I come to this without you when you say you would follow me even to Vulcan's flames? Hold fast to your religious life at least in this, so that you and I will never be apart as I go "striding off to God," as you believe[29]—and do it gladly, my dear sister, for where we must come is blessed, and our company should be as gracious as it will be full of joy. Remember what you have said, recall what you have written about the way I turned to God, that although he seemed my enemy, he proved my friend.[30] Be reconciled to his will at least in this, for it has been so thoroughly to my good—no, to my good *and* to yours, if you can admit the claims of reason in your grief. Do not torment yourself that you have been the cause of this great good, or doubt that God created you for this.[31] And do not grieve over what I may have suffered, except when the blessings that flow from the suffering of the martyrs and the death of our Lord himself will also make you sad. Would you find it any less offensive or any easier to bear if what happened to me had happened in accord with perfect justice? Surely if this had been the case, it would redound more to my discredit and more to my enemies' honor, for the justice of their act would bring them praise and my guilt would bring me scorn, and no one then would blame what they had done or be moved by compassion for me.

---

[29] Cf. the First Letter, p. 60.

[30] Cf. the Third Letter, p. 80.

[31] Cf. the Third Letter, p. 76.

Nonetheless, it may relieve the bitterness of your grief if I demonstrate to you that what happened to us was both in accord with justice and to our advantage as well,[32] and that God acted more properly against us after our marriage than he had done before. After you and I were married and you were living with the nuns at Argenteuil, you know how I came to visit you one day and what my lust then did with you even within the walls of the refectory itself, when there was nowhere else for us to go. You know how shamelessly we acted in that holy place, consecrated to the Blessed Virgin. Now even if there were no other sins, that one alone deserves a heavy retribution. But do I need to remind you of those shameful and polluting acts that came before our marriage? Or of my treachery toward your uncle, whom I so foully deceived about you even while I kept living in his house? Could anyone think that, when I had broken faith, his broken faith toward me was in any way unjust? Do you imagine that the momentary pain I suffered from my wound is enough to atone for all these sins? Or rather, that all the *good* that I derived from it is really proper payment for the wrongs that I have done? What wound do you suppose would be enough to satisfy God's vengeance for the pollution of his mother's precinct? Unless I am badly in error, it was not so much that soul-preserving wound that became my punishment as it is all *these* that I suffer every day without an end.

[And on the journey to Brittany when you were pregnant, you know how you disguised yourself in the habit of a nun and with that pretense mocked the religious calling that now is yours. Consider then how appropriately God's justice—or rather, it was God's grace—dragged you against your will to the calling you were not afraid to mock, wanting you to atone for that desecration while wearing the same habit you once profaned, to answer the lie with the truth of the event and correct the falsehood of your pretense.][33]

---

[32] Abelard is adapting the familiar double-pronged appeal of deliberative rhetoric, that a proposed course of action is (or is not) both ethical and advantageous.

[33] This short paragraph, which interrupts the steady rhetorical crescendo and anticipates the shift accomplished in the following paragraph from God's justice to his grace, is most likely a later addition to the text. If taken at its face value, it could have been added only by someone in a position at least to pretend to know the facts, although it is unlikely to have been Heloise, who never exhibits this kind of religious sensibility in her own writings. But the story may also derive from a garbled version of Abelard's dressing Heloise "in the garments of monastic life" when he first brought her to Argenteuil, as described in the *Calamities*.

But if you look beyond God's justice to see the advantages we have gained, you can no longer call what he did for us his justice, but only properly his grace. Then, *look,* my dearest, *look and see* how the nets of God's mercy have fished us up from the depths of that dangerous sea, and how the Lord has drawn our shipwrecked souls safely from the whirlpool of Charybdis—yes, even despite our will—so that each of us may break out in that cry, "The Lord taketh thought for me!"[34] Think and think again about the dangers we were in and how we found our rescue in the Lord. And always with the deepest gratitude proclaim what great things he hath done for our soul.[35] Use the force of our example to console the unrighteous who despair of the goodness of God: let all of them know what may be done for suppliants in prayer, when such blessings come to sinners against their will. Ponder the high purpose of God's compassion—with what mercy he turned his judgment to our correction, with what wisdom he used these evils for our good, with what piety he then threw down all our impiety, and with a stroke of justice to one part of my body he began to work the healing of two souls. Measure our danger against the manner of our deliverance. Measure our illness against its cure. Examine the cause, what our actions deserve; stand in awe of the effect, which is his mercy.

You know to what vile corruption my lust enslaved our bodies, how no reverence for God or any self-respect could keep me from wallowing in filth even on the days of the Passion of our Lord or on any holy day, however sacred—but when you resisted and you argued and you struggled to the limits of your strength, I would force you to my will with greater strength. I was welded to you by desire so hot that I set those low and degenerate pleasures—which we are at a loss even to name—ahead of both God and myself. His mercy had no other way, it seemed, but to sever me entirely from those pleasures and set them forever beyond my reach. And so with perfect justice and with perfect clemency—the treachery of your uncle not withstanding—I was lessened in that part of my body where lust had its dominion and desire its root cause, to become a greater man in many ways. What justice that those organs should lament all they had done to us and expiate in pain when they had sinned in taking pleasure, cutting me off from the loathsome filth in

---

[34] Ps. 39:18. Charybdis is the whirlpool from which Ulysses escaped; cf. also its use as an image of sensuality in the *Calamities*.

[35] Cf. Ps. 66:16.

which I had been sunk to leave me circumcised in mind as well as body.[36] It then would make me only the more fit to approach the altar of God with no stain of pollution in my flesh to call me back again. What mercy, too, that God should have me suffer only in that organ whose loss would advance the salvation of my soul but not disfigure my body or debar me from any exercise of the Offices.[37] On the contrary, it only made me readier in all the things that can be done in decency and honor, once I was free of the yoke of that desire.

I was purged, not deprived, of those organs—so vile they are called the parts of shame for what they do and have no proper name of their own—and the grace of God did nothing else but rid me of corruption to leave me purified and clean. Many of the wise, in fact, have longed for this same purity, even to the point of laying hands upon themselves to be rid of the shame of desire. Saint Paul, we read, repeatedly begged the Lord to remove this thorn in his flesh, though his prayers were never answered.[38] But there is also the example of Origen, the great Christian philosopher, who was unafraid to do violence to himself to extinguish all trace of the fire within him[39]—as though he read too literally what is written about those who have made themselves eunuchs for the kingdom of heaven, and believed that they fulfilled the Lord's command to pluck out and cast away any organ that is our undoing; as though he understood Isaiah's prophecy not as the veiled mystery it is but as simple fact declaring the Lord's special love for eunuchs:

> If they shall keep my Sabbaths and shall choose the things that please me . . . , I will give to them in my house and within my walls a place and a name better than sons and daughters. I will give them an everlasting name which shall never perish.[40]

---

[36] Cf. Rom. 2:25–29.

[37] Despite Abelard's anxiety in the *Calamities* about biblical prohibitions (in the *Calamities*), canon law does not preclude eunuchs from the priesthood, except in cases of self-mutilation. See Muckle 1954, 89 n. 94.

[38] See 2 Cor. 12:8, in which Paul reports that he offered this prayer three times. Abelard understands Paul's "thorn in the flesh" to mean sexual desire.

[39] See Eusebius, *Historia Ecclesiae* 6.7.

[40] Cf. Matt. 19:12, 18:8–9; Isa. 56:4–5.

But Origen deserves our blame for seeking an answer for blame in the punishment of his body—an act of zeal for God, no doubt, but not in accord with knowledge[41]—becoming guilty of homicide through his self-mutilation. For surely it was at the suggestion of the devil, or else by some most serious mistake, that he did to himself what, through the mercy of God, was done to me by others. I escaped that blame, I did not incur it. And I deserve death, yet I live. I am called, I refuse, I persist in my wrongs and am dragged to God's forgiveness against my will. And yet the Apostle prayed and was not heard; and yet he persisted in prayer and did not prevail. Yes, truly the Lord taketh thought for me: I will go and proclaim what great things he hath done for my soul.[42]

And you come, too, my inseparable companion, and join me in this common act of thanks, my partner in God's grace as you once were my partner in our sins. Indeed God is thinking of your salvation as well—no, he is thinking of your salvation most of all, having marked you as his own with a sacred token of his name when he named you *Heloise,* that is to say, *Of God,* from the name that he himself bears, *Heloim.*[43] In his merciful plan he provided for the two of us in one when the devil was contriving one destruction for us both. It was only a short time before that event took place that he joined us together in the bond of holy matrimony when I wanted to keep you forever for myself, beloved beyond measure. But God himself prepared this means to bring us both to him; for if you had not already been bound to me in marriage, you easily would have clung to the world after I had withdrawn from it, succumbing to the pressures of your family or yielding to the pleasures of the flesh.[44]

Then, see how the Lord hath taken thought for us, as if he would keep us for some great use and be grieved if the great sums of learning he had lent us were not dedicated to the glory of his name. Or perhaps he was afraid for his poor servant, so lacking in the power of self-restraint, for "women make even the wise fall away," as we

---

[41] Cf. Rom. 10:2.

[42] Ps. 39:18, 66:16.

[43] There is no basis other than the pun for connecting Heloise's name to the Hebrew *Elohim* or for taking its meaning as Abelard does here.

[44] Abelard's account here of his motives for marriage differs from the one he gives in his *Calamities,* but he may be revealing a significant reason for his insistence that Heloise take the veil, that is, his fear that she might remarry.

know happened to Solomon, the wisest man of all.[45] But the sum of *your* wisdom earns the Lord interest every day in the form of the daughters in the spirit you have borne him—while I remain forever barren, laboring without issue among these sons of perdition. What a waste it would be, what a hateful sorry loss if you spent your life amid the pleasures of the flesh just to bear a few children in sorrow to the world,[46] when now you can give birth to a multitude of off-spring in joy and exultation to heaven. You would not then transcend the state of women, as you now surpass all men and have turned the curse of Eve into the blessing of Mary. What a sad misuse of your sacred hands, which now turn the pages of Holy Writ, to be slaves to the sordid business of women's work. God himself saw fit to lift us from that mire, from that filthy sink of pleasure, and to bring us to himself—even if he used some force, as he once struck Paul at the hour of his conversion.[47] [And perhaps by our example he could deter other learned men from their presumption.][48]

But none of this should trouble you, my sister, or move you to resentment of our Father, who has only corrected us as a father should. Remember what is written: "Whom the Lord loveth he chastiseth, and he scourgeth every son whom he receiveth," and "He that spareth the rod hateth his son." This is but a temporary punishment, not eternal, our purgation, not our damnation. And take some comfort in the words of the prophet that the Lord will not judge twice the same offense: "There shall not rise a double affliction." Remember, too, what the Lord himself has said, his greatest and his highest exhortation: "In your patience you shall possess your souls." Think also of the words of Solomon: "The patient man is better than the valiant, and he that ruleth his spirit better than he that taketh cities."[49]

Instead, you should be troubled and moved to tears by God's only-begotten Son, who for your sake and the sake of all mankind was taken up by the wickedest of men, led off and scourged, blindfolded, mocked and beaten, spat upon and crowned with thorns, and finally, in what was then the basest form of punishment, hung

---

[45] Ecclus. 19:2; see 3 Kings 11:1 ff. for Solomon's fall.

[46] Cf. Gen. 4:16.

[47] See Acts 26:14.

[48] A moralistic tag which, interrupting the flow of argument through to the next paragraph, is most likely a later interpolation.

[49] Heb. 12:6; Prov. 13:24; Nah. 1:9; Luke 21:19; Prov. 16:32.

on a cross between two thieves to die there in such appalling agony. *He* is your true Bridegroom, my sister, and the Bridegroom of all the Church. Keep *him* always before your eyes, hold *him* always in your mind. See how he goes to be crucified for you, see how he carries his cross. Be present there yourself among the "multitude of people and of women who bewailed and lamented him," as Luke has said. And then he turned to the women in his kindness, and in mercy he foretold the destruction that would come as vengeance for his death and how they might escape it if they were wise. "Daughters of Jerusalem," he said,

> weep not over me, but weep for yourselves and your children. For behold, the days shall come wherein they will say, "Blessed are the barren and the wombs that have not borne and the paps that have not given suck." Then they shall begin to say to the mountains, "Fall upon us," and to the hills, "Cover us." For if in the green wood they do these things, what shall be done in the dry?[50]

Pity him who suffered willingly to redeem you. Save your remorse for his death upon the cross. In your mind be ever present at his sepulcher, mourning and lamenting with the women who "sat at the tomb, weeping and lamenting the Lord."[51] Prepare the oils for his burial—but let them be far better oils, the oils of the spirit, which he requires, not the oils of the body, which he did not take. Let all of your remorse and your devotion be for this, as he himself told the faithful when he spoke through Jeremiah, "All ye that pass by the way, attend, and see if there be any sorrow like to my sorrow";[52] that is to say, "When I in my innocence alone must pay the price for the sins of others, for whom else should you grieve?" Yes, he is the way out of exile for the faithful, the way to their home country. And his is the cross from which he calls out to us, and which he has made a ladder for our use. Here, the only-begotten Son of God died for your sake, "offered because it was his will."[53]

Pity him in your grief, grieve for him in your pity. Fulfill the prophecy Zachariah spoke about devoted souls: "And they shall

---

[50] Luke 23:27, 28–31.

[51] From the antiphon to the *Benedictus* in the Roman Breviary for Holy Saturday.

[52] Lam. 1:12.

[53] Isa. 53:7.

mourn for him as for an only son, and they shall grieve for him as for the death of the firstborn."[54] See, my sister, how those who love the King mourn the death of his first and only Son. See how the household mourns, how all the court is consumed with grief. And when you come to the widowed bride of God's only-begotten Son, you will not be able to bear her wails of sorrow. These should be *your* wails, my sister, these *your* cries of grief, for you are joined in marriage to this Bridegroom. Your brideprice was not his property but himself, for he bought you and redeemed you with his blood. See what claim he has on you, look what price he has set on your worth. When Paul considered how little *he* was worth the price paid out for him and the debt he owed such grace in return, he said, "God forbid that I should glory, save in the cross of our Lord Jesus Christ, through whom the world is crucified to me, and I to the world."[55] But you are more than the heavens, you are more than the world, whose price was the Creator of the world. What did he see in you, I ask, when he himself lacked nothing, that he would buy you with the agony of his death? What does he seek in you except yourself? He is a true friend who wants nothing of what you own, but you yourself,[56] a true friend who, when coming to his death for your sake, could say, "Greater love than this no man hath, that he lay down his life for his friends."[57]

It was he who truly loved you—I did not. My love, which brought us both to sin, was lust, which is not worthy of the name of love. I glutted my wretched pleasures in you, and that was all I loved. You say I suffered for you, and perhaps that may be true; but more, I suffered *through* you and unwillingly at that, and not from love of you but from my own compulsion, and then not for your good but for your grief. *He* suffered for you willingly to bring you your salvation. *His* suffering heals all sickness and puts an end to suffering. To *him,* I beg of you, and not to me do you owe all your devotion, your compassion, your remorse. Lament the savage injustice worked against his innocence, not the just vengeance brought to bear on me—or what I must call instead, that most extraordinary grace that has come upon us both. You are unjust if you do not love his justice, and most unjust if you knowingly stand

---

[54] Zac. 12:10.

[55] Gal. 6:14.

[56] Cf. the First Letter, p. 55.

[57] John 15:13.

against the will, indeed against the grace, of God. Weep for your Savior, not for your seducer, for your Redeemer, not for the man who used you as his whore. Weep for the Lord who died for you, not his servant who is still living, or I should say, who only now has been truly freed from death. And, I beg of you, beware that the words that Pompey spoke to Cornelia in her grief not be said of you, and to your shame:

> After the battle, Pompey is alive.
> His fortune, though, is fallen. It is for *that*
> You shed your tears and *that* which you have loved.[58]

Yes, remember this and blush, unless you really would commend our former, foul ways.

Accept it then, my sister, I beg of you. Accept with patience what has come upon us through the mercy of God. It is the rod of our Father that strikes us, not the sword of our oppressor, and a father strikes to correct that an enemy not strike to kill. With his wound he forestalls death, he does not bring it. He wields the knife to cut out the disease. He wounds the body and heals the soul. He ought to have killed and he gives life. He cuts away the unclean to leave only the clean, and he punishes once, not to punish forever. One of us endures his wound that both may be spared death. One alone was punished while the two of us were at fault. This too was through God's mercy—his indulgence of the weakness of your nature—and in its own way just, for inasmuch as you are by nature weaker in your sex and yet stronger in your self-restraint, you were not liable to further penalty.[59]

For this I thank the Lord, that he exempted you from punishment at the time and so preserved you for a crown. When I myself was seething with the lust that would consume me, he chilled me once and for all with what I suffered in my body, and so he kept me from my ruin. But what you suffer in your heart from all the longing of the flesh, which certainly is far greater for your youth, he left intact and kept you then in readiness for your crown. I know it wearies you to hear it and you have told me not to say it, but still the truth is plain—where there is struggle, there is also a crown: "No one is

---

[58] Lucan, *Pharsalia* 8.84–85. With this Abelard responds to Heloise's invocation of Cornelia as he had cited it in the *Calamities*.

[59] Cf. the Third Letter, p. 76.

crowned who does not strive."[60] For me there is no crown, for there is no cause for strife, no grounds for struggle when the thorn of desire is gone.

Yes, I will win no crown, but even so, I still must think it something if I am spared some pain, if through that single momentary pain I may perhaps be pardoned many pains that last forever. It is written about the men of this most miserable life, "The beasts have rotted in their dung."[61] But I do not complain that my merit is diminished so long as I can trust that yours is growing greater. For we are one in Christ, one flesh through the law of marriage: whatever is yours must then be mine as well. And Christ is yours because you are his bride, and as I said, I am now your servant who was once your lord, but a servant joined with you in spiritual love, not bound over in obsequious fear. I place myself under your protection, then, fully trusting that through your prayers for me I yet may gain what I cannot gain alone. I do this now and now above all, when the dangers I face and my own deep agitation press on me every moment and give me no time to live, much less to pray. They will not let me follow the example of the eunuch of Ethiopia, that most blessed and powerful man who had charge over all the queen's treasure and had come from so far to worship in Jerusalem.[62] For when he was returning home, an angel sent Saint Philip to convert him to the faith since, though he was a rich man and a pagan, his prayers and constant reading of our scriptures had made him worthy. And even on his journey the goodness of God would not have him distracted from his reading, but instead it came to pass by God's great will that a passage of scripture was open before him, which gave the apostle the means for his conversion.

Now nothing must impede my request or delay its fulfillment, so I have been quick to compose a prayer for you to offer to the Lord on behalf of us both. I send it to you now:

God,
who at the beginning of the human race
sanctified the sacrament of marriage,

---

[60] 2 Tim. 2:5; and see the Third Letter, p. 83.

[61] Joel 1:17.

[62] See Acts 8:27 ff.

creating woman from the rib of man;
who, with your birth from a woman given in marriage
and again with the first of your miracles,[63]
raised up the bond of marriage to honors without measure;
and who granted relief as it has pleased you
for my weakness and my lack of self-restraint—
do not despise the prayers of your poor handmaid,
which I pour out to you in the sight of your majesty
for my own transgressions
and those of someone dear to me.

O most beneficent Lord,
indeed Beneficence itself,
forgive our sins, so many and so great.
May your mercy without measure
test the multitude of our faults.
Punish the guilty now, I beg of you,
that you may spare us in the future.
Punish us for a time
and do not punish us forever.
Take up against your servants the rod of correction,
not the sword of wrath.
Afflict our flesh that you may preserve our souls.
Come to cleanse our sins, not to avenge them.
Be beneficent more than just,
our merciful Father more than our stern Lord.

Prove us, Lord, and test us,
as the prophet asked for testing of himself:[64]
Examine my strength and lighten the burden
of my temptations according to what it will bear.
As Saint Paul said to the faithful, "God is faithful,
who will not suffer you to be tempted
beyond what you are able,
but with temptation he will make release,
that you may be able to bear it."[65]

---

[63] That is, at the wedding feast at Cana, John 2:1–11.
[64] Cf. Ps. 25:2: "Prove me, Lord, and test me: burn my heart and mind."
[65] 1 Cor. 10:13.

You have joined us together, O Lord,
and you have put us asunder
when it has pleased you and how it has pleased you.
What you once began in mercy
now complete in perfect mercy,
and those whom you have sundered in the world for a time
join together with you in heaven for all time.

For you are our hope and our portion,
our comfort and our expectation,
our Lord who are blessed forever.
Amen.

Now, bride of Christ, farewell in Christ; in Christ may you live
and be well.

# FIFTH LETTER

## HELOISE TO ABELARD

*To him who is hers in species*
*From her who is his as particular.*[1]

**S**ince there must never be the slightest cause
for you to find fault with my obedience,
a bridle has been set upon my words,
although my grief itself is still untamed.
Your order now is that I moderate myself
and refrain at least from writing
what is not difficult but impossible
to guard against in speech.
Nothing is less in our power than the heart,
which is more apt to command us than to obey.
And so when the heart's passions rouse us,
no one can contain their sudden surge of pressure
and keep them then from having their effects.

---

[1] *Suo specialiter, sua singulariter.* Heloise is using the terminology of formal dialectic, perhaps responding to Abelard's formal language in the Fourth Letter. The phrase presents difficulties not only because of its clipped form. The word *specialiter,* "in species," may have a limiting sense when the reference point is the larger category of *genus*—compare English "especially" or "specifically" to "generally" or "generically." Here, however, it is opposed to the more limiting *singulariter,* "as particular," "as individual," "singularly," or "uniquely," and therefore points to *species* as the universal that applies to particulars or individuals. A single manuscript presents the variant reading *Domino specialiter,* which should be understood as "To her lord in species."

In Abelard's metaphysics there is no thing except for particulars, which are unique and distinct from all else, and Heloise's use of the terms of dialectic here may be an apt way of indicating that, even if Abelard should insist on maintaining an abstract or generic posture toward her, her stance toward him would remain concrete and personal.

No, they will easily burst out
and still more easily spill over into words,
which are the ready symbols of the motions of the heart:[2]
as it is written,
"Out of the abundance of the heart the mouth doth speak."[3]
I therefore will restrain my hand from writing
what I cannot keep my tongue from saying aloud.
If only the heart that grieves
were as ready to obey as the hand that writes.

And yet you have it in your power
to palliate my grief to some extent,
even if you cannot remove it all.
For as one nail drives out another,[4]
so a new thought drives out an old,
and the heart, which had been set in one direction,
is forced to lay aside or to abandon
its memories of what once was.
And the more this thought—of anything at all—
occupies the heart and distracts it from other things,
the more we think it an honorable thought,
and the new direction in which we turn our hearts
then seems more necessary and compelling.

So then—

All of us, the handmaids of Christ and your daughters in Christ,
now approach you as our father with two requests.[5] We see them

---

[2] An understanding of words that is common in Latin treatises on dialectic, deriving ultimately from Aristotle, *De Interpretatione* 1. Cf. Heloise's description of her involuntary utterances in the Third Letter, p. 80.

[3] Matt. 12:34.

[4] Cf. Cicero, *Tusculan Disputations* 4.35.75, and Jerome, *Epistulae* 125.14.

[5] The inclusive plural "all of us" should be taken seriously. What follows from this point in the letter seems an orchestrated fugue of different voices developing a set of different themes connected to the central question of women's religious life: the inapplicability of the Benedictine Rule to women; the historical contingency of the Benedictine and similar Rules; the distinction between formal compliance and the inward disposition seen as proper to a Christian; the general importance of moderation and discretion in the Rule, and some specific areas in which accommodation for women's nature should be made; the need for better instruction in whatever Rule may be

both as necessary to us. One is that you teach us how the order of nuns began and tell us of the origin and foundation of our calling. The other is that you institute a rule for us to follow, a written directive suitable for women, detailing in full the condition and habit of our own way of life. This has not been done by any of the Fathers, and because of this failure, it now is the case that both men and women are received into monasteries to profess the same rule, and the same yoke of monastic regulation is laid upon the stronger and the weaker sex alike.

At present, throughout the Latin Church women profess the Rule of Saint Benedict on the same basis as men. But as this rule was written only for men, its instructions can be followed only by men, whether they apply to subordinates or superiors in our orders. For example, the regulations about cowls, scapulars, and breeches— what can they have to do with women?[6] Or the ones about wearing tunics and woolen clothing next to the skin, when the monthly purgation of excess humors makes this something women must avoid? Then, what does it imply for a convent of women that the abbot himself is required to read the lesson from the Gospel before proceeding to the hymn?[7] And what about the abbot's table, where he is required to dine with pilgrims and guests?[8] Will *either* be suitable for our religious practice—that an abbess never offer hospitality to men, or that she sit and take her meals with her male guests? On the one hand, the situation of women and men interacting in easy proximity is hazardous for the soul, but certainly most so at table, where gluttony and drunkenness are the rule and wine is consumed for

---

adopted; and the need for a convent's material support. Some of the voices appear to have been introduced at a later date, as certain comments and sections seem to derive from Abelard's reply in the Seventh Letter and from other subsequent texts. In all, the main part of the letter, like *The Questions of Heloise*, has the air of a collective research project, which Heloise could be imagined to have set for the nuns of the Paraclete to help educate them more fully in the principles and particulars of their religious practice and which may well have continued for some time. The translation makes no attempt to distinguish the separate voices; however, passages that appear most plainly to have been composed at a later date are enclosed in brackets.

[6] Cf. *Rule of St. Benedict*, chapter 55.

[7] Cf. *Rule of St. Benedict*, chapter 11. As indicated at the end of the letter when the issue briefly returns, the difficulty is that the Gospel readings should be conducted by a priest or a deacon and are scheduled for the Night Office, a time when inviting a man into the convent is especially unsuitable.

[8] Cf. *Rule of St. Benedict*, chapter 56.

pleasure ["wherein is lechery"].[9] "It is hard to preserve your modesty at a feast," Saint Jerome warned a mother and her daughter,[10] and Ovid, the learned poet of seduction, described exactly the kind of opportunities a banquet affords, in the book he entitled *The Art of Love*:

> When wine soaks Cupid's wings, he cannot fly
> But sits there sluggish, rooted to the spot. . . .
> A time for laughter, when even a poor man
> Unpuckers his brow, all care and sorrow gone. . . .
> That's when girls make off with young men's souls;
> Mixing love and wine adds fuel to the fire.[11]

But on the other hand, if only the women guests are invited to table, is there not some risk in that, too? There is nothing that so leads a woman astray as feminine finery, and a woman will spread her corruption of mind most easily to another woman—which is why Jerome so vigorously urged women in religious orders to avoid contact with women of the world.[12] Also, if we do invite only women and exclude all men from our hospitality, will that not seriously offend the men on whose kind services all women's convents must depend, especially if we seem to give so little, or nothing at all, to the men from whom we receive so much? If in the end, however, it turns out to be impossible for us to observe the tenor of the Rule in full, then, I'm afraid, we risk the condemnation of the apostle James: "Whoever shall keep the whole law but offend in one point is become guilty of all."[13] [That is to say, if someone fulfills many parts of the law but does not fulfill them all, he still is guilty in the one part he has left unfulfilled: unless he has fulfilled all parts, because of this one part he becomes a transgressor of the whole. As James goes on to say:

> For he that said, "Thou shalt not commit adultery," also said, "Thou shalt not kill. Now if thou do not commit adultery, but thou shalt kill, thou art a transgressor of the law.

---

[9] A tag from Eph. 5:18, most likely an interpolation imported from Abelard's reply in the Seventh Letter, where it is also cited.

[10] *Epistulae* 117.6.

[11] *Ars Amatoria* 1.233–34, 239–40, 243–44.

[12] Cf. *Epistulae* 22.16.

[13] Jas. 2:10.

In other words, someone becomes guilty by transgressing any one precept of the law, because the Lord who set one precept also set the other, and whatever precept of the law is violated will show disdain for God, who made the law not in one but in all of its requirements.][14]

But I do not want to dwell on those parts of the Rule which we cannot observe in full, or cannot without some risk; instead, here are some other points. Where in the world has it ever been the practice for a convent of nuns to work the harvest?[15] Or to test the constancy of the women we accept through the probation of just a single year? Or to instruct them with just three readings of the Rule, as the Rule itself prescribes?[16] What can be more foolish than entering on a path that is both unknown and as yet unexplained? Is there any more presumptuous act than committing yourself to a way of life you do not know or taking vows you have no capacity to fulfill? If discretion is the mother of all virtues and reason the mediator of all good, can something be a virtue or a good which seems so at odds with discretion and with reason? Virtues that exceed the mean and measure should be counted among the vices, Jerome says.[17] Where, then, is the discretion or the reason in loading burdens on the backs of those whose strength has not first been tested to make sure that the tasks assigned to human beings are in line with their natural constitutions? Would anyone give a donkey the same load as an elephant? Or the young or very old the same loads as full adults? Can the frail bear as much as the hardy, or the sickly as much as the well? Can women, who are the weaker sex, bear as much as men, who are the stronger? [Saint Gregory addressed this issue in Chapter 24 of his *Pastoral*, where he distinguished between women and men regarding both admonition and instruction:

> Men should be admonished in one way and women in another, in that heavy burdens should be placed on men and lighter ones on women. Let men take up the greater tasks, but let women be corrected gently with the light ones.][18]

---

[14] This redundant section is a close paraphrase of Abelard's answer to the second of Heloise's *Questions*, which postdates this letter. Evidently, it is a later interpolation, imported from that source.

[15] Cf. *Rule of St. Benedict*, chapter 48.

[16] Cf. *Rule of St. Benedict*, chapter 58.

[17] Cf. *Epistulae* 130.11.

[18] *Regulae Pastoralis Liber* 3.1. The comment apparently derives from Abelard's reply in the Seventh Letter.

The men who wrote the rules for monks were entirely silent about women, but they also laid down regulations which they knew did not suit women in the slightest. Bull and heifer were *not* to fit their necks to the same yoke of the Rule: those whom nature had *not* created equal must *not* have equal work. Saint Benedict himself was consistently aware of the importance of careful distinctions, steeped as he was in the spirit of all things just. In fact, he tempered everything in the Rule to suit the character of the person involved and the season of the year, and in one passage concluded, "Let all things be done in moderation."[19] Beginning with the abbot himself, he instructed him to preside over his subordinates "according to the character and understanding of each, adjusting and adapting himself to all in such a way that he may not only suffer no loss in his flock, but may even rejoice in its increase,"[20] and later continued:

> Let him always keep his own frailty before his eyes and remember not to "break the bruised reed. . . ." Let him be discreet and moderate, bearing in mind the discretion of Jacob, who said, "If I should cause my flocks to be overdriven, in one day they all will die." Following this and other examples of discretion, the mother of virtues, he should temper all things in a way that the strong may have something to strive for and the weak may not be discouraged.[21]

All of the allowances he made—for the young, the old, and the infirm in general; for feeding the lector and the weekly kitchen workers before the other monks; and for the provision of different kinds and amounts of food to meet the different needs of different men—were based on moderation, and all of them were carefully written down.[22] He even relaxed the statutory periods of fast in accord with the season of the year and the amount of labor to be done, as natural weakness would require.[23]

---

[19] *Rule of St. Benedict*, chapter 48.

[20] *Rule of St. Benedict*, chapter 2.

[21] *Rule of St. Benedict*, chapter 64. Internal quotations are from Isa. 42:3 and Gen. 33:13.

[22] Cf. *Rule of St. Benedict*, chapters 34–41.

[23] Cf. *Rule of St. Benedict*, chapter 48.

Now, if this is the case, what would he do, Saint Benedict, who tempered everything to suit the character of the person involved and the season of the year in such a way as to enable everyone to follow the regulations without complaining[24]—what provision would he make for women if he were to institute a rule for them, as he did for men? If he found himself compelled to ease the rigor of his rule in certain parts to accommodate the weakness of the young, the old, and the infirm, how would he accommodate the fragility of our sex, whose natural lack of strength is obvious?

You will need, then, to consider how far it is from reason and discretion to insist that women follow the same rule as men, that the weak bear as much as the strong. It seems to me that we do well enough in our weakness if we equal the leaders of the Church and other clerics in Holy Orders in the virtues of abstinence and self-restraint: "Everyone shall be perfect," the Lord has said, "if he be as his master."[25] If we could equal even the most devout among the laity, I think it would be taken as no small thing, for what seems of little moment in the strong is something we all admire in the weak:[26] "Power is made perfect by weakness," the Apostle says.[27] And of course, no one should disparage the devout among the laity, men like Abraham, David, and Job, simply because they were married. As Chrysostom reminds us:

> There are many things . . . a man can do to charm that beast, things such as work, reading, and keeping vigils. "But what are they to us, who are not monks?" That is not a question for me but rather for Paul. "Keep vigil in patience and prayer," he said, and "Make not provision for the flesh in its concupiscences." He was not writing only for monks but for all men. A layman should have no more latitude than a monk—except that he may lie with his wife: he has dispensation for that, but for nothing else—and should act in every other way as a monk acts. And Christ did not address the Beatitudes only to monks. . . . For if he had and if laymen in fact cannot obey them, . . . it will mean the destruction of the world, for then Christ has confined virtue within

---

[24] Cf. *Rule of St. Benedict*, chapter 39.

[25] Luke 6:40.

[26] Cf. Gregory, *Regulae Pastoralis Liber* 3.1, quoted in the Seventh Letter.

[27] 2 Cor. 12:9.

very narrow limits. If marriage by itself so hinders us, how can it be called honorable?[28]

The clear inference is that whoever adds the virtue of self-restraint to the precepts laid down in the Gospel will attain monastic perfection. I only wish our own religious practice reached the heights where it simply fulfilled the Gospel—no need to surpass it, nor for us to try to be anything more than Christians. So, unless I am mistaken, this is why the Fathers decided not to set down a general rule for us, as they did for men, a rule which then would be like some new law, burdening our weakness with a multitude of vows: they obeyed Saint Paul, who said, "The law worketh wrath, for where there is no law, neither is there transgression," and "The law entered in that sin might abound." But even he, that great preacher of self-restraint, understood our weakness and urged younger widows to remarry: "I would have it, therefore, that the younger should marry, bear children, be mistresses of families, and give no occasion to the adversary to speak evil."[29] And Saint Jerome agreed, telling Eustochium about the ill-considered vows some women take:

> But if, because of some other faults, even those who are virgins are not saved, what will happen to those who have prostituted the body of Christ and turned the temple of the Holy Spirit into a brothel? . . . Better for a person to have married and to have walked on level ground than to strain for the heights and plunge into the depths of hell.[30]

Saint Augustine, too, wrote of women's thoughtlessness in entering orders, in the book he addressed to Juliana on a widow's self-restraint:

> A woman who has not begun on this path should think again; a woman who has begun should persevere. No opening should be given to the devil, and no offering taken from Christ.[31]

---

[28] *Homiliae in Epistulam ad Hebraeos* 7.4, cited in the sixth-century Latin translation of Mutianus, not in the original Greek. Internal quotations are from Eph. 6:18 and Rom. 13:14.

[29] Rom. 4:15 and 5:20; 1 Tim. 5:14.

[30] *Epistulae* 22.6.

[31] *De Bono Viduitatis* 9.13.

Accordingly, Church regulations do not allow women to be ordained as deaconesses before the age of forty, and then only after careful probation, while men may become deacons at age twenty—it is another recognition of our weakness.

There are also those who call themselves the Canons Regular of Saint Augustine.[32] They too live in monasteries, claim to follow a rule of sorts, and consider themselves in no way inferior to monks—and yet we see they are permitted to eat meat and wear linen clothing. Now, if we in our weakness could match their virtue, no one would see that as trivial at all. But any allowance made for *us* in food or drink would only need to be minor and could be made without much risk, since we are protected by a greater natural power of sobriety. Women, it is recognized, can be maintained at less cost and with less nourishment than men, and medical science indicates that we are also less easily intoxicated. As Macrobius writes in Book 7 of the *Saturnalia:*

> Aristotle says that old men are often drunk, but women very rarely. . . . The female body is extremely moist—witness the lightness and clarity of a woman's skin and, especially, the regular purgation of her excess humors. So, when wine has been swallowed and incorporated into this great general moisture, it loses its strength . . . and does not easily strike the seat of the brain, once its force has been dissipated.

And again:

> The female body, designed as it is for frequent purgation, is pierced with several holes, so that channels and passageways are open for the humors to drain out. Through these holes the fumes of wine quickly evaporate. In old men, on the other hand, the body is quite dry, as is indicated by the roughness and dullness of the skin.[33]

So allowances made for us in food and drink are more appropriate to our weakness and our nature and can be made without much risk, since women are less prone to gluttony and drunkenness, as we require less food and are protected by the constitution of our bodies.

---

[32] See p. 3, n. 5.

[33] *Saturnalia* 7.6.16–17.

Now, it should be enough in our weakness—and may even be thought a great thing—if, living in poverty and self-restraint and occupied with our duties to God, we could equal the leaders of the Church or devout laymen in our own mode of life, or match the so-called canons regular, who pledge themselves to follow the apostles' way. But in the end, it shows considerable foresight if those who bind themselves to God actually vow *less* than they perform, in order that there may always be something they can add over and above what they are already bound to do, something of their own accord. The Lord said, "When you shall have done all those things that are commanded you, say, 'We are unprofitable servants; we have done that which we ought to do'"—in other words, "We are unprofitable, unworthy, and of no account if we rest content with what we ought to do, adding nothing of our own accord"—and he promised in a parable elsewhere, "Whatsoever thou shalt spend over and above, I, at my return, will repay thee."[34]

If those who rush blindly into their religious vows—and there are many of them in these times—were to watch more carefully what they were doing, consider beforehand the calling they professed, and actually study the import of the Rule, they would offend less through their ignorance and sin less through their neglect. But as it is, nearly everyone alike comes running to monastic life with little thought at all, and once received in disorder, they proceed to live in disorder, and, as easily as they profess a rule they do not know, will ignore the same rule, substituting customs they prefer for existing law. We must be careful, then, to avoid burdening woman with the load we see causing nearly every man to stagger and collapse. The world has now grown old, we see, and human beings, along with all the other creatures of the world, have lost the ancient vigor of their nature. "The love not of many but nearly of all has grown cold," to adapt a phrase of the Lord's.[35] In accord with people's character, then, it is necessary to change, or at least to temper, the Rule that once was written for people to follow.

Saint Benedict, in fact—consistently aware of the importance of careful distinctions—admits that he has already tempered the rigor of monastic regulations in such a way that, in comparison with

---

34 Luke 17:10, 10:35.
35 Cf. Matt. 24:12.

earlier systems, his Rule is little more than a guide to upright living and the first step in the religious life:

> I have written this Rule that we may show in its observance
> that we have reached a degree of upright living and the
> rudiments of the religious life. For the one, though, who
> would hasten towards the perfection of this life there are the
> teachings of the holy Fathers, whose observance will lead
> him to the pinnacle of perfection. . . . And so, whoever you
> are who are hastening to your home in heaven, with
> Christ's help fulfill this minimal Rule, which is the first step,
> and at length you will attain the greater heights of doctrine
> and virtue under the protection of God.[36]

For example, he explains, there was a time when the Fathers used to
complete the entire Psalter in a single day. He adjusted the recitation
of psalms, however, to the needs of the "lukewarm," spreading
them over the course of a week, so that now monks are content with
a smaller number of psalms, as secular clerics are.[37]

Or another example—What is most inimical to a monastery's
devotions and repose? What most foments lechery and sows the
seeds of discord, or destroys reason, which is the image of God in
man and our chief distinction from beasts? I mean of course *wine,*
the item of food which scripture condemns beyond any other.
Solomon, the wisest of the wise, writes in the Book of Proverbs:
"Wine is a luxurious thing, and drunkenness riotous: whosoever is
delighted therein shall not be wise."[38]

> [Who hath woe? Whose father hath woe? Who hath contentions?
> Who falls into pits? Who hath wounds without cause? Who hath
> redness of eyes? Surely they that pass their time in wine and
> study to drink off their cups. Look not upon the wine when it is
> red, when its color shineth in the glass: it goeth in pleasantly, but
> in the end it will bite like a snake and will spread poison abroad
> like a basilisk. Thy eyes shall behold strange women and thy
> heart perverse things. And thou shalt be as one sleeping in the
> midst of the sea, and as a pilot fast asleep when the stern is lost.

---

[36] *Rule of St. Benedict*, chapter 73.

[37] Cf. *Rule of St. Benedict*, chapter 18.

[38] Prov. 20:1.

And thou shalt say, "They have beaten me, but I was not sensible of pain. They drew me, and I felt not. When shall I wake and find wine again?]39

And:

Give not wine to kings, O Lamuel, because there is no secret where drunkenness reigneth, and they might drink and forget judgments and pervert the cause of the children of the poor.40

In Ecclesiasticus we read, "Wine and women make even the wise fall away,"41 and when Jerome wrote to Nepotianus about the cleric's way of life, he seemed outraged that the priests of the old law could surpass our own in their abstinence from drink:

Never smell of wine, or else the words of the philosopher will be spoken about you, "This is not offering a kiss, but proffering a cup." Saint Paul condemned drunken priests, as does the old law before him: "Whoever serve at the altar shall not taste wine or *sikera*." In Hebrew, *sikera* means anything that can intoxicate, whether it is made by fermentation, or pressing dates, or boiling down apples or honey into a rough, sweet drink, or brewing roasted grain in water. Whatever can intoxicate and disturb your mental balance—stay away from it as you would wine.42

So, here is something that kings must not touch, priests must avoid, and everyone agrees is thoroughly pernicious. And yet Saint Benedict, that most spiritual of men, is obliged by the conditions of the present age to allow it to monks. "Yes," he says,

we read that wine is not a thing for monks. But since the monks of our day can never be convinced of this, let us at

---

39 Prov. 23:29–35, cited also in the Seventh Letter, from which it seems to be imported here.

40 Prov. 31:4–5.

41 Ecclus. 19:2.

42 *Epistulae* 52.11. Cf. 1 Tim. 3:3 and Lev. 10:9, 10:35. The source of "the words of the philosopher" has not been identified.

least agree to drink sparingly and not to the point where we are sated, because "wine makes even the wise fall away."[43]

[Unless I am mistaken, he had been reading this passage in the *Lives of the Fathers*: "Abbot Pastor was once told about a monk who did not drink wine, and he replied that wine is not a thing for monks." And just afterward:

> Once there was a celebration of the Mass on Abbot Anthony's mountain, and they found a jar of wine left over. One of the elders filled a cup and brought it to Abbot Sisoi, who drank it off. Then he brought him a second cup, which he also took and drank off. But when he brought him a third cup, he refused it, saying, "Peace, brother, don't you know that this is Satan?"

And another story about Abbot Sisoi:

> So his disciple Abraham asked him, "If it happens in church on the Sabbath or the Lord's Day, is it still too much to drink three cups?" And the old man answered, "If it were not Satan, it would not be too much."][44]

[Where, I ask, did God ever condemn meat or forbid it to monks?][45]

See how he had to temper the Rule even in what he knew was pernicious and not for monks, because in his day he could not persuade them to abstain. In our day, too, I would call for a similar dispensation, that the same moderation apply in all matters that fall between good and evil and are therefore called *indifferent*. What persuasion cannot now enforce, our vows should not exact. Once all of

---

[43] *Rule of St. Benedict*, chapter 40. The manuscripts quote the sentence only through "can never be convinced of this," indicating the rest with "etc." The internal quotation is from Ecclus. 19:2.

[44] This string of quotations from *Vitae Patrum* 5.4.31, 5.4.36, and 5.4.37 is found in the same form and with the same connecting phrases in the Seventh Letter, from which it seems to be imported here.

[45] This short question most likely has its origin as a reader's query, possibly inspired by a discussion in the Seventh Letter. Its inclusion as part of the text has made it appear that the subject has shifted, and also that Benedict had come to the same sort of accommodation with eating meat as he had with drinking wine. He had *not*, however, as chapter 36 of the *Rule* makes clear—the use of meat may occasionally be granted to the sick who are very weak; otherwise, "let all abstain from meat as usual"—and the subject here continues to be wine.

these indifferent things are permitted that can be done without offense, it will be enough to forbid the sins alone. In food and clothing both, whatever can be purchased most cheaply will serve, so long as our concern is always for what is necessary and never more than that. We should not give too much thought to what neither commends us to God nor prepares us for his kingdom, for they are only outward things, common to both the chosen of God and his rejected, to the righteous and to hypocrites alike.[46]

This, in fact, more than anything else, is what separates Christian from Jew, the distinction made between inward and outward works—especially since it is love alone that distinguishes the children of God from the children of the devil, the love Saint Paul calls the fulfillment of the law and the end of the commandment.[47] This is why he disparages the glory of works in favor of justification by faith when he addresses the Jew:

> Where then is thy boasting? It is excluded. By what law? Of works? No, but by the law of faith. For we account a man to be justified by faith without the works of the law. . . . For if Abraham was justified by works, he hath whereof to glory, but not before God. For what saith the scripture? Abraham believed God, and it was reputed to him unto justice. . . . But to him that worketh not, yet believeth in him that justifieth the ungodly, his faith is reputed to justice, according to the purpose of the grace of God.[48]

At the same time, he allows Christians to eat any kind of food, distinguishing this from what is truly righteous:

> The kingdom of God is not food or drink, but justice and peace and joy in the Holy Spirit. . . . All things are clean, but it is evil for that man who eateth with offense. It is good not to eat flesh and not to drink wine, nor anything whereby thy brother is offended, weakened, or undone.[49]

---

46 Cf. Heloise's words in the Third Letter, pp. 82–83.

47 Cf. Rom. 13:10 and 1 Tim. 1:5.

48 Rom. 3:27–8, 4:2–3, 4:5.

49 Rom. 14:17, 20, 21.

Here he does not forbid any food as such but only the eating of what would offend some of the converted Jews when they saw foods being eaten which the law did not allow. Saint Peter was also trying to avoid this kind of offense when Paul corrected him, as Paul reports in his letter to the Galatians. In writing to the Corinthians, however, Paul said, "Food does not commend us to God. . . . Eat whatever is sold in the markets . . . for the earth is the Lord's and the fullness thereof"; and then to the Colossians:

> Let no man judge you in food or in drink. . . . If, with Christ, you be dead to the elements of this world, why do you yet decree as though living in the world, Touch not, taste not, handle not those things which are all unto destruction by their very use, according to the teachings and the precepts of men?[50]

By "elements of this world" he means the principles of the law concerning worldly practices. In its early days, the world—that is, a people as yet worldly—was concerned with teaching these practices, somewhat as it would be with teaching the basic elements of the alphabet. But Christ and those who belong to Christ are dead to these elements—dead, that is, to these worldly practices—when they admit no further obligation to them, that is, when they are no longer living in the world among men who take note of outward forms and decide among them, distinguishing between foods or between one thing and another, saying, "Do not touch this, do not touch that," and so on. The things that are touched or tasted or handled are destructive of the soul "by their very use," he says, when we put them to use "according to the teachings and the precepts of men"—that is, of worldly beings who understand the law in a worldly sense—and not according to the teachings of Christ and his disciples.

When Christ sent the apostles out to preach, it was a time when he had to guard most against offense. Nonetheless, he allowed them to eat any kind of food, which would enable them to live in the same manner as their hosts, "eating and drinking such things as they have."[51] Paul was able to foresee that they would fall away from the proper teaching about this, and he wrote to Timothy:

---

[50] Gal. 2:11 ff.; 1 Cor. 8:8, 10:25–26; Col. 2:16, 20–22.
[51] Luke 10:7.

Now the Spirit manifestly saith that in the last times some shall depart from the faith, giving heed to spirits of error and doctrines of devils, speaking lies in hypocrisy . . . , forbidding marriage or commanding abstinence from the foods which God hath created to be received with thanksgiving by the faithful and by them that have known the truth. For every creature of God is good, and nothing is to be rejected that is received with thanksgiving: for it is sanctified by the word of God and by prayer. Proposing these things to the brethren, thou shalt be a good minister of Christ Jesus, nourished in the words of faith and of the good doctrine which thou hast attained unto.[52]

If someone, then, is determined to make a display of his own outward abstinence, would he ever look to Christ and his disciples as a model? Or would he look instead to John and to John's followers, who were known to be extreme in their fasting? They once took even Christ to task in their apparent devotion to Jewish observances, asking him, "Why do we and the Pharisees fast often, but thy disciples do not fast?"[53] But when Saint Augustine examined the difference between virtue and its display, he concluded that such outward works add nothing at all to merit. In his book on the good in marriage he wrote:

Self-restraint is not a virtue of the body but of the soul.[54] There are times when the virtues of the heart are evident in actions and times when they lie hidden in the propensities of character, as the virtue of the martyrs *became* apparent in the way they endured suffering. . . . For example, patience already existed within Job, as the Lord knew and even spoke about, but it came to the notice of men only through the evidence of Job's temptation. . . .

Or, to make it clearer how virtue can exist in character even if it is not seen in actions, here is an example no Catholic will question: the Lord Jesus hungered, thirsted, ate, and drank in the truth of the flesh—this no one faithful to the Gospel doubts. Can it ever be said, though, that the Lord's

---

[52] 1 Tim. 4:1 ff.

[53] Matt. 9:14.

[54] Cf. the Third Letter, p. 80.

virtue of restraint in food and drink was not as great as John the Baptist's? "For John came neither eating nor drinking, and they said, 'He hath a devil.' And the Son of man came eating and drinking, and they said, 'Behold a man that is a glutton and a wine drinker, a friend of publicans and sinners. . . .'" And the Lord added, "Wisdom is justified by her children,"[55] that is, by those who see that the virtue of self-restraint must always exist in the propensities of the heart although it becomes manifest only through the opportunity of time and circumstance, as is also true of the virtue of patience in the holy martyrs. . . . Just as the merit of patience is not greater in Peter, who endured martyrdom, than in John, who did not, so the merit of self-restraint is not greater in John, who remained unmarried, than in Abraham, who had many children. John's self-restraint was in his actions and Abraham's in his character alone, but the celibacy of one and the marriage of the other each battled for Christ according to the circumstances of the times.

In those times and even after the days of the Patriarchs, the law cursed whoever did not raise up seed in Israel,[56] and so a man with the propensity toward self-restraint was not allowed to show it, even though he did possess it. But the fullness of time was come[57] when it could be said, "He that can take, let him take";[58] that is, whoever has the propensity toward virtue should act accordingly, and whoever does not wish to act should not claim falsely that he has it.[59]

The inference is that virtue alone wins merit in the eyes of God: those who are equal in virtue will win equal merit, though they may be unequal in their actions. This is why true Christians are concerned entirely with the inward man, with adorning him with virtue and keeping him clean of vice, caring little or nothing about the outward man. And this is why we read that the apostles behaved in such an uncouth—we can almost say disreputable—manner even

---

[55] Matt. 11:18–19.

[56] Cf. Deut. 25:5–10.

[57] Cf. Gal. 4:4.

[58] Matt. 19:12.

[59] *De Bono Conjugali* 21, 25–26.

in the company of the Lord, as if oblivious to all propriety and reverence, to pluck and strip the grain in the fields and eat it like little boys with no sense of shame at all.[60] They also did not bother to wash their hands before their meals, which led some to accuse them of uncleanness. The Lord defended them, though, saying, "To eat with unwashed hands doth not defile a man," and he added that, in general, the soul is not defiled by outward things but only by what may proceed from the heart, that is, by "evil thoughts, murders, adulteries," and so on.[61] Unless the heart is first corrupted by a depraved will, what is done outwardly in the body cannot be sin. And so, he says that murder and adultery proceed from the heart and can exist even where there is no injury or physical contact: "Whosoever look on a woman to lust after her hath already committed adultery with her in his heart,"[62] and "Whosoever hateth his brother is a murderer."[63] And physical contact or injury *per se* does not make for these crimes, as in cases where violence forces a woman against her will or the law compels a judge to execute a criminal. But no *murderer,* it is written, has a share in the kingdom of God.[64]

We must consider, then, not what is done but what is in the heart if we seek to please him who searches heart and mind and sees in all the secret places.[65] The Lord, Paul tells us, "shall judge the secrets of men according to the Gospel."[66] And so, he preferred the widow's offering of just two mites to the most lavish offerings of the rich.[67] "Thou hast no need of my goods," he was told, and he loves the gift for the giver more than the giver for the gift. It is written, "The Lord had respect to Abel and to his offerings,"[68] for he looked first to the man's devotion before he was pleased with his gift. God is more pleased with the devotion of the heart, the less the heart is taken up with outward things; and the less we put our trust

---

[60] Cf. Matt. 12:1 ff. The apostles' behavior won the Pharisees' disapproval because it happened on the Sabbath; however, this plays no part in the argument here.

[61] Matt. 15:20, 19.

[62] Matt. 5:28.

[63] 1 John 3:15, but said by John and not Jesus.

[64] Cf. 1 John 3:15.

[65] Cf. Prov. 24:12; Ps. 7.10; Jer. 11:20, 17:10, 20.12; etc.

[66] Rom. 2:16.

[67] Cf. Mark 12:42–44.

[68] Ps. 15:2; Gen. 4:4.

in outward things, the more humbly do we serve him and think the more of what we owe him. And so, after writing about the allowances made for food, Saint Paul tells Timothy about the exercise of the body, saying:

> Exercise thyself unto godliness, for bodily exercise is profitable to little, but godliness is profitable to all things, having promise of the life that is now and of the life that is to come.[69]

The mind's devotion to God earns from him what is necessary to us in this life and what is eternal in the next. What else do we learn from this but Christian wisdom—like Jacob, to make a meal for our Father from our domestic flock and not, like Esau, to go out hunting wild game or act like Jews in regard to outward things?[70] The Psalmist said, "In me, O God, are vows to thee, which I will pay, my praises to thee."[71] To which the poet Persius added, "Beyond yourself seek nothing."[72]

There are, however, countless testimonials from the learned in both the Church and the secular world which point to this one lesson: we must care nothing for the outward things, which are indifferent, or else we would find the works of the law and what Peter called the unbearable yoke of its slavery[73] preferable to the freedom of the Gospel and the sweet yoke and easy burden of Christ.[74] Yet Christ himself has called us to this yoke: "Come to me," he said, "all you that labor and are burdened, and I will refresh you."[75] And Peter rebuked those who had turned to Christ but still kept to the observance of the law:

> My brethren, men, . . . why tempt you God to put a yoke upon the necks of the disciples which neither our fathers

---

[69] 1 Tim. 4:7–8.

[70] See Gen. 27:6 ff.

[71] Ps. 55:12.

[72] *Satires* 1.7.

[73] Cf. Acts 15:10.

[74] Cf. Matt. 11:30.

[75] Matt. 11:28. The manuscripts quote only through the words "and are burdened," adding "etc."

nor we have been able to bear? But by the grace of the Lord
Jesus Christ we believe we shall be saved, in like manner as
they also.[76]

And so I beg of *you*—who would imitate not only Christ but Saint
Peter in your discretion as you do in your name—temper the practices set for us in a way that will suit our weak nature. Let us then be
free for the service of offering praise to God, which is the offering he
commends to us, rejecting all our outward sacrifices:

> If I should be hungry, I would not tell thee: for the world is
> mine and the fullness thereof. Shall I eat the flesh of bul-
> locks? Shall I drink the blood of goats? Offer to God the sac-
> rifice of praise and pay thy vows to the Most High. And call
> upon me in the day of trouble: I will deliver thee, and thou
> shalt praise me.[77]

Of course, we are not saying that we should be exempt from
labor when necessity requires it, only that we should not put undue
importance on what serves the body but interrupts our celebration
of the Office. This is particularly true when the authority of Paul
grants women in religious orders a special means of sustenance
apart from manual labor. As he writes to Timothy:

> If any of the faithful have widows, let him minister to them
> and let not the Church be charged, so that there may be suf-
> ficient for them that are widows indeed.[78]

By "widows indeed" he means all women who are devoted to
Christ; for not only is their Husband dead but the world is crucified
to them and they to the world.[79] And so it is right that they find support at Church expense, as if from the private wealth of their own
husbands. This is why the Lord himself put his mother under the
protection of an apostle instead of her husband,[80] and why the apostles arranged for seven deacons, the ministers of the Church, to look

---

[76] Acts 15:7, 10–11.

[77] Ps. 49:12–15.

[78] 1 Tim. 5:16.

[79] Cf. Gal. 6:14.

[80] Cf. John 19:26.

after the needs of these devoted women.[81] Now, certainly we know that in his letter to the Thessalonians Saint Paul laid down the rule against idlers who mind everyone's business but their own—"If any man will not work, neither let him eat"[82]—and that Saint Benedict prescribed manual labor as the best safeguard against idleness.[83] But we also know that Mary sat in idleness to listen to Christ's words while Martha continued working both for her and for the Lord, grumbling about her sister's leisure as if she envied it and as if she alone "bore the burden of the day and the heats."[84] People still will grumble when they minister to the needs of those who are busy with their duties to God. Often they complain less about the taxes of a tyrant than their obligations to the lazy and the idle, as they call them, even though they see them not only listening to Christ's words but continually reading and chanting those same words. They do not know that it is only a small thing, as Saint Paul has said, to supply material goods to those from whom they receive such spiritual goods,[85] or that it is only fitting for those who are concerned with earthly matters to serve others who are concerned with matters of the spirit. Even the old law granted this leisure to the ministers of the Church: the tribe of Levi received no inheritance in land but was to take its tithes and offerings from the labor of others, so that it might better serve the Lord.[86]

There is also the matter of fasting, which Christians see as abstinence from vice more than from food—you must consider whether you think anything should be added to what the Church has established, and institute what is fitting for us.

You should also give some thought to two matters in particular: the ordering of the psalms and our conduct of the ecclesiastical Offices. In the first, at least, we need some accommodation to ease the burden on our weakness—if it seems right to you. As we complete the Psalter through the week, it should not be necessary to

---

[81] Cf. Acts 6:5.

[82] 2 Thess. 3:10.

[83] Cf. *Rule of St. Benedict*, chapter 40.

[84] For this account of Mary and Martha, see Luke 10:38 ff.; for the quotation, see Matt. 20:12.

[85] Cf. 1 Cor. 9:11.

[86] Cf. Num. 18:21.

repeat the same psalms. When Saint Benedict arranged the weekly order to suit his purposes, he also left it open for others to arrange the psalms differently if it seemed best to them,[87] no doubt aware that the beauty of the Church would grow with time, becoming a splendid edifice where there was once a rough foundation. Before all else, however, we ask you to decide for us how we are to arrange for the reading of the Gospel at the Night Office.[88] It seems unsafe to bring into our presence the priests or deacons who must read the lesson at a time when we should be most secluded from the sight of any man in order to be freer from temptation and to give ourselves wholeheartedly to God.

It now lies with you, my lord,
while you remain alive,
to institute a rule for us,
a rule which then will bind us for all time.
For you, after God, are the founder of this place,
you, through God, are the planter of our congregation,
and you, with God, should be the guide of our religious life.[89]
Perhaps we will have some other after you,
who then will build on the foundation of another,[90]
and so, we are afraid, will be less concerned with us
or less worthy to be obeyed,
and although he may be equally as willing,
he then will not be equally as able.

Speak and we shall hear.

Farewell.

---

[87] Cf. *Rule of St. Benedict*, chapter 18.
[88] Cf. *Rule of St. Benedict*, chapter 11.
[89] Cf. the First Letter, p. 52.
[90] Cf. Rom. 15:20.

# SIXTH LETTER

## ABELARD TO HELOISE

Love, my dearest sister, divine love leads you to ask about the origin of your calling and how the religious life of nuns began. I will respond to you and to your daughters in the spirit as directly and succinctly as I can.[1] The order of monastics, of nuns and monks alike, took the form of its religious life most fully from Jesus Christ, our Lord. Even before his incarnation, though, the rudiments of this way of life existed among men and women both; hence, Jerome can

---

[1] Only the first half of the letter, in fact, responds directly to Heloise's request, offering a roughly chronological account of the women followers of Jesus and the parity of women's and men's roles in the institutions of the early Church, with continual backward glances at Jewish precedents. The remainder may be described, as Abelard describes it in the final paragraph, as praise of the "proper dignity" of nuns, although it is somewhat more than that—a wide-ranging assertion of the nature of women's virtue in general and the prerogatives and privileges of women in the religious life of pagans, Jews, and Christians. At times the letter takes on the character of an exhortation or a catalog of exempla similar to what Abelard in the Second Letter claims Heloise does not need. To judge by its repetitions, rough transitions, tangential remarks, gross disproportion of emphasis and treatment, and other inconsistencies of its internal organization, much of the letter seems to have been cobbled together by Abelard from texts composed for other purposes (parts resemble in their rhetoric and structure the extant sermons Abelard wrote for audiences at the Paraclete and elsewhere), then overlaid with comments and additions by others sympathetic to his project and imitative of his methods. Since some transitions in the text appear to have been modified to accommodate these additions, it is often very difficult to disentangle layers of the text with confidence. However, sections that are most likely later additions and not by Abelard himself have here been enclosed in brackets. This should not, though, attest to the completeness or secure authenticity of everything left unbracketed.

Some of these sections were identified and used by John F. Benton (1975) to support an argument against Abelard's authorship of this letter and others in the collection. Benton later (1980) retracted many of his claims, but problems remain. The letter shows signs of having been extensively reworked, and I have put forward the most conservative suggestions I believe are consistent with making sense of the text as it exists.

write to Rusticus about "the sons of the prophets, the monks we read of in the Old Testament,"[2] and the Gospel speaks of the widow Anna, who devoted herself to God and the temple and, alongside Simeon, was found worthy to receive the Lord in the temple and to prophesy about him when he came.[3] But Christ is the end of righteousness and the consummation of all good, and in the fullness of time he came to reveal the good that had been hidden and to perfect what as yet had only been begun. And coming as he did to summon men and women both to their redemption, he thought it best to unite each sex in the true monkhood of his community. In this, then, lies the source and the foundation of the calling for men and women both, its perfection of life set out for all to follow.

Already in the Gospel we read of a gathering of holy women who, along with the apostles and other disciples and the mother of the Lord herself, renounced the world and all of their possessions to be possessed of Christ alone. "The Lord is the portion of my inheritance," it is written, and they fulfilled the precept the Lord laid down, by which all those who turn from the world may enter into this communal life: "Every one of you that doth not renounce all that he possesseth cannot be my disciple."[4] They followed Christ devotedly—these most blessed women, these nuns in the true sense—winning honor and favor from Christ himself and later from the apostles, as our sacred histories carefully record. We read in the Gospel, for example, that the Lord rebuked the Pharisee who had invited him to his table and then complained that his hospitality was valued less than the service of the woman who had sinned.[5] We also read that, when the resurrected Lazarus sat with the others among the guests, his sister Martha served at supper alone, and that Mary poured a pound of precious oil on the feet of the Lord and dried them with her hair—the fragrance of the oil filled the house, angering the disciples with its seeming vanity and cost, and leading Judas finally into greed.[6] So, while Martha was busy with the food, Mary dispensed the oil: one inwardly, one outwardly, they both attended to the Lord.

---

[2] *Epistulae* 125.7. For Jerome's reference, see 4 Kings 6:1; cf. also the *Calamities*, p. 32.

[3] See Luke 2:25–38.

[4] Ps. 15:5; Luke 14:33.

[5] See Luke 7:36–50.

[6] A conflation of Matt. 26:8 ff., Mark 14:3 ff., Luke 10:38 ff., and John 12:1 ff.

Only women ministered to the Lord, according to the Gospel, devoting their resources to his daily maintenance and providing the necessities of this life. He himself would serve the disciples at table and wash their feet as an example of complete humility;[7] but we never hear of any disciple, or in fact of any *man*, doing this for him, only of women, as I've said, rendering him these and other services his humanity required. Martha, we see, did it in one way and Mary in another; and Mary served the Lord with all the more devotion, the more sinful her earlier life had been. When he washed the disciples' feet, the Lord poured water out into a basin; Mary used the tears of her inner remorse. He dried their feet with a linen cloth; she used her hair in place of linen. And she added oil over and above, which is nothing we read the Lord had ever done. The woman then so presumed upon his favor that she also anointed his head with oil, not simply letting it pour from an alabaster bottle but breaking the bottle open, it is said, in her desire to show her great devotion, so that once it had been used for such a service, it never could be put to use again. In this she fulfilled the prophecy of Daniel, that the time would come when the Holy of Holies would be anointed.[8] And see—it was a *woman* who anointed the Holy of Holies and by her act proclaimed that he was the one whom the prophet had predicted and the one in whom she placed her faith. I ask you then, What is this benevolence of the Lord? Or what is this intrinsic dignity of women, that the Lord would offer his head as well as his feet to no one but to *them* to be anointed? What is this prerogative of the weaker sex, that the supreme Christ, who from his very conception had been anointed by all the oils of the Holy Spirit, should be anointed again, and by a woman, as though she consecrated him priest and king with these material sacraments and made him the *Christ* in body, that is to say, the *Anointed One?*

We know that the patriarch Jacob first anointed a stone in *type* of the Lord,[9] and that afterward only men could anoint priests and kings or celebrate any rite of unction—although women may at times perform baptisms. As the patriarch once sanctified a stone, the bishop now sanctifies a temple and an altar with oil. Men thus enact these sacraments in symbols, but a woman wrought in truth itself,

---

[7] See John 13:5 ff.

[8] Dan. 9:24.

[9] See Gen. 28:18. For the typological reading of scripture, see the Fourth Letter, p. 86.

as the Truth himself proclaimed, "The woman wrought a good work upon me."[10] Christians are anointed by men, Christ himself by a woman; the members of the Church by men, its head by a woman. And she let the oil pour upon his head not drop by drop, it is said, but in full flow, in accord with what the bride in Canticles sings: "Thy name is as oil poured out." The veiled speech of the Psalmist, too, prefigures this abundance: "Like the precious oil on the head that ran down upon the beard, the beard of Aaron, which ran down to the hem of his garment."[11]

We read that David was anointed three times over, as Jerome points out in his commentary on Psalm 26, and Christ and Christians also three times over. For Christians it is at baptism, confirmation, and the anointing of the sick. For the Lord it was when a woman anointed his feet and then his head with oil, and when Joseph of Arimathea and Nicodemus prepared his body with spices after his death, as the Gospel of John reports.[12] Consider, then, the dignity of the woman who anointed Christ twice while he was still alive, his feet and then his head, as she consecrated him priest and king. The myrrh and aloes used to preserve the bodies of the dead prefigured the incorruptibility of his body, which at their resurrection the chosen of God will share; but his earlier anointings by a woman express the dignity unique to Christ as priest and king, the higher dignity by the anointing of his head and the lower by the anointing of his feet. He accepted the sacrament of kingship from a woman when he had rejected a kingdom offered him by men and even fled when they came to seize him and force him to be king.[13] But it was as heavenly, not as earthly, king that she anointed him, for as he later said, "My kingdom is not of this world."[14] Our bishops strut in all their pride when they anoint earthly kings, and all the populace watches and applauds; or they dress themselves in their fine golden robes when they consecrate mortal priests, and in fact they often bless those whom God cursed. But the woman was humility itself—no change of garment, no elaborate rite, and the apostles even took offense— when she performed this sacrament for Christ, invested with no office of the Church but only with the merit of her devotion. How

---

[10] Mark 14:6.

[11] Cant. 1:2; Ps. 132:2.

[12] See John 19:38.

[13] See John 6:15.

[14] John 18:36.

great is the constancy of faith, how priceless the fervor of charitable love, which "believeth all things, hopeth all things, endureth all things."[15] The Pharisee complained when a sinner anointed the feet of Christ, and the apostles were outraged that a woman had dared anoint his head. But a woman's faith remained unmoved on each of these occasions, trusting in the goodness of the Lord, and thus she won his favor. Her oils were acceptable and pleasing to the Lord, and when Judas objected, he said to him, "Let her alone, that she may keep it against the day of my burial."[16] In other words, "Do not dismiss her service to the living, or you deny her devotion to the dead."

Women prepared the spices for the burial of the Lord—this is certain—which this woman would not have done with the same intense devotion if her earlier service had been refused. But when the disciples turned on her in anger, Mark recounts, the Lord answered them with mild words and praised her act of kindness, even saying it should be included in the Gospel, that wherever the Gospel itself would be proclaimed, her act would also be proclaimed as her memorial, praise for the woman who had done this daring thing.[17] Nowhere do we read of any act of any other person receiving such commendation from the Lord. Then—and earlier when he praised the poor widow's gift over any other offerings to the temple[18]—he showed how thoroughly acceptable to him was the devotion of women. Peter once boasted that he and his fellow apostles had renounced all things for Christ,[19] and Zacchaeus, who received the Lord at his coming, gave half of all his riches to the poor and returned fourfold whatever he might have taken deceitfully;[20] and there were many others who had given even more on Christ's behalf, had made far richer offerings to God, or had renounced even more to follow Christ. But none of them won such praise from the Lord as the praise he gave to women.

We see their devotion to him most clearly toward the end of his life. When Peter, the prince of the apostles, denied the Lord and John, the beloved apostle, ran away, when the rest of the apostles

---

[15] 1 Cor. 13:7.

[16] John 12:7.

[17] See Mark 14:9.

[18] See Mark 12:41–44.

[19] See Matt. 19:27.

[20] See Luke 19:1–10.

then were scattered, these women remained firm.[21] No terror, no despair could keep them from Christ, not in his Passion nor in his death, and to them in particular the words of the Apostle apply: "What then shall separate us from the love of God? Shall tribulation or distress? Shall famine, nakedness, danger, persecution, or the sword?"[22] Matthew says of himself and the others, "Then all of the disciples left him and fled," but he also says that the women were undaunted, staying with the crucified Lord so long as it was allowed them—"There were many women there afar off, who had followed Jesus from Galilee, ministering unto him"—and waiting without stirring from his tomb: "Mary Magdalene and the other Mary sat against the sepulcher." Mark, too, speaks about these women:

> And there were also women looking on afar off, among whom was Mary Magdalene, Mary the mother of James the younger and of Joseph, and Salome, those who followed him when he was in Galilee and ministered to him, and many other women that came up with him to Jerusalem.[23]

John tells how he was there beside the cross, standing by the crucified Lord although he had run away before; but before he mentions himself, he mentions the resolution of the women, as though it were the force of their example that heartened him and called him back:

> There stood by the cross of Jesus, his mother and his mother's sister, Mary of Cleophas, and Mary Magdalene. When Jesus therefore had seen his mother and the disciple standing whom he loved, he saith to his mother, "Woman, behold thy son." After that, he saith to the disciple, "Behold thy mother." And from that hour the disciple took her into his home.[24]

Now the failure of the disciples and the constancy of the women had already been predicted long before, that is, by Job, who was

---

[21] For Peter's denial of Jesus, see Matt. 26:69 ff.; for the flight of John and the other disciples, see Matt. 26:56 and Mark 14:50.

[22] Rom. 8:35, where the Vulgate reads "the love of Christ." The manuscripts include the passage only through the word "distress," adding "etc."

[23] Matt. 26:56, 27:55, 61; Mark 15:40–1.

[24] John 19:25–27. The manuscripts break off with "etc." after "his mother and the disciple standing."

speaking in the persona of the Lord: "The flesh being consumed, my bone hath cleaved to my skin, and nothing but lips are left around my teeth."[25] The strength of the body lies in the bone, which supports the flesh and skin. In the body of Christ, which is the Church, the bone is the foundation of the faith or the fervor of that charitable love about which it is sung, "Many waters cannot quench charity, neither can the floods drown it,"[26] and which, the Apostle says, "beareth all things, believeth all things, hopeth all things, endureth all things."[27] The flesh is the inward part of the body and the skin its outward part; and so, the apostles, who looked to the inward nourishment of the soul, and the women, who supplied the necessities of the body, can be compared to the flesh and skin. When the flesh was consumed, the bone of Christ cleaved to the skin; that is to say, while the apostles fell away at the Passion of the Lord and yielded to despair at his death, the dedication of these holy women remained unmoved, not drawing back from the bone of Christ even to the slightest extent. It held so firm in faith, hope, and love that they never could be apart from him in body or in mind, even after his death. Since men are by nature stronger than women both in body and in mind, masculine nature is signified by the flesh, which is nearer the bone, and feminine weakness by the skin. The apostles are also called the *teeth* of the Lord, since it is their duty to bite, as it were, at the faults of others. And so, only the lips had been left for them—that is to say, their words and not their deeds—since in their despair they more spoke of Christ than they acted on his behalf.

Such were the disciples, then, to whom the Lord appeared as they went out to Emmaus, talking with each other about what had happened and earning his reproach for their despair.[28] Peter and the others had nothing else but words when the Lord foretold their failure at his Passion:

"Even if they all shall fall away on thy account," Peter said, "I will never fall away. . . . Yea, though I should die with thee, I will not deny thee." And all of the disciples said the same.[29]

---

[25] Job 19:20.

[26] Cant. 8:7. The manuscripts quote only through "charity," indicating the rest of the verse by "etc."

[27] 1 Cor. 13:7.

[28] See Luke 24:13 ff.

[29] Matt. 26:33–35.

Yes, they all *said* the same but did not act. And so, the first and greatest of the apostles—the one whose constancy to the Lord in words could lead him to pronounce, "I am ready to go with thee, both into prison and to death," the one into whose hands the Lord had just entrusted his Church, saying, "And thou, being once converted, confirm thy brethren"—this very one denied the Lord at a single sound from a serving-maid.[30] Not once but three times did he do it, denying Christ while he was still alive; and all of the disciples, too, deserted him while he was still alive.

The women, on the other hand, would not part from the Lord in body or in mind, even after his death. The blessed sinner, Mary Magdalene, searched for his body, proclaiming him her Lord: "They have taken away the Lord out of the sepulcher," she said; "if thou hast taken him hence, tell me where thou hast laid him and I will take him away."[31] The rams all flee and the shepherds of the flock, but the ewes are unafraid. For their weakness of the flesh the Lord reproached the men because even at the moment of his Passion they could not stay awake with him one hour.[32] But the women spent a sleepless night in tears beside his tomb, and thus they were found worthy to be first to see the glory of the risen Lord. By their devotion after his death, by their deeds and not only their words, they showed how much they had loved him while he was still alive.[33] From their concern about his Passion and his death, they became the first to rejoice in his resurrection to life. Joseph of Arimathea and Nicodemus wrapped his body in linen along with spices for his burial, according to John, but Mark tells how Mary Magdalene and Mary the mother of Joseph were watching to see where the body was laid.[34] Luke also speaks of them: "And the women that were come with Jesus from Galilee, following after, saw the sepulcher and how his body was laid. And returning, they prepared spices and ointments"—since the spices of Nicodemus would not have been enough if they had not added their own—"and on the Sabbath day they rested, according to the commandment."[35] And then, Mark tells us, when the Sabbath was over, in the earliest morning on the

---

[30] See Luke 22:33, 32; see Matt. 26:69 ff.

[31] John 20:2 and 20:15.

[32] Matt. 26:41.

[33] Cf. Abelard's request of the women of the Paraclete in the Second Letter, p. 70.

[34] See John 19:38–40 and Mark 15:47.

[35] Luke 23:55–56.

very day of his resurrection, Mary Magdalene, Mary the mother of James, and Salome came to his tomb.[36]

That was their devotion—now for the honor they won. First, they saw an angel, who brought them comfort in the news that he had risen. Then they saw the Lord himself and touched him with their hands. The very first was Mary Magdalene, whose devotion was more fervent than the rest. Soon after they saw the angel, she and the others

> went out from the sepulcher . . . running to tell his disciples about the resurrection of the Lord. And behold, Jesus met them, saying: "All hail." But they came up and took hold of his feet and worshiped him. Then Jesus said to them: . . . "Go, tell my brethren that they go into Galilee. There they shall see me."[37]

Luke says, "It was Mary Magdalene and Joanna and Mary mother of James and the other women that were with them, who told these things to the apostles," and Mark says that they were sent to the apostles by the angel: "He is risen" the angel said, "he is not here. . . . But go, tell his disciples and Peter that he goeth before you into Galilee."[38] But first the Lord himself appeared to Mary Magdalene and told her, "Go to my brethren and say to them: I ascend to my Father and to your Father, to my God and to your God."[39] From this we conclude that these holy women were appointed female apostles, so to speak, to the apostles,[40] being sent—whether by angels or by the Lord—to announce the joy of his resurrection and to bring the apostles the first tidings of what they would later preach to all the world.

After the resurrection, Matthew tells us, the Lord greeted the women as a mark of his great favor and concern. We never read that he gave the formal greeting of "All hail" to anyone but them—on

---

[36] See Mark 15:1.

[37] Matt. 28:8–10.

[38] Luke 24:10; Mark 16:6–7.

[39] John 20:17. The manuscripts quote only through "to my Father" and add "etc." The inconsistencies, real or apparent, among these Gospel accounts become the subject of the fifth question in Heloise's *Questions*.

[40] Abelard's qualification "so to speak" refers to his use of the feminine form *apostolae*, "female apostles," not to the fact that he calls them apostles.

the contrary, he had ordered his disciples to refrain from any greet-ing: "Greet no one by the way," he said, as if he would reserve for devout women the privilege he himself would show them when he had attained the glory of his immortality. Then, after his ascension, when the apostles had returned from the Mount of Olives and assembled in that sacred gathering in Jerusalem, the women joined them in their constant devotion, as the Acts of the Apostles tell: "All these were persevering with one mind in prayer with the women and with Mary the mother of Jesus."[41]

Now these Hebrew women had turned to the faith while the Lord was still preaching and living in the flesh, and they first adopted the form of this religious life; but there were also the wid-ows of the Greeks who were received by the apostles afterward, and we must now consider them as well. Their care was entrusted to Stephen, first martyr and glorious standard-bearer in the army of the Lord, and to other men of the Holy Spirit, as the Acts of the Apostles record:

> The number of the disciples increasing, there arose a mur-muring of the Greeks against the Hebrews, for that their widows were neglected in the daily ministration. Then the twelve, calling together the multitude of the disciples, said: "It is not reason that we should leave the word of God and serve tables. Wherefore, brethren, look ye out among you seven men of good reputation, full of the Holy Spirit and wisdom, whom we may appoint over this business. But we will give ourselves continually to prayer and to the ministry of the word." And the saying was liked by all the multitude. And they chose Stephen, a man full of faith and of the Holy Spirit, and Philip and Prochoros and Nicanor, and Timon and Parmenas and Nicolas of Antioch. These they sat before the apostles, and they, praying, imposed hands on them.[42]

It was the highest tribute to Stephen's self-restraint that he would have been selected for the task. Ministering to holy women was a noble service in the eyes of God and the apostles, as they indicated by their prayer and laying on of hands: those whom they appointed

---

[41] Luke 10:4; Acts 1:14.

[42] Acts 6:1–6.

were solemnly entreated, as it were, by blessing and by prayer to act as faithfully as they could in aiding them. In fact, Saint Paul would claim this service as his own to help him fulfill his duties as apostle: "Have we not the power to carry about a woman, a sister as well as the rest of the apostles?" he said.[43] In other words, "May we too not bring holy women with us when we preach? The other apostles do this, and the women provide the necessities for them from their substance." As Augustine says in his book on the work of monks:

> Faithful women of means would go with them and provide for them from their substance so that they would lack none of the necessities of life. . . . If anyone doubts that women of holy life traveled with the apostles wherever they preached the Gospel . . . , let him but read the Gospel itself and learn that in this they had the example of the Lord. . . . In the Gospel of Luke it is written: "And it came to pass afterwards that he traveled through the cities and towns, preaching and evangelizing the kingdom of God, and the twelve with him and certain women who had been healed of evil spirits and infirmities: Mary who is called Magdalene . . . , and Joanna the wife of Chusa, Herod's steward, and Susanna, and many others who provided for him from their substance."[44]

Again we see how women sustained the bodily needs of the Lord when he went out to preach and how they traveled with him and the apostles as their inseparable companions.

Soon after the beginning of the Church, the number of women living the religious life, like the number of men, had grown to the point where women, like men, took up residence in monasteries of their own. The *History of the Church* records the praise the learned Jew Philo gave the church of Alexandria under Mark; in Book 2, Chapter 17 we read:

> There are people leading this life in many parts of the world. . . . In each place there is a house of prayer called a *semneion*, a holy place or monastery. . . . There they not only

---

[43] 1 Cor. 9:5.

[44] Augustine, *De Opere Monachorum* 4.5 and 5.6; the internal quotation is from Luke 8:1 ff. The passage is also cited in this form in Abelard's *Calamities*.

learn the hymns of the ancient sages but compose new hymns to God in a range of different melodies and meters, singing them in sweet and solemn arrangement.

He spoke at length about their austerity and their worship of God, and then continued:

Along with the men I have mentioned, there are also women, most of them elderly virgins who maintain their chastity not out of some necessity but out of devotion. They consecrate themselves body and soul to the pursuit of wisdom and think it unworthy to give over to lust the vessel which had been prepared to receive that wisdom, or to bring forth mortal children when their relations ought to be the sacred and immortal intercourse with God's word, which leaves no offspring subject to the corruption of death.

"Philo also wrote about their meetings, about the segregation of men and women living in a single place, and about the vigils they kept in the way that we still do."[45]

The *Tripartite History* has this to say in praise of the Christian philosophical life, that is, the monastic privilege taken up no less by women than by men:

Some say the founder of this most scrupulous philosophy was the prophet Elijah; others say it was John the Baptist. Philo the Pythagorean says that the outstanding Hebrews of his time came from all over to take up the practice of philosophy on an estate overlooking the Lake of Mary. Their dwellings, food, and discourse are of the kind we now see among the monks of Egypt. He also writes that they . . . touched no food before sunset . . . , completely abstained from meat and wine, ate only bread flavored with hyssop and salt, and drank only water. Women lived among them, older virgins who, from their love for philosophy, abstained from marriage of their own accord.[46]

---

[45] Eusebius, *Historia Ecclesiae* 2.17. Abelard cites Eusebius' Greek text in the Latin paraphrase of Rufinus.

[46] *Historia Ecclesiastica Tripartita* 1.11, formerly attributed to Cassiodorus.

[And Jerome has this to say in praise of Mark and his church in Chapter 8 of his book on distinguished men:

> The first to bring the news of Christ to Alexandria, he established a church of such rigor and self-restraint that all the followers of Christ were led to take up his example. Philo, the most eloquent among the Jews, saw that the church of Alexandria continued Jewish practices at first, and so he wrote a book on its way of life, as if in praise of his own people. As Luke tells of the communal life of the faithful in Jerusalem, Philo records what he observed in Alexandria under the tutelage of Mark.

And in Chapter 11:

> Philo, an Alexandrian by birth and from a priestly family of Jews, is nonetheless considered among the historians of the Church because he praises our people in the book he wrote about the church in Alexandria, established by the evangelist Mark. He speaks about them not only in Alexandria but in many different regions, and he calls their residences monasteries.[47]

Monastics now strive to follow the ways of the early Church, holding no property of their own, none of them rich, none of them poor, sharing their inheritance with those in need, devoting themselves to prayers and psalms, to learning and self-restraint—as Luke recounts of the first believers in Jerusalem.][48]

In earlier history, too, no distinction is made between women and men in any matter that pertains to God or in any particular of the religious life. Women sang hymns, as men did, and composed them as well. In fact, the very first song the people of Israel sang to the Lord on their deliverance from bondage was sung by men and women both, which became the source and precedent for the role of women in the divine services of the Church:

> Miriam the prophetess, the sister of Aaron, took a timbrel in her hand, and all the women went forth after her with

---

[47] *De Illustribus Viris* 8 and 11.

[48] This section, which takes up further comments on Philo and the early church of Alexandria but veers away from the main subject of the letter, is most likely a later addition to the text.

timbrels and with dances. And she began the song to them, saying, "Let us sing to the Lord, for he is gloriously magnified, the horse and his rider he hath thrown into the sea."[49]

There is no mention here of Moses acting as a prophet or singing as Miriam did, and no mention of men taking up timbrels and dancing as the women did. When Miriam is called a prophetess in her song, it is not because she recited or dictated what she sang but because her voice was lifted in prophetic utterance. When it is said that she *began the song to them,* we understand that they all chanted in concord and fine order. That they sang *with timbrels and with dances* and not with the voice alone suggests their great devotion, certainly, but also signifies in veiled speech the form of song particular to monastic congregations. We too are urged to the same form of song by the Psalmist who tells us, "Praise him with timbrel and dance," that is, in the mortification of the flesh and the concord of that charitable love about which it is written, "The multitude of believers had but one heart and one soul."[50] That *all the women went forth* in song signifies the joys of the contemplative soul, which, so long as it is fixed on heavenly things, abandons, as it were, the tabernacle of its earthly dwelling and makes a hymn to the Lord from the inner sweetness of its own contemplation. Hence, in the Old Testament we also have the songs of Deborah, Hannah, and the widow Judith, and in the Gospel the song of Mary, mother of the Lord.[51] [Hannah's offering of her son Samuel to the tabernacle of the Lord set the precedent for accepting children into monasteries, as Isidore writes to the monks of the Honorian abbey, Chapter 5:

> Whoever has been designated for the monastery by his parents must know that he will remain there in perpetuity. For Hannah gave her son Samuel to God, and he remained in the service of the temple as his mother had intended, serving where he was established.][52]

---

[49] Exod. 15:20–21. The manuscripts quote only through "gloriously magnified"; "etc." indicates the rest of the verse.

[50] Ps. 150:4; Acts 4:32.

[51] For Deborah, see Judg. 5:2–31; for Hannah, see 1 Kings 2:1–10; for Judith, see Jth. 16:2–21; for the song of Mary, see Luke 1:46–55.

[52] A likely later addition to the text, prompted by the mention of Hannah. The figures of Hannah and Samuel apparently evoked considerable interest at the Paraclete, becoming the subject of no fewer than seven of Heloise's *Questions* (31–37). The passage quoted here is not actually by Isidore, as Muckle (1955, 261 n. 19) points out, but was accepted as Isidore's on the authority of Smaragdus and Gratian.

Clearly the daughters of Aaron belonged to the sanctuary and shared with their brothers in the portion of Levi, the means the Lord established for their maintenance. As he said to Aaron in the Book of Numbers:

> All the first fruits of the sanctuary which the children of Israel offer to the Lord, I have given to thee and to thy sons and daughters by a perpetual ordinance.[53]

Hence, women in religious life, it seems, were not distinct from the order of clerics. Their titles also clearly were the same, since we speak of deaconesses along with deacons, recognizing, as it were, both male and female members of the tribe of Levi. In the Book of Numbers, too, we read how the consecration of Nazirites of the Lord, which entailed the strictest form of religious vow, applied to women as well as men. As the Lord said to Moses:

> Speak to the children of Israel and say to them, "When a man or woman shall make a vow to be sanctified and will consecrate themselves to the Lord, they shall abstain from wine and from every thing that may make a man drunk. They shall not drink vinegar of wine or of any other drink, nor any thing that is pressed out of the grape, nor shall they eat grapes either fresh or dried. All the days that they are consecrated to the Lord by vow, they shall eat nothing that cometh of the vineyard, from the raisin even to the kernel.[54]

It was women of this way of life, I believe, who watched at the door of the tabernacle, and from whose mirrors Moses made a basin for Aaron and his sons to wash themselves. It is written:

> Moses set out a bronze vessel for Aaron and his sons to wash themselves . . . which he fashioned from the mirrors of the women who watched at the door of the tabernacle.[55]

---

[53] Num. 18:19.

[54] Num. 6:2–4.

[55] Cf. Exod. 30:18–19 and 38:8. The exact form of the passage as quoted is found in Gregory, *Homiliae in Evangelia* 17.10, which also introduces the image of the mirrors of remorse taken up later in the paragraph.

We read of their fervor and devotion as they watched outside the closed door of the tabernacle, praying and keeping vigil through the night, while the men were asleep. That the door was closed to them signifies the life of penitents, who keep themselves apart from the rest to afflict themselves with harsher penance—indeed, the monastic calling in particular is said to be just such a life, nothing, that is, but a relatively mild form of penance. The tabernacle also must be understood symbolically, as the Apostle understood it in his letter to the Hebrews: "We have an altar whereof they have no power to eat who serve the tabernacle"[56]—that is to say, no one is fit to have a share in the altar who indulges in the pleasures of the body while serving in this life on earth as in a camp. The door of the tabernacle is the end of this life on earth, when the soul goes forth from the body to enter into the life to come. Those who watch at the door are those who are concerned with the transit from this life and by repentance so arrange their death as to be worthy of eternal life. [The Psalmist refers to this daily entering in and going out of the holy Church in his prayer, "May the Lord keep thy coming in and thy going out."[57] He keeps our coming in and going out when, once we have left this life and have been purged through our repentance, he leads us directly to that other life. The Psalmist very properly places "coming in" before "going out," acknowledging its priority in value, if not in time, since we leave this mortal life in pain but come to that eternal life in highest exaltation.] [The women's mirrors are the outward works by which the beauty or ugliness of the soul is judged, like a human face by a material mirror. So, the vessel in which Aaron and his sons wash themselves is fashioned from these mirrors when the works of holy women and the constancy of their sex become a rebuke to the negligence of priests and bishops and move them to tears of remorse: if they look after the women as they should, the women's works will win them pardon for their sins. Saint Gregory turned these mirrors into a vessel of remorse for himself when he marveled at the virtue of holy women and at their victory in martyrdom, asking with a groan:

> What will big bearded men have to say when these delicate girls
> bear such burdens for Christ and the members of the fragile sex

---

[56] Heb. 13:10.

[57] Ps. 120:8.

triumph in a struggle that wins them the double crown of virginity and martyrdom?][58]

I have no doubt that the blessed Anna belonged among those women standing watch outside the door, the ones who had consecrated their widowhood to the Lord as if they were his female Nazirites. For she, no less than Simeon, was found worthy to receive the unique Nazirite of the Lord, the Lord Jesus Christ himself, and to recognize him through the Holy Spirit at the same hour Simeon did, becoming something greater than a prophet as she revealed his presence and publicly proclaimed him to the world. [As Luke recounts:

> There was one Anna, a prophetess, the daughter of Phanuel, of the tribe of Aser. She was far advanced in years and had lived with her husband seven years from her virginity. And she was a widow until fourscore and four years, who departed not from the temple, by fastings and prayers serving night and day. Now she, at the same hour, coming in, confessed to the Lord, and spoke of him to all that looked for the redemption of Jerusalem.[59]

Note each thing he says and how he praises her in such detail. The grace she was granted with the gift of prophecy, her father, her tribe, the seven years she lived with her husband, the long period of her widowhood, which she devoted to God, her dedicated service to the temple, her fasting and her prayers, her praise of the Lord and her thanks to him, her public proclamation of the Savior who had been promised and now was born—all this the evangelist carefully sets down. He had praised Simeon earlier, but for his righteousness and not his prophetic gift, and he made no mention of his austerity or self-restraint nor said anything about his speaking of Christ to others.]

Also among the women of this calling are the true widows Saint Paul described to Timothy:

> Honor widows that are widows indeed. . . . She that is a widow indeed and desolate, let her trust in God and continue

---

[58] Not Gregory's actual words, but very like his *Homiliae in Evangelia* 11.3. The stress on outward works throughout this passage seems so at odds with the thrust of Abelard's arguments elsewhere that it may be enough in itself to cast doubt on his authorship of the section.

[59] Luke 2:36–38, in which the Vulgate has "the redemption of Israel."

in prayer night and day. . . . And this give in charge, that they may be blameless. . . . If any of the faithful have widows, let him minister to them and let not the Church be charged, so that there may be sufficient for them that are widows indeed.[60]

The true widows, *widows indeed,* are those who have not disgraced their widowhood by a second marriage and have dedicated themselves to God out of devotion, not necessity. They are *desolate* having renounced the world and all their earthly possessions with no one to care for them. Such women, Paul instructs us, must be honored and supported by the Church, as if from the property of Christ, their Husband; and from their number women should be chosen for the ministry of the diaconate, as he says:

Let a widow be chosen of no less than threescore years of age, who hath been the wife of one husband, having testimony for her good works, if she have brought up children, if she have offered hospitality, if she have washed the saints' feet, if she have ministered to them that suffer tribulation, if she have diligently followed every good work. But the younger widows avoid.[61]

[Jerome comments on this passage: "Avoid appointing to the diaconate someone who would set a bad example for others."[62] Younger widows are more likely to set this bad example, being less steady and more open to temptation through their lack of experience, as Paul had learned from his own observation.][63] He goes on to explain:

For when they have grown wanton in Christ, they will marry, having damnation because they have made void their first faith. And being idle, they learn to go about from house to house, and are not only idle but tattlers also and busybodies, speaking things which they ought not. I will,

---

[60] 1 Tim. 5:3–7.

[61] 1 Tim. 5:9–11.

[62] Actually from Pelagius' *Expositions of the Epistles of Paul,* which had been attributed to Jerome; see Muckle 1955, 264 n. 70.

[63] A likely later addition, perhaps derived from Abelard's Sermon 31, which it paraphrases.

therefore, that the younger should marry, bear children, be mistresses of families, and give the adversary no occasion to speak evil. For some are already turned aside after Satan.[64]

And Saint Gregory agrees, writing to Maximus, bishop of Syracuse:

We strictly forbid young abbesses. Bishops should only give the veil to virgins at least sixty years of age whose life and character have been thoroughly tested.[65]

Those we now call abbesses were once called deaconesses, that is, ministers rather than mothers. The word deacon itself means *minister* or *servant,* and deaconesses were named for the ministerial function of their service rather than their rank. This is in accord with both the words and the example of the Lord: "He that is greatest among you shall be your servant," he said, and "For which is greater, he that sitteth at table or he that serveth? Is not he that sitteth at table? But I am in the midst of you, as he that serveth," and "Even as the Son of man is not come to be ministered unto, but to minister."[66] So, when Jerome objected to the use of the term abbot, knowing how many gloried in the name, he relied on the authority of the Lord. Commenting on the phrase, "Crying, 'Abba, Father,'" in Paul's Letter to the Galatians, he said:

*Abba* is the Hebrew word for father . . . and the Lord said that only God should be called father. I do not understand, then, how we can use that term in monasteries, of ourselves or of someone else. The Lord also told us not to swear oaths, so if we do not swear oaths, we should not call any man father. If we understand *father* otherwise, we will have to think otherwise about swearing oaths.[67]

The Phoebe whom Saint Paul commended to the Romans was certainly one of these early deaconesses:

---

[64] 1 Tim. 5:11–15.

[65] *Epistulae* 4.11.

[66] Matt. 23:11; Luke 22:27; Matt. 20:28.

[67] *Commentarii in Epistulam ad Galatas,* 2.4.451. Paul's phrase is in Gal. 4:6. Cf. also Matt. 23:9 and 5:34.

I commend to you Phoebe, our sister, who is in the ministry of the church in Cenchrae, that you receive her in the Lord as becometh saints and that you assist her in whatsoever business she shall have need of you. For she also hath assisted many, and myself also.[68]

In their commentaries on this passage, both Cassiodorus and Claudius assert that Phoebe was indeed a deaconess of her church. Cassiodorus says:

He means she was a deaconess of her mother church, an office which still exists today in parts of the Greek world as a kind of training. In that church deaconesses are allowed to perform baptisms.

And Claudius:

The passage tells us on apostolic authority that women also may be ordained in the ministry of the Church. Phoebe had such an office in the church of Cenchrae, and the Apostle praises her highly.[69]

When Paul writes to Timothy about the ranks of the Church ministry, he discusses these women along with deacons and holds them to a similar moral standard:

Deacons should be chaste, not double-tongued, not given to much wine, not greedy of filthy lucre, holding the mystery of faith in a pure conscience. And let them also first be proved, and so let them minister, having no crime. The women also should be chaste, not slanderers but sober and faithful in all things. Let deacons be the husbands of one wife, who rule their children and their own houses well; for they that have ministered well shall purchase to themselves a good degree and much confidence in the faith which is in Christ Jesus.[70]

---

[68] Rom. 16:1–2.

[69] Abelard cites these passages to the same purpose in his Sermon 31. Cassiodorus' commentary is now lost, Claudius' not published.

[70] 1 Tim. 3:8–13.

Deacons must not be *double-tongued*, he says, and deaconesses not be *slanderers;* deacons must not be *given to much wine* and deaconesses must be *sober*—all the other details he summarizes as *faithful in all things*. Deacons, like bishops, cannot have been married more than once, nor can deaconesses, as we noted before:

> Let a widow be chosen of no less than threescore years of age, who hath been the wife of one husband, having testimony for her good works, if she have brought up children, if she have offered hospitality, if she have washed the saints' feet, if she have ministered to them that suffer tribulation, if she have diligently followed every good work. But the younger widows avoid.

In fact, Paul is more precise in his requirements of deaconesses than he is in his requirements of deacons or of bishops. A deaconess must *have testimony for her good works* and must *have offered hospitality*, but not a deacon. Of a deaconess he says *if she have washed the saints' feet* and so on, but says nothing of a deacon or bishop beyond their *having no crime*. A deaconess should be *blameless*, he insists, but he adds that she should *have diligently followed every good work*. He also is cautious in stipulating her age—*no less than threescore years*—eager for her to have a general authority and command respect for her years as well as her mode of life.

[For a similar reason, the Lord set Peter over all the other disciples despite his greater love for John. There is less resentment at the preferment of an elder: we are more willing to obey him since his precedence derives not only from his character but from the passage of time and the order of nature itself. As Jerome says of the choice of Peter:

> A single one is chosen, one head appointed to reduce the chance of schism. But why wasn't it John? Well, Peter was the elder, and deference was paid to age to keep someone who was young—still almost a boy, in fact—from being preferred to men of advanced years. The good master forestalled quarrels among his students, as he should, giving them no cause to envy the youngster whom he loved.[71]

Similarly, the abbot in the *Lives of the Fathers* transferred seniority from a younger to an elder brother even though the younger had joined the

---

[71] *Contra Jovinianum* 1.26.

monastery first: the elder would take it hard, he was afraid, if his younger brother in the flesh took precedence over him.[72] The abbot remembered how even the apostles were annoyed when two among them seemed to have gained some privilege with Christ at their mother's request, especially since one of them was younger than the rest, in fact, this same John of whom we spoke just now.][73]

[Saint Paul was certainly careful about the appointment of deaconesses, but he also showed remarkable concern for widows of the holy calling in general and how to isolate them from temptation. Just after "Honor widows who are widows indeed," he wrote:

> But if any widow have children or grandchildren, let her learn first to govern her own house and to make a return of duty to her parents. . . . But if any man have not care of his own and especially those of his house, he hath denied the faith and is worse than an infidel.[74]

Here he looked to both a human need and the needs of the religious life at once. No woman should leave her children in poverty on the pretext of her calling: her feeling for them could well interfere with her vows, causing her to look back or even leading her into sacrilege if she steals from the community to provide for her own. And so, he added this necessary caution, that before they pass to true widowhood and become entirely free for their service to God, women with family ties must first return the duty they owe their parents; that is, they must provide for their children out of the same obligation that had bound their parents to provide for *them*. While his emphasis was on their religious life, with instructions to "continue in prayer night and day," nonetheless he remained concerned with their material needs: "If any of the faithful have widows," he said, "let him minister to them and let not the Church be charged, that there may be sufficient for them that are widows indeed."[75] In other words, "If a widow has family with the means to provide for her, it must do so, in order to allow the public funds of the Church to provide for the needs of others." If a family is reluctant to fulfill this obligation, it then should be compelled, upon the authority of Paul. This is not only a matter of a widow's needs but also of her honor: "Honor widows," he said, "who are widows indeed."]

---

[72] See *Vitae Patrum* 5.10.113.

[73] See Matt. 20:24 ff. and Mark 10:35 ff.

[74] 1 Tim. 5:4–8.

[75] 1 Tim. 5:5, 15.

[We also can count among these women both the one whom Paul called "mother" and the one whom John called "lady" out of respect for her calling. Writing to the Romans, Paul said, "Greetings to Rufus, chosen of the Lord, and to his mother and mine," and in his second letter John wrote, "To the lady chosen of God and to her children. . . . I ask thee, my lady, . . . that we love one another."[76] Jerome later followed John's precedent when, writing to Eustochium, a virgin of your calling, he addressed her without embarrassment as "my lady"—indeed why should he have been embarrassed at all? "I write to you as 'My lady Eustochium,'" he said, "because, surely, I ought to call my Lord's own bride 'my lady.'"][77]

[Later in the letter, he set the privilege of the religious life above every earthly glory:

> Avoid contact with married women. Avoid visiting the mansions of the rich. Avoid looking upon what you once despised when you chose to be a virgin. . . . If there is a crush to greet the emperor's wife, why insult your Husband and join it? You are the bride of God: why fawn over the wife of man? Learn a bit of holy pride in this and know that you are better than they.][78]

Jerome also wrote about the heavenly blessedness and earthly dignity belonging to virgins consecrated to God:

> We learn from scripture and the ways of the Church the blessedness virginity has in heaven and the special merit subsisting in those who have been consecrated in the spirit. All believers receive an equal gift of grace, and all glory alike in the blessings of the sacraments, but *they* have something of their own beyond all others. Out of the pure and holy flock of the Church, these holier and purer victims come, chosen by the Holy Spirit for their merits and of their will, to be offered by the high priest on the very altar of God. . . . Virginity, then, has what others do not have, a special grace and the joy of its own privileged consecration.[79]

---

[76] Rom. 16:13; 2 John 1:1–5.

[77] *Epistulae* 22.2.

[78] *Epistulae* 22.16.

[79] Cf. *Virginitatis Laus* 1, once attributed to Jerome.

Except when there is imminent danger of death, the consecration of virgins is reserved for only a few days in the year—Epiphany, Pentecost, and the nativities of the apostles—and only a high priest, that is, a bishop, may sanctify them or their veils. Monks, on the other hand, may be blessed at any time whatever, and they receive their own religious garments, that is, their cowls, from their abbot, even though monks are of the same order as nuns and the male sex has a higher dignity. Priests and those of lesser rank may be ordained throughout the fasts of Ember Days, and bishops may be ordained on any Sunday. The consecration of virgins, though, is as precious as it is rare, claiming the leading festivals for itself, when all the Church rejoices in their virtue, as the Psalmist said: "After her shall virgins be brought to the king. . . . They shall be brought with gladness and rejoicing . . . into the temple of the king."[80] [It is also said that the apostle and evangelist Matthew wrote about their consecration, as one reads in his *Passion*, which tells of his martyrdom in defense of their consecration and their calling.[81] No apostle, though, has left us a written blessing either for clerics or for monks.]

The religious life of women alone is marked with the name of sanctity, for nuns are known as *sanctimoniales*. As women are the weaker sex, their power is more perfect and finds greater favor with God. For this we have the testimony of the Lord himself, who urged Saint Paul in all his weakness on to win the crown: "My grace is sufficient for thee," he said, "for power is made perfect in weakness."[82] Through the same apostle in the same letter [—the first to the Corinthians—][83] he spoke as if to praise the weaker members of his body, that is to say, the weaker members of the Church:

> Those members of the body that seem to be the weaker are also the more necessary, and what we think to be the less honorable members of the body, we adorn with more abundant honor. Those that are our uncomely parts have more abundant comeliness, for our comely parts are not in need. But God hath tempered the body together, giving the more

---

[80] Ps. 44:15–16.

[81] Cf. *Acta Sancti Matthaei* 2.19.

[82] 2 Cor. 12:9.

[83] The citation "in the same letter" is an error and the phrase "the first to the Corinthians" was apparently added to correct it.

abundant honor to what was in need, that there might be no schism in the body, but its members might be mutually careful one for another.[84]

It is in the weakness of the female sex, debased by sin and nature, that the grace of God fulfilled these words completely. Look around at each of the conditions of the sex—at virgins and widows, married women, yes, but also at the hatefulness of whores—and you see the grace of Christ most fully there, in accord with what the Lord and his Apostle have said: "So shall the last be first and the first last" and "Where sin abounded, grace did more abound."[85] If we look for the benefits of that grace and the honor shown to women at the origin of the world, we find that, in one respect at least, the creation of woman had a higher dignity than that of man: woman was created inside Paradise but man outside. Paradise, then, is women's natural home, as women should take note, and the celibate life of Paradise more fit for them to lead. As Ambrose wrote in his book on Paradise:

> God took the man he made and set him in Paradise. . . . You see how man already existed when God took him and set him in Paradise. . . . Note then that man was created outside Paradise but woman inside. . . . In the inferior place man is found to be superior and woman, who was created in the superior place, is found to be inferior.[86]

[Moreover, the Lord restored Eve in Mary before he repaired Adam in Christ—as sin began in woman, so grace began in woman and the privilege of virginity flowered again—and the form of women's holy calling was revealed in Anna and Mary before the pattern of men's religious life was set by the apostles or by John.]

But if, beyond Eve, we look at Deborah, Judith, Esther and *their* power, we will surely feel ashamed for the powerful male sex. Deborah, a judge of the people of the Lord, gave battle when the courage of men failed; she conquered her enemies, freed her people, and won a mighty triumph. Judith went unarmed and alone against a

---

[84] 1 Cor. 12:22.

[85] Matt. 20:16; Rom. 5:20.

[86] *De Paradiso* 4.24. Cf. also Abelard's hymn "After the Virgin's Highest Honor," which also makes reference to Deborah, Judith, the anonymous mother in the Book of Maccabees, and Jephtha's daughter.

fearsome army with only her maidservant at her side; she cut off the head of Holofernes with his own sword, destroyed the entire army, and set her people free. At the secret prompting of her spirit, Esther married a pagan king against the precept of the law; but she thwarted the designs of Haman and the edict of the king, and, in almost an instant, turned the import of the cruel decree into its opposite.[87] That David could overcome Goliath with no more than a sling and stone is set down as a mark of his great virtue. The widow Judith, on the other hand, went out against the enemy with not even sling and stone, in fact with no weapon at all, and she did battle. Esther freed her people with only a word—her enemies fell by a plot of their own devising—and her deed is remembered every year in a joyous festival among the Jews, something no act of a man has ever achieved, no matter how splendid it was.

And who has read the story in the Book of Maccabees of the mother of seven sons and does not marvel?[88] There was no equal to her constancy when the godless King Antiochus caught them all and tried in vain to force them to eat pork, which the law did not allow. Forgetting her maternal nature and blind to human feeling, she kept only the Lord before her eyes. One by one she sent her sons ahead, urging them all to win the sacred crown; and one by one she triumphed in their martyrdom until at last she won a martyrdom of her own. Throughout all of the Old Testament we find nothing to compare with the constancy of this woman. The great Seducer, violent to the last against Job, thought human nature weak in the face of death: "Skin for skin," he said, "and all that a man hath he will give for his life."[89] All of us shrink so naturally from death that to defend one limb we will often risk another, deterred by nothing if it will save our lives. But *she* could face the loss of all she had, of her sons' lives and her own, rather than offend against the law. And what was the transgression forced upon her? Renouncing God? Burning incense before idols? No—the only thing demanded of them was that they eat some meat in contravention of the law.

Let me ask my brothers and my fellow monks, who every day gape after meat in violation of the Rule that governs their calling: What will *you* have to say to the constancy of this woman? Are you

---

[87] For the story of Deborah, see Judg. 4:4 ff.; for Judith, see Jth. 8 ff.; for Esther and the festival of Purim, see Est. 2:5 ff.

[88] See 2 Macc. 7.

[89] Job 2:29.

really so entirely without shame that you can hear her story and not blush? Remember the Lord's reproach of unbelievers, that the queen of the south shall rise in judgment and condemn this generation,[90] and know, my brothers, that even more will the constancy of this woman rise in judgment against *you*; for her deeds were so much greater than the queen's, and you are bound more strictly by your religious vows. Her virtue was tested in such a struggle that her martyrdom deserved the honor of a Mass and solemn lessons in the Church, something never granted to any of the holy who died before the coming of the Lord.[91] [As the Book of Maccabees relates, however, the venerable scribe Eleazar had already won the crown of martyrdom for much the same reason.[92] But it did not deserve commemoration in a feast because women's virtue is more honorable and acceptable to God, that sex being naturally weaker, as we said, and in this martyrdom no woman was involved. It is as though it were considered no great matter for the stronger sex to endure with strength. Hence, scripture praises the woman all the more:

> Now the mother was to be admired beyond measure and worthy to be remembered by good men, who beheld her seven sons slain in the space of one day and bore it with a good courage, for the hope that she had in God. And she bravely exhorted every one of them . . . being filled with wisdom and joining a man's heart to a woman's thought.][93]

The daughter of Jephtha, too, his only one, deserves a place in the praise of virgins.[94] Rather than see her father break his word and defraud God's grace of the sacrifice he promised, she offered her own throat to her father's knife and urged him on to cut it. Imagine, then, what she would have done if she were faced with the struggle of the martyrs and ever forced by infidels to deny God. If asked about Christ, could she ever say, "I know him not," as Peter did, who at the time was already prince of the apostles?[95] Her father released her for two months, but when the time had passed, she

---

[90] Matt. 12:42.

[91] Cf. also the Seventh Letter.

[92] Cf. 2 Macc. 7:18 ff.

[93] 2 Macc. 7:20–21.

[94] See Judg. 11:30–40; also cf. the Second Letter, and Abelard's "Lament of the Virgins of Israel for the Daughter of Jephtha."

[95] Luke 22:57.

returned to him to meet her death willingly and unafraid—she even demanded it. Her father repented of his foolish vow, but she saved him from a lie in her supreme devotion to the truth. If she could not bear such a lapse in her father, how much would she have despised it in herself? If this was her love for her earthly father, what must it have been for her Father in heaven? By her death she kept Jephtha's word intact and insured that God would have his sacrifice. And so, the courage of the girl deserved the memorial it received, as every year the daughters of Israel assemble to commemorate her death with solemn hymns and lament her suffering with pious tears.

But to pass over other examples, was anything more essential to our redemption and the salvation of the world than the female sex, which gave birth to the Savior? The woman who dared approach Saint Hilarion defended herself with this special honor: "Why avert your eyes?" she said, "why run away? Do not look on me as a woman but as a wretched being. This sex, remember, gave birth to the Savior."[96] Can anything compare with the glory this sex won in the mother of the Lord? If he had wished, the Redeemer could well have taken his bodily form from a man, as he formed the first woman from the body of a man, but he brought the grace of his humility to the honor of the weaker sex. He also could have been born from another part of her body and a worthier part than where other men are born, that is to say, from the place where they are conceived. But to the incomparable honor of the weaker body, he consecrated the genitals of woman by his birth far more than the genitals of man by circumcision.

But to leave aside this special honor of virgins, let me write, as we proposed, of the rest of womankind.[97] Consider the grace which the coming of Christ brought to Elizabeth, who was married, or to Anna, who was a widow.[98] While her husband Zachariah remained afflicted with the muteness he incurred through his lack of faith,

---

[96] Jerome, *Vita Sancti Hilarionis* 13.

[97] It is hard to reconcile this transition with the text of the letter as it has been transmitted: the immediately preceding subject is not in fact virgins. The indication of a proposal to treat the "rest of womankind" may refer to the earlier division of women into the various "conditions" of virgin, married woman, etc., but the paragraph begins a larger section on the gift of prophecy among women, which may derive from a work originally separate in conception.

[98] For Elizabeth, see Luke 1:5 ff.; for Anna, Luke 2:25 ff.

Elizabeth felt her child leap inside her womb as soon as Mary came to greet her. Filled with the Holy Spirit, she proclaimed her prophecy about Mary's conception and so proved herself more than a prophet; for immediately she knew that the virgin had conceived and urged her then to magnify the Lord. In her the gift of prophecy was more complete than it was in John, for Elizabeth could recognize the Son of God from the time of his conception while John revealed him only after he was born. As we called Mary Magdalene the apostle of apostles, so the title prophet of prophets belongs to Elizabeth [or maybe to the widow Anna, who was treated more fully above].

And if we extend the grace of prophecy to include the pagans, we must also bring the Sibyl to the fore and have her reveal her prophesies of Christ.[99] In any comparison of prophets—including Isaiah, who, as Jerome said, was more an evangelist than a prophet[100]—woman far surpasses man in this grace as well. In his treatise against five heresies, Augustine says:

> Let us also hear what the Sybil has to say: "The Lord has offered another to be worshipped by men of faith." And: "Know that your Lord is the Son of God." Elsewhere she calls the Son of God the *symbolum*, that is, *Counsel* or the *Counselor*. And the prophet says: "They will call his name *Wonderful, Counselor*."[101]

[In Book 18 of the *City of God*, the same Father Augustine writes:

> Some say the Sibyl of Erythrae was prophesying at that time . . . though others believe it was the Sibyl of Cumae. . . . One passage contains a poem of twenty-seven lines . . . which in Latin translation runs:

> Justice will soak the earth with its standard;
> Enduring forever, the king will come,
> Sent in the flesh to judge the world at its end. . . .

---

[99] There were several Sibyls, prophetesses of great authority and fame installed at various oracular centers throughout the pagan world. In the second or third century Christians took up the practice of composing Sibylline prophecies of Christ after the fact, which were taken as genuine by some Church Fathers.

[100] See the Prologue to his *Commentarii in Isaiam Prophetam*.

[101] *Adversus Quinque Hereses*, chapter 3, no longer considered to be by Augustine.

The initial letters of the lines yield an acrostic in Greek reading, "Jesus Christ the Son of God, the Savior" . . . Lactantius also introduces a Sibylline prophecy of Christ . . . :

> He will later fall into the hands of unbelievers, who will beat him with their unclean hands and spit on him with their poisoned spittle. He will offer his back to their blows in meekness and endure their beatings in silence—no one may learn what word he speaks in hell or whence he comes—and he will be crowned with thorns. They have given him vinegar to drink and gall to eat, spreading for him their inhospitable table. You have not known your God, you ignorant nation, but have mocked him with the minds of mortal men. You have crowned him with thorns and have fed him with gall. But the veil of the temple will be rent, and at midday it will be as night for three hours, and he will fall into death for three days. But returning from hell, he will come to the light and be revealed at the beginning of his resurrection.][102]

[Unless I am mistaken, our greatest poet, Virgil, had also heard a prophecy of the Sibyl, which he then recorded in his fourth Eclogue. It foretold the miraculous birth soon to take place in the consulship of Pollio under Augustus Caesar, the birth of a child, sent to earth from heaven to take away the sins of the world and establish, as it were, a whole new age. His source, he says, was the prophecy of Cumaean song, that is, the Sibyl of Cumae, and he writes as if to call upon the world to rejoice in the birth of the child, in comparison to which all else seems low and mean:

> Now I would lift my song to a loftier plane,
> For the lowly woodland shrubs do not please all. . . .
> The final age foretold in Cumaean song
> Has come, the cycle of time begins again:
> The Virgin returns and the realm of Saturn,
> A child, new and wondrous, descends from heaven. . . .][103]

---

[102] *De Civitate Dei* 18.23 ff., citing Lactantius, *Divina Institutio* 4.18 ff. The subject of the acrostic poem is the last judgment, and Augustine includes the poem in its entirety. The manuscripts of this letter, the translator is happy to say, include only its first three lines.

[103] *Eclogues* 4.1–7, the so-called Messianic Eclogue, widely held among the Fathers of the Church to be a Christian prophecy. The section seems to be an interpolation within an interpolation, since the comments that follow it in the text refer to the earlier Sibylline prophecy cited by Lactantius.

[See each thing the Sibyl says, how completely she embraces Christian teaching about Christ. She includes his humanity and his divinity, his first and second coming, his first and second judgment—that is, the Passion in which he was unjustly judged and the majesty in which he will justly judge the world—his descent to hell and his resurrection. In this, she seems to surpass not only the prophets but the evangelists as well, who actually wrote little about the descent to hell.]

And who does not marvel at the woman of Samaria and her private conversation with the Lord?[104] The apostles themselves were amazed when he spoke to her alone, carefully instructing her, a gentile and an unbeliever, rebuking her for the number of her husbands, and even asking for something to drink, which he never asked of anyone else. The apostles come offering him food they have bought: "Rabbi, eat," they say, but he replies, "I have food to eat which you know not," and their offerings are not accepted. But he asks *her* for something to drink, while she even would decline his gracious favor:

> How dost thou, being a Jew, ask of me to drink, who am a Samaritan woman? For the Jews do not communicate with the Samaritans. . . . Thou hast nothing wherein to draw and the well is deep.[105]

I ask you then, What is this grace shown to the weaker sex, that he who has given life to all men should now seek water from this woman? Does it not plainly indicate that the weaker the virtue of women is by nature, the more it is pleasing to him, and the more astonishing their virtue, the deeper his thirst for their salvation? When he asks the woman for something to drink, he indicates that his thirst can be satisfied best by the salvation of women. "I have food to eat which you know not," he says and adds, "My food is to do the will of my Father,"[106] as if the salvation of the weaker sex is the Father's particular will. Nicodemus, ruler of the Jews, also had a private conversation with the Lord, coming in secret for instruction about salvation, but it never bore the same fruit.[107] For the spirit of prophecy filled this woman, and she proclaimed that Christ had

---

[104] See John 4:7 ff.

[105] John 4:9–11.

[106] John 4:34, in which the Vulgate reads "the will of him who sent me."

[107] See John 3:1–21.

come to the Jews and soon would come to the gentiles as well: "I
know that the Messiah cometh, who is called Christ," she said;
"therefore, when he is come, he will tell us all things." And at her
words, a crowd came from the city and believed in Christ, and he
stayed with them two days, despite his telling the disciples, "Go ye
not into the way of the gentiles, and into the city of the Samaritans
enter ye not."[108] John elsewhere says that there were gentiles who
had come to worship in Jerusalem and sent word to Christ through
Andrew and Philip that they wanted to see him.[109] He does not say,
however, that any were admitted or were granted the abundance of
Christ that this woman received, even though they sought it and she
did not. Christ's preaching to the gentiles began with her: she both
turned to the faith herself and was the means through which he
brought others to believe.[110] The Magi came to Christ as they were
guided by the star but are not said to have brought any others to
him.[111] But she ran to her city to announce his coming and won
many converts from her people, and in doing so she won herself
grace from Christ among the gentiles.

[Throughout the pages of the Old Testament and Gospel, we will find
that the greatest miracles of God's grace, the miracles of raising the dead, all
were performed especially for women, either at their request or on their
bodies. First, we read of the men Elijah and Elisha raised from death and
restored at the entreaties of their mothers. And the Lord himself also performed this miracle for women, resurrecting the son of a widowed mother,
the daughter of the ruler of the synagogue, and Lazarus at the request of his
sisters. And so, the Apostle wrote to the Hebrews, "Women received their
dead raised to life again," since on her return to life, the girl took back the
body she had, as those women took back the bodies of the dead men they
had mourned.[112] The grace the Lord has always shown to women is clear,
first, in his resurrection of them and their kinsmen and, later, in his own resurrection where he exalted women, as we said, by appearing earliest to
them. Women were found worthy because of their natural compassion
toward the Lord, amid a people who had persecuted him. While men were
leading him out to crucifixion, their women followed bewailing and

108 John 4:25; Matt. 10:5.

109 See John 12:20 ff.

110 See John 4:41.

111 See Matt. 2:12.

112 This section closely paraphrases a section in the Second Letter; see p. 66 and the
references there.

lamenting him, as Luke has said. And he turned to them in mercy and in pity, even at the moment of his Passion, and told them how to escape the destruction he foretold:

> Daughters of Jerusalem, weep not over me, but weep for yourselves and your children. For behold, the days shall come wherein they will say, "Blessed are the barren and the wombs that have not borne and the paps that have not given suck." Then they shall begin to say to the mountains, "Fall upon us," and to the hills, "Cover us." For if in the green wood they do these things, what shall be done in the dry?[113]

Matthew explains how the wife of Pilate, Christ's most unjust judge, worked faithfully for his release:

> As he was sitting in the place of judgment, his wife sent to him, saying, "Have thou nothing to do with that just man, for I have suffered many things this day in a dream because of him.[114]

And while the Lord was preaching, a woman from the crowd lifted her voice in praise of him, saying: "Blessed is the womb that bore thee and the paps that gave thee suck." Although her declaration was most true, still she was found worthy to hear his holy correction: "Yea rather, blessed are they who hear the word of God and keep it."[115]]

[Among all of Christ's apostles John alone was called beloved of the Lord, but John himself writes, "Jesus loved Martha and her sister Mary and Lazarus."[116] The same apostle who records that he alone had the privilege of being beloved of the Lord distinguished these women with the privilege he ascribes to no other apostle. If he included Lazarus in this honor, he nonetheless put the women's names before their brother's because he believed that they came first in love.][117]

---

[113] Luke 23:28–31. The manuscripts quote only through "wombs that have not borne," indicating the remainder by "etc." The preceding section closely paraphrases a section in the Fourth Letter; see p. 99.

[114] Matt. 27:19.

[115] Luke 11:27–28.

[116] John 11:5.

[117] The preceding two paragraphs are very spottily preserved in the manuscripts, only two of the surviving seven retaining them in full.

To return to women of the Christian faith,[118] we finally must speak in wonder and must wonder in our speech about the mercy God has shown even to common whores. Was anything more abject than the early life of Mary Magdalene or Mary the Egyptian?[119] But afterward God's grace raised them both in honor and in merit, the first remaining all her days in the communal life of the apostles, as I've mentioned,[120] and the second contending beyond the bounds of human virtue in the solitary struggle of the anchorites. We then can see how much in both these modes of monastic life the virtue of women excels, and how the Lord's words to unbelievers apply also to men of faith: "The harlots go before you into the kingdom of God." In the differences of sex and way of life, the last shall be first and the first last.[121]

Women embraced the words of Christ and the guidance of the apostles with such a love for chastity that, to preserve the integrity of their minds and bodies, they offered themselves to God in martyrdom and, now victorious with a double crown, sought to follow the Lamb, the Bridegroom of virgins, wherever he might go.[122] This perfection is rare in men, but we know it is common among women. There even have been some who have so longed for this privilege of the flesh that they laid violent hands upon themselves to preserve the purity they vowed to God and to come as virgins to their Virgin Bridegroom. And God so loves their devotion that he saved a throng of pagans from the fires of Mount Etna, when they sought the protection of Saint Agatha's veil.[123] Never do we hear of a monk's cowl winning grace like this. We may read of the Jordan River being divided at the touch of Elijah's cloak, allowing him and Elisha to cross over on dry ground;[124] but a virgin's veil saved a throng of unbelievers and turned them to the pathway to heaven. It also commends the dignity of holy women, that they are consecrated with the

---

[118] Implying a direct transition, perhaps, from the Sibyls and the woman of Samaria.

[119] Mary the Egyptian (possibly of fifth-century date) was a prostitute of Alexandria who, after her conversion, lived as a solitary penitent in the wilderness.

[120] It is not clear where in the letter this is.

[121] Matt. 21:31; cf. Matt. 20:16

[122] Cf. Apoc. 14:4.

[123] Agatha was said to have been martyred in 251 in Sicily. Her veil was taken several times from her tomb and carried in procession as protection against eruptions of Mt. Etna.

[124] See 4 Kings 2:8 ff.

words, "He has espoused me with his ring: I am his bride." These
are the words of Saint Agnes, and virgins of her calling are wed to
Christ in them.[125]

Now if anyone would search among the pagans for the dignity
and form of your religious life, there are many examples that can
be found and used for your encouragement. For among the
pagans, as among the Jews, there were many early forms of institutions which the Church retained but transmuted for the better.
From the Synagogue, the Church derived the clerical ranks from
doorkeeper to bishop, the use of tonsure, the fasts of Ember Days,
and the sacrifice of unleavened bread, not to mention the orna-
ments of priestly vestments and other sacraments and ceremonies
of dedication. From pagans who converted to the faith, the Church
adopted the secular ranks of kings and other rulers, some ranks of
ecclesiastical authority, many legal decrees and philosophical
teachings, as well as a scrupulous form of bodily cleanliness and
self-restraint. Hence, where once there had been flamens and arch-
flamens, bishops and archbishops now preside, and temples once
dedicated to pagan idols now are consecrated to the Lord and the
memory of saints.

The privilege of virginity, too, flourished among the pagans in
the days when the law enforced marriage among the Jews,[126] and
the purity of the flesh was so valued among them that many
women would dedicate themselves to the celibate life in their temples. Jerome, then, writes in his commentary on Paul's Letter to the
Galatians:

> What should we do, then, when Juno has her Women-of-
> One-Husband to hold against us, and Vesta has her Virgins,
> and other idols their other women of self-restraint?[127]

[What he calls "Women-of-One-Husband" and "Virgins" are our monastic
women, those who have been married and those who are virgins; for the
word "monastic," meaning "solitary," derives from *monos*, meaning

[125] The words are from the response to the seventh Lesson of the Feast of St. Agnes in
the Roman Breviary. The manuscripts preserve a second version of this paragraph,
although with a different conclusion, as the penultimate section of the letter.
[126] See Deut. 25:5.
[127] *Commentarii in Epistulam ad Galatas* 3.6.528.

"one."][128] In his first book against Jovinian, he also sets out many examples of chastity and self-restraint among pagan women, and concludes:

> I know I have made a long list of women . . . but it was to allow those women who despise the Christian faith at least to learn some chastity from the pagans.[129]

He so praised self-restraint that it seems as if the Lord particularly approved of purity of the flesh among all peoples and had exalted it even among some unbelievers by rewarding them with his gifts and manifesting miracles through their virtues:

> There is the Sibyl of Cumae, the Sibyl of Erythrae, and eight others. Varro claims that there were ten in all, each distinguished by her virginity and each rewarded for it by the power of prophecy.

And:

> To vindicate her chastity, the Vestal Virgin Claudia is said to have drawn a large vessel, which thousands of men could not move, simply with her girdle alone.[130]

[Sidonius, bishop of Clermont, writes in his preface:

> This was no Tanaquil, this was no Lucretia,
> This was no Vestal, who, against the tide of Albula,
> Could draw a vessel with her virgin's hair.[131]

Augustine, *City of God*, Book 22:

---

[128] This comment is in apparent response to an earlier manuscript corruption. The word *univiras*, "Women-of-One-Husband," had prompted the copyist's error of *univirgines* for *virgines*, "Virgins." The difficult form *univirgines*—"Single-virgins"? "Women-of-One-Virginity"?—would then demand some sort of explanation that also could apply to *univiras*.

[129] *Contra Jovinianum* 1.6.

[130] *Contra Jovinianum* 1.41.

[131] Sidonius Apollinaris, Poem 24.39–43. Tanaquil and Lucretia were heroines of early Rome; Albula was another name for the Tiber.

The claims of pagan miracles held up against our martyrs will redound to our advantage in the end. Among the great miracles of their gods is one that Varro relates about a Vestal Virgin whose chastity was falsely challenged. She is said to have drawn water from the Tiber in a sieve and carried it to her judges without losing a drop. But who was it who kept the water in the sieve . . . despite its open holes? . . . Cannot Almighty God . . . move the heaviness of an earthly body so that the quickened body may exist in whatever element the quickening spirit wishes?][132]

It is not strange at all that God should honor the chastity even of unbelievers with these miracles or allow it to be exalted through the agency of demons: it could only inspire the faithful all the more toward what they see is exalted among unbelievers. We know that the grace of prophecy was bestowed on the office, not the person, of Caiaphas,[133] and that even spurious apostles might occasionally succeed in working wonders[134]—again, through their office, not their persons. Why then should it seem strange if God should grant—not to the persons of unbelieving women but to the virtue of their self-restraint—the exculpation of an innocent virgin and the disproof of a false charge against her? The love of self-restraint is a good even among infidels, as respect for the bond of marriage is God's gift among all peoples. It is not strange if God should honor his gifts—his gifts and not the error of unbelief—through the signs he sends to unbelievers, especially when it also means that innocence will be vindicated, wickedness defeated, and all people urged to extol this good: that even unbelievers sin the less, the more they refrain from pleasures of the flesh. So, Jerome is right to conclude in his book against the heretic Jovinian that what does not surprise him in a Christian makes him blush to find among the pagans. The power enjoyed by pagan rulers—no matter if they do not use it well—their love of justice, the clemency they derive from natural law, or any of the other things that rulers ought to have—who would deny that these are gifts of God? Is a good no longer a good because it may be mixed with evil? Does not Augustine argue and does not reason agree that evils cannot exist except in a good nature?[135]

---

[132] *De Civitate Dei* 22.11.

[133] See John 11:49–52.

[134] Cf. Matt. 24:24.

[135] See, e.g., *De Civitate Dei* 12.6.

Would anyone condemn the thought of Horace—"Out of a love of virtue do the good hate sin"[136]—or the miracles of healing the blind and lame which Suetonius says Vespasian performed,[137] or what Saint Gregory reportedly did for the soul of the emperor Trajan?[138] Men can find a pearl in the mire and tell the wheat from the chaff; and God cannot be ignorant of his gifts, even when they are joined with unbelief, nor can he hate anything he has made. The more brightly they glow with his signs, the more he shows that they are his, and that what is his can never be corrupted by any depravity of men. If this is how he shows himself to unbelievers, what must he be in the hope of all believers?

The chastity women vowed in pagan temples was held in high enough esteem to have called down a terrible penalty on its violation. Juvenal writes about it in his satire against Crispinus—

> With whom a sacred Vestal recently lay,
> And soon she'll lay again, her blood still hot,
> Beneath the earth[139]

—as does Augustine in Book 3 of the *City of God:*

> The ancient Romans used to bury alive . . . any Vestal Virgin proved guilty of sexual misconduct. They punished adulterous wives, certainly, but not with death, so much more heavily did they avenge what they considered a divine sanctuary than a human bed.[140]

The care that Christian rulers devote to protecting your chastity likewise indicates the sanctity with which it is regarded. The law of the emperor Justinian provides:

---

[136] *Epistles* 1.16.52.

[137] *Vitae Caesarum*, Vespasian 7.

[138] As reported, e.g., by Paul the Deacon, *Vita Gregorii* 27, and John the Deacon, *Vitae Gregorii* 2.44, Gregory was so moved by an example of Trajan's kindness toward a widow that he prayed for the soul of the pagan emperor to be spared the pains of hell. His prayers, it seems, were answered—at least to judge from the testimony of Dante's *Paradiso* 20.44 ff.

[139] *Satires* 4.8–9.

[140] *De Civitate Dei* 3.5.

If anyone dares, I do not say to rape, but merely to make an attempt upon the holy virgins with a view toward matrimony, let him be sentenced to death.[141]

The sanction of the Church, which stresses penance and not death, is also unambiguous in the severity with which it responds to any lapses on your part. In the words of the decree of Pope Innocent, Chapter 13, addressed to Bishop Victricius of Rouen:

If those who are spiritually married to Christ and veiled by a priest either openly marry or secretly become corrupted afterwards, they shall not be admitted to a course of penance, unless the one to whom they had been joined has already departed this life.[142]

And those who have not taken the veil but have consistently asserted a wish to remain virgins will undergo a course of penance, even though they have not been veiled, because their vow to the Lord remains intact. Now, if it is the practice among men that a contract made in good faith cannot be broken for any reason, how much less can a promise made to God be broken without some penalty? And if, as the apostle Paul has said, those who have left their widowhood for a second marriage are to be condemned "because they have made void their first faith,"[143] how much more should those virgins be condemned who have not kept the faith of their earlier vow? As Pelagius says to the daughter of Mauritius:

Adultery against Christ incurs more guilt than adultery against a husband. The Roman Church, then, properly has decreed a sentence for this crime that is severe enough to judge them hardly fit for penance who have polluted with lust a body sanctified to God.[144]

If we turn now to consider the Doctors of the Church, the diligent attention and the love they have always shown devoted women, we

---

[141] *Codex Iustinianus* 1.3.5.

[142] *Epistula* 2 to Victricius, chapter 13.

[143] 1 Tim. 5:12.

[144] From the work known as *Virginitatis Laus, Praise of Virginity,* surviving under the names of various authors but not Pelagius. See Muckle 1955, 278 n. 99.

find that, like the Lord and the apostles, they embraced women's devotion with enthusiasm, continually seeking to foster and advance their religious life through various forms of teaching and encouragement. I will leave aside the rest and bring only the most important to the fore, namely, Origen, Ambrose, and Jerome. The first, the greatest Christian philosopher, embraced the religious life of women with such zeal that he even dared lay hands upon himself, as the *History of the Church* records, in order to place his teaching and encouragement of women beyond any suspicion.[145]

And who is unaware of that great harvest of books Jerome wrote for Eustochium and Paula? In a sermon he composed for them on the assumption of the mother of the Lord, he told them, "I cannot deny you anything you ask, bound as I am by your great love. I will, then, attempt to do what you request."[146] And yet we know that many of the greatest learned men, men of the highest eminence of rank and moral conduct, would write to him from the corners of the world, asking without success for some short, simple piece of writing. One of them was Saint Augustine, who in the second book of his *Retractions* says:

> I sent two books I had written to Jerome in Bethlehem—one on the origin of the soul, the other about the dictum of the apostle James, "Whoever shall keep the whole law but offend in one point is become guilty of all"—eager to consult him about them. In the first I knew I did not solve the question I posed, although in the second I put forward what seemed to me a likely solution; nonetheless, I wanted his opinion about both. He wrote back, glad that I had consulted him, but said that he had no time to reply. I held off publishing the books as long as he was alive, in the hope of eventually including his reply. I published them only after his death.[147]

Now here is a man of enormous distinction waiting for the smallest piece of writing from Jerome but never receiving it. The women, on the other hand, we know inspired book after book from him, as he sweated over his writings and transcriptions, showing them far

---

[145] Eusebius, *Historia Ecclesiae* 6.8 ff.

[146] This sermon is now attributed to Paschasius Radbertus.

[147] *Retractiones* 2.79. The internal quotation is from Jas. 2:10.

more respect in this than he ever showed Augustine. Perhaps it was that he embraced their virtue all the more because of their weak nature and could not bear to see them disappointed. At times his love toward women of this calling seemed to lead him in his praise of them a bit beyond the limits of the truth—as if he were speaking from his own experience when he wrote "Love knows no bounds."[148] He begins his *Life of Paula,* in fact, by directing the reader's attention to himself:

> If all the members of my body were turned to tongues and all its limbs could speak with a human voice, nothing I could say would yet be worthy of the virtues of this saintly and venerable woman.[149]

Jerome could recount the lives of many venerable Fathers—lives which shine with the light of miracles and far more remarkable events—but he never spoke of them with such warm praise as he spoke of the widow Paula. The beginning of his letter to Demetrias is another place where he seems to fall into excessive adulation:

> Of all things I have written from my childhood to my old age, whether I have dictated it to a scribe or wrote it out with my own hand, nothing has been more difficult than the present work. In writing to Demetrias, virgin of Christ and foremost in nobility and wealth in all the city of Rome, I should be called a flatterer if I should attempt to say everything her virtue deserves.[150]

It was the greatest pleasure for Jerome to use all the verbal art at his command in rousing a weak nature to the pursuit of virtue. But in the end it is his actions, not his words, that offer the best argument for the love he had for these women, reaching the point where his very saintliness imperiled his reputation. Writing to Asella about his false friends and detractors, he said:

> Some think I am wicked and overwhelmed with vice. . . . You, however, do well to think that even bad men are good.

---

148 *Epistulae* 46.1.

149 *Epistulae* 108.1.

150 *Epistulae* 130.1.

It is dangerous to judge another's servant and a grievous fault to speak evil of the just. . . . Some men have kissed my hand and then attacked me with a serpent's tongue. There is grief on their lips but joy in their hearts. And yet can they say that they have seen anything in me but what is proper to a Christian? My only crime is my sex, and even that is not an issue except when Paula comes to Jerusalem. . . . Before I knew the house of that saintly woman, all of Rome sang my praises and thought I was worthy of the highest priestly office. But since I began to revere the woman, to honor her and take her in my charge for the sake of her sanctity and merit, all my virtues have deserted me, it seems. . . . Still, greet Paula and Eustochium for me: whether they will it or not, they are mine in Christ.[151]

We read that even the Lord incurred suspicion for associating with Mary Magdalene: the Pharisee began to doubt him in his heart, saying, "This man, if he were a prophet, would surely know who and what manner of woman this is that toucheth him, that she is a sinner."[152] Can it then be any wonder if, inspired by Christ's example, his followers do not hesitate to risk their reputations for the sake of souls like these? Origen, as I said, risked even more.

[Not only did the charity of the Fathers leave its mark in their teaching and encouragement of women but in their consolation of women as well. At times their compassion has been so great that, in their eagerness to console, they seemed to promise things contrary to the faith. One example is the consolation Ambrose wrote for the sisters of the emperor Valentinian. There he assured them that their brother had been saved when he had died only a catechumen, and this is at variance with the truth of the Gospels and the Catholic faith.][153]

They understood how acceptable to God is the virtue of the weaker sex. Hence, many women follow the mother of the Lord in the excellence of this way of life, although only a few men have gained the grace of chastity by which they might follow the Lamb

---

[151] *Epistulae* 45.1–2 p. 39.

[152] Luke 7:39.

[153] Cf. *De Obitu Valentiani Consolatio* 5.1. An orphan paragraph and a likely later comment.

wherever he might go. There even have been women who laid violent hands upon themselves to preserve the integrity of the body they vowed to God—this is nothing we should blame in them: their martyrdom has earned them the dedication of many churches in their name. (Betrothed virgins, too—if they have decided on the monastery and have rejected their partners in favor of Christ before they have known them carnally—are allowed a freedom of action in this, a freedom which is denied to men.) And there also have been many who, inflamed with their desire for chastity, have dared to violate the law, to put on male attire and enter into monasteries, where they so surpassed the monks themselves in virtue that they were thought worthy of election as abbot. This was the case of Saint Eugenia, who, with the knowledge, even the encouragement, of her bishop Saint Helenus, put on men's clothing, received baptism from her bishop, and was taken into a monastery of monks.[154]

My dearest sister in Christ, I have, I think, written enough in response to the first of your requests. I have described the source and the foundation of your order and have praised its proper dignity in the hope that all of you can embrace your calling with greater warmth and in fuller recognition of its excellence. And now, God willing, for me to address the second, I must rely on your merit and your prayers.

Farewell.

---

[154] For this episode in the life of Eugenia, see *Vitae Patrum* 1.7–9. The paragraph contains an alternate version of material presented earlier in the letter; see p. 160. It seems to have been set at the end of the letter as if in storage, either in anticipation of an integration of the text that never occurred or out of an editorial piety that could not discard something Abelard had written.

# SEVENTH LETTER

## ABELARD TO HELOISE

Now that I have responded to one part of your request, I will turn, God willing, to the other. You and your daughters in the spirit have asked me to provide a directive for your order that would function in its way as a rule, some written instructions which, more securely than custom, would guide you on an appropriate path. Relying in part on scripture, in part on reason, and in part on the best of our traditions, I have brought these disparate elements together to allow me to adorn God's spiritual temple, which you are, with only the choicest paintings, as it were, and out of these imperfect parts to compose a single work.[1]

In this, I have followed the procedure of the ancient painter Zeuxis, who worked in a material temple as I propose to work in a spiritual one. As Cicero tells the story, the people of Croton asked Zeuxis to decorate a temple they held in high esteem with the finest paintings he could devise.[2] He approached the task with care, selecting five of the town's most beautiful women to sit beside him as he worked and model their beauty for his painting. There were several good reasons for this. Zeuxis, we know, was a master in portraying women's beauty, which by nature is more elegant and delicate than men's. But as Cicero makes it a point to explain, he chose *several* women because he did not think he could find *one* who was uniformly lovely in all her parts. Nature, he thought, had never conferred such beauty on a single woman that all her parts should have an equal share: nothing composed by nature is complete in all

---

[1] The extant rule of the Paraclete in fact disregards many of the suggestions Abelard will make, in favor of a somewhat stricter and more traditional regime. For that rule, see Waddell 1987; for some significant divergences from Abelard's proposals, see McLeod 1971, 219–24.

[2] See *De Inventione* 2.1.

respects, as if, in bestowing all her bounties in one place, nature would have none left to bestow elsewhere.

Similarly, in my depiction of the beauty of the soul and the perfection of the bride of Christ—in which, as in a mirror of one spiritual virgin, you can all see your true ugliness or beauty—I have sought to guide your religious life by drawing from different teachings of the Fathers as well as from the best monastic customs, taking up each thought as it comes to mind and gathering them all like flowers in a wreath appropriate to the sanctity of your order. I have included some instructions to monks as well as nuns, since as monastics we are united in our name and our common dedication to self-restraint, so nearly everything that has applied to monks will also be applicable to you. Selecting from all these flowers, as I said, to set off the lilies of your chastity, I then should be able to depict the bride of Christ with greater warmth than Zeuxis could depict a pagan idol. For him, five women were enough to model a share of their beauty; but I will have a far greater store in the teachings of the Fathers, and trusting in the assistance of the Lord, I have no doubt that I will leave you with a far more finished work. Through it, I hope, you will be able to attain the state of the five wise virgins whom the Lord put forward to depict the virgin of Christ.[3] But if I am to accomplish all I would like, I must ask the help of your prayers.

Now, brides of Christ, farewell in Christ.[4]

The treatise I have planned for your instruction, to detail and reinforce your religious practice and organize your worship of the Lord, is in three parts, constituting, in my judgment, the whole of monastic life, I mean, chastity, poverty, and silence. These, in turn, follow from the teaching of the Lord about girding the loins, renouncing all possessions, and refraining from idle or empty speech.[5]

About chastity, Saint Paul says, "The unmarried woman and the virgin thinketh on the things of the Lord, that she may be holy both in body and in spirit." Note that he speaks of the whole body, not

---

[3] See the parable of the wise and foolish virgins in Matt. 25:1–13.

[4] The formal close of a letter introducing the main body of the text, similar to the letters accompanying the collections of sermons and hymns Abelard composed for use at the Paraclete and the Introductory Letter to *The Questions of Heloise*.

[5] Cf. Luke 12:35, Luke 14:33, and Matt. 12:36.

one part, for she must not succumb to licentiousness of word or deed in any part whatever. She is *holy in spirit* when pride does not puff her up and when consent does not lead her mind to sin like the foolish virgins of the parable, who ran off to buy their oil and were shut outside the door: although they knocked and shouted, "Lord, Lord, open to us," they heard their Bridegroom answer, "I say to you, I know you not."[6]

And about poverty—We become like the apostles and follow naked a naked Christ[7] not simply when we renounce all our possessions and earthly attachments for his sake but when we put our will itself behind us and live, that is, not by our own lights but at the command of our superior, obeying for the sake of Christ the one who rules in place of Christ as we would Christ himself; for as he says, "He that heareth you heareth me, and he that despiseth you despiseth me." If it so happens—though I pray it never will—that our superior lives an evil life though his teachings themselves are good, still we must not reject the word of God because of the sins of man: "Whatsoever they say to you, observe and do, but according to their works do ye not." This spiritual turning from the world to God the Lord himself describes: "Every one of you that doth not renounce all that he possesseth cannot be my disciple," and "If any man come to me and hate not his father and mother and wife and children and brethren and sisters, yea and his own life also, he cannot be my disciple."[8] To hate one's father, mother, and so on, is to renounce one's earthly attachments, and to hate one's life is to renounce one's will, as he says elsewhere, "If any man will come after me, let him deny himself and take up his cross and follow me." We follow him most closely, then, when we take him for our model in his saying, "I came not to do my own will but the will of him that sent me"[9]—in other words, when obedience governs all our actions.

What else is self-denial but subordinating our own will and earthly attachments to the will of another? We carry our own cross, through which the world is crucified to us and we to the world,[10] when we forbid ourselves our earthly desires by the free profession of our calling, and so renounce our will. What else do the worldly

---

[6] 1 Cor. 7:34; Matt. 25:11–12.

[7] Cf. Jerome, *Epistulae* 125.20.

[8] Luke 10:16; Matt. 23:3; Luke 14:33 and 14:26.

[9] Luke 9:23; John 6:38.

[10] Cf. Gal. 4:14.

seek but the satisfaction of their will? What else is earthly pleasure but the fulfillment of that will, even when it involves us in great suffering and risk? And what else is it to bear the cross, to suffer some crucifixion, but to act in a way *against* the will, though it seems so easy or advantageous? As the other, lesser Jesus says in Ecclesiasticus, "Go not after thy lusts, but turn away from thy own will. If thou give to thy soul her desires, she will make thee a joy to thy enemies." But when we renounce our possessions and ourselves, then truly is our property cast aside and truly do we enter on the life of the apostles, in which all things are held in common. "The faithful had but one heart and one soul," it is written. "None said of anything he possessed that it was his own, but all things were common unto them. . . . And distribution was made to each according to his need."[11] They did not have equal need nor an equal share of things, but each received *according to his need*—one heart in faith, for belief comes from the heart, and one soul in their mutual charity, for each wanted for the other what he wanted for himself, not seeking more for himself than for another. All things were for the common good and no one sought what was his own but only what was Christ's. There was no other way they could live without property, which consists more of desires than possessions.

And, finally, about silence—An idle or unnecessary word is the same thing as excessive speech; hence, Augustine says in the first book of his *Retractions,* "I cannot call it excessive speech when what is said is needed, no matter how many words are used."[12] Solomon tells us, "In excessive speech sin shall not be wanting, but he that refraineth his lips is most wise."[13] Where *sin shall not be wanting,* we must especially beware and guard against the condition all the more when it is so dangerous and difficult to avoid. This is what Saint Benedict did, saying, "Monks should study silence at all times."[14] *Studying silence* is something more than simply *keeping silent,* for study is the pointed application of the mind to accomplish a given task. We do many things in negligence or even against our will, but we cannot *study* a thing without acting with purpose and will.

---

[11] Ecclus. 18:30–31; Acts 4:32–35.

[12] *Retractiones* 1, preface.

[13] Prov. 10:19.

[14] *Rule of St. Benedict,* chapter 42.

The apostle James, however, tells us how difficult it is to curb the tongue, but also how beneficial it will be. "We all offend in many things," he says,

> but if any man offend not in word, then he is a perfect man. . . . For every nature of beasts and birds and serpents and the rest is tamed, and hath been tamed, by the nature of man, but the tongue no man can tame. . . . The tongue is indeed a small part of the body . . . but see how small a fire can kindle a great wood. . . . It is a world of iniquity . . . , an unquiet evil, full of deadly poison.[15]

Nothing is more dangerous than poison or more to be avoided. But as poison will destroy a life, so babbling will destroy religious practice. As James says earlier, "If any man think himself to be religious, not bridling his tongue but deceiving his own heart, this man's religion is vain." And as it is written in Proverbs, "As a city that lieth open and is not compassed with walls, so is a man that cannot restrain his spirit in speech."[16]

I am reminded of the old man who once came to visit the abbot Anthony with a group of babbling monks. When Anthony asked him, "Father, have you found some good companions in these monks?" he answered, "Very good companions, I suppose, but it seems to me their barn still needs a door. Anyone can come into their stable and let loose the ass inside."[17] It is as though our soul were tethered to the manger of the Lord, feeding on holy meditations there; but it is loose to run at random in its thoughts if silence does not restrain it. Words impart understanding to the soul, but with the end of directing it toward what it understands and having it hold fast by means of thought. Thought is the means we use to speak with God, as we speak with men through words; and so long as our minds are on the words of men, they *must* be misdirected, for we cannot direct our minds to men and to God at the same time.

We must avoid not only idle words but even speech that seems to have some purpose—from the necessary to the idle, from the idle to the harmful are easy steps. "The tongue is an unquiet evil," as James

---

[15] A collage of phrases from Jas. 3:2–8, here minimally restored with other phrases from the passage to allow at least for an intelligible sequence.

[16] Jas. 1:26; Prov. 25:28.

[17] *Vitae Patrum* 5.4.1.

said,[18] smaller and subtler than other parts of the body, quicker in motion but not fatigued by use—rest, in fact, will sap its strength. And the subtler and more pliant it is because of the softness of your female bodies, the quicker it is in motion and the readier in words, the seedbed of every evil, to be sure. Because he saw this vice especially in women, Saint Paul strictly forbade them to speak in church or even to ask questions about God, except of their husbands at home: in what they were to learn and what they were to do, women were enjoined to total silence. As he wrote to Timothy, "Let the woman learn in silence with all subjection. I suffer not a woman to teach or have authority over a man, but to exist in silence."[19]

These instructions were for married women and the laity, but what, then, is appropriate for you? Paul argued—again, to Timothy—that women are talkative by nature, prone to speaking when they should not. So, if we are to find a remedy for this, we should discipline the tongue with complete silence at least at certain times and in certain places: at prayer, at meals, in the hours after compline, in the kitchen, the dormitory, the refectory, and the cloister. There, if it is necessary, you should use signs in place of words. Teach and learn these signs with special care, and when words are indispensable, use the signs to summon someone to a conversation in an appropriate place designated for the purpose. Then, after only the briefest and most necessary use of words, you should both return directly to your tasks.

Excessive use of words or signs should be disciplined severely, but the overuse of words more so, since the greater danger is there. As Saint Gregory says in Book 7 of his *Moralia:*

> If we are not careful about idle words, we soon will slip into harmful words, and there the seeds of discord are sown, quarrels arise, the flames of hatred are kindled, and all peace is extinguished in the heart. Solomon is surely right to say, "The beginning of quarrels is as when one letteth out water." For letting out water is releasing the tongue in a flood of speech. He does say, on the other hand, "Words from the mouth of a man are as deep water." But "the beginning of quarrels is as when one letteth out water" because whoever does not restrain his tongue also destroys concord.

---

[18] Jas. 3:8.
[19] 1 Tim. 2:11–12.

And so it is written, "He that putteth a fool to silence, appeaseth anger."[20]

We must then be strict in correcting this vice and prompt in punishing it, for it seriously endangers religious practice, bringing slander, strife, and calumny, and sometimes spawning the conspiracies and plots which do not so much undermine as overthrow the entire structure of religious life. Cutting off the vice may not eliminate evil thoughts completely, but it will stop them from corrupting others. In fact, the abbot Macharius thought that avoiding this one vice is almost all there is to religious practice, as the following story shows:

> In far-off Scythia, Macharius the Elder told his monks, "After Mass is said, my brothers, I want you all to withdraw from the church." "But Father," one of the monks replied, "to what place of solitude can we withdraw that is further than this wilderness around us?" The abbot put his finger on his lips and said, "*This* is what I am telling you to flee," and with that he went into his cell, closed the door, and sat down there alone.[21]

Silence will make a man perfect, as James says; Isaiah calls silence "the service of justice"; and the Fathers pursued silence with such deep passion, it is said, that the abbot Agatho "kept a stone in his mouth for three whole years until he finally learned to keep silent."[22]

A place in itself cannot bring us salvation, but the location of the monastery can facilitate religious life and aid in its reinforcement, becoming a help or a hindrance as may be. This is why the sons of the prophets, whom Jerome calls the monks of the Old Testament, retired to the wilderness and built huts for themselves on the banks of the Jordan.[23] And John and his followers, who were the founders of our calling, and Paul and Anthony and Macharius after them, and all those other flowers of the monastic way of life—this is why they fled the world with all of its temptations and brought their beds of contemplation to the quiet of the wilderness, where they

---

[20] *Moralia* 7.37. The internal quotations are from Prov. 17:14, 18:4, and 26:10.

[21] *Vitae Patrum* 5.4.27.

[22] See Jas. 3:2; Isa. 32:17; *Vitae Patrum* 5.7.

[23] *Epistulae* 125.7; see 4 Kings 6:1.

could devote themselves more wholeheartedly to God. Even the
Lord himself, who certainly feared no temptation, set us the example of leaving crowds of men behind and going off to lonely places
whenever he had a thing of great importance to do. He consecrated
the wilderness with his forty days of fasting; he refreshed the people
in the wilderness and would withdraw there to the purity of prayer,
not only from the crowds of men but even from the apostles.[24] But
he also led the apostles to a mountain to appoint them; on a mountain he was transfigured in their presence; on a mountain he
revealed to them his glorious resurrection; and from a mountain he
ascended into heaven—everything he did of great importance he
did in the lonely places of the wilderness.[25] He came to Moses and
the patriarchs in the wilderness; through the wilderness he led his
people to the promised land; for forty years he kept them in the wilderness, where he delivered his law, rained down his manna, drew
water from a rock, consoled his people, appeared to them, and
worked his miracles to show how much his Oneness loves a place of
solitude, a place where we as well can devote ourselves to him in all
the greater purity of prayer.

In the veiled speech he spoke to Job, the Lord praised the freedom of the onager, which loves the wilderness:

> Who hath sent out the onager free, and who loosed his
> bonds, to whom I have given a house in the wilderness and
> dwellings in the barren land? He scorneth the multitudes of
> the city, he heareth not the cry of the driver, he looketh
> round about the mountains of his pasture, and seeketh for
> every green thing[26]

—in other words, "Who has done this, if not I?" The onager, which
we know as the wild ass, represents the monastic who has been
*loosed from the bonds* of worldly things, has retired to the tranquil
freedom of the solitary life, and, fleeing from the world, has not
remained within the world. He lives *in the barren land* where his
body is parched and dry through abstinence. He *heareth not the cry of
the driver* but only his quieter voice when he provides his belly with
nothing more than what it needs. No driver is as constant and as

---

[24] See Matt. 4:2 and Mark 8:1 ff.
[25] See Luke 6:12; Matt. 17:1, 28:16; and Acts 1:9.
[26] Job 39:5–8.

urgent as the belly, whose cry is the demand for extravagance in food and not merely for what is needed; and to that cry he never should give ear. The *mountains of his pasture* are the lives and lofty teachings of the Fathers, which restore us by our reading and meditation. And what he calls *every green thing* are the writings of the life in heaven that will not ever fade.[27]

Saint Jerome in particular urged us to this solitary life, as he wrote to the monk Heliodorus, "You are called a monastic, but think what that word means. If you are truly *alone*, then what are you doing among the crowd of men?"[28] And he distinguished our monastic way of life from the life that clerics lead, writing to the priest Paul:

> If you want to function as a priest, if the duties of a bishop—though I should call them the burdens—appeal to you, then by all means live in the towns and cities and make the salvation of others a source of profit to your soul. But if you want to be what you say you are, a *monastic*—that is to say, *alone*—what are you doing in the city, where no man can live alone but only among the many? Every way of life has its forefathers. When it comes to the religious life, let priests and bishops follow the example of the apostles and men like them—they already have their honors: let them strive to have their merit. But *we* have forefathers of our own to follow: the Pauls, the Anthonies, the Hilarions, Macharius, and—to go back to the scriptures—Elijah and Elisha, leaders of the prophets, who lived in the fields and the wilderness and built themselves huts on the banks of the Jordan, and the sons of Rechab who lived in tents and drank no *sikera* or wine, and heard Jeremiah tell them of God's praise, that they shall never lack a man of their stock to stand before the Lord.[29]

If we too are to stand before the Lord and better attend to his worship, then we too must build our huts in the wilderness, where the

---

[27] Abelard interprets the allegory at greater length, while making similar points, in his Sermon 33 on John the Baptist.

[28] *Epistulae* 14.5.

[29] *Epistulae* 58.5. For the sons of Rechab, see Jer. 35.

society of men can never shake the bed of our repose, disturb our quiet, or distract our minds from the holiness of our calling.

When the Lord led Saint Arsenius to the tranquil freedom of this life, he gave to all of us an example in this one man:

> While he still lived in the palace, Abbot Arsenius prayed to the Lord, saying, "Lord, lead me to my salvation." And a voice came to him, saying, "Arsenius, retire from mankind and you will be saved." Then after he retired to monastic life, he prayed the prayer again, "Lord, lead me to my salvation." This time he heard a voice that said, "Arsenius, retire, keep silent, and be still: these are the roots of avoiding sin."

And so, he was instructed in the single rule of God's teaching: not only did he avoid all men but he drove them all away. One day, the archbishop came to him along with a certain judge to ask for some instruction. Arsenius said to them:

> "If I answer you, will you follow my advice?" They promised him they would, and then he told them, "Wherever you hear Arsenius may be, do not come near him." A second time the archbishop wanted to see him, but he first sent word to ask if he would be admitted. "If you come, I will admit you," Arsenius sent word back, "but if I admit you, I admit all men, and then I can no longer stay here." When the archbishop heard this, he said, "If my going means I persecute him, I will never go to see this holy man."[30]

There is also what Arsenius told a woman who came to visit him from Rome:

> "How could you have dared make this long journey? Don't you know that, as a woman, you should never leave your home? Or is it that you want to go back to Rome and tell the other women, 'I have been to see Arsenius,' and they will make the sea a women's highway leading to my door?" She said, "If it is God's will that I return to Rome, I will not allow another woman to come here. But pray for me and remember me always." Arsenius answered, "I pray that

---

[30] *Vitae Patrum* 5.2.3–4.

God will wipe your memory from my mind." Dismayed by
this reply, she went away.[31]

And when the abbot Marcus asked him why he withdrew from
men, he told him, "I love men, as God knows, but I cannot be with
them and be with God."[32]

Some of the holy Fathers went so far in their aversion to the company of men that they pretended to be mad or—strange to say—
even spread the word that they were heretics. You can read in the
*Lives of the Fathers* how Abbot Simon prepared for a visit from the
provincial judge by sitting in the doorway to his cell and nibbling
on a handful of bread and cheese, all the while keeping hidden
under a sack.[33] Or how a hermit, seeing men with lanterns on their
way to visit him, stripped off all his clothes, threw them in the river,
and stood there washing them, stark naked:

> The man who looked after him blushed at this and told the
> visitors, "Please go away, for you see our old man has lost
> his mind." Then he turned and asked the hermit, "Father,
> why have you done this? Everyone who saw you said you
> were possessed by a demon." And the old man answered,
> "That's just what I wanted to hear."[34]

Or how Abbot Moses ran off into a swamp to avoid a visit by the
provincial judge:

> The judge and his company caught up with him and asked,
> "Tell me, old man, where can I find the cell of Abbot
> Moses?" "What do you want *him* for?" Abbot Moses
> replied. "The man is crazy and a heretic."[35]

There was also Abbot Pastor, who would not see the provincial
judge even to free his sister's son from prison.[36] See how the great
men of this world seek out the presence of the saints with the

---

[31] *Vitae Patrum* 5.2.7.

[32] *Vitae Patrum* 5.17.5.

[33] *Vitae Patrum* 5.8.18.

[34] *Vitae Patrum* 7.12.7.

[35] *Vitae Patrum* 5.8.10.

[36] For the story, see *Vitae Patrum* 5.8.13.

utmost veneration and respect, and how the saints drive them away, even if it means their public shame.

Your own sex, too, has shown its virtue in this matter. Can there be adequate praise for the virgin who refused a visit from the most holy Saint Martin so that she could devote herself completely to her contemplation? As Jerome wrote to the monk Oceanus:

> Sulpicius tells us in his life of Saint Martin that he traveled to see a virgin outstanding in her chastity and moral way of life. She refused to see him but sent him a guest-gift instead and spoke to him through her window. "Pray from where you are, my father," she said, "for I have never been visited by any man." Saint Martin then gave thanks to God that here was a woman of such moral conduct who could preserve the chastity of her will. He blessed her and went away, filled with joy.[37]

She would not rise, this reverend woman, from her bed of contemplation but was prepared to say to her beloved at the door, "I have washed my feet; how shall I defile them?"[38]

Now, imagine how the bishops and other prelates of our day would respond if Arsenius or this woman treated *them* in such a way. Imagine their offense at the rebuff. The monastics in the wilderness—if there still are any left—should be ashamed to welcome the company of bishops as they do, erecting special houses to entertain them. Not only do they not avoid the so-called great men of this world who come with their huge retinues to visit, but they actually *invite* them to come, using hospitality as a pretext to set up building after building and turn the solitude they once sought into a city. Nearly all the monastic houses of our time have succumbed to this temptation of the devil: first founded to escape society, as their early fervor for religious life has cooled, they now invite society, assembling a mass of servants, men and women both, heaping up vast villages on their monastic sites, and in this way returning to the world, or I should say, attracting the world to them. Embroiled in the greatest misery, enslaved to ecclesiastical and secular powers, and living at ease on another's labor, these monks do not live *alone* at all but

---

[37] The anecdote does not in fact appear in Sulpicius' *Life of St. Martin,* and the source of the quotation has not been identified.

[38] Cant. 5:3.

have abandoned their very name as well as their own proper mode of life. The troubles of the world so press on them that, in their struggle to safeguard their followers' possessions, they often come to lose what truly is their own. And when nearby houses burn, their monasteries too go up in flames.[39]

Yet even this does not curb their ambition in the world. There are some monks who submit to no monastic restriction at all but go off by twos and threes into villages, towns, and cities, or even live by themselves outside any rule, and in this apostasy from their calling become worse than men of the world. The places where they live they abuse by calling them *obedientaries*, though they observe no rule and obey nothing but the belly and the flesh, and there they stay with their friends and kin and act as freely as they like, far even from the fear of their own conscience. In these shameless apostates sins are criminal which in other men might be forgiven. The lives of men like these—I would not have you even hear about them, much less follow their example. On the contrary, women's weakness requires isolation from the world all the more, a place where the temptations of the flesh are less severe and the senses less distracted toward bodily things. As Saint Anthony said:

> Whoever resides in the wilderness and at rest is exempt from the three great wars of hearing, speech, and sight. Only one war remains for him to fight, and that is the war of the heart.[40]

And so, the great Doctor of the Church, Jerome, recommended a dwelling in the wilderness. "The wilderness rejoices in God's presence," he told Heliodorus. "What then, my brother, are you doing in the world when you yourself are more than the world?"[41]

Now that I have spoken of the proper location of the monastery, I should also say a word about the *kind* of place it should be. As Saint Benedict advised, the monastery should be established in a place which, if possible, will allow for the inclusion in its precincts of the things most necessary to it: a garden, a source of water, a mill, a bakery

---

[39] Abelard makes a similar point in his Sermon 33 on John the Baptist.

[40] *Vitae Patrum* 5.2.2.

[41] *Epistulae* 14.10.

with an oven, and various other work places where the sisters may perform their daily tasks without the need for going about outside.[42]

As in the military camps of the world, so in the camps of the Lord—that is to say, our monastic communities—there must be certain persons who have charge of the others. In a military camp, a single individual is in overall command. Because of the size of the army and the sheer diversity of duties, however, he delegates responsibility to subordinates who look after different tasks or different troops of men. So, too, in the convent—one senior woman must preside and all the others do their work under her auspices and according to her judgment: no one must presume to oppose her in any matter or demur from any of her instructions. Without this unity of governance under a single head, no community can remain intact, not even the smallest household. [Hence, the ark of Noah, which provides the model for the Church, was many cubits in length and breadth but was finished in a single cubit.][43] Hence, it is written in Proverbs, "Because of the sins of the land, many are the princes thereof."[44] When Alexander died and his kingdom was divided, the number of ills increased in proportion to the new number of kings. And when Rome was entrusted to multiple rulers, it also lost the harmony it had. As Lucan says:

> With your three masters,
> Rome, you brought these evils on yourself:
> There is no concord in realms divided
> Among a multitude. . . .
> So long as earth supports the sea and air
> Supports the earth, so long as Titan rolls
> Across the sky and night comes after day,
> Distrust will reign when rule is shared: all power
> Detests a partner.[45]

Compare the situation that developed with the seventy followers of the abbot Saint Frontonius. So long as he remained in their monastery in his native town, he won great favor in the eyes of God and

---

[42] Cf. *Rule of St. Benedict*, chapter 66.

[43] See Gen. 6:15–16. This sentence, included in one manuscript, is most likely a later interpolation.

[44] Prov. 28:2.

[45] *Pharsalia* 1.84–93.

men, but when he brought them to the wilderness with only their portable goods, they started to complain like the people of Israel complaining to Moses that he led them to the desert away from the fleshpots of Egypt. "Is there chastity only in the wilderness," they asked him, "and none in the cities?"

> Then why don't we return to the city we left? Or will God hear prayers offered only in the wilderness? Do you think we can survive on the food of angels, or take pleasure in the company of flocks and wild beasts? Why can't we go back and bless the Lord in the place where we were born?[46]

As the apostle James once warned, "Be ye not many masters, my brethren, knowing that you receive the greater judgment."[47] And as Jerome wrote to Rusticus:

> No art is ever learned without a master. Even dumb animals and wild herds follow leaders of their own. Bees fly after their queen; cranes line up in their V-formation behind a single bird. There is but one emperor and one judge to a province. At the founding of Rome, two brothers could not act as king at one and the same time, so Rome began with an act of fratricide. Jacob and Esau battled in Rebecca's womb. Each church has a single bishop, a single archpriest, a single archdeacon; and every ecclesiastical order is subject to its ruler. One pilot to a ship, one master to a house. No matter how large the army, it looks to the standard of just one man. My aim in all of this is to tell you not to follow your own lights: live in a monastery under a single father's control but with many companions around you.[48]

For the sake of harmony and good governance, then, there must be one woman at the head of the convent, whose instructions all the others will obey. But there should be several others under her, as she herself determines, to function as magistrates, as it were, in charge of the duties she assigns them and acting as she sees fit—captains,

---

[46] Loosely paraphrased from the *Life of St. Frontonius* 2–3, contained in *Vitae Patrum* 1.
[47] Jas. 3:1.
[48] *Epistulae* 125.15.

we might call them, or lieutenants in the army of the Lord, and all the rest like knights or foot soldiers fighting against the minions of the enemy under the careful watch of these officials.

Seven women, I believe, will be needed for the management of the convent, and seven should be enough: a portress, a cellaress, a wardrober, an infirmarian, a chantress, a sacristan, and, over them all, a deaconess, who in these times is called an abbess.[49] In this camp, this army of God—for you know that it is written, "The life of man upon earth is a warfare," and "terrible as an army in array"[50]— the deaconess functions as commander, obeyed implicitly by all. The six others under her—the officials, as I called them—hold the positions of captains or lieutenants. All the others, the nuns of the cloister, duly perform their service to God after the fashion of knights. And the lay sisters—those who have renounced the world and devoted themselves to the service of the nuns, wearing a kind of religious garb but not the full monastic habit—hold the lower rank of foot soldiers.

Now, if the Lord inspires me, I will set these ranks in order, so that they may truly constitute an army in array against the assaults of the devil. I will begin with the head, the one I called a deaconess when I traced the history of this calling, and I will marshal her duties as she is to marshal the duties of the others. As I noted in my previous letter, Saint Paul required that she be proven and distinguished in her sanctity:

> Let a widow be chosen of no less than threescore years of age, who hath been the wife of one husband, having testimony for her good works, if she have brought up children, if she have received to harbor, if she have washed the saint's feet, if she have ministered to them that suffer tribulation, if she have diligently followed every good work. But the younger widows avoid. . . .[51]

He also spoke of deaconesses when he considered the life of deacons: "The women also should be chaste, not slanderers but sober

---

[49] For Abelard's objection to the titles abbess and abbot and his preference for the term deaconess, see the Sixth Letter.

[50] Job 7:1; Cant. 6:9.

[51] 1 Tim. 5:9–11.

and faithful in all things."[52] The intelligence and good sense of these requirements I have already discussed in my earlier letter, especially Paul's stipulation that she have been married and be advanced in age; so I am not a little surprised at the offensive and dangerous practice that has developed in the Church of electing virgins rather than women who have been married and of putting younger women in charge of their elders, as now is often the case. The Book of Ecclesiastes speaks against it: "Woe to thee, O land, when thy king is a child," and also the Book of Job: "In the ancient is wisdom, and in length of days prudence," the Book of Proverbs: "Old age is a crown of dignity when it is found in the ways of justice," and the Book of Ecclesiasticus:

> O how comely is judgment for a gray head, and for ancients to know counsel! O how comely is wisdom for the aged, and understanding and counsel to men of honor! Much experience is the crown of old men, and the fear of God is their glory.[53]

[Also:

> Speak, thou that art elder, for it becometh thee.

> Young man, scarcely speak in thy own cause. (*This one was needed, too.*) If thou be asked twice, let thy answer be short. In many things, be as if thou wert ignorant, and hear in silence and withal seeking. In the company of great men take not upon thee, and when ancients are present, speak not much.

In this way, the presbyters, or priests, who have charge of the people, are also understood to be "elders," showing by their titles the kind of men they ought to be. And those who recorded the lives of the holy men we now call abbots referred to them as "elders."][54]

---

[52] 1 Tim. 3:11.

[53] Eccles. 10:16; Job 12:12; Prov. 16:31; Ecclus. 25:6–8.

[54] The additional quotations, from Ecclus. 32:4 and 32:10–13, and subsequent remarks are evident interpolations in the text. The comment, *enim necesse fuit*, "This one was needed, too," is parenthetical and refers to the second quotation; McLaughlin omits it from his text of the letter. The final comment in the paragraph, "And those who recorded the lives of the holy men . . . ," takes notice of the fact that four books of the *Vitae Patrum* are known as the *Verba Seniorum*, "Sayings of the Elders."

Every care must be taken, then, to see that Paul's counsel is followed in the election and consecration of the deaconess. Her life and doctrine should justify the charge she will have over others, her age should guarantee the ripeness of her character, and her own obedience should have earned her the right to govern. She should have learned the rule through daily practice, not merely by hearing it read. If she is not trained in letters, she should know how to apply herself, not to the logical wrangles of the philosophical schools, but to the doctrine of life as manifested in her deeds. It is written of the Lord, "He began to do and to teach,"[55] by which we understand that *doing* is prior to *teaching*, since teaching is more perfect through action than through speech, better through the deed than through the word. What Abbot Ipitius said will help confirm this: "He is truly wise who teaches others by his deed, not by his words."[56] And there is also the argument of Saint Anthony, by which he confounded all the windy philosophers who laughed at his teaching as the teaching of a fool and a man untrained in letters:

> "Now, answer me this," he said, "which comes first, sense or letters? Which is the beginning of the other? Does sense arise from letters or do letters arise from sense?" When they replied that sense was both the source and the foundation of letters, he went on, "So, whoever is whole in sense will not need letters. Then let him hear the word of the Apostle and be strengthened in the Lord: 'Hath not God made foolish the wisdom of this world?' and 'But the foolish things of the world hath God chosen, that he may confound the wise; and the weak things of the world hath God chosen, that he may confound the strong. And the base things of the world and the contemptible hath God chosen, and things that are not, that he might bring to naught things that are, that no flesh should glory in his sight.' For the kingdom of God, as he afterwards said, is not in speech but in virtue."[57]

But if she needs to turn to scripture for fuller knowledge of any point, she should not be ashamed to ask the educated and take

---

[55] Acts 1:1.

[56] *Vitae Patrum* 5.10.75.

[57] Athanasius, *Life of Anthony*, in *Vitae Patrum* 1.45. The internal quotations are from 1 Cor. 1:20, 27–29.

instruction from them. She should never reject an education in let-ters but rather should accept it diligently, as even Peter took correc-tion from his fellow apostle Paul, for as Saint Benedict remarked, "The Lord often reveals to the lesser man what is better."[58]

The better to fulfill the Lord's command which Saint Paul noted above, we should never elect a deaconess from a noble or powerful family, except when there is the most pressing need and the clearest possible reason. With their easy confidence in their origins, people of this sort become too proud or too boastful or presumptuous in their conduct. Especially if they are native to the area, their prelacy may be harmful to a convent: the proximity of their relations may make them much more proud, their frequent visits may disrupt or burden the convent, and this familiarity may breed contempt for religious life and the prelates themselves, according to what the Lord has said: "A prophet is not without honor, save in his own country."[59] Saint Jerome raised these and similar problems when he listed for Heliodorus the difficulties facing monks who remain in their own country. "In sum," he concluded, "a monk in his own country cannot be perfect, and not to wish to be perfect is a sin."[60]

Think what a great loss of souls it would be if the woman who has charge of the teaching of religion should fall short in her own religious life. If she shows her virtues individually to each of her individual subordinates, that certainly is enough; but in her *all* vir-tues ought to shine, so that all those things she teaches to the others she may evince herself through her example. She must not undo in conduct what she teaches or destroy in deeds what she builds in words; she must not let the word of rebuke be taken from her mouth by her shame to correct in others what she herself is known to do. It was the Psalmist's prayer that this never happen to him. "Take not the word of truth utterly from my mouth," he said, for he knew it was the harshest of God's punishments: "But to the sinner God hath said, 'Why dost thou declare my justices and take my covenant in thy mouth, seeing thou hadst hatest discipline and hast cast my words behind thee?'" And Saint Paul said, "But I chastise my body and bring it into subjection, lest perhaps, when I have preached to others, I myself should become cast out." Whoever's life has been despised will see his preaching and his doctrine both condemned.

---

[58] *Rule of St. Benedict*, chapter 3, and see Gal. 2:11 ff.

[59] Matt. 13:57.

[60] *Epistulae* 14.7.

When someone ought to heal another of a sickness he himself is suffering from, the sick man then will charge him properly, "Physician, heal thyself."[61]

Whoever has high position in the Church must always be aware of the ruin his fall will cause if he himself ever comes to the brink and brings his followers with him. "He that shall break the least of these commandments and so teach men, shall be called the least in the kingdom of heaven."[62] To break a commandment is to act against it, and if someone corrupts others by example, he becomes an instructor of evil. But if that makes him *least in the kingdom of heaven*—that is to say, in the Church on earth—then what should we call that contemptible prelate whose carelessness has led the Lord to seek not his blood only but the blood of all souls under him? The Book of Wisdom rightly curses such a man:

> For power is given to you by the Lord, and strength by the Most High, who will examine your works and search out your thoughts because, being ministers of his kingdom, you have not judged rightly, nor kept the law of justice, nor walked according to the will of God. Horribly and speedily will he appear to you, for a most severe judgment shall be for them that bear rule. For to him that is little, mercy is granted, but the mighty shall be mightily tormented. . . . and a greater punishment is ready for the more mighty.[63]

It is enough for a subordinate to see to his own sins, but for superiors, there is death in the sins of others as well. When gifts increase, the reasons for those gifts also increase, and to whom more is given, of him more is demanded. And so the Book of Proverbs warns against this danger:

> My son, if thou be surety for thy friend, thou hadst engaged fast thy hand to a stranger. Thou art ensnared with the words of thy mouth, and caught with thy own words. Do therefore, my son, what I say, and deliver thyself because thou art fallen into the hand of thy neighbor. Run about,

---

61 Ps. 118:43, 49:16–17; 1 Cor. 9:27; Luke 4:23.

62 Matt. 5:19.

63 Wis. 6:4–9.

make haste, stir up thy friend. Give not sleep to thy eyes, neither let thy eyelids slumber.[64]

We become *surety for a friend* whenever our charitable love receives someone into the life of our community; we extend to him our supervisory care, as he extends to us his obedience. And we *engage fast our hands* when, by becoming surety for him, we commit ourselves to working for his benefit. But we also are *fallen into his hands* because, unless we guard against him, we will find him to be the destroyer of our souls. And so, the words *run about, make haste,* and so on, provide advice against the danger.

So let her now run all about her camp, first here, then there, like a watchful and untiring commander, checking to see if, through someone's negligence, a way has been left open for the adversary, who "goeth about as a roaring lion seeking someone he may devour."[65] She should be first to see all the evils of her house and correct them before anyone can follow their example. She must always beware of the charge Saint Jerome laid at the door of the negligent and foolish: "We are the last to learn the evils of our own house or the faults of our wives and children, and the first to turn a deaf ear to what all the neighbors are saying."[66]

The woman who presides in the convent must recognize that she has become the guardian of both bodies and souls. About the guardianship of bodies the Book of Ecclesiasticus says:

Hast thou daughters? Have a care of their body and do not show thy countenance light-hearted toward them. . . . The father waketh for his daughter . . . and the care for her taketh away his sleep . . . lest she should be corrupted.[67]

But bodies are corrupted not only by fornication but by doing anything unseemly with them—I mean with any part, including the tongue—or by misusing our senses for any vanity. "Death comes through our windows," it is written, meaning that sin comes to the soul through our five senses.[68]

---

64 Prov. 6:1–4.

65 1 Pet. 5:8.

66 *Epistulae* 147.10.

67 Ecclus. 7:26 and 42:9–10.

68 Cf. Jer. 9:21.

No death, though, is more fearful than the death of souls, and no guardianship is more fraught with risk. The Lord said, "Fear ye not them that kill the body and have no more that they can do to the soul."[69] But will anyone hear these words and still not fear the body's death more than the soul's? Who is less afraid of a sword than a lie? And yet it is written, "The mouth that belieth killeth the soul."[70] What can be killed more easily than the soul? What arrow can be fashioned more quickly than a sin? Who can guard himself against a thought? Who is strong enough to guard against his own sins, much less another's? What fleshly shepherd can protect his spiritual flock against wolves of the spirit, guarding what cannot be seen against what cannot be seen? Who would not fear a predator who never ceases from his prowl, whom no wall will keep out and no sword slay? His snares are always set and, above all, for men and women of the religious life. "His portion is made fat and his meat dainty," the prophet Habakkuk said, and the apostle Peter: "Your adversary the devil goeth about as a roaring lion seeking someone he may devour." The Lord told Job about the adversary's great presumption in devouring us: "He will drink up a river and not wonder, and he trusteth that the Jordan may run into his mouth."[71] For what would he then *not* presume to do, when he also dared to tempt the Lord himself, when he lured our first forefathers from paradise, and when he snatched away from the company of apostles an apostle whom the Lord himself had chosen? What place is ever safe from him? What cloister can he not penetrate? Who can guard against his snares? Who can resist his strength? For he is the wind that shook the corners of Job's house and at one blast crushed his innocent sons and daughters.[72]

Then what can the weaker sex do to stand against him? No one should fear his seduction more than a woman, since it was a woman he first seduced and through her ensnared her husband and descendants: the desire for a greater good robbed woman of a lesser. And now by this same artfulness, he will easily seduce a woman who, in her love for wealth or honor, is more attracted by supremacy than service. But which it was that first attracted her, the aftermath will prove. If she lives in greater luxury as a superior than she had as a

---

[69] An amalgam of Matt. 10:28 and Luke 12:4.

[70] Wis. 1:11.

[71] Hab. 1:16; 1 Pet. 5:8; Job 40:18.

[72] See Job 1:19.

subordinate, or if she claims something special for herself beyond her needs, then doubtless this was always her desire. If she seems more interested in costly adornments after her election than before, then plainly she is puffed up with vainglory. Whatever she had been before will later be revealed, and whether it was her virtue or only a charade that led to her election, her conduct in her office will show.

She should be forced to her position and not come to it on her own, for the Lord said, "All who have come are thieves and robbers,"[73] and Jerome observed, "Note *who have come,* not *who were sent.*"[74] That is, she should be taken for the honor and not take it to herself, according to the words of Paul: "Neither doth any man take the honor to himself but he that is called by God, as Aaron was."[75] If called, she should lament, as if being led to death; if rejected, she should exult, as if reprieved. If we hear it said that we are better than the others, we modestly blush at the words; but if these words are proven true by the fact of our election, we carry on without any shame at all. Most certainly, the better should be chosen over others—hence, Saint Gregory says in Book 24 of his *Moralia:*

> No one ought to undertake the leadership of others who is not in a position to correct them. Nor should someone who is elected to correct the faults of others do himself what ought to be rooted out[76]

—but if to avoid this shamelessness we only voice some weak refusal, we open ourselves to the charge of merely wanting to appear more righteous and deserving.

How many have we seen at their election, tears in their eyes and laughter in their hearts, proclaiming their unworthiness but currying men's favor all the more. They take note of the words, "The just is first accuser of himself,"[77] but afterward, when it comes their turn to be accused and they have the chance to retire from the field, with what supreme, tenacious impudence do they assert their claims to those same honors which, with false tears but with truthful accusations of themselves, they originally said they were unwilling to

---

[73] John 10:8.

[74] *Dialogus Contra Pelagianos* 2.17.

[75] Heb. 5:4.

[76] *Moralia* 24.25.

[77] Prov. 18:17.

accept. Think of all the canons we have seen in our churches who resist their bishops' call to take holy orders, avowing their unworthiness for such a sacred office, entirely unwilling to accept. But if a little later those same canons should be chosen for a *bishopric* by some chance, how weak will their refusal appear then—if in fact we hear a refusal at all. Those who only yesterday protested that the danger to their soul must force them to decline a deaconship, become reconciled to the higher office overnight and now no longer fear the precipice. About such men the Book of Proverbs says, "A fool will clap his hands when he is surety for his friend."[78] For only a wretch will exult at what ought to make him lament, when, coming to the governance of others, he is bound by his calling to the care of his subordinates, by whom he should be loved rather than feared.

We must guard against this evil as securely as we can. Therefore, we strictly forbid the superior to live in greater comfort than her subordinates. She should not have private rooms for sleeping or eating, but should do everything alongside her flock: the more she is with them, the better she can look after them. I know that Saint Benedict had assigned a separate table for the abbot to dine with pilgrims and guests.[79] Although he acted out of a pious concern for the monastery's visitors, a more recent and sensible practice has developed in some monasteries by which the abbot does not separate himself from the community at large, but rather delegates the care of pilgrims to some other responsible person. Yes, it *is* easy to sin at table and discipline should be enforced especially during meals, but there are additional reasons for it. Many people use hospitality as an opportunity to cater to themselves more than their guests, and it is chiefly from a suspicion of this that those who are not present feel offended and complain. The authority of the superior is weakest when his life is not open to his followers, and further, any privation becomes easier to bear when it is shared equally by all, including— and especially—the superior. This we learn from the example of Cato, who, as Lucan tells it, would not accept the water offered to him "when the people in his ranks were thirsty," and so "the stream became enough for them all."[80]

---

[78] Prov. 17:18.

[79] *Rule of St. Benedict,* chapters 53 and 56. Abelard here begins to address one of Heloise's specific concerns from the Fifth Letter; see p. 107.

[80] Lucan, *Pharsalia* 9.498 ff.

Since sobriety is necessary for all prelates, they must live frugally to allow provision for the rest. They must not turn their office, a gift conferred by God, into a source of pride, nor ever lord it over their subordinates. Instead, they must attend to what is written: "Be not as a lion in thy house, terrifying them of thy household and oppressing them that are under thee." "Pride is hateful before God and men." The beginning of pride is man's turning from God, as the beginning of sin is pride, for then his heart withdraws from his Creator. "The Lord hath overturned the thrones of proud princes and hath set up the meek in their stead." "Have they made thee ruler? Be not lifted up. Be among them as one of them." And as Saint Paul instructed Timothy about his subordinates, "Rebuke not an ancient man but entreat him as a father, young men as brothers, old women as mothers, young women as sisters." And the Lord said, "You have not chosen me, but I have chosen and appointed you that you should go and bring forth fruit."[81] All other prelates are chosen by their subordinates, created and constituted by them for service, not for lordship. The Lord alone is truly Lord and chose his own subordinates for his service; yet he showed himself as servant, not as lord, and by his own example corrected those of his followers who aspired to high honors, saying:

> The kings of the gentiles lord it over them and they that have power over them are called beneficent. But you are not so. He that is the greater among you should become as the lesser, and he that is the leader as he that serveth.[82]

Someone follows the way of the kings of the gentiles, then, if he strives for lordship and not service among his subordinates, if he seeks to be feared more than loved, and if, swollen with the authority of his office, he loves "the first places at feasts and the first chairs in the synagogues, and greetings in the market place and to be called Rabbi by men." We should not glory in that title or in any titles at all but should look to humility in all things, as the Lord said, "But be not you called Rabbi . . . and call none your father upon

---

[81] Ecclus. 4:35, 10:7, 10:17, 32:1; 1 Tim. 5:1–2; and John 15:16 (the manuscripts include only the first phrase, adding "etc.").

[82] Luke 22:25–26. The manuscripts include the passage only through the words "But you are not so," indicating the rest by "etc."

earth." And then, forbidding all boasting, he continued, "Whoever shall exalt himself shall be humbled."[83]

We must also insure that the absence of the shepherds does not endanger the flock, letting discipline grow slack when they are away. I have resolved, therefore, that the deaconess, with her attention more on spiritual than on worldly things, is not to leave the convent for any business outside its walls. Her constant presence among her women will demonstrate her greater care, and her appearance in the world will be as honored as it is rare, as is written, "If thou be invited by one that is mightier, withdraw thyself, for so he will invite thee the more."[84] If the convent requires any mission sent abroad, it should be monks or lay brothers who undertake it. Men always must see to the needs of women, and the greater women's religious life becomes and the more they devote themselves to God, the more they will need the protection of men. Hence, the angel told Joseph to watch over the mother of the Lord, though he was not permitted to lie with her, and the Lord at his death found for his mother a second son, as it were, to care for her in worldly things.[85] The apostles, too, arranged for the care of holy women and appointed the seven deacons to serve them, as I have already discussed at length.[86] So, following their authority and aware of the real necessity, I have determined that in matters which concern the outside world the needs of women's convents should lay in the hands of monks and lay brothers, after the manner of the apostles and first deacons. Monks will be needed chiefly for the Mass, lay brothers for their physical labor.

It is therefore necessary—as was the practice under Mark in Alexandria at the very beginnings of the Church—that women's convents be located near monasteries of men, and that all their business outside the walls be conducted through men who share the religious life. It is also my belief that women's convents adhere more securely to the tenets of their practice if they are guided by the wisdom of spiritual men and if a single shepherd watches over rams and ewes alike, that is to say, if the man presiding over the men also presides over the women. For always, as Paul says, "Let

---

[83] Matt. 23:6–7, 8–9, and 12.

[84] Ecclus. 13:12. Cf. also Abelard's comments on Heloise in the *Calamities*, p. 136 ff.

[85] See Matt. 1:20 and John 19:26.

[86] See Acts 6:5 and the Sixth Letter.

the head of every woman be the man, as the head of every man is Christ and the head of Christ is God."[87] It was for this reason that the convent of Saint Scholastica, which had been built on land belonging to a monastery of monks, was also guided by a monk and received his frequent visits, or his brothers', for its consolation and instruction.[88]

The Rule of Saint Basil endorses the wisdom of this system:

> *Question:* Should the presiding monk ever speak with the nuns to offer them instruction except in the presence of the woman who directs the sisters?
>
> *Answer:* How then will we follow Saint Paul's command, "Let all things be done decently and according to order"?

And in the next chapter:

> *Question:* Should the presiding monk often speak with the woman who directs the sisters if it offends some of the brothers?
>
> *Answer:* As Saint Paul says, "Why is my liberty judged by another man's conscience?" But it is also good to follow him when he says, "I have not used my power . . . lest I should hinder the gospel of Christ." He should see the women, then, as little as possible and all their conversations must be brief.[89]

There is also the decree of the Council of Seville:

> It is decided by our common consent that women's convents in the province of Baetica be guided by the supervisory ministry of monks. It is only to the good of these devoted women if we choose spiritual fathers to protect and

---

[87] 1 Cor. 11:3.

[88] St. Scholastica was the sister, and by tradition the twin, of St. Benedict. They were buried in the same grave, as Heloise and Abelard also were to be.

[89] Basil was a fourth-century bishop of Caesarea in Cappodocia, a leading light in eastern monasticism, and a Doctor of the Church. Abelard cites his "Greater Rule," not in the original Greek, but in the Latin translation of Rufinus; see Rufinus, *Regula Fusius Tractata,* 197 and 199. The internal quotations are from 1 Cor. 14:40, 10:29, and 9:12.

instruct them. Yet we caution the monks to keep far from
the women's quarters, not coming even so close as the
entryway. Neither the abbot nor any man set in authority
shall speak with the nuns to instruct them in morals, except
in the presence of the woman who directs the sisters, nor
should he often speak with her alone, but only in the presence of two or three sisters. Their visits should be infrequent
and their conversations brief. Far be it from us to wish that
the monks become familiar with the virgins of Christ—it is
improper even to speak of it—but the men must be kept
separate and apart, in accord with our canons and our rule.
We entrust the women only to their guidance, calling for the
selection of a single man, the most tested of the monks, to
have charge over the management of their town or country
properties, the construction of their buildings, and the provision of anything else the convent may require. This will
free the handmaids of Christ to live for the worship of God
alone and see to their own tasks, concerned only for what
will benefit their souls. The man chosen for this office by the
abbot will of course be subject to the approval of the bishop.
For their part, the nuns will make clothing for the monks
who look over them, receiving in exchange both their support and the fruits of their labor, as we said.[90]

Accordingly, I would have it that convents of women always be
subject to monasteries of men, that brothers see to the care of their
sisters, and that a single man preside as father over both communities. Both should look to his judgment, making "one fold and one
shepherd" in the Lord.[91] Indeed, such a spiritual family will be
more pleasing to God and men when it can more fully accommodate anyone of either sex who would enter religious life, that is,
when monks take in the men and nuns take in the women and the
whole provides for every soul who is looking toward salvation. If a
man with a wife or a mother, a daughter or a sister, or any other
woman in his charge wishes to turn to the religious life, he can find
full comfort there; and charitable love would bind the two communities more closely to each other if their members are united by family connections as well.

---

[90] Canon 11 of the second Council of Seville, convened in 619.
[91] John 10:16.

The one they call the abbot should preside over the nuns in recognition that they are brides of Christ, who is his lord, and that each of them, as such, is now his lady.[92] He should exult in his service to them, not in his supremacy, acting as a steward in the house of the king, a steward who does not bend his lady to his command but is always attentive to her interests, who obeys her at once in what is necessary but declines in what may do her harm, and who sees to all external matters in such a way that he never need enter her chamber unless ordered. This is how the servant of Christ should see to the brides of Christ, attending them faithfully for the sake of Christ. All important matters he should discuss with the deaconess and, without consulting her, should not decide anything about the nuns or their affairs; nor should he presume to instruct them or speak to them except through her. Whenever the deaconess summons him, he should come without delay, and whatever she advises him about her or her charges' needs, he should carry out as quickly as he can. And when the deaconess summons him, he should not speak with her except in the open and in the presence of other responsible persons. He should never draw too close to her or engage her in long conversations.

The sisters will collect all food and clothing and any money there may be and set it aside; whatever they have in excess they will make over to the brothers as needed. The brothers, then, will supply all outside goods, and the sisters only do what is fit for women to do within the confines of the walls, for example, sewing and washing their own and the brothers' clothes, and kneading, baking, and handling bread. They will also take charge of the cows and the poultry and whatever else that women can do more easily and suitably than men.

When the man takes up his appointment as superior, he will swear in the presence of the sisters and the bishop that he will be a faithful steward in the Lord and will scrupulously preserve them from any carnal contact. If he is ever found negligent—and I pray he never is—he should immediately be deposed for perjury. Likewise, all the monks, when they make their vows, must bind themselves to the sisters by this sacrament that they will never allow them to be wronged and will protect their chastity with all their power. No man will approach the sisters without permission of the superior; nothing will be sent to them without going through the superior. No

---

[92] Cf. the Fourth Letter, p. 86.

sister will leave the precincts of the convent, but rather, as I said, the brothers will supply all outside goods as is only fitting, the hard sex sweating in its hard work. No brother will ever enter the convent grounds without permission of the superior *and* the deaconess, and then only for a virtuous and compelling reason. If anyone dares act in any way against this rule, he will summarily be expelled from the monastery.

To insure that the men with their greater strength do not wrong the women in any way, I have resolved that they, too, should be subject to the deaconess and carry out her will in every matter. *All* members of these communities, the men and women alike, will make their profession to her and vow her their obedience. Peace will be more lasting and concord better preserved if the strong are set strict limits, while, on the other hand, the stronger sex will not feel wronged by its obedience to the weaker as it has no reason to fear the weaker's violence. The more a man is humbled before God, the more he is sure to be exalted.

I think I have said enough about the deaconess for the moment. I will turn, then, to the other officials.

The sacristan, or treasurer, will look after the oratory and everything connected with the place of prayer. She will keep all its keys and safeguard its necessary items, and if there are any offerings, she will receive them. She will have charge over the manufacture and repair of items needed in the oratory and over all of its furnishings. It is also her responsibility to look after the hosts, the vessels and books of the altar and all of its furnishings, the relics, the incense, the lights, the clock, and the striking of bells. The nuns will prepare the hosts, if it is feasible, purify the flour from which they are made, and also wash the altar-cloths. But neither they nor the sacristan herself must ever touch the relics or the vessels of the altar or even the altar-cloths, unless they are brought to them to wash. For this they will rely on the monks and lay brothers. When it becomes necessary, certain worthy men will be appointed to act under the sacristan's supervision, and they will be the ones to remove the items from the chests, which she will have unlocked, and return them to their place again. The woman who presides over the sanctuary should be outstanding in the purity of her life, whole both in body and in mind, if possible, and proven in austerity and self-restraint. She also should be trained in lunar calculation, so that she may look after the oratory according to the order of the seasons.

The chantress will look after the choir, set the order of worship, and have charge over the teaching of reading and singing in the convent and everything connected to writing. She also will have custody of the convent's books, taking them to and from their storage, and either arrange for their copying and decoration or undertake it herself. She will organize and assign the seats in choir, allocate the spoken or sung parts, and make the list of weekly duties to be read each Saturday in chapter. She should, therefore, be well trained in letters and especially knowledgeable in music. She also will see to all the education in the convent, after the deaconess; if she happens to be busy with other matters, she will act as her deputy in this.[93]

The infirmarian will tend the sick, keeping them from both bodily privation and sin. Whatever their illness demands in the way of food, baths, or anything else, should be allowed them, for as the saying goes, "The law was not made for the sick." Meat, too, should be permitted them, except on Fridays and the chief vigils or during the fasts of Ember Days and Lent. But they also should be cautioned against sin all the more since illness is a time for them to be thinking about death, a time for silence and insistent prayer, as it is written, "My son, neglect not thyself in thy sickness, but pray to the Lord and he shall heal thee. Turn away from sin and order thy hands aright, and cleanse thy heart from all offense."[94] There must always be an attendant for the sick, someone who can rush to their aid if the need arises, and the house should be equipped with everything necessary for their illness, including a supply of medicines so far as the convent's resources will allow. This, of course, is more easily done if the infirmarian has some medical knowledge. Her charge also extends to the women who are issuing blood. It is important as well that she be skilled in bloodletting, so that no man will have to come among the women for that purpose. There should also be provision for the sick to celebrate the Offices of the Hours and take communion on Sundays at the least, but always after their confession and whatever atonement they are able to make. About the anointing of

---

[93] In the single manuscript that preserves this section, the word *infirmaria* is added at the end of the sentence, apparently anticipating the paragraph to come. McLaughlin, however, includes it as part of the text, according to which reading, then, the infirmarian would act as deputy of the chantress in matters of convent discipline.

[94] Ecclus. 38:9–10.

the sick, the words of the apostle James should be strictly observed, especially when the patient is beyond hope of recovery.[95] For this, two of the elder priests and a deacon from the monastery should be admitted to the convent, bringing the consecrated oil with them, and they should administer the sacrament with the sisters in attendance, separated from them, however, by a partition wall. When the need arises, a similar procedure should be followed with communion. The infirmary, therefore, must be so arranged that the monks can easily come in and go out without seeing the nuns or being seen by them.

At least once each day, the deaconess and cellaress will visit the sick woman as if she were Christ himself to look after her physical and spiritual needs, and so they may deserve to hear the Lord say, "I was sick and you came to me."[96] If the woman is near the end and has come to her death struggle, one of the attendants will run to the convent as quickly as she can, beating on a board to proclaim her sister's departure. The whole convent then must rush to the dying woman's side, no matter the hour of the day or night, unless the Offices of the Church prevent it. Since "nothing must be set before the work of God,"[97] it is enough in this circumstance that the deaconess go herself with a few chosen women and that the convent as a whole follow later. But whoever comes running at the beating of the board should at once begin the litany down through the invocation of the male and female saints and then continue with the psalms or other texts appropriate to a death. As the Book of Ecclesiastes tells us:

> It is better to go to the house of mourning than to the house of feasting, for in that we are put in mind of the end of all, and the living thinketh what is to come. . . . The heart of the wise is where there is mourning, and the heart of fools where there is mirth.[98]

The nuns then will wash their dead sister's body, clothe it in sandals and a clean but common garment, and place it on a bier, wrapping

---

[95] See Jas. 5:14: "Is any man sick among you? Let him bring in the priests of the church, and let them pray over him, anointing him with oil in the name of the Lord."

[96] Matt. 25:36.

[97] *Rule of St. Benedict*, chapter 43.

[98] Eccles. 7:3–5.

her head in her veil. They will stitch or tie the clothes tightly to the body and not move them afterward. And they will carry the body to the church for the monks to bury at the proper time, during which they themselves, retired to the oratory, will chant the psalms or meditate in prayer. The burial of a deaconess will have only one distinction: her body will be wrapped in a shroud and the whole stitched together, as if in a sack.

The wardrober will look after everything concerning clothing, including shoes as well as everything else. She will arrange for the shearing of the sheep and will receive the leather for making sandals. She will spin the flax and wool, collect it, and see to all the weaving, and she will provide the others with their scissors, needles, and thread. She also will have charge of the dormitory and will see to all the beds. The table coverings, hand cloths, and every other article of cloth along with their cutting, sewing, and washing—all this is her responsibility, and to her in particular these words apply:

> She hath sought wool and flax and hath wrought by the counsel of her hands. . . . She hath put out her hand to the distaff and her fingers have taken hold of the spindle. . . . She shall not fear for her house in the cold of snow, for all her domestics are clothed with double garments . . . and she shall laugh in the latter day. . . . She hath looked well to the paths of her house and hath not eaten her bread idle. Her children rose up and called her blessed.[99]

She will keep the implements needed for her tasks and assign the sisters their own share of the work, since she also will have charge over the novices until they are received into the community.

The cellaress will oversee everything having to do with food: the cellar, the refectory, the kitchen, the mill, the bakery and oven, the gardens, the orchards, the beehives, the cows, the sheep, and the poultry—whatever is needed in the way of foodstuff will be her responsibility. It is especially important, then, that she be generous in nature, ready and willing to furnish what is needed, "for God loveth a cheerful giver."[100] She is strictly forbidden to favor herself

---

[99] Prov. 31:13–28.
[100] 2 Cor. 9:7.

over others in carrying out her duty, to prepare food for herself alone, or to keep something for herself and so cheat the others. "The best steward," says Jerome, "keeps nothing for himself,"[101] unlike Judas, who abused his stewardship of the purse and was lost to the company of the apostles, or Ananias and his wife Saphira, who received the sentence of death for holding back part of the price of the land.[102]

The portress, or gatekeeper, will have the responsibility of receiving guests and anyone else who comes to the convent, announcing them, bringing them to the appropriate place, and taking general charge over hospitality. She should be discreet in mind and years, know how to receive and to give a message, and be able to determine whom to admit, whom to turn away, and the manner appropriate for each. Since acquaintance with the convent begins with her, she must be an adornment to its religious life, as if she herself were the vestibule of the Lord. She therefore should be soft in speech and mild in address, eager to increase the good will even of those she turns away by giving them a suitable reason—as it is written, "A mild answer breaketh wrath, but a harsh word stirreth up fury," and "A sweet word multiplieth friends and appeaseth enemies."[103] Because she will be the one to see the poor most often and come to know them best, she also should distribute whatever food or clothing there is to distribute. If she or any other official needs assistance or relief, the deaconess will appoint deputies for her, choosing them mainly from the lay sisters, so that none of the nuns need ever be absent from divine worship or from the refectory or chapter.

The portress will have a small lodge by the gate, where either she or her assistant will always be on hand to meet people as they arrive. But that is not a place for them to be idle or forget their study of silence, especially since it is that much easier for outsiders to overhear their talking from there. It is her responsibility, in fact, to keep the convent closed not only to unsuitable visitors but also to gossip of any kind—none must come inside without control, and for any lapse in this the portress should be held accountable; if she does hear some important news, however, she should bring it to the deaconess in private for her to act on as she herself sees fit. When someone

---

[101] *Epistulae* 52.16.

[102] See John 13:29 and Acts 5:1–10.

[103] Prov. 15:1 and Ecclus. 6:5.

knocks or calls out at the gate, the woman stationed there will ask who it is and what they want and, if it is appropriate, open the gate immediately and take them in. Only women may be received as guests in the convent; men should be directed to the monks. No man will be admitted for any reason without the prior consultation and order of the deaconess, but women will have entry at once. The portress then will have the women—or any men who have occasion to enter—wait in her lodge until the deaconess can come to greet them, or some other sisters if it is necessary or more convenient. If the visiting women are poor and require washing of their feet, the deaconess herself or some of the sisters should perform this act of hospitality. The Lord himself was called a deacon for performing this service for the apostles, as is mentioned in the *Lives of the Fathers:* "On your account, O man, . . . did the Savior become a deacon, gird himself with a linen towel, and wash his disciples' feet, and in this way teach them to wash their brothers' feet."[104] For this reason, Saint Paul required that the deaconess "have offered hospitality and have washed the saints' feet." And the Lord himself said, "I was a stranger and you took me in."[105]

All of these officials, except for the chantress, should be selected from the women who do not study letters if there are others in the convent better suited to spend their time on reading.

All the furnishings of the oratory should be necessary, not extravagant, and clean rather than costly. There should be nothing of gold or silver except for a single silver chalice, or more than one if needed, and nothing of silk except the stoles and maniples. There should be no carved images. A wooden cross should be set above the altar, nothing more, with a painting of the Savior, if desired, but no other images. The convent should be content with a single pair of bells. Outside the entrance to the oratory, there should be a vessel of holy water, where the women can bless themselves as they come in in the morning and go out after compline.

The nuns will all be present in the oratory at each canonical Hour. As soon as the bell is struck, they will put aside any other business and come to the Divine Office at a swift but modest pace. They will

---

104 *Vitae Patrum* 6.4.8; cf. John 13:4 ff.

105 1 Tim. 5:10; Matt. 25:35.

enter the oratory quietly, but those who can should recite the words, "I will come into thy house and worship at thy holy temple in fear of thee."[106] No book will be kept in the choir except the one needed for the current service. The words of the psalms should be pronounced clearly and distinctly so as to be understood, and the music should be slow enough to allow the weaker voices to keep up. No text is to be read or sung in church except what is taken from authoritative scripture, and from the Old and New Testaments in particular; these will be so divided among the lessons that they may be read in their entirety over the course of a year. Other instructional texts, including the commentaries and sermons of the Doctors of the Church, will be read in chapter or at meals; in other circumstances that call for reading, any other book will be permitted. No one will read or chant a text that she has not prepared, and if someone makes a mistake of pronunciation in the oratory, she will make open atonement then and there by saying quietly, "Forgive me for my carelessness, O Lord, this time as well."

At midnight, they will rise for the Night Office, as the prophet has commanded.[107] For this, they must retire early enough to enable their weak nature to sustain the vigil and continue with the Offices of the day when it is light, in the manner Saint Benedict prescribed.[108] After the Night Office, they will return to the dormitory until the bell is struck for morning lauds. For the remainder of the night, they may sleep if they like, for sleep refreshes a weak and weary nature, preparing it for toil and keeping it steady and alert. If any of them, however, feel the need to meditate on the psalms or other readings, as Saint Benedict suggests,[109] they should take up their study in such a way that no one is disturbed—in fact, he speaks of *meditation* and not *reading* in that passage to insure that the sounds of reading will not keep anyone awake. When he speaks of "any brothers who feel the need to meditate," he does not require meditation of everyone. At times there may be need for singing practice, for example, but in such cases those who need the practice should see to it that no one is disturbed.

---

[106] Ps. 5:8.

[107] See Ps. 118:62: "I rose at midnight to give praise to thee." Cf. *Rule of St. Benedict,* chapter 16.

[108] The Offices of the day being the Morning Office or lauds, prime, terce, sext, none, vespers, and compline; for the manner of their celebration, see *Rule of St. Benedict,* chapter 8 ff.

[109] *Rule of St. Benedict,* chapter 8.

The Morning Office will be celebrated as soon as it is light, the bell rung at sunrise if it can be arranged. At the end of the service, they will return to the dormitory. During the summer months, when the nights are short and the mornings long, they may sleep a little before prime until awakened by the bell. There is a reference to this morning nap after lauds in the second chapter of Saint Gregory's *Dialogues*, where he recounts a story of the venerable Libertinus:

> But on the following day, there was a court case to be heard which would mean much for the monastery's benefit. So, after the morning hymns had been sung, Libertinus came to the bedside of the abbot and humbly asked his blessing.[110]

The morning nap should be permitted from the time of Easter to the autumn equinox, when the nights begin to be longer than the days.

When they leave the dormitory, the nuns will wash, then sit in the cloister with their books, reading or singing until the bell for prime. After prime, they will go to their chapter, where the phase of the moon will be announced and a portion of the martyrology will be read. This should be followed by an instructional sermon or the reading and exposition of a portion of the Rule. Then, if there are things to be set in order and corrected, this is the proper time.

We must recognize that a monastery or any other house should not be called disorderly simply because disorderly things may happen there, but rather because when such things happen, they pass without correction. No place is entirely free from fault, as Saint Augustine reminds us:

> The discipline of my house can be as watchful as you like—I am still a man and live among men. I dare not claim that my house is better than the ark of Noah, where of the eight people aboard only one was found to be a sinner; or the house of Abraham, where it was said, "Cast out this bondwoman and her son"; or the house of Isaac, where Jacob was loved but Esau hated; or the house of Jacob, where a son defiled the bed of his father; or the house of David, where one son lay with his sister and another took up arms against the indulgence of his father; or the company of the

---

[110] *Dialogi*, 1.2.

apostle Paul, who if he lived among good men would never say, "Combat without and terror within," or "There is no man of the same mind who is solicitous for you: all seek the things that are their own and not the things of Christ"; or the company of Christ himself, where eleven good men put up with the treachery and theft of Judas; or, finally, better than heaven itself, which saw the fall of angels.[111]

But urging a vigorous pursuit of discipline, he added this:

> I confess before God that, from the day I first became his servant, I have seen few men better than those who have prospered in monasteries. But I also have seen few men worse than monks who have fallen.[112]

[As I believe is written in the Book of Apocalypse, "He that is just, let him become more just, and he that is filthy, let him be filthy still."][113]

Strict discipline must therefore be enforced. Whoever witnesses a fault in another but conceals it will be subject to a harsher punishment than the one who committed the original fault. No one must be remiss in pointing out a failing, whether it is another's or her own; but if she comes forward to accuse herself first, she will deserve a lighter punishment if her negligence has ceased, for "the just is first accuser of himself."[114] No one must make excuses for another, unless the deaconess questions her about the truth of a matter she alone may know. No one must ever strike another for any fault whatever, unless the deaconess so orders it. Some passages about discipline and correction:[115]

> My son, reject not the correction of the Lord, and do not faint when thou art chastised by him. For whom the Lord loveth, he chastiseth, and as a father in the son he pleaseth himself.

---

[111] *Epistulae* 78.8. The internal quotations and references are to Gen. 9:22 ff., 21:10; Mal. 1:2–3; Gen. 25:22; 2 Kings 13:11, 15; 2 Cor. 7:5; Phil. 2:20–21; John 13:29; and Apoc. 12:9.

[112] *Epistulae* 78.9.

[113] A close but inexact citation of Apoc. 22:11, included in one manuscript and a likely later interpolation.

[114] Prov. 28:17.

[115] It is not possible to determine which, if any, of these passages might belong to Abelard's original text and which might be later additions.

He that spareth the rod hateth his son, but he that loveth him correcteth him betimes.

When the wicked man is scourged, the fool shall be wiser.

When the pestilent man is scourged, the little one will be wiser.

A whip for a horse, a snaffle for an ass, and a rod for the back of fools.

He that rebuketh a man shall afterward find favor with him more than he that deceiveth him with flattering tongue.

Now all the chastisement for the present indeed seemeth not to bring with it joy but sorrow. But afterwards it will yield to them that are exercised by it the most peaceable fruit of justice.

A son ill taught is the confusion of the father, and a foolish daughter shall be to his loss.

He that loveth his son frequently chastiseth him that he may rejoice in his latter end. . . . He that instructeth his son shall be praised in him, and shall glory in him in the midst of his household.

A horse not broken becometh stubborn, and a child left to himself will become headstrong. Give thy son his way, and he shall make thee afraid. Play with him, and he shall make thee sorrowful.[116]

In the advisory discussions of the chapter, anyone may offer her opinion; but whatever may seem best to everyone else, the decision of the deaconess will be final, for everything is subject to her will, even if she is in error and her decision turns out for the worse, as I pray will never be the case. "To disobey one's superiors in any matter is a sin," Augustine says in his *Confessions*, "even if one chooses better things than he has been ordered to do."[117] It is far better to do *well* than to do *good*, since we should not weigh *what* is done so much as *how* it is done and what is in the heart.[118] Whatever is done

---

[116] Prov. 3:11–12, 13:24, 19:25, 21:11, 26:3, 28:23; Heb. 12:11; Ecclus. 22:3, 30:1–2, 8–9.

[117] The passage cannot be found in Augustine's *Confessions*.

[118] Cf. the First and Fifth Letters and Abelard's *Ethics* (Luscombe 1971, 24).

in obedience is done well, no matter if what is done seems the least good. However great the material harm, it is right to obey superiors in all things, so long as it does not entail a danger to the soul. A superior must see that he *orders well* since for subordinates it is enough to *obey well* and follow not their own will but the will of their superiors, according to the terms of their profession.

In these discussions, we strictly forbid that custom ever be valued over reason, that any action be justified by tradition rather than by reason or because it is the practice rather than because it is good. The better a thing is, the more warmly we should embrace it; otherwise, we act like Jews, who reject the Gospel, preferring their old law. Saint Augustine speaks to this matter, drawing on the counsel of Saint Cyprian:[119]

> Whoever dares scorn truth to follow tradition is acting either out of envy of his brothers, to whom the truth has been revealed, or out of an ingratitude to God, whose inspiration has instructed his Church.

> In the Gospel, the Lord said, "I am truth," not "I am tradition." And so, let tradition yield to truth, now that the truth has been made plain.[120]

> Now that truth has been revealed, let error yield to truth, as Peter, who had been circumcised, yielded to Paul, who preached the truth.

> Those who are vanquished by reason now plead custom against us, but in vain—as though custom were greater than truth, or what the Holy Spirit has revealed for the better were not to be followed in spiritual things. But plainly reason and truth must be valued over custom.[121]

And Gregory VII wrote to Bishop Wimund:

> And surely, to use the words of Saint Cyprian, no custom, however ancient or widespread, is ever to be valued over

---

[119] Reading *consilio Cypriani* with two of our three manuscripts against *Concilio Cypriani*, "the Council of Cyprian," which McLaughlin accepts.

[120] *De Baptismo* 3.5, 3.6. The internal quotation is from John 14:6.

[121] *De Baptismo* 3.7, 4.5.

truth, and practices which are contrary to the truth must be abolished.[122]

We are told in Ecclesiasticus how much we should love truth in our words as well:

> For thy soul, do not be ashamed to speak the truth.
>
> In nowise speak against the truth, but be ashamed of the lie of thy ignorance.
>
> In all thy works let the true word go before thee, and steady counsel before every action.[123]

Nothing must be taken as authority because it is done by the many but because it is proven by the wise and the good. As Solomon says, "The number of fools is infinite," and according to the Lord, "Many are called but few are chosen."[124] What is rare is precious, and as things become more common they also diminish in price. No one, then, should follow the majority but rather what is best, not looking toward a person's age but to that person's wisdom, and not regarding friendship but the truth; hence Ovid's saying, "It is right to learn even from an enemy."[125]

Meetings should be called whenever there is need for counsel or serious matters to decide. Less important matters the deaconess may discuss with a few of the senior sisters alone. Some passages about counsel:[126]

> Where there is no governor, the people shall fall, but there is safety where there is much counsel.
>
> The way of a fool is right in his own eyes, but he that is wise hearkeneth unto counsels.
>
> My son, do nothing without counsel, and thou shalt not repent when thou hadst done.[127]

---

[122] The origin of the text is uncertain, as McLaughlin notes 1956, 266 n. 55.

[123] Ecclus. 4:24, 4:30, 37:20.

[124] Eccles. 1:15; Matt. 22:14.

[125] *Metamorphoses* 4.428.

[126] It is not possible to determine which, if any, of these passages might belong to Abelard's original text and which might be later additions.

[127] Prov. 11:14, 12:15; Ecclus. 32:24.

A thing done without counsel may turn out well by chance, but for-tune's gift does not excuse man's presumption. A thing done with counsel at times may go astray, but the power that asked for counsel is not guilty of presumption. The man who took advice is less to blame than those to whom he yielded in his error.

When the chapter meeting is over, the women will turn to the tasks that are suited to them—reading, singing, or handiwork—until terce. Afterward, Mass will be said. To celebrate the service one of the monks from the monastery should be appointed priest for the week. If their community is large enough, he should have a deacon and a subdeacon to assist him in his duties, but they also may per-form their own offices. The sisters must not be able to see their com-ing in or going out. If more than these are needed, provision should be made for them, but only if it can be arranged without taking the monks from the Divine Offices in their own monastery on account of the masses they say for the nuns.

If the sisters will receive communion, an older priest should be cho-sen to administer the sacrament after Mass, during which time the dea-con and subdeacon will have withdrawn to remove any opportunity for temptation. The convent as a whole will receive communion at least three times a year, at Easter, Pentecost, and Christmas, as the Fathers established for the laity as well. They will prepare for these commun-ions in the following way: three days before, they will offer confession and do appropriate penance; then for three days they will purify them-selves with a fast of bread and water and frequent prayer, taking to heart, in all humility and awe, those fearsome words of the Apostle:

> Whoever shall eat this bread or drink this cup of the Lord unworthily shall be guilty of the body and blood of the Lord. But let a man prove himself, and so let him eat of that bread and drink of the cup. For he that eateth and drinketh unworthily eateth and drinketh judgment to himself, not discerning the body of the Lord. Therefore are there many infirm and weak among you, and many sleep. But if we would not judge ourselves, we should not be judged.[128]

After Mass, they will return to their work until sext. At no time will anyone be idle, but each will do what she can and what is

---

[128] 1 Cor. 11:27–31.

appropriate for her. After sext, they will go to their meal, unless it is a fast day when they must wait until none or even until evening during Lent. There will be someone reading to them throughout every meal; when the deaconess wishes her to end, she will say, "It is enough," and then all will rise and give thanks to God. In the summer, they will rest in the dormitory until none and afterward return to their work until vespers. Immediately after vespers, they will take something to eat or drink, or, depending on the season, go on to collation.[129] Before collation on Saturdays, however, they will wash their hands and feet, the deaconess acting as their servant in this task, assisted by the kitchen workers for the week. After collation, they will go straight to compline and then retire to sleep.

About food and clothing, the dictum of Saint Paul must be observed: "But having food and covering, with these we are content."[130] That is to say, what is necessary is enough: we must not seek more than that. Whatever can be purchased most cheaply or had most easily should be permitted, and whatever can be used without offense. For in matters of food, Saint Paul avoided only what would cause offense to his own or another's conscience, knowing that the fault is in the appetite and not in the food itself:

> Let not him that eateth despise him that eateth not; and he that eateth not, let him not judge him that eateth. . . . Who art thou that judgest another man's servant? . . . He that eateth, eateth to the Lord, for he giveth thanks to God. . . . Let us not therefore judge one another any more. But judge this rather, that you not offend your brother nor put a stumbling block in his way.
>
> I know and am confident that nothing is unclean in itself in the Lord Jesus but to him that esteemeth it unclean. . . . For the kingdom of God is not meat and drink, but justice and peace and joy in the Holy Spirit. . . . All things indeed are clean, but it is evil for that man who eateth with offense. It is good not to eat flesh and not to drink wine, nor anything whereby thy brother is offended, weakened, or undone.[131]

---

[129] That is, the evening readings instituted by Benedict, which on fast days are to follow vespers directly after a short interval; see *Rule of St. Benedict*, chapter 42.

[130] 1 Tim. 6:8.

[131] Rom. 14:3–21.

After discussing the offense to his brother, Paul continues with the offense a man commits against himself when he eats in violation of his conscience:

> Blessed is he that condemneth not himself in that which he alloweth. But he that discerneth is condemned if he eat, because he eateth not of faith. For all that is not of faith is sin.[132]

We sin in everything we do against our conscience and against what we believe. And we judge and condemn ourselves in what we *allow*—by the terms, that is, of a law we accept and approve—if we eat the foods which we *discern*—that is, distinguish as unclean and exclude according to the law. So powerful is the witness of our conscience that this, above all, will condemn or acquit us before God. Hence, John remarks in his first letter:

> Dearly beloved, if our hearts do not reprehend us, we have confidence toward God. And whatever we shall ask we shall receive of him, because we keep his commandments and do those things which are pleasing in his sight.[133]

Paul, then, spoke correctly when he said above, "Nothing is unclean in Christ but to him that esteemeth it unclean," or impure and forbidden to the man who believes it so. We apply the term *common,* or *unclean,* to foods which are called *impure* according to the law,[134] because when the law forbids these foods to its adherents, it makes them available or public, as it were, to those outside its jurisdiction; hence, *common* is also a term for impure women, and anything cheap or less valuable which is made public is also known as *common.*[135] And so, Paul says that in Christ no food is *common,* or impure,

---

[132] Rom. 14:22–23.

[133] 1 John 3:21–22.

[134] Reading *immundi* with mss. C and E against *mundi* of ms. T, which McLaughlin accepts.

[135] Much of what seems to be an odd punctiliousness about language in this paragraph derives from a divergence between the usage of the Vulgate and the normal Latin usage of Abelard's time. The word the Douay-Rheims version reasonably translates as "unclean" in Rom. 14:14 is *commune*, normally "common." Abelard then feels a need to gloss what would appear to be a strained meaning at the least.

because the law of Christ forbids no food, except to avoid an offense to one's own or another's conscience. As he says elsewhere:

> Wherefore, if meat be an offense for my brother, I will never eat meat, lest I set a stumbling block in his path. Am not I free? Am not I an apostle? Have I not seen Christ Jesus our Lord?[136]

In other words, "Do I not have the freedom which the Lord gave the apostles to use what others offer and eat any food at all? For when he sent out the apostles, as he says, 'eating and drinking such things as they have,'[137] he did not distinguish one food from another." And so, Paul carefully proceeds to say that every sort of food—even the food of unbelievers which has been consecrated to idols—is lawful for Christians to eat, so long as it does not constitute an offense to another's conscience. "All things are lawful to me," he said, "but not all things are expedient."

> All things are lawful for me, but all things do not edify. Let no man look to his own, but to that which is another's. Eat whatever is sold in the markets, asking no questions for conscience's sake, for "the earth is the Lord's and the fullness thereof." If any unbeliever invite you and you be willing to go, eat of anything that is set before you, asking no questions for conscience's sake. But if any man say, "This has been sacrificed to idols," do not eat of it for the sake of him that told it and for conscience's sake—conscience, I say, not thy own but the other's. . . . Do no offense to the Jews and to the gentiles and to the church of God.[138]

The clear inference from his words is that we are forbidden nothing we may eat without offense to our own or another's conscience. Now, we act without offense to our conscience if we believe that we are keeping that calling in life that enables us to be saved; and we act without offense to another's if we are believed to be living such a life. Indeed, we *will* live such a life if we keep away from sin while allowing for the requirements of our nature, if we stay within our

---

[136] 1 Cor. 8:13–9:1.

[137] Luke 10:7.

[138] 1 Cor. 10:22–29, 32. The internal quotation is from Ps. 23:1.

strength and do not bind ourselves by our calling to such a heavy yoke that, overburdened, we collapse. And our fall will be the worse, the steeper the ascent of our calling has been.

To forestall such a collapse and the foolish taking of a vow, the Book of Ecclesiastes says:

> If thou hadst vowed anything to God, defer not to pay it, for an unfaithful and foolish promise displeaseth him: whatsoever thou hadst vowed, pay it. But it is much better not to vow than after a vow not to perform the things promised.[139]

Saint Paul adds this counsel against the danger:

> I would have it, therefore, that the younger widows marry, bear children, be mistresses of families, and give no occasion to the adversary to speak evil. For some are already turned aside after Satan.[140]

He considers what is natural to women's weakness at that age and weighs the remedy of a looser life against the risks inherent in a better. In the end, he advises remaining in the low places to keep from falling from the heights. And Saint Jerome agrees, saying in his letter to Eustochium:

> But if, because of some other faults, even those who are virgins are not saved, what will happen to those who have prostituted the body of Christ and turned the temple of the Holy Spirit into a brothel? . . . Better for a person to have married and to have walked on level ground than to strain for the heights and plunge into the depths of hell.[141]

Throughout all of Saint Paul's writings, it is only women who are permitted this second marriage—men are urged to the highest self-restraint: "Is any man called who has been circumcised? Let him not then seek to be uncircumcised," he says, and "Art thou loosed from a wife? Then seek not a wife." Moses gave men more latitude than

---

[139] Eccles. 5:3–4.

[140] 1 Tim. 5:14–15.

[141] *Epistulae* 22.6. The passage is also quoted in this form in the Fifth Letter, where it also directly follows Paul's words from 1 Tim. 5.

women, allowing a man more than one wife but a woman only one
husband, and setting stricter penalties for adultery on a woman
than a man. But Paul said, "A woman, if her husband be dead, is
delivered from the law of her husband, so that she is not an adulter-
ess if she be with another man"; and elsewhere, "But I say to the
unmarried and to the widows, it is good for them if they continue
so, even as I. But if they do not restrain themselves, let them marry,
for it is better to marry than to burn"; and again, "If her husband
die, a woman is at liberty. Let her marry whom she will, but only in
the Lord. More blessed shall she be if she abide according to my
counsel."[142] And he allowed them not only a second marriage but
any number of marriages: if their husbands have died, they may
marry again. No limit is set on the number of times, so long as they
do not incur the guilt of fornication. Let them marry again and
again rather than fornicate once; let them discharge their carnal
debts to many husbands rather than prostitute themselves even to
one man. For although the payment of the marital debt is not
entirely without sin, still the lesser sins are permitted them to keep
them from the greater.

Is it any wonder, then, if, to keep women from sin, something is
permitted them in which there is no sin at all—that is, whatever food
they like, so long as it is necessary and nothing more than that? The
fault is not in the food itself but in the appetite, as I said, by which I
mean, in taking pleasure in what is unlawful, desiring what is forbidden, and using it without shame even when it creates the greatest
possible offense. In fact—of all our foods is there one so dangerous
to us, so condemned, or so inimical to our devotions and repose as
*wine?* Solomon, the wisest of the wise, would keep us from it more
than anything else: "Wine is a luxurious thing, and drunkenness
riotous: whosoever is delighted therein shall not be wise."[143]

> Who hath woe? Whose father hath woe? Who hath conten-
> tions? Who falls into pits? Who hath wounds without
> cause? Who hath redness of eyes? Surely they that pass
> their time in wine and study to drink off their cups. Look
> not upon the wine when it is red, when its color shineth in
> the glass: it goeth in pleasantly, but in the end it will bite
> like a snake and will spread poison abroad like a basilisk.

---

[142] 1 Cor. 7:18, 27; Rom 7:3; 1 Cor. 7:8–9, 39–40.
[143] Prov. 20:1.

Thy eyes shall behold strange women and thy heart perverse things. And thou shalt be as one sleeping in the midst
of the sea, and as a pilot fast asleep when the stern is lost.
And thou shalt say, "They have beaten me, but I was not
sensible of pain. They drew me, and I felt not. When shall I
wake and find wine again?[144]

And:

Give not wine to kings, O Lamuel, because there is no
secret where drunkenness reigneth, and they might drink
and forget judgments and pervert the cause of the children
of the poor.[145]

In Ecclesiasticus we read:

A workman that is a drunkard shall not be rich, and he that
condemneth small things shall fall little by little. Wine and
women make even the wise fall away.[146]

And Isaiah mentions no other food, blaming wine alone for the cap-
tivity of his people:

Woe to you that rise up early in the morning to follow
drunkenness and to drink till the evening to be inflamed
with wine. The harp and the lyre and the timbrel and the
pipe and wine are in your feasts, and you regard not the
work of the Lord nor consider the work of his hands. Therefore is my people led away captive, because they had not
knowledge. . . . Woe to you that are mighty at drinking wine
and stout men at drunkenness.[147]

He then extends his complaint to the prophets and the priests:

But these also have been ignorant through wine and through
drunkenness have erred. The priest and the prophet have

---

[144] Prov. 23:29–35.
[145] Prov. 31:4–5.
[146] Ecclus. 19:1–2.
[147] Isa. 5:11–13 and 5:22.

218 THE LETTERS AND OTHER WRITINGS

been ignorant through drunkenness; they are swallowed up
with wine; they have gone astray in drunkenness; they have
not known him that seeth; they have been ignorant of judgment. All their tables were full of vomit and filth, so that
there was no more place. Whom shall he teach knowledge,
and whom shall he make to understand the hearing?[148]

And the Lord said through the prophet Joel, "Awake, ye that are
drunk, and weep all ye that take delight in drinking sweet wine,"
though he did not forbid the use of wine when it is necessary, as
Saint Paul advised Timothy, "for thy stomach's sake and for thy
frequent infirmities"—not only "infirmities," note, but *frequent*
infirmities."[149]

Noah first planted the vine, perhaps still unaware of the evils of
drunkenness, but he became drunk and uncovered his loins—
since lust is connected to wine—then cursed the son who mocked
him to a life of slavery, which we never hear happening before.
Lot, who was a holy man, would never have been induced to commit incest with his daughters if they had not first arranged that he
was drunk. And the blessed widow Judith, too, thought that only
by this trick could Holofernes be deceived and undone. The angels
who appeared to the patriarchs, we read, were offered meat but
never wine. And Elijah, too, the first and greatest forefather of our
calling, was brought meat and bread by ravens in the morning and
the evening, but we never read that they brought him any wine. The
people of Israel even fed on the sumptuous meat of quails in the
desert, but took no wine and did not wish for it; and the meals of
loaves and fishes which sustained the people in the wilderness are
never said to have included wine.[150] Only a wedding, where some
loosening of self-restraint is permitted, saw the miracle of wine,
"wherein is lechery."[151] But the wilderness, which is the proper
habitation of monastics, has known the gift of meat but not of
wine.

---

[148] Isa. 28:7–9.

[149] Joel 1:5; 1 Tim. 5:23.

[150] For Noah, see Gen. 9:20 ff.; for Lot, see Gen. 19:31 ff.; for Judith, see Jth. 13; for the
patriarchs' receiving angels, see, e.g., Gen. 18:7–8; for Elijah, see 3 Kings 17:6; for the
feasts of quails, see Exod. 16:13; for the meals of loaves and fishes, see Matt. 14:13 ff.,
Mark 6:31 ff., Luke 9:10 ff., and John 6:5 ff.

[151] See the wedding at Cana in John 2:1–10. The quoted phrase is from Eph. 5:18.

The single most important point in the rule by which the Nazirites consecrated themselves to God was that they stay away from
wine or anything else that can intoxicate.[152] There is no virtue and
no good in intoxication, and so the priests of former days were forbidden not only wine but anything that can intoxicate. [So, when Jerome wrote to Nepotianus about the cleric's way of life, he was outraged
that the priests of the old law could surpass our own in their abstinence
from drink:

> Never smell of wine, or else the words of the philosopher will be
> spoken about you, "This is not offering a kiss, but proffering a
> cup." Saint Paul condemned drunken priests, as does the old law
> before him: "Whoever serve at the altar shall not taste wine or *sik-
> era*." In Hebrew, *sikera* means anything that can intoxicate, whether
> it is made by fermentation, or pressing dates, or boiling down
> apples or honey into a rough, sweet drink, or brewing roasted
> grain in water. Whatever can intoxicate and disturb your mental
> balance—stay away from it as you would wine.][153]

The Rule of Saint Pachomius tells us, "Let no one touch wine or
liquor except in the infirmary."[154] And who has not heard that wine
is not a thing for monks and that they used to avoid it with such
horror they called it Satan? In the *Lives of the Fathers* we read, "Abbot
Pastor was once told about a monk who did not drink wine, and he
replied that wine is not a thing for monks." And just afterward:

> Once there was a celebration of the Mass on Abbot
> Anthony's mountain, and they found a jar of wine left over.
> One of the elders filled a cup and brought it to Abbot Sisoi,
> who drank it off. Then he brought him a second cup, which
> he also took and drank off. But when he brought him a third
> cup, he refused it, saying, "Peace, brother, don't you know
> that this is Satan?"

---

[152] See, e.g., Num. 6:3.

[153] *Epistulae* 52.11; cf. 1 Tim. 3:3 and Lev. 10:9, 35; the source of "the words of the philosopher" has not been identified. The passage is quoted with virtually the same
introductory words in the Fifth Letter, from which it is likely to have been imported
as an interpolation here.

[154] Pachomius was a fourth-century Egyptian monastic and the first to organize
monks in communal life according to a written rule. Abelard here quotes chapter 45
of Pachomius's Rule in the Latin translation of Jerome.

And another story about Abbot Sisoi:

> So his disciple Abraham asked him, "If it happens in church
> on the Sabbath or the Lord's Day, is it still too much to drink
> three cups?" And the old man answered, "If it were not
> Satan, it would not be too much."[155]

And Saint Benedict was aware of this, even while he allowed wine
to his monks by a special dispensation:

> Yes, we read that wine is not a thing for monks. But since
> the monks of our day can never be convinced of this. . . .[156]

For monks to be completely barred from what Saint Jerome
strictly forbids to women would not in fact be strange, since
women's nature, though weaker in itself, is nonetheless stronger
against the effects of wine. Jerome wrote sternly to the virgin of
Christ, Eustochium, about the importance of preserving chastity:

> If my counsel has any force with you or my experience any
> credit—before anything else, I warn the bride of Christ to
> keep away from wine as she would from poison. It is the
> devil's first weapon against youth. Greed does not unsteady
> us so much, nor pride so puff us up, nor ambition so lead us
> on—we can forgo these other vices easily. But *this* enemy is
> within us, and we carry him with us wherever we go. Wine
> and youth together make a double conflagration. So why
> throw oil on the flames or add fuel to a young body, which
> is already on fire?[157]

Yet medical writers agree that wine has much less effect on women
than on men. In Book 7 of his *Saturnalia* Macrobius explains why:

> Aristotle says that old men are often drunk, but women very
> rarely. . . . The female body is extremely moist—witness the
> lightness and clarity of a woman's skin and, especially, the
> regular purgation of her excess humors. So, when wine has

---

[155] *Vitae Patrum* 5.4.31, 36, and 37.

[156] *Rule of St. Benedict,* chapter 40. The interrupted sentence is continued below.

[157] *Epistulae* 22.8.

been swallowed and incorporated into this great general moisture, it loses its strength . . . and does not easily strike the seat of the brain, once its force has been dissipated.

And:

The female body, designed as it is for frequent purgation, is pierced with several holes, so that channels and passage-ways are open for the humors to drain out. Through these holes the fumes of wine quickly evaporate.[158]

If this is the case, then what can be the sense in allowing to monks what is denied to the female sex? Madness, it seems, to permit it to those who would suffer most harm while denying it to these others. Is there anything more foolish than for religious life *not* to shrink in horror from what is most contrary to it and most makes us turn away from God? Is there any greater audacity than for the abstinence of Christian perfection *not* to shun completely what was forbidden even to kings and the priests of the old law? But no, we see it even takes the greatest pleasure in it. For we all know how devoted the monks of our time—and the clerics even more—are to the contents of their cellars, how they stock them with wines of different sorts, how they flavor them with honey, herbs, and spices to increase their pleasure in the taste as they get increasingly drunk, how they sharpen their lust as they grow hotter in their wine. It is not so much a lapse as lunacy that those who bind themselves most tightly by their vows of self-restraint should prepare themselves least carefully to keep those very vows—or I should say, that they should so arrange it that their vows are certainly least likely to be kept. Their bodies may be walled inside a cloister, but their hearts are filled with lust and on fire for fornication.

When Saint Paul wrote to Timothy, "Do not still drink water, but use a little wine for thy stomach's sake and thy frequent infirmities,"[159] it was clearly because Timothy would take no wine when he was in good health. So, if we profess the apostles' way of life and vow abstinence as a form of penance, if our calling is to renounce the world, then why do we take most pleasure in what is

---

[158] *Saturnalia* 7.6.16–17.
[159] 1 Tim. 5:23.

most hostile to our calling and in what is the most enjoyable of all foods? In his book on penance, Saint Ambrose condemns no food except for wine:

> Would anyone call it penance when we still seek worldly honors, when wine still flows and we still enjoy the pleasures of the marital bed? No, we must renounce the world. I have always thought it easier to find someone who has kept his innocence intact than someone who has done a proper penance.[160]

And in his book on renouncing the world, he says:

> Your renunciation is well done if your eye also renounces the sight of cups and flagons and does not become voluptuary as it lingers over wine.[161]

Wine is the only food he mentions, and he makes our renunciation of the world subject to our renunciation of wine, as if every worldly pleasure depended on it alone. He does not in fact speak of the palate renouncing the taste of wine but of the eye renouncing its sight, to prevent its being caught by pleasure and desire for what it sees—as Solomon said in the words noted above, "Look not upon the wine when it is red, when its color shineth in the glass."[162] But what will we say, I ask you, when, to gratify the palate as well as the eye, we flavor our wine with honey, herbs, and spices and even want to drink it up by flagons?

When Saint Benedict felt obliged to allow wine to his monks, he did so with this limitation: "Let us at least agree to drink sparingly and not to the point where we are sated, because 'wine makes even the wise fall away'"[163]—though I would call for a limit *at* the point where we are sated, to keep us from the greater sin of drinking to excess. Saint Augustine, too, in the Rule he wrote for clerics in monastic life, allowed them wine but limited it to Saturday and Sunday—"On Saturday and Sunday, those who wish may take some

---

160 *De Poenitentia* 2.10.

161 *De Fuga* 9.

162 Prov. 23:31.

163 *Rule of St. Benedict*, chapter 40, the continuation of the interrupted sentence above. The internal quotation is from Ecclus. 19:2.

wine, as is the custom"[164]—out of respect for the Lord's Day and its vigil, which is Saturday, but also because the brothers would be gathering at those times, when otherwise they lived separately in their cells, [as Saint Jerome also noted in the *Lives of the Fathers* when he wrote of the place he called The Cells: "They remain in their individual cells except on Saturday and Sunday, when they come together in church and greet one another as if they had been restored to each other's sight in heaven."[165] So it was meet to grant them this allowance, to allow them to rejoice with some refreshment when they meet,[166] each one thinking, although not saying aloud, "See how good and how pleasant it is for brethren to dwell together in unity."[167]]

See, though, how important many people seem to find it if we simply abstain from meat, no matter how far we may exceed any limit when we feed on other foods. Even if we spend vast sums to buy our platters of fish, even if we season them with pepper and other spices, even if, when we are drunk on the strongest unmixed wine, we add cups and flagons of mulled and herbed wine over and above—everything—so long as we devour these meals in private—everything is pardoned by our abstinence from meat, as though the fault lay in the kind of food and not in the excess. The Lord himself, however, prohibited "surfeit and drunkenness" alone, that is to say, not the kind of food or wine but *only* its excess.[168]

But Saint Augustine understood this well and, opposed to nothing in food except for wine and excluding no kind of food in itself, believed that a single principle would suffice for abstinence, which he expressed succinctly: "Subdue your flesh with fasts and abstinence from food or drink so far as your health permits."[169] Now, unless I am mistaken, he had been reading this passage in Saint Athanasius's exhortation to monks:

---

[164] *Regula Secunda Augustini*, fragmentary fifth-century work once attributed to Augustine.

[165] From Rufinus, *Historia Monachorum* 22, which forms the second book of *Vitae Patrum*, and had been attributed to Jerome.

[166] The English pun on "meet" reflects the Latin, I'm afraid: "*conveniens* erat haec indulgentia ut . . . *convenientes* . . . congauderent."

[167] Ps. 132:1.

[168] Luke 21:34.

[169] *Epistulae* 211.8.

> There should be no fixed limit on fasts for the willing, but only so far as possibility allows and not to the point of suffering; and, except on Sunday, they always should be solemnized if they have been vowed.[170]

In other words, if fasts are undertaken in fulfillment of a vow, they must be performed devoutly at all times, excepting Sundays. The term of fasts is not fixed here except as health permits; as it is said, "He looks only to the capacity of our nature and allows it to set its own limits, aware that there can be no delinquency if moderation is observed."[171] That is to say, we must not become relaxed by our pleasures beyond what is right, as was written about the people fed "with the marrow of wheat and the purest wine": "The beloved grew fat and kicked."[172] But on the other hand, we must not waste away from abstinence beyond the proper measure and then collapse completely, or squander by our complaining any good we might have gained, or glory in what we take to be our own special distinction. As the Book of Ecclesiastes says, "A just man perisheth in his justice. . . . Be not over just, and be not more wise than is necessary, lest thou become stupid" and swell with pride at your sense of your own distinction.[173]

Instead, it must be discretion, the mother of all virtues, that governs our diligence in this. It must carefully take note what burdens are placed on whom and allot to each individual only what his strength will bear, following rather than forcing nature, and preserving the good use of being sated while destroying the abuses of excess. Vices should be rooted out without injuring nature. For the weak it is enough to keep from sin even if they do not reach the summit of perfection; and, yes, it is enough to find a corner of paradise if you cannot claim a place among the martyrs.[174] There is no risk in making only modest vows, in order to add something of your own accord beyond what you are already bound to do; for as it is written, "When you shall have done all those things that are commanded you, say, 'We are unprofitable servants; we have done

---

[170] Athanasius, *Exhortatio ad Monachos*, an appendix to the *Codex Regularium* of Benedict of Aniane.

[171] The source of this passage is unknown.

[172] Deut. 32:14–15; reading *dilectus*, "beloved," with the Vulgate and mss. C and E against *dilatatus*, "distended," with ms. T, which McLaughlin accepts.

[173] Eccles. 7:16–17.

[174] Cf. the Third Letter, p. 83.

that which we ought to do.'"[175] As Saint Paul said, "For the law
worketh wrath. Where there is no law, neither is there transgression." And also:

> For without the law sin was dead. And I lived some time
> without the law. But when the commandment came, sin
> revived, and I died. And the commandment that was
> ordained to life was found to be unto death to me. For sin,
> taking occasion by the commandment seduced me, and by
> it killed me . . . so that sin . . . might become sinful above
> measure.[176]

[Augustine to Simplician: "Forbidding desire has made it sweeter, and so it
has undone me." And in his book of eighty-three questions: "Pleasure per-
suades us to sin all the more when the pleasure is forbidden." And as Ovid
writes, "We desire the forbidden and denied."[177]]

This should give pause to anyone who would take on the yoke of
monastic rule as if he were professing some new law.[178] Let him
choose only what he is able to do and avoid what he is not. No one
becomes guilty of breaking a law which he has not professed. So,
*think* before you enter into orders, but once you have entered orders,
*persevere*; what first is voluntary, afterward becomes obligatory.[179] "In
my Father's house there are many mansions," and many paths lead
to it.[180] The married are not damned, but those who practice self-
restraint are more easily saved. The rules of the holy Fathers were not
laid down in order that we may be saved, but in order that we may
be *more easily* saved and with *greater* purity devote ourselves to God.
"And if a virgin marry," Saint Paul says, "she hath not sinned: never-
theless, such shall have tribulation of the flesh. But I spare you."

> The unmarried woman and the virgin thinketh on the
> things of the Lord, that she may be holy both in body and in

---

[175] Luke 17:10.

[176] Rom. 4:15, 7:8–13.

[177] Augustine, *De Quaestionibus ad Simplicianum* 1.1.5, *De Diversis Quaestionibus
LXXXIII* 66.5; Ovid, *Amores* 3.4.17. These later interpolations miss the point that Paul
and Abelard are making: the issue is not in fact psychological but structural.

[178] See Heloise's discussion in the Fifth Letter, p. 112.

[179] Cf. Augustine, *De Bono Viduitatis* 9.13, cited in the Fifth Letter, p. 112.

[180] John 14:2.

spirit. But she that is married thinketh on the things of the world, how she may please her husband. And this I speak for your profit, not to cast a snare upon you, but for that which is decent and which may give you power to attend upon the Lord without impediment.[181]

And this, of course, is most easily done when we retire to the cloisters of our monasteries, physically withdrawing from the world so that none of the world's troubles may disturb us.

Likewise, whoever makes the law must not create a multitude of sins by laying down a multitude of strictures. In coming to earth, the Word of God curtailed the word on earth. The words of Moses were many, yet Paul says, "The law brought nothing to perfection"[182]—yes, his words were many and so onerous that Peter admits no one could endure all of his commandments: "Men, brethren," Peter says,

> why do you tempt God to put a yoke upon the necks of the disciples, which neither our fathers nor we ourselves have been able to bear? But by the grace of the Lord Jesus Christ, we believe we are saved in like manner as they were.[183]

Christ's words on ethical conduct and the holy life were few, and yet he taught perfection. Eliminating the harsh and onerous, he commanded what was sweet and light, and thereby brought religious practice to its full consummation:

> Come to me, all you that labor and are burdened, and I will refresh you. Take up my yoke upon you and learn of me, because I am meek and humble of heart, and you shall find rest to your souls. For my yoke is sweet and my burden light.[184]

What often happens in worldly business also happens in our good works. There are many people, we know, who work hard in their business but with only diminishing returns. And there also are

---

[181] 1 Cor. 7:28, 34–35.
[182] Heb. 7:19.
[183] Acts 15:7–11.
[184] Matt. 11:28–30.

many who afflict themselves the more in outward acts of penance but earn less reward from God, who looks more to our hearts than to our deeds. In fact, the more these people are taken up with outward things, the less they can devote themselves to inward things; and the more they receive the attention of men, who judge by outward things, the more they seek out glory among them and more easily are beguiled by their esteem. Saint Paul corrects this error by disparaging outward works in favor of justification by faith:

> For if Abraham were justified by works, he hath glory, but not glory before God. For what saith the scripture? "Abraham believed God, and it was reputed to him unto justice." . . . What then shall we say? That the gentiles, who followed not after justice, have attained to justice, even the justice that is of faith. But Israel, by following after the law of justice is not come unto the law of justice. Why so? Because they sought it not by faith, but as it were of works.[185]

Those who scour the outside of the platter or the cup are looking less to the cleanliness within, and when they guard the body more closely than the soul, they become more worldly than spiritual themselves. But when *we* desire that Christ live in the inner man through faith, we count as only little those outward things which are common to God's chosen and rejected alike, taking to heart what is written: "In me, O God, are vows to thee, which I will pay, my praises to thee." And so, we do not follow that outward abstinence of the law which cannot justify us, to be sure. In matters of food, the Lord forbids us nothing but "surfeit and drunkenness" alone,[186] that is to say, excess; and what he allowed us, he was not ashamed to exhibit in himself, although many were offended and reproached him severely for it, as he said:

> For John came neither eating nor drinking, and they said, "He hath a devil." And the Son of man came eating and drinking, and they said, "Behold a man that is a glutton and a wine drinker, a friend of publicans and sinners."[187]

---

[185] Rom. 4:2–3, 9:30–32. The internal quotation is from Gen. 15:6.
[186] Ps. 55:12; Luke 21:34.
[187] Matt. 11:18–19.

He defended his followers, who did not fast like the followers of John nor even care if they washed their hands before they ate:

> Can the children of the bridegroom mourn as long as the bridegroom is with them? But the days will come when then bridegroom shall be taken from them, and then they shall fast.[188]

And:

> Not what goeth into the mouth defileth a man, but what cometh out of the mouth. . . . The things that proceed from the mouth come forth from the heart, and those things defile a man. . . . But to eat with unwashed hands doth not defile a man.[189]

No food in itself defiles the soul, but only the appetite for foods that are forbidden. As the body cannot be defiled except by some physical stain, the soul cannot be defiled except by a spiritual stain. We should never waste our fear on what may happen in the body if the heart has not been forced to give consent; we should never dare to trust in any cleanness of the flesh if the mind has been corrupted by the will. The life and death of the soul, therefore, lie entirely in the heart. Hence, Solomon in the Book of Proverbs says, "Keep thy heart with all watchfulness, because life issueth out from it."[190] And there *come forth from the heart* the things that can defile a man, as the Lord said just above, because the soul is saved or damned by good or evil desires. But since the union of body and soul within a person is so close, it is especially important to see that the pleasures of the flesh do not lead the soul to give consent, and that the flesh itself, becoming lawless with immoderate indulgence, does not struggle against the soul and begin to take command when it should obey.[191] Now, we will be able to accomplish this if we permit all that is necessary but entirely eliminate excess, as I've often said, not denying the weaker sex the *use* of any foods but denying them the *abuse* of them all. Let them take and consume anything at all, but nothing

---

[188] Matt. 9:11. The manuscripts include only the first sentence of this passage, indicating what follows by "etc."

[189] Matt. 15:11, 18, 20.

[190] Prov. 4:23.

[191] Cf. the Fifth Letter, p. 105.

outside the bounds of moderation. "For everything made by God is good," the Apostle says,

> and nothing is to be rejected that is received with thanksgiving, for it is sanctified by the word of God and prayer. Proposing these things to the brethren, thou shalt be a good minister of Jesus Christ, nourished up in the words of faith and the good doctrine which thou hast attained unto.[192]

So let us then, like Timothy, follow this teaching of Saint Paul, avoiding nothing in food but "surfeit and drunkenness" alone, according to the word of the Lord. But let us also temper everything in such a way that we support the weak nature in all things and do not encourage its vice: whatever can do more harm must be limited more strictly. Eating in moderation is in fact more worthy of praise than total abstention. Hence, Augustine says in his book on the good in marriage during his discussion of the sustenance of the body:

> No one uses these things well unless he can refrain from using them. For many, in fact, it is easier to abstain and thereby not use them at all than to temper their use and thereby use them well. But no one can use them wisely unless he can exercise self-restraint and *not* use them.[193]

And Paul spoke, too, out of the same disposition: "I know both how to have plenty and how to suffer need."[194] Any sort of man can suffer need, but only the great *know how* to suffer need; and any man can have plenty, but to *know how* to have plenty is only for those whom plenty does not corrupt.

Now, since "wine is a luxurious thing and riotous," as it is said,[195] contrary both to self-restraint and silence, women should either abstain completely for the sake of God—as the wives of the gentiles did out of fear of committing adultery—or temper their wine with water in such a way that it will quench their thirst and serve their health without having the strength to do them harm—I

---

[192] 1 Tim. 4:4–6.

[193] *De Bono Coniugali* 21.

[194] Phil. 4:12.

[195] Prov. 20:1.

recommend a mixture of at least a fourth part water. But it is extremely difficult, when the wine is right there before us, to keep from drinking to the point where we are sated, as Saint Benedict would have it.[196] Therefore, to avoid the greater risk, I think it is safer *not* to prohibit being sated, as I've said, for the fault does not lie in being sated but rather in excess. And herbed wine may be prepared as medicine, and even unmixed wine may be drunk—neither should be forbidden—but this is only for the sick and never for the convent as a whole.

[We also forbid the use of pure wheat flour; when the nuns have wheat flour, it must always be mixed with at least a third part coarser grains. And they should never indulge themselves with bread hot from the oven, but only after it has been sitting at least a day.][197]

As for all the other kinds of food, the deaconess should see to it that the women's needs are met by whatever can be purchased most cheaply or had most easily. [Is it not the height of foolishness, when our own goods will suffice, for us to go and buy the goods of others? Or when we have what we need at home, for us to seek something more outside the walls? Or when we have enough at hand, for us to struggle for what would be excess?][198] Indeed, for this lesson in moderation and discretion we have the teaching, not only of mortal men, but also of angels and the Lord himself, that in serving the needs of this earthly life, we should not be particular about the kind of food we eat but should rest content with whatever is before us. The angels ate the meat which Abraham set out for them, and the Lord Jesus fed the hungry multitude with fish found in the wilderness[199]—from which we learn that the eating of meat or fish indifferently is not to be condemned: any food may be eaten which does not give offense, which presents itself freely, is most easily had, and involves the least expense.

This is also the teaching of Seneca, who of all philosophers was the foremost teacher of ethical conduct and the greatest exponent of austerity and self-restraint. "My idea," he said, "is to live in accord with nature."

---

[196] *Rule of St. Benedict*, chapter 40.

[197] One manuscript includes these later comments.

[198] These rhetorical questions, included in one manuscript, emphasize a different point and are most likely later interpolations.

[199] See Gen. 18:1–8; Mark 8:1–8; and John 6:1–9.

But it is against nature to torment the body, to despise clean-liness and seek out squalor, to eat food that is not only cheap but loathsome and disgusting. If it is luxury to crave expensive things, it is lunacy to thumb your nose at ordi-nary things that are available for only little cost. Philosophy calls for thrift, not penance, but there is such a thing as thrift without disorder, and that is what I like.[200]

Gregory, too, teaches us to look less to our food than our hearts; in Book 30 of his *Moralia*, he distinguishes among the different appeals of the palate. "At times," he says, "the palate may want more sumptuous food or, at times, a dish that requires more elabo-rate preparation."[201] But sometimes what it desires is more hum-ble, yet still it sins by the heat of its desire. The people of Israel succumbed in the desert because they scorned God's manna and longed for meat instead, which they considered a more sumptuous kind of food. But Esau, on the other hand, lost the glory of his birthright because he longed for a simple dish of lentils, which in the great heat of his desire meant more to him than the sale of his own birthright. The fault is in the appetite, not the food itself. We often can eat a humble food and incur substantial guilt, but still can take the more sumptuous food without any sin at all, just as Esau lost his birthright for some lentils while Elijah in the wilderness kept his physical strength intact by eating the meat which God had sent him. So, knowing that the desire for food and not the food itself can lead to our damnation, the old adversary tempted the first man with an apple, not with meat, and tempted the second man with bread alone.[202] Since we often commit the sin of Adam when we eat humble or simple foods, we must eat only those foods that the requirements of our nature demand and not those foods that pleasure may suggest. Our desire, though, is less intense for what we take as less valuable, for what is plentiful and can be cheaply bought, and this is the case with common meat. Meat also strengthens a weak nature better than fish, is less expensive, and is easier to prepare.

---

[200] *Epistulae ad Lucilium* 5.4.

[201] *Moralia* 30.18.

[202] For Esau, see Gen. 25:29; for Elijah, see 3 Kings 17:2–6; for the temptation of Jesus, "the second man," see Matt. 4:1–4.

The use of wine or meat—like marriage itself—is a matter that falls between good and evil and is therefore called *indifferent*,[203] though the marriage bond is not entirely without sin and wine remains the most dangerous kind of food. But if the moderate use of wine is not forbidden in religious life, why do we forbid any other kind of food, so long as it too is used in moderation? If Saint Benedict admits that wine is not a thing for monks, yet is compelled to allow it by a special dispensation in these times when the initial fervor of charity has cooled,[204] why should we not allow women all those things which none of their vows now forbids? If popes and other leaders of the Church may all eat meat, if canons regular in their monasteries too may all eat meat because none of their vows prevent it, what reason can there be to find fault in allowing the same to women, especially if they are bound more strictly in every other thing? It is enough for the disciple if he be as his master;[205] and it seems a great injustice if what monasteries of clerics have is forbidden to convents of women. It also should not be taken as a small thing if women, with all the other strictures of the monastery, could equal the devout among the laity in this single matter of having access to meat. Chrysostom says, "A layman should have no more latitude than a monk—except that he may lie with his wife";[206] and in Saint Jerome's judgment, the religious obligations of clerics are not less than the obligations of monks: "Whatever is said against monks reflects also upon clerics, who are the forefathers of monks."[207]

For the weak to bear the same burdens as the strong, for women to be bound to the same standards of abstinence as men, is at odds with the principle of discretion. If someone needs an authority beyond the teaching of nature, let him consult Saint Gregory, who, while not a Doctor of the Church himself, instructed other Doctors. In Chapter 24 of his *Pastoral*, he notes:

> Men should be admonished in one way and women in another, in that heavy burdens should be placed on men and lighter ones on women. Let men take up the greater

---

[203] See the Fifth Letter, pp. 117–18.

[204] See *Rule of St. Benedict*, chapter 40.

[205] Cf. Matt. 10:24.

[206] *Homilia in Epistulam ad Hebraeos* 7.4. Cf. the Fifth Letter, pp. 111–12.

[207] *Epistulae* 54.5.

tasks, but let women be corrected gently with the light ones. . . .[208]

For what seems of little moment in the strong is something we all admire in the weak. Moreover, eating common meat affords less pleasure than eating the flesh of birds and fish, which Saint Benedict does not in fact forbid.[209] Now, Saint Paul distinguishes among different kinds of flesh, saying, "All flesh is not the same flesh, but one is the flesh of men, another of beasts, another of birds, and another of fish,"[210] and since the law includes the flesh of beasts and birds among permitted sacrifices to the Lord but does not mention fish, no one would suppose that the eating of fish was cleaner in the sight of God than the eating of other flesh. Fish also imposes a greater burden on our poverty than meat because it is more expensive, being in scarce supply, and does less than meat to strengthen a weak nature, so that one presents the greater burden, the other the greater sustenance.

So, considering both human nature and resources, I forbid nothing in the way of food, as I've said before, nothing but excess. But I also place such limits on the eating of meat and other foods, that, with every kind of food permitted them, the abstinence of nuns may be greater than the abstinence of monks, who still are forbidden certain kinds of food. The nuns will not eat meat at more than one meal a day; no more than one dish will be prepared for any person; no separate dish of condiments will be added to the meat; and under no circumstances will anyone eat meat more than three times in a week—on Sundays, Tuesdays, and Thursdays, that is— no matter how many feast days the week contains. In fact, the greater the feast, the greater should be the abstinence that honors it. As Gregory of Nazianzus, that great Doctor of the Church, tells us in the third book of his treatises, "On Lamps, or Second Epiphany," "Let us celebrate a feast by exulting in the spirit, not by indulging the belly";[211] and in his fourth book on Pentecost and the Holy Spirit:

---

[208] *Regulae Pastoralis Liber* 3.1; cf. the Fifth Letter, p. 109.

[209] *Rule of St. Benedict,* chapter 39, specifies only the flesh of four-footed animals as prohibited.

[210] 1 Cor. 15:39.

[211] *Oratio 39, In Sancta Lumina* 20. Abelard cites Gregory in the Latin translation of Rufinus, where it is presented as the third of a set of treatises.

This is our feast: let us lay down in the treasure-house of the soul something that will last forever, not transient things that will melt away. The body has enough in its own evil, it does not need anything more; and the insolent beast of the belly does not need another meal to make it both more insolent and insistent.[212]

A feast should rather be celebrated in the spirit, as Gregory's follower, Saint Jerome, also remarks:

So, we must be careful to celebrate a feast day less with an overflow of food than with an exultation of the spirit. How thoroughly absurd to gorge ourselves in remembrance of a martyr who we know had honored God by fasting.[213]

Augustine, *On the Remedy of Penance:*

Think of the thousands of martyrs. Why does it please us to celebrate their births with all these worthless banquets and *not* please us to follow their example with our conduct?[214]

At meatless meals, however, the nuns may have two vegetable dishes of any sort, and fish may be added to these. No expensive flavorings will be served at the convent: the nuns must be content with whatever grows locally. Fruit will only be eaten at the evening meal, but it may be served, along with roots, herbs, and other things of the sort, to those who require it for medicinal reasons. If there is a visiting nun at table, received as the convent's guest, let her feel the kindness of its charitable love by being offered an additional dish; if she wishes to share any of it, she may. But she—and any other visitors there may be, no matter the number—will sit at the high table, where the deaconess will serve her before taking her own meal with the others who are serving at table. A sister who wishes to subdue the flesh with a leaner, more sparing diet must not presume to do so without permission; if her wish seems grounded in virtue and not caprice, and if her physical strength can bear it, permission should

---

212 *Oratio 41, In Pentecosten* 1.

213 *Epistulae* 31.3.

214 *Sermons* 351.4.

not be withheld, but no one will be permitted to leave the convent for this purpose or spend a whole day without eating.

The nuns will not use animal fat to flavor their meals on Fridays but must be content instead with Lenten fare, enduring some abstinence out of compassion for their Bridegroom, who died on that day of the week. And they are not only forbidden but must absolutely shun the custom that is practiced in some monasteries of wiping food-stained hands and knives on some part of the bread that is held back for the poor: merely to spare their hand-cloths, they pollute the bread of the poor—no, not in fact *their* bread but *his,* who said, "What you have done for the least of my brethren, you have done also for me."[215]

On the matter of fasting, what the Church has established for the general populace will be enough. I do not presume to impose a burden on nuns beyond what is observed by the devout among the laity, and would not dare set their weakness in this above the strength of men. From the time of the autumn equinox to Easter, though, I think one meal a day will be enough—not, however, for the sake of religious abstinence, but because of the shortness of the days, and here I make no distinction among the different kinds of food.

The rich clothing which scripture condemns must also be avoided, as the Lord himself warns against it, condemning the pride of the rich while praising the humility of John. Saint Gregory knew this well, saying in his sixth homily on the Gospels:

> What does it mean to say, "They that are clothed in soft garments are in the houses of kings"? It means that they are soldiers in an earthly, not a heavenly, kingdom, who will not suffer hardships for God but devote themselves to outward display, seeking the softness and pleasure of this, our present life.[216]

And in his fortieth homily:

> Some think there is no sin in the love of fine, rich dress. But if there were not, the Lord would not have made the point

---

[215] Matt. 25:40.

[216] *Homiliae in Evangelia* 6. The internal quotation is from Matt. 11:18.

that the rich man tortured in hell had been "clothed in purple and fine linen." For no one wants or needs expensive clothing except to seem superior, that is, for the sake of the empty pomp and glory of the world. Here is the proof: no one adorns himself like this in private, but only where he can be seen.[217]

[The first letter of Peter also warns married women and the laity against this vanity:

> In like manner, also let women be subject to their husbands, that if any believe not the word, they may be won without the word by the conversation of the wives, considering your chaste conversation with fear. Let their adornment not be the outward plaiting of the hair, or the wearing of gold, or the putting on of apparel, but the hidden man of the heart in the incorruptibility of a quiet and meek spirit, which is rich in the sight of the Lord.[218]

The warning is properly directed more toward women than toward men because, women's minds being weaker, they are more susceptible to the lures of luxury. But if secular women are to be so warned, what then is appropriate for women devoted to Christ, whose adornment consists in remaining unadorned? A woman who seeks out adornment, or who does not refuse it when it is offered, forgoes this witness to her chastity and should be thought readying herself for fornication, not religious practice, less nun, that is, than whore. Her adornment itself announces her whoredom, betraying an unchaste heart, as it is written, "The attire of the body and the laughter of the teeth and the gait of the man show what he is."] [219]

As I noted above, the Lord praised John more for the roughness and cheapness of his clothing than for his rough food. "What went you into the desert to see?" he said, "A man clothed in soft garments? But they that are clothed in soft garments are in the houses of kings."[220] At times there may in fact be reason to eat expensive

---

[217] *Homilia in Lucam,* 40.16. The internal quotation is from Luke 16:19.

[218] 1 Pet. 3:1–4.

[219] Ecclus. 19:27. The stress in this passage on outward forms, so at odds with Abelard's consistent position elsewhere, may be enough in itself to cast doubt on his authorship.

[220] Matt. 11:8. The manuscripts quote only through "a man clothed in soft garments," inserting "etc."

food, but there never is a use for expensive clothing. The more expensive the clothing, in fact, the more carefully it must be protected; and the less it is then used, the less use it will be, creating only problems for its owner: its fabric can be easily be ruined and affords only little warmth. Black cloth is most appropriate for the garb of penitence, and lamb's wool best for the brides of Christ, who in their very habit may be seen, or reminded, to be clothed in the Lamb, who is their Bridegroom.

Their veils should not be silk, but dyed linen. I recommend two different kinds of veils, one for nuns who have already been consecrated by the bishop, the other for the sisters who will not be. The first should bear the sign of the cross to indicate that they belong to Christ in the chastity of their bodies: as they are set apart by consecration, so their habits will be distinguished by this sign, a warning to the faithful not to burn with lust for them. The virgin will wear this mark of purity detailed in white thread at the top of her head, but she will not presume to wear it before her consecration, and no other veils will bear this sign.

The women should wear clean shifts next to the skin and always sleep in them as well. They may use soft mattresses and sheets because of the weakness of their nature, but each of them must sleep and eat alone. No one ever must presume to take offense if an item of clothing or anything else allotted for her use is made over to a sister who needs it more. Instead, she should be glad to have realized the fruit of her charity in meeting the needs of her sister and also to have recognized that she is living for others and not for herself alone. Otherwise, she is not part of a sisterhood of holy community but is guilty of the sin of claiming possessions.

For covering the body, I think a shift and woolen gown will be enough, and an outer cloak when it is very cold, which may also be used as a coverlet in bed. Because of the need to wash them and to treat them against vermin, there should be two of each article of clothing, exactly as Solomon says in his praise of the strong and prudent housewife: "She shall not fear for her house in the cold of snow, for all her domestics are clothed with double garments."[221] The cloaks should not be more than ankle-length, so as not to stir up dust, and their sleeves should not extend beyond the arms and hands. Shoes and stockings will be worn; no one must ever go barefoot on the pretext of religious practice. A single mattress, cushion,

---

[221] Prov. 31:21.

pillow, blanket, and sheet should be enough for their bedding. They should wear a white headband with a black veil over it and a lamb's wool cap if needed, because of their close-cropped hair.

Not only in matters of food and dress but in buildings and other material possessions, excess must be avoided. What constitutes excess in buildings is in fact easy to see—if they are larger and more beautiful than we need or if they are ornamented with paintings and sculptures, not humble dwellings for the poor, that is, but stately palaces for kings. Jerome once said, "'The son of man hath not where to lay his head,' but you lay out wide porches and vast expanses of roof."[222] The pleasure we take in beautiful, expensive things betokens vanity as well as excess. When we multiply our herds of cattle or extend our holdings of land, our ambition swells for outward things; and the more things we possess on earth, the more we are forced to give them our attention and so are called away from thoughts of heaven. While our bodies may be walled inside a cloister, our hearts are compelled to follow what they are attached to in the world outside, and become widely scattered like the things themselves. And the more things we possess that can be lost, the more we are tormented by the fear that we may lose them; and the more costly they are, the more they can attach us and the more ensnare the wretched heart with ambition to possess them.

For this reason, we must fix limits on our households and expenditures, never going beyond what is needed, not in our desires, nor in the offerings we receive, nor in what we keep for ourselves of what we gather. Everything we have beyond our needs, we have by theft, and we are guilty of the deaths of as many of the poor as we might otherwise have been able to sustain. Each year, therefore, when all the food has been collected, a determination should be made of how much will be needed for the year, and anything beyond that should be given, or rather *returned,* to the poor.

There are some for whom economy has no meaning, who despite their meager revenues, still rejoice in the grandeur of their household. In their struggle, then, to secure its maintenance, they shamelessly go begging or use violence to extort from others what they do not have themselves. We see many such monastic fathers in these times, who glory in the size of their monasteries and work to increase the number, if not the virtue, of their sons, anxious to

---

[222] *Epistulae* 14.6. The internal quotation is from Matt. 8:20.

seem superior in their own esteem by becoming the superiors of a multitude. They attract these crowds with the promise of ease—when they should be talking of the hardships they will face—accepting anyone without discrimination, without scrutiny or standards, and losing them all easily, as they all fall away. The Lord said of such men, "Woe to you who go round land and sea to make one proselyte, and when he is made, you make him the child of hell twice more than yourselves."[223] They would surely glory less in the number of souls if they cared more about their salvation and put less reliance on numerical strength in the final accounting of their rule.

The Lord himself chose few apostles and of these only one fell away, of whom he said, "Have not I chosen you twelve, and one of you is a devil?"[224] Just as Judas was lost to the apostles, Nicolas was lost to the seven deacons;[225] and when the apostles had not yet assembled many followers, Ananias and his wife Saphira were found worthy of the sentence of death.[226] Many of his disciples turned away from the Lord while a few remained with him, for "strait is the way that leadeth to life, and few there are that find it," but wide and broad is the way "that leadeth to destruction, and many there are who go in thereat." As the Lord himself bears witness, "Many are called, but few are chosen," and as Solomon confirms, "The number of fools is infinite." So, whoever rejoices in the number of his subordinates must be afraid that only few of them are chosen, and that he himself, in increasing his flock beyond the proper limit, may fail in his guardianship of souls; in the words of the prophet, "Thou hast multiplied the nation but hast not increased the joy."[227] While they glory in the size of their monasteries, they are compelled to go out in the world again and again, scurrying about for handouts to supply their own and their subordinates' needs. Their concerns are now for material things and not for the things of the spirit, and while they look for glory in the world, they find there only infamy and scorn.

---

[223] Matt. 23:15.

[224] John 7:71.

[225] Nicolas is named as a deacon in Acts 6:5. The tradition that he was "lost" to them apparently derives from the identification of the "Nicolaites" condemned in Apoc. 2 as his followers. Abelard refers to his downfall more pointedly in his Sermon 31.

[226] See Acts 5:1–10.

[227] Matt. 7:13–14, 20:16; Eccles. 1:15; Isa. 9:3.

For women, there is even more shame in this scurrying through the world, more shame, to be sure, and considerably more risk. Whoever would lead a life of tranquility and honor, devoted to the Offices of God, whoever would be held as dear to God as to the world, must never assemble a flock whose needs he cannot meet, nor rely for his expenditures on the depths of another's purse. His attention must be set on giving alms, not on receiving them. Even the apostle Paul, that great preacher of the Gospel, who had power from the Gospel to accept offerings, did manual labor himself because he would not "be chargeable to any" and "make his glory void."[228] If that is so, then how can *we*, whose business is not preaching but lamenting our sins, go out begging through the world in recklessness and shame merely to support a mass of followers, which we have so thoughtlessly assembled? Look how we erupt into such madness that, unable to preach ourselves, we bring preachers along with us and go out through the world with these spurious apostles, toting our reliquaries and crosses to sell these things and the word of God itself—and even figments of the devil—to those poor, ignorant Christians who are simple enough to credit whatever promises we make to extort their money.[229] And by this greed—which has no shame, which seeks only its own and not the things of Christ—our order and the preaching of God's word are both debased—how much debased, I think is plain to all.

And so, these abbots and so-called superiors go knocking at the doors of earthly princes and soliciting at the gates of worldly courts. They become more courtiers than common monks, using every art and charm to curry favor and gossiping with men more than they talk to God.[230] Perhaps they read but never paid attention, perhaps they heard but never stopped to listen to the warning of Saint Anthony:

> If fish try to live on dry land, they die. If monks try to live outside their cells or spend their time among men of the world, they weaken their ties to the tranquil life. Just as fish must return to the sea, so we must hasten back to our cells

---

[228] 1 Thess. 2:9; 1 Cor. 9:12.

[229] Abelard describes a similar scene in his Sermon 33 on John the Baptist.

[230] Making a similar point in his Sermon 33 on John the Baptist, Abelard says (also with rhetorical alliteration), "They become more citizens than solitary monks."

or else, in our lives outside, forget our guardianship of what lies within.[231]

But the author of the monastic Rule, Saint Benedict, knew this well and, not only by his writings but by the force of his example, taught abbots to keep careful watch over their flock by their constant presence at the monastery. Once, when he was away from his monks on a visit to his most holy sister, she begged him to remain with her, at least for a single night, to continue her education, but he refused; there was no way, he said, that he could remain away from his cell. He did not say that *they* could not, only that *he* could not, because the monks in fact could do so, given his permission, but he himself could not, except by a revelation from the Lord, as did happen afterward.[232] For this reason, then, when he wrote the Rule, he never referred to the abbot's absence from the monastery, but only to the absence of the monks. His provision for the abbot's constant presence is implied by his insistence that the Gospel readings at the Night Office on Sundays and feast days, and other matters that pertain to them, are to be done by the abbot himself.[233] His requirement that the abbot take his meals with pilgrims and guests or, "when there are no guests, with whomever of the brothers he chooses to invite, leaving one or two senior monks with the others,"[234] implies the abbot's presence at all meals, never forgoing the daily bread of his subordinates in a preference for the luxurious food of princes, unlike those who "bind heavy burdens on men's shoulders but do not move a finger themselves," as the Lord said. And as he also said about false preachers, "Beware of false prophets, who come to you in the clothing of sheep, but inwardly they are ravening wolves."[235] For they are not sent by God, he says, but come of themselves in the expectation of an offering. John the Baptist, our founder and forerunner, to whom the priesthood passed by right of inheritance, left the city for the wilderness—that is to say, the priesthood for the monkhood—only once, withdrawing from the towns to the lonely places; and the people came out to him, he did not go in to the people. When he became so

---

[231] *Vitae Patrum* 5.2.1.

[232] See Gregory, *Dialogi* 2.33.

[233] See *Rule of St. Benedict*, chapter 11.

[234] *Rule of St. Benedict*, chapter 56.

[235] Matt. 23:4, 7:15. The manuscripts quote only through "who come to you," indicating the rest of the verse by "etc."

great that he even was believed to be the Christ and able to put right many things that were wrong in the cities of the world, he was already on the narrow bed of contemplation and was prepared to say to the beloved at the door, "I have put off my garment; how shall I put it on? I have washed my feet; how shall I defile them?"[236]

And so, whoever longs to withdraw to the tranquility of monastic life should rejoice that his bed is narrow and not wide. From the wide bed, the Lord says, "The one shall be taken, and the other shall be left." But the narrow bed, we read, belongs to the bride of the Lord, that is to say, to the contemplative soul, which is closely bound to Christ and clings to him with the most intense desire; and once someone has come into that narrow bed, we do not read that he ever has been left. For of him the bride herself says, "In my bed by night I sought him whom my soul loveth."[237] But she does not deign to rise from that bed but rather speaks to her beloved at the door as I have said, for she knows that there is no stain except out of that bed, and she does not want to defile her feet.

Dinah went out into the world to see the women of a strange country, and was defiled.[238] And as the captive monk Malchus heard from his abbot and later discovered for himself, the sheep that leaves the fold quickly becomes prey to the wolf.[239] We should never, then, assemble a great number in our monasteries and use its maintenance as a reason—or excuse—to go out into the world, acquiring wealth for others while we bring harm to ourselves and are consumed, as lead is in a furnace, for the sake of a little silver; for the lead and silver both will be consumed in the furnace of temptation. They will object that the Lord has said, "Him that cometh to me, I will not cast out," but I do not want to cast out those we have already accepted, only that we provide for them without casting out ourselves when we accept them. For the Lord himself did not cast out anyone he had accepted, but rejected anyone who too eagerly offered himself; when the scribe said, "Master, I will follow thee wherever thou shalt go," he replied, "The foxes have holes, and the birds have nests, but the son of man hath not where to lay his head."[240]

---

[236] Cant. 5:3. The point is elaborated in Abelard's Sermon 33 on John the Baptist.

[237] Luke 17:34; Cant. 3:1.

[238] For the story of Dinah, daughter of Jacob and Leah, see Gen. 34:1 ff.

[239] See Jerome, *Vita Malchi*.

[240] John 6:37; Matt. 8:19–20. The manuscripts quote only through "foxes have holes," adding "etc."

He also told us to look to the charges that are necessary before we consider any action:

> For which of you having a mind to build a tower doth not first sit down and reckon the charges that are necessary, whether he hath the means to finish it, lest after he hath laid the foundation and is not able to finish it, all that see it begin to mock him, saying, "This man began to build but could not finish"?[241]

If someone has the means to save himself alone, that certainly is a great thing, but it is dangerous to provide for others when one hardly has the means to look after himself. No one can be careful in looking after others if he has not been cautious in accepting them; and no one can persevere in a task he has undertaken as well as someone who is slow and deliberate in beginning. Indeed, the caution of women must be all the greater as their strength to bear burdens is less and their need to foster stillness is more.

Scripture is the mirror of the soul, it is agreed. We live through its reading and thrive through its understanding. In it each of us sees the beauty or ugliness of his character, endeavoring to increase the one and remove the defects of the other. As Saint Gregory says in his *Moralia*:

> Holy Scripture is like a mirror held up before the eyes of the mind, in which our inner aspect can be seen. In it we see our faults and look upon our beauty. In it we realize how far we have advanced and how far we are from advancing.[242]

But someone who looks at scripture without understanding is like a blind man holding up a mirror to his eyes. He does not have the means to see who he is and does not seek to learn what scripture teaches, which is its only purpose. Like an ass with a lyre, he sits idly with the book,[243] as if he had some bread set down before him that does not satisfy his hunger. He cannot enter God's word

---

[241] Luke 14:28–30; cf. the *Calamities*, p. 37.

[242] *Moralia* 2.1.

[243] See the proverb cited by Jerome, *Epistulae* 61.4.

through his own understanding or use another's teaching to break his way in. His bread does him no good; he does not thrive.

This is why the Apostle calls us all to the study of scripture. "For whatsoever things were written," he says, "were for our learning, that through patience and the comfort of the scriptures, we might have hope." And elsewhere: "Be ye filled with the Holy Spirit, speaking to yourselves in psalms and hymns and good songs of the spirit." A man speaks *to himself* or *with himself* when he understands what is to his good and can reap from his understanding the harvest of his words. Paul also said to Timothy, "Till I come, attend to reading, to exhortation, and to doctrine," and:

> But continue in those things which thou hast learned and which have been committed to thee, knowing from whom thou hast learned them, and because from thy infancy thou hast known the holy scriptures, which can instruct thee to salvation by the faith which is in Jesus Christ. All scripture inspired by God is profitable to teach, to reprove, to correct, to instruct in justice, that the man of God may be perfect, furnished to every good work.[244]

He also urged the Corinthians to understand scripture to be able to expound what others say about it:

> Follow after charity, be zealous for spiritual gifts, so that you may prophesy. For he that speaketh in a tongue, speaketh not unto men but unto God, for no man heareth. . . . But he that prophesieth, edifieth the church. . . . And therefore he that speaketh in a tongue, let him pray that he may interpret. I will pray with the spirit, I will pray also with the understanding; I will sing with the spirit, but I will also sing with the understanding. Else, if thou shalt bless with the spirit, how shall he that holdeth the place of the unlearned say "Amen" to your blessing because he knoweth not what thou sayest? For thou indeed givest thanks well, but the other is not edified. I thank my God I speak with all your tongues, but in the church I had rather speak five words with my understanding that I may instruct others also than ten thousand words in a tongue.

---

244 Rom 15:5; Eph. 5:18–19; 1 Tim. 4:13; 2 Tim. 3:14–17.

Brethren, do not become children in sense, but in malice be children and in sense be perfect.[245]

*To speak with a tongue* means to form words with the mouth alone and not minister to others by an explanation that operates through the understanding. But *to prophesy*, or *interpret*, means to understand what one says and so be able to explain it to others, in the manner of the prophets, who are also called seers, and those who see are those who understand. *To pray* or *sing with the spirit* is to form words with a certain prolongation of the breath alone without fitting them to the understanding of the mind. But when our spirit prays—that is, forms words only with the prolongation of our breath without conceiving in the heart what is uttered by the mouth—our mind loses the benefit it ought to have from speech, that is, to be impelled toward God through its own understanding. So, Paul tells us to realize this full perfection in our words, so that we may not, like children, merely utter words but know how to understand their sense. Otherwise, he indicates, all our prayers and singing bear no fruit.

[Saint Benedict also follows him in this, saying, "Let us approach our singing in such a way that our mind may be in harmony with our voice."[246] And the Psalmist tells us, "Sing ye wisely," that is to say that the savor of understanding should be added to our song so that we may say in truth along with him, "How sweet are thy words to my palate, more than honey to my mouth." And elsewhere he says, "The Lord shall not take pleasure in the legs of a man,"[247] for the *tibia*, or the leg bone, that is to say, the flute, produces sounds for the pleasure of the senses, not for the understanding of the mind. So, people are said to sing well or to play well on the flute but not to please God by their music if their pleasure in the melody is such that they derive no understanding from it.]

[And, the Apostle asks, how can someone say "Amen" to the blessings offered in church if he does not understand what the blessings pray for?[248] He couldn't know if it is for something good or not. We often see many people in church who do not know any Latin, and they could end up praying for something harmful by mistake. For example, the words, "That we may so pass through temporal things that we lose not eternal things,"

---

[245] 1 Cor. 14:1–20.

[246] *Rule of St. Benedict*, chapter 19.

[247] Ps. 46:8, 118:103 (the manuscripts quote only through "palate," indicating the rest of the verse by "etc."), 146:10.

[248] See 1 Cor. 14:16.

could be confused with "we *choose* not eternal things" because they sound so much alike, or maybe "*use* not eternal things." But the Apostle says something to prevent it: "Else, if thou shalt bless with the spirit"—that is, if you form the words of a blessing with the prolongation of the breath but do not instruct the mind of your hearer with its sense—"how shall he that holdeth the place of the unlearned"—that is, somebody nearby who is supposed to answer and give an answer that the unlearned couldn't or shouldn't give—"say 'Amen'?" and so forth—that is, when he doesn't know if you're making him give a blessing or a curse? And finally, how can women even edify *themselves* with a sermon, or understand and explain the Rule, or correct someone's bad pronunciation, if they do not understand what the writing says?][249]

So, I cannot help but wonder what wiles of the devil have brought it about that there is no study of scriptural interpretation in our monasteries, although there is formal education in singing alone and in the formation of words alone, but not in their understanding. It is somewhat as if the bleating of sheep were considered more useful than the feeding of them. But the soul has its own food, its own spiritual nourishment, and that is the understanding of God's scripture. When the Lord sent out Ezekiel to preach, he first caused him to eat a book, which suddenly "became as sweet as honey in his mouth." And of such food it is written in the Lamentations of Jeremiah, "The children have asked for bread, but there was none to break it unto them." To break bread unto children is to open the meaning of the letter to the ignorant, but *these* children ask for their bread to be broken when they long to feast their souls on the understanding of scripture. As the Lord bears witness elsewhere, "I will send forth a famine into the land, not a famine of bread, nor a thirst for water, but of hearing the word of the Lord."[250]

But our ancient enemy has sent forth into our cloisters a famine and a thirst for hearing the words of men and the swiftly passing rumors of the world. As we devote ourselves to this vain, empty talk, the more tiresome we think the word of God, more stale and flat and tasteless to us without the spice or sweetness of understanding. And so, the Psalmist says, "How sweet are thy words to my palate, more than honey to my mouth," and the source of that sweetness he reveals in the next verse, "By thy commandments I

---

[249] Likely later additions to the text by readers eager to try their own hands at scriptural exegesis.

[250] Ezek. 3:3; Lam. 4:4; Amos 8:11.

have had understanding—that is to say, I have taken understanding from your commandments and not the commandments of men, and they have taught me and instructed me. The result of this understanding follows next: "Therefore, I have hated every way of iniquity." The ways of iniquity are many and so open in themselves that they are hated and contemned by all, but only by the word of God do we recognize these ways and become able to avoid them. And so, he says, "Thy words have I hidden in my heart that I may not sin against thee."[251] They are *hidden in the heart,* not merely sounded on the lips, when our thought retains the understanding of them. But the less we apply ourselves to this understanding, the less we can recognize and avoid those evil ways, and the less we can protect ourselves from sin.

Such negligence is reprehensible, especially in monks, who aspire to perfection and have all the facilities for learning at hand: their libraries abound in sacred books, and they have all the tranquil leisure they can use. But those who glory in the number of their books but still refrain from reading deserve the stinging rebuke from the elder in the *Lives of the Fathers:*

> The prophets composed the books, and your forefathers came after them and added many things. Their successors then committed them to memory. Then the present generation came and copied them out on paper and on parchment, and put them back to sit idle on the shelves.[252]

And Abbot Palladius calls us both to learn and to teach: "It is fitting for the soul that lives according to Christ's will either to learn faithfully what it does not know or to teach plainly what it knows."[253] But if, when it can, the soul will do neither, it suffers under a madness; for the first step in withdrawing from God is a weariness with learning, and when the soul has lost an appetite for what the soul forever craves, how can it love God?

In his exhortation of monks, Saint Athanasius recommended reading and learning to the point where he allowed it even to interrupt prayer. "I will trace the course of our way of life," he said:

---

[251] Ps. 118:103, 11.

[252] *Vitae Patrum* 5.10.114.

[253] *Vitae Patrum* 5.10.67.

First, the cultivation of abstinence, endurance of hunger, persistence in prayer and reading—or, for someone who has not yet learned to read, let him have the desire to hear, born from an eagerness to learn. These are the first stages, as if of nurselings in the cradle, of our progressive knowledge of God.

But soon he continues, saying first, "But we must become so insistent in our prayers that scarcely any time should come between them," and adding finally, "And nothing should interrupt them, except for intervals of reading."[254]

[The apostle Peter would offer no different advice: "Be always ready to satisfy every one that asketh you a reason of the word of hope and faith."[255] And the apostle Paul: "We do not cease to pray for you and to beg that you be filled with the knowledge of his will in all wisdom and spiritual understanding." And again: "Let the word of Christ dwell in you abundantly in all wisdom." In the Old Testament, too, God's word inspired men with a similar concern for his teaching; so David says, "Blessed is the man who hath not walked in the counsel of the ungodly. . . . But his will is in the law of the Lord. . . ." And the Lord says to Joshua, son of Nun, "Let not this book depart from thy hands and thou shalt meditate upon it day and night."[256]]

[The slippery ways of evil thoughts often work themselves into these matters as well. Constant diligence may prepare the heart for God, but the cares of the world gnaw at us and make us apprehensive for them. If a man must endure this without end who is devoted to the struggles of religious life, surely the indolent man will never be free from them.][257]

And Pope Gregory says in Book 19 of his *Moralia:*

We lament the fact that the time has already begun when we see many with positions in the Church who do not act on what they understand, or who even scorn to understand and know the holy word itself. They turn their attention from the truth and listen only to fables, and "all seek the things that are their own, not the things that are Jesus

---

[254] Athanasius, *Exhortatio ad Monachos.*

[255] Cf. 1 Pet. 3:15, in which the Vulgate reads, "a reason of that hope which is in you."

[256] Col. 1:9, 3:16; Ps. 1:1–2; cf. Josh. 1:8, in which the Vulgate reads, "Let not the book of this law depart from thy mouth."

[257] A series of comments on a variety of points made over the last several pages, most likely added by later hands.

Christ's." The scriptures of God are everywhere and are set before their eyes, but men think it beneath them to come to know his word. There is hardly a man who seeks to know what he has believed.[258]

Both the Rule that governs their calling and the examples set by the Fathers strenuously urge them to this reading. Benedict says nothing about the practice and teaching of singing, but lays down many instructions about reading, even setting fixed times for reading as he does for manual labor. He also makes provision for the teaching of writing and composition, including tablets and a pen among the necessary articles the abbot should supply the monks.[259] And when among other things he commands, "At the beginning of Lent, each monk will receive a book from the library, which he will read straight through from the beginning,"[260] what can be more absurd than to spend this time on reading without troubling to understand? [The proverb of the wise man is well known: "Reading without understanding is not reading at all," and to such a reader the words of the philosopher apply: "An ass set in front of a lyre."][261] For a reader with a book but without the capacity to fulfill its purpose is like an ass confronted with a lyre. Far better for him to turn to other things, in which there may be some use, than to sit there dumbly staring at the letters and then idly flip the page, for we see in such a reader the words of Isaiah fulfilled:

> And the vision of all shall be unto you as the words of a book that is sealed, which when they shall deliver to one that is learned, they shall say, "Read this," and he shall answer, "I cannot, for it is sealed." And the book shall be given to one that knoweth no letters, and it shall be said to him, "Read," and he shall answer, "I know no letters."
> And the Lord said, "As much as this people draw near me with their mouth and with their lips glorify me, still their heart is far from me, and they have feared me with the commandment and with the doctrines of men. Therefore,

---

[258] *Moralia* 19.30. The internal quotation is from Phil. 2:21.

[259] See *Rule of St. Benedict,* chapters 48 and 55.

[260] *Rule of St. Benedict,* chapter 48.

[261] *Distichs of Cato,* prologue (Chase 1922, 12); cf. Jerome, *Epistulae* 61.4. One manuscript includes this passage, most likely added by later hands.

behold I will proceed to cause an admiration in this people
by a great and wonderful miracle. For wisdom shall perish
from their wise men, and the understanding of their prudent men shall be hid."[262]

These days in our cloisters men are said to know letters who have
learned only to make the sounds. But as far as understanding is concerned, they might as well not know how to read, since for them the
book remains as sealed as it is for those they call illiterate. The Lord
rebukes these men, saying *they draw near him with their mouth and lips*
but not with their heart, for the words which they can pronounce in
a fashion they cannot understand at all. In their ignorance of the
word of God, they tamely follow the customs of men rather than the
useful value of scripture. Because of this, the Lord threatens that
those who are considered wise and sit as doctors among such men
also will be blinded.

The greatest true Doctor of the Church and the glory of our
monastic calling, Saint Jerome, calls us to a love of reading—"Love
knowledge of the scriptures and you will hate sins of the flesh"[263]—
and we know from his own testimony the labor and expense he
incurred to learn. Among the many things he wrote about his own
course of study to help teach us through the force of his example, he
wrote this to Pammachius and Oceanus:

> When I was young, I burned with a love of learning, but I
> was not so presumptuous, as some men are, as to try to
> teach myself. I heard Apollinaris often at Antioch, and I
> honored him because he made me learned in scripture. I
> already had some gray in my hair—more like a teacher
> myself than a student, I'm afraid—but I went off to Alexan-
> dria to study with Didymus; I am still grateful to him for
> many things, for I found out how much I didn't know. They
> thought I'd put an end to all this schooling but, back to
> Jerusalem, back to Bethlehem—the work! the *cost!*—where I
> took lessons from the Hebrew Baranina. The lessons had to
> be at night because he was afraid of the Jews, but he turned
> out to be a second Nicodemus.[264]

---

[262] Isa. 29:11–14.

[263] *Epistulae* 125.11.

[264] *Epistulae* 84.3. For Nicodemus, who came to Jesus secretly at night, see John 3:1.

Surely, he remembered what he had read in Ecclesiasticus: "My son, from thy youth receive instruction and even to thy gray hairs thou shalt find wisdom."[265] But he himself found instruction not only in the words of scripture but in the example of his monastic fathers; to his rich praises of that most excellent monastery, he added this on its practices in scriptural education: "I never saw such study or understanding of sacred knowledge and scripture. You would have thought that almost every one of them was an orator on divine learning."[266] The Venerable Bede also, who was taken into a monastery as a boy, has this to say in his history of the English:

> Spending all the remaining time of my life in that same monastery, I wholly applied myself to the study of scripture, and along with my observance of the discipline of the Rule and my daily singing in church, I always took delight in both learning and writing.[267]

But those who are educated in monasteries nowadays remain so stubbornly foolish that, content with the sound of the letters, they ignore the meaning of the words, happy to instruct the tongue and leave the heart alone. As Solomon says in Proverbs, "The heart of the wise seeketh instruction, and the mouth of fools feedeth on foolishness."[268] And the less these men are able to love God, the further they would keep us from an understanding of him and from the meaning of the scripture that teaches us about him.

I think there are two main reasons for this: the envy of the lay brothers or the superiors themselves, and the empty talk of idleness, which has captured the devotion of so many monastic cloisters in these times. When they want to have us concentrate, as *they* do, on earthly rather than spiritual things, these men act like the Philistines who persecuted Isaac, continually filling his wells with earth, even as he dug them, and stopping the flow of water.[269] As Saint Gregory explains in Book 16 of his *Moralia*:

---

[265] Ecclus. 6:18.

[266] Rufinus, *Historia Monachorum* 21, formerly attributed to Jerome.

[267] *Historia Ecclesiastica* 5.24.

[268] Prov. 15:14.

[269] See Gen. 26:14 ff.

> When we concentrate on the holy word, we often have to put up with the intrigues of malignant spirits, who throw the dust of earthly thoughts on our mind to darken the eyes of our concentration against the light of inner vision.[270]

The Psalmist had put up with this too long when he said, "Depart from me, ye malignant, and I will search the commandments of my God,"[271] indicating that he could not observe the commandments of God while he had to put up with the intrigues of malignant spirits in his mind. In the work of Isaac this is signified by the wickedness of the Philistines, who kept filling the wells he dug with earth. For we are digging wells of our own when we penetrate the depths of holy scripture for meanings that are hidden there. But the Philistines—in the hidden or symbolic sense—fill these wells with earth when unclean spirits heap thoughts of earthly things upon us as we strive for these depths, and they keep us, as it were, from the water of sacred knowledge we have found. No one overcomes these enemies by his own strength, as we hear from Eliphaz: "And the Almighty shall be against thy enemies, and silver shall be heaped together for thee,"[272] or in other words, "So long as the strength of the Lord keeps malignant spirits from you, the great treasure of his word will shine in you the brighter."

But unless I am mistaken, Saint Gregory had been reading the homilies of Origen, the great Christian philosopher, and had drawn from Origen's wells what he now is saying about Isaac's. For Origen worked hard to dig wells of the spirit and urged us both to drink from them and to dig others of our own. As he says in his twelfth homily:

> Let us try to do what wisdom advises: "Drink water from thy wells and from thy springs, and let thy spring be thine own." And you, my listener, even you, try to have a well of your own and a spring of your own, so that when you take up a book of scripture, even you may begin to bring forth some understanding derived from your own sense and following what you have learned in the church. And try, even you, to drink from the spring of your inborn intelligence.

---

[270] *Moralia* 16.18.
[271] Ps. 118:115.
[272] Job 22:25.

Inside you is a source of living water, veins that never cease to flow, running channels of rational understanding—if only they are not clogged with earth and stones. Dig away your earth, clear away the rubble that is blocking your intelligence, rid yourself of sloth, shake off the torpor of the heart. For hear what scripture says: "Prick the eye and bring forth tears, but prick the heart and bring forth understanding." Free your intelligence from rubble, even you, so that someday you may drink from your own springs, swallow drafts of living water from your wells. For if you have taken the word of God into yourself, if you have received the living water from Jesus and have received it with faith, it will become in you a spring of water flowing to eternal life.[273]

In his next homily he writes of the springs of Isaac:

The wells the Philistines had filled with earth are, no doubt, men who are blocked in their spiritual understanding; they do not drink themselves nor allow any others to drink. Hear what the Lord has said: "Woe to you Scribes and Pharisees, for you have taken away the key of knowledge; you yourselves have not entered in, and those that were entering in you have hindered." And the passage continues: "And as he was saying these things to them, they began violently to oppress him and to stop his mouth about many things, lying in wait for him and seeking to catch something from his mouth that they might accuse him."[274]

But we must never give up digging wells of living water but, by arguing all things, disputing all things—sometimes new things, sometimes old—become like the scribe, instructed in the kingdom of heaven, of whom the Lord said, "He bringeth forth out of his treasure both new things and old." Let us then return to Isaac and dig wells of living water as he did. And even if the Philistines stop these wells, and even if they fight, let us continue digging nonetheless, so that we too may hear it said, "Drink water from thy cisterns and thy wells." And let us dig them deep, and let the

---

273 *Homilia in Genesim* 12.5. Internal quotations are from Prov. 5:15 and Ecclus. 22:24.

274 Luke 11:52. The manuscripts quote only through "you have hindered," indicating by "etc." the rest of the passage, which Abelard, of all people, surely knew.

water overflow, not only so that the knowledge of scripture may be enough for ourselves alone but so that we may educate others and teach all men to drink. Yes, let them drink, and the beasts of the fields as well. In the words of the prophet, "Thou wilt preserve both men and beast, O Lord."

And then:

A Philistine knows earthly things but does not know where in all the earth to find water, where to find rational sense. What is the good in having education but not knowing how to use it, in having language but not knowing how to speak? That is the condition of the children of Isaac, who dig for living water across the earth.[275]

But it must not be that way with *you*. Those of you who, standing aloof from vain and idle talk, have attained the grace of some learning must apply yourselves to become deeply learned in those things that pertain to God, as it is written of the man called blessed in the psalm: "His will is in the law of the Lord, and on his law he shall meditate day and night." The good that results from this study follows next: "And he shall be like a tree which is planted near the running waters, which shall bring forth its fruit in due season." For a tree is dry and barren which is not watered by the rivers of God's word, of which it is written, "From his belly shall flow streams of living water." These are the streams the bride in Canticles describes as part of her praise of the Bridegroom: "His eyes are as doves on brooks of waters, which are washed with milk and sit beside the plentiful streams."[276] And you as well, washed with the milk that is the whiteness of your chastity, must sit like doves beside these streams and drink drafts of wisdom from them—not only to learn but to teach, to show others, as it were, the way to turn their eyes; not only to know the Bridegroom for yourself but to have the means to speak of him to others.

It is written of the matchless bride of God, who was found worthy to conceive him through the ears of her heart, "But Mary kept all

---

[275] Origen, *Homilia in Genesim* 13.2–4. Internal quotations are from Matt. 13:52, Prov. 5:15, and Ps. 35:7.

[276] Ps. 1:2, 3 (the manuscripts quote only through "waters," indicating the rest of the verse by "etc."); John 7:38; Cant. 5:12.

these words, pondering them in her heart."[277] And so, the great mother of the highest Word itself, *keeping these words in her heart*, not on her tongue, then *pondered* them all carefully, arguing every one, weighing each against the other, to determine how they might all be consistent. She knew that, according to the veiled speech of the law, every animal was called unclean which did not ruminate, or chew the cud, and have divided hooves. For, in fact, no soul is clean which does not, by meditating to the best of its ability, ruminate, or chew the cud of God's commandments, and which does not display discretion in following them, so as not only to do good but to do well, that is, to act with correct intention. This discretion of the heart is the division of the hooves of all clean animals, and of it, it is written, "If thou offerest rightly but dividest not rightly, thou hast sinned."[278]

"Anyone who loveth me will keep my word," the Truth has said.[279] But who can keep the words and the commandments of the Lord in all obedience without first understanding them? No one will be diligent in observance who has not been attentive in her listening. Think of that blessed woman who put aside all other things and sat at the feet of the Lord to hear his words;[280] and she heard them with the ears of her understanding, which is precisely what the Lord himself demands: "He that hath ears to hear," he tells us, "let him hear."[281]

[But if you cannot be fired to such intense devotion, at least follow in your study of holy scripture the example of Paula and Eustochium, those blessed students of Saint Jerome, at whose request he brought light to the Church with so many volumes of his writings.][282]

---

[277] Luke 2:19.

[278] Gen. 4:7 in its Septuagint version.

[279] John 14:23.

[280] That is, Mary, sister of Martha; see Luke 10:38–42.

[281] Matt. 11:15.

[282] This anticlimactic passage, which also segues a bit too neatly into Abelard's letter on the nuns' studies and *The Questions of Heloise*, is likely a later addition.

# THE QUESTIONS OF HELOISE

## INTRODUCTORY LETTER

## HELOISE TO ABELARD

The text known as *The Questions of Heloise* (*Heloisae Problemata*) consists of forty-two short queries on scripture together with Abelard's replies. Although it is not transmitted as part of the canonical letter collection, its introductory letter follows directly from Heloise's words in the Fifth Letter and Abelard's in the Seventh.

Saint Jerome would praise Marcella with extraordinary praise,
offering encomia to her studies,
her passion for scripture,
and her ever-questioning mind.
As he wrote in his commentary on Galatians:

"I know her ardor, I know her faith,
I know the fire she has in her heart
to surpass her sex, forget mankind,
beat the drum of Holy Writ,
and cross the raging Red Sea of this world.
While I lived in Rome, she never came to me so fast
as when she had some question about scripture—
not like some tractable Pythagorean,
to accept every word I said because I said it.[1]
Authority without reason had no power over her.

---

[1] Ancient Pythagoreans were notorious for their reliance on the authority of the master's word. *Ipse dixit*—"He himself said it"—became a catchphrase sufficient to resolve all their disputes.

She left nothing unexamined or unweighed,
nothing unsubjected to the keenest critical spirit.
She seemed less like my student than my judge."[2]

The progress she had made in her studies
even led him to appoint her as a teacher
over others who shared her passion for this learning.
As he once wrote to Principia:

"You have Marcella and Asella both there with you,
as you pursue scripture and the sanctity of body and mind.
One will lead you through the meadows of Holy Writ
to him who sings,
'I am the flower of the field and the lily of the valleys.'
The other is a flower of the Lord herself,
like you, and worthy of the words,
'As a lily among thorns, so my love among the maidens.'"[3]

All this your wisdom knows far better than I.

Then, why do I repeat it, my beloved,
my heart's own,
dear to us all but dearest to me?
Take it not as schooling but a reminder
not to neglect your obligations
nor be slow in discharging your debt.
We are the handmaids of Christ
and your daughters in the spirit.
You have gathered us together in your oratory
and bound us to the service of God.
You have always counseled us to turn our minds
to the word of God and the reading of his scriptures,
calling it the mirror of the soul,
in which we can see our true ugliness or beauty,
and which no bride of Christ should be without
if she seeks to please the one
to whom she has given her life.
You also told us that reading without understanding

---

[2] *Commentarii in Epistulam ad Galatas* 1.

[3] *Epistulae* 65.2. The internal quotations are from Cant. 2:1 and 2:2.

is like holding up a mirror before the blind.[4]
My sisters and I have taken this to heart
and have acted in obedience to your words
as fully as we could,
until we have completely fallen in love
with the learning about which Jerome said,
"Love knowledge of the scriptures
and you will hate sins of the flesh."[5]

But now we are disturbed by many questions,
which has made us slower in our reading.
We cannot love what we do not understand,
and as we labor in this field, it does not seem
that we can make much progress on our own.
So, we send our humble questions on to you—
    your students to their teacher,
    your daughters to their father—
and we ask and we implore you,
    we implore you and we ask,
that you do not think it beneath your dignity
to address yourself to answering them for us,
for it was at your urging—
no, it was at your command—
that we came to take up this study above all.

    You will see we have not arranged them in the order of the scriptures, but only as they occurred to us each day. But here we have set them out, and we anticipate your reply.

---

[4] Cf. the Seventh Letter, p. 243.
[5] *Epistulae* 125.11.

# ABELARD'S CONFESSION OF FAITH

## ABELARD TO HELOISE

This short letter was preserved by Berengar of Poitiers, one of Abelard's students, in his *Apologeticus,* a spirited defense of Abelard addressed to Bernard of Clairvaux and Abelard's other opponents at the Council of Sens in 1140, after which Abelard was condemned for heresy and sentenced to perpetual silence, all copies of his writings ordered destroyed.

My sister Heloise, once dear to me in the world, now dearest to me in Christ:

Logic has made me hateful to the world, for those twisted men who twist all things and are wise only to destroy claim that I stand alone when it comes to logic but badly stumble when it comes to Paul. And when they praise the brilliance of my intellect, they slander the purity of my Christian faith; and in all, they come to judgment led by prejudice and not by what experience should teach them. I would not be the philosopher who would challenge Paul; I would not be the Aristotle who is barred from Christ, for there is no other name under heaven in whom I must be saved. I worship Christ who rules at the right hand of the Father. With the arms of faith I embrace him who works as God in the glorious flesh of the Virgin which he assumed from the Paraclete. And to dispel all doubts and anxiety from your heart, hold fast to this assurance: that my conscience is founded upon that rock on which Christ has built his church. To what is inscribed on that rock I will briefly bear witness for you.

I believe in the Father and the Son and the Holy Spirit, one in nature and true God, who in the persons of the Trinity preserves his Unity in substance forever. I believe that the Son is co-equal with the Father in all things, in eternity and power, in will and operation. I do not hold with Arius, who, driven by a twisted intellect or led astray by some demoniacal spirit, establishes degrees within the Trinity, teaching that the Father is greater and the Son is less,[1] oblivious to the precept of the law, "Thou shalt not go up by steps unto my altar."[2] For he goes up by steps unto the altar of God who posits a first and last in the Trinity. And I bear witness that the Holy Spirit is consubstantial with the Father and the Son and co-equal with them in all things and is the one who, as my books declare, is known by the name of Goodness. And I condemn Sabellius, who claimed that the person of the Father is the same as the Son and that the Father suffered the Passion of the Cross, and whose followers are then called Patripassians.[3]

And I believe that the Son of God became the Son of man; that his single person is of and in two natures; and that, after he fulfilled the mission he undertook by becoming man, he suffered and died and was resurrected and rose into heaven, whence he will come to judge the living and the dead. And I assert that in baptism all sins are remitted; that we are in need of grace, in which we may begin and persevere in good; and that, though fallen, we may through penance be made whole. I will not speak of the resurrection of the body— what is the need?—for if I did not believe in resurrection, all my boasts of being a Christian would be vain.

This then is the faith on which I rest, from which I draw the firmness of my hope. Anchored here in safety, I do not fear the barking of Scylla, I laugh at the whirlpool of Charybdis, I do not shrink from the song of the Sirens that brings death.[4] In the howling storm I am unshaken, in the onrushing winds I am unmoved, for I am founded on this rock, and it is firm.

---

[1] Arius (c. 250–336) was a heretic who claimed that the Son was not of one nature and substance with the Father but of a lesser and derivative nature.

[2] Exod. 20:26.

[3] Sabellius (fl. 215) was a heretic who claimed that God was a single indivisible substance with three modes rather than three distinct persons; the word "Patripassian" denotes the Passion, or suffering, of the Father.

[4] Scylla, Charybdis, and the Sirens were dangers that confronted Ulysses on his epic sea voyage home.

# LETTERS OF HELOISE
## AND
# PETER THE VENERABLE

# PETER TO HELOISE

*To the abbess Heloise, his revered sister, most beloved in Christ
From Peter, abbot of Cluny, her humble brother:*
  *The salvation God has promised those who love Him.*

**I** was pleased to have received the recent letter which you sent me
through my son Theobald; I welcomed it with every warm feeling
for its sender. I did want to write back right away and tell you what
had been in my heart, but with the constant demands of urgent
business—to which, I'm afraid, I must surrender most, if not all, of
my time—it simply proved impossible. At last, though, I have a day
that is relatively free and have set myself to do what I first
intended.[1]

I wanted, first, to reciprocate at least in words the good will you
have shown me both in your letter and earlier with your kind gifts,
and to let you know the place of love in the Lord I keep for you in my
heart. But, you know, I did not begin to love you only now; my love
in fact goes back for many years. I remember I was very young—still
too young to be considered a young man, but somewhere near the
upper edge of adolescence—when I first began to hear your name,
not yet, of course, in connection with your religious life but in connection with your admirable studies.[2] People at the time would talk
about a woman, who, while not yet disentangled from the bonds of

---

[1] Peter was on an extended trip to Spain when Abelard died on April 21, 1142. The let-
ter dates from after his return in 1143 and most probably from 1144. The letter of
Heloise to which he refers does not survive. Theobald was a monk of Cluny, whom
Peter used as a messenger on at least one other occasion; see Constable 1967, vol. 2, 177.

[2] Peter was born in 1092 or 1094; Heloise, evidently somewhat older, would have
been born perhaps in 1090, perhaps a few years earlier. At the time Peter remembers—say, 1115 or a year or two before Heloise's affair with Abelard began—Peter
would have been in his early twenties, Heloise in her mid-twenties at the youngest.
He was just beginning as prior at Vézelay in Burgundy, over 100 miles from Paris;
Heloise's fame must have been widespread, indeed.

the world, still devoted all her energies to literature and the pursuit of secular wisdom—something very rare, indeed—and none of the world's pleasures with its trifles and delights could distract her from her commitment to these good and useful arts. While nearly all the world is sunk in indifference to these studies, and wisdom can hardly find a place to stand—I will not say among women alone, who seem to have rejected it completely, but even among the hearts of men—you outstripped every woman and surpassed nearly every man by holding to your studies, by persisting.

But soon you turned these studies in a far better direction, when, as the Apostle says, it pleased the Lord who separated you from your mother's womb to call you by His grace.[3] Where there had been logic, now there was the Gospel; where there had been metaphysics, now there was Saint Paul. Plato you exchanged for Christ, the Academy for the cloister, now a woman of philosophy in the full and truest sense.[4] You beat the enemy and robbed him of his spoils. You left the treasure-house of Egypt behind and embarked on a pilgrimage through the wilderness, building a precious tabernacle to God in your own heart. You sang a song of praise with Miriam when Pharaoh was cast down, taking in your hands, as she once did, the timbrel of blessed mortification,[5] and sending a new melody to the very ears of God, a skillful and a scholarly musician. By the beginning you have made, you set your heel on the head of the old serpent, who is always the enemy of women. By persisting now through the grace of the Almighty, you will crush him and so destroy him he will never again dare to hiss against you. You have made a mockery of the proud prince of the world, this "king over all the children of pride," in the words of God to Job,[6] and you will do so in the future, forcing him to wail and groan, as you bind him for yourself and the handmaids of God who are with you.[7] "The cedars in the paradise of God were not higher than he, the fir trees did not equal his top,"[8] and yet the most wondrous thing of all, a wonder to be set above all wonders, is that he is beaten by the weaker sex, the mightiest archangel mastered by a fragile woman. Your battle brings

---

[3] Cf. Gal. 1:15.

[4] Peter speaks in very similar terms of Abelard in the epitaph he composed for him.

[5] See Exod. 15:20–21.

[6] Job 41:25.

[7] Cf. Job 40:24.

[8] Ezek. 31:8.

great glory to God, deep disgrace to the Deceiver, whose arrogant hopes to equal God's sublimest majesty will now appear absurd, when he has failed in his brief fight with woman's weakness. And the victor in that struggle—her head awaits a jeweled crown from heaven's King, and rightly so for such a victory: for as weak in body as she was throughout the battle, she will only appear more glorious in her eternal reward.

I do not say these things to flatter you, my dearest sister in the Lord, but to exhort you and encourage you to remember the great good in which you have persisted for some time and to become fiercer in your purpose to preserve it. Fire the hearts of your company of women with all the words and examples at your command; they serve the Lord with you by virtue of the grace you have received: now rouse them to fight in that same struggle. You are one of the living creatures of the prophet Ezekiel's vision, though as a woman you must burn and give off light, not like a coal of fire, but like a lamp.[9] You are a student and disciple of the truth, to be sure, but to the women entrusted to your care, you are also a teacher and a master of humility—yes, a master of humility and all of heavenly learning, appointed so by God—and as such, must be responsible not only for yourself but for your flock. Your burden is that much greater, but so is your reward. The palm of victory belongs to you on their behalf since, as you know, all those who, under your command, have subdued the world and vanquished its proud prince will win you many triumphs, many glorious trophies in the eyes of the eternal Judge and King.

It is nothing new in human history for women to be commanders over women or even to take up arms and fight side by side with men. If indeed "it is right to learn even from an enemy,"[10] we can read from among the pagans that Queen Penthesilea often led her Amazons into battle at the time of the Trojan War, and the Amazons were women and not men.[11] And among God's chosen people, the prophetess Deborah fired the heart of Barach, judge of Israel, against the gentiles.[12] Then why should women of virtue and strength not be allowed to captain armies of the Lord, marching at

---

[9] See Ezek. 1:13: "And the appearance of the living creatures was like that of burning coals of fire and like the appearance of lamps."

[10] Ovid, *Metamorphoses* 4.428.

[11] For Penthesilea, see, e.g., Virgil, *Aeneid* 1.491 and 11.662.

[12] See Judg. 4:9 ff.

their head against a powerful armed foe, if the Amazon queen could fight the enemy hand to hand—and wasn't *this* unbecoming to a woman?—and our own Deborah stirred men to battle, put weapons in their hands, and fired their hearts for the fighting of God's war? And after, when King Jabin was defeated, his general Sisara killed, and the entire godless army overpowered, she began to sing her song, her hymn of praise to God. But when you have won your victory over far more powerful foes, yours will be a far more glorious song, and you will sing with such rejoicing that you will never stop rejoicing and never stop singing your song. What Deborah was for the people of Israel, you will be for the handmaids of God, your own army of heaven, and you will never cease the struggle that will bring such great rewards, no matter what may come, until you triumph.

You will be a second Deborah in another way as well, since, as you know, her name means "bee" in Hebrew, and that is what you will become, a bee; for you also will make honey, and not for yourself alone.[13] All the good things you have gathered from the flowers of your reading you will render in the form of your example and your words and in every way you can both to your sisters at home and to others everywhere. For the short span of this mortal life, you will fill yourself with the private sweetness of the scriptures and your sisters with your public teaching, until that day when, in the prophet's words, "The mountains shall drop down eternal sweetness, and the hills shall flow with honey and with milk."[14] I know that this was spoken about the time of grace, but nothing prevents us from taking it as about the time of glory. In fact, I think it is even sweeter so.

I myself would find it sweet to talk with you at greater length on such a subject. Your learning enchants me, your religious life even more, which I have heard so much about from many quarters. If only you lived here with us at Cluny, or at the joyous prison of Marcigny[15] with the other handmaids of Christ who are awaiting their release into heavenly freedom. I would rather have had the riches of your knowledge and devotion than the greatest treasures of any king, and would rejoice to see that brilliant college of our sisters shine even brighter for your presence. And you would have derived

---

[13] Cf. *Anthologia Latina* 257.2: "You bees do not make honey for yourselves."

[14] Joel 3:18.

[15] Site of a noted Cluniac convent about twenty-five miles southwest of Cluny.

no little benefit from them. You would marvel, I know, to see the pomp and arrogance of the world trodden underfoot, every sort of luxury and excess transmuted to a marvelous austerity, and once-soiled vessels of the devil become the purest shrines of the Holy Spirit. You would watch young girls of God, stolen as it were from Satan and the world, erecting high walls of virtue on the bedrock of their innocence and raising to the very heights of heaven the rooftop of a blessed edifice. Your heart would smile to see them flower in angelic chastity in company with the most virtuous of widows, and all of them alike awaiting the glory of that great and blessed resurrection, their bodies enclosed so snugly in their houses as if already in a tomb of blessed hope. You may already have all this and more in the colleagues God has given you; there may be nothing we could add to help advance your sacred studies. I only know that our commonwealth here would be very much enhanced by the addition of all your gracious talents.

But God's providence ordains all things, and you have been denied us. We were allowed the presence, though, of someone dear to you—I mean the man whose name I must speak often and always with honor, Christ's servant and true philosopher, Master Peter, whom providence brought to Cluny in the last years of his life and enriched it with his presence "far above gold and topaz."[16] No brief account can do justice to the holiness, the humility, and the devotion of his life among us—all Cluny is its witness. I cannot remember ever seeing his like in the modesty of his dress or his demeanor—not even Germanus could have seemed more lowly or Martin himself more poor.[17] At my insistence, he took on a higher rank in our community than his recent entry would normally have warranted, but he always looked the least of all our monks in the extreme simplicity of his clothing. I often wondered at this and, seeing him in our processions—where according to our custom he would walk with the others ahead of me—I found myself nearly speechless that a man of his enormous reputation could comport himself with so little self-importance, so little self-regard. There are some in our religious life, of course, who are more than eager to assume an undue opulence even in the religious garb they wear, but for this very reason, I suspect, he was absolutely spartan in his

---

[16] Ps. 118:127.

[17] Peter most likely has in mind St. Germanus of Paris (sixth century) and St. Martin of Tours (fourth century), both major figures in early French monasticism.

dress, content with a simple garment of each kind, and wanting
nothing more.

In food and drink and in all his physical needs, he was the
same: a rebuke in words and mode of life to everything but the
barest of necessities for both others and himself. He was constant
in his reading, steadfast in his prayer, unbroken in his silence
except when a private conference among the monks or a public
address on divine matters to their assembly would force him to
speak. And he was regularly present at the holy sacraments, offering the sacrifice of the immortal Lamb to God whenever he could,
and after he was restored to apostolic favor through my labor and
my letters, this became his normal practice.[18] But why say more?
All his mind was devoted to meditation about God, all his speech
to the teaching of philosophy, all his work to the affirmation of
learning.

He lived with us like this for quite some time, an upright and
straightforward man, fearing God and shunning evil, devoting his
remaining days to God. When the disease of his skin became worse
and he developed other ailments as well, I sent him for some rest to
our priory near Chalons.[19] The climate there is pleasant, perhaps the
best in Burgundy, and I thought the place would suit him, being
close to the town but on the opposite bank of the Saône. There he
renewed his old studies, at least so far as his health would permit,
always bending over his books, never letting a moment go by without "either praying or reading or writing or composing," as was
said of Gregory the Great.[20]

And that is where the good angel came upon him, in the midst of
his holy work; and he found him, not asleep, as are so many, but alert
and wide awake. He found him truly wide awake, and he called him
to the wedding feast that is eternal life as a wise, not a foolish, virgin,
for he took with him a lamp full of oil, that is, a conscience filled with

---

[18] Peter had written to Pope Innocent II, probably in July 1140, after Abelard's condemnation at the Council of Sens, requesting that Abelard be allowed to remain at
Cluny under "the shield of apostolic protection"; see Letter 98 in the edition of Constable. No papal response survives, but Peter's words here indicate that his request
was granted.

[19] Peter speaks of sending him to "Cabilo," that is, the priory of St. Marcellus, about
thirty miles north-northeast of Cluny.

[20] John the Deacon, *Vita Gregorii*, 1.8. None of Abelard's writings can be securely
dated to this period, and Peter's comments here, as elsewhere in the letter, may be
more gracious than exact.

the testimony of his holy life.[21] As he came to discharge the common debt of mortal beings, his sickness became worse and brought him quickly to the end. Then, how he made his profession of faith, and then his confession of sins, with piety, devotion, and a truly Catholic spirit; how he received with open heart and deep emotion the viaticum for his journey and the pledge of eternal life that is the body of our Lord and Redeemer; how he commended his body and soul to Him both now and forever in faith—to all of this his brothers in religion can bear witness, and the community of that monastery where the body of the martyr Saint Marcellus lies.

So did Master Peter end his days, renowned throughout the world for his teaching and his knowledge, and known everywhere as a student of Him who said, "Learn from me, for I am meek and lowly of heart."[22] For remaining meek and lowly of heart did he make his way to Him, as I believe. And so, my revered, my dearest sister in the Lord, this man, to whom you clung after your marriage in the flesh with the stronger, finer bonds of divine love, your partner and your guide throughout your long service to God, God now enfolds in His embrace in place of you, as another you, and He keeps him there for you until the coming of the Lord, and the voice of the archangel, and the trumpet blast that signals the descent of God from heaven, when through grace he will be restored to you again.

Remember him in the Lord, and, if you will, remember me. And commend to the prayers of your holy sisters all the brothers of our community and the sisters who, with all their might, serve the same Lord as you throughout the world.

---

[21] See the parable of the wise and foolish virgins, Matt. 25:1–13.
[22] Matt. 11:29.

# HELOISE TO PETER

*To Peter, revered abbot of Cluny, her most venerable father and lord*
*From Heloise, his own humble handmaid and God's:*
    *The spirit of saving grace.*

To us, the coming of your worthiness
was the coming of God's mercy.
We are grateful, kindest father,
and we glory that your greatness
has descended upon us,
for we are small;
indeed, your coming would be cause for glory
to anyone, however great.
Others know what good they may derive
from the good of your high presence.
I myself do not have the words to say,
or even the intellect to comprehend,
all the good your visit brought to us,
all the personal pleasure to me.

My abbot and my lord:

You celebrated Mass in our presence
on the sixteenth of November of last year.[1]
You commended us to the Holy Spirit in that Mass.
You feasted us in our chapter
with your preaching of God's word.
You restored to us the body of our master

------

[1] For all Heloise's precision here, the year of Peter's visit to the Paraclete is not
known. In the period following Abelard's death, it could have been in 1144, 1146–
1149, or 1152–1154, and an earlier date is certainly more likely than a later; see Constable 1967, vol. 2, 210.

and extended to us the kindness of Cluny.[2]
And to me,
whom you in your high humility
condescended to call your sister
both in writing and in speech,
though I am not even worthy of the name handmaid,
you gave a singular token of sincerity and love,
a trental of masses to be sung after my death
by the entire community of Cluny.[3]

You indicated you would confirm this gift
with a document marked with your seal.
What you granted to your sister—
or, let me say, your handmaid—
may you fulfill now as her brother—
or, let me say, her lord.

May it please you to send me a second document,
also marked with your seal,
containing the absolution of our master
in letters for all to read,
to be displayed above his tomb.

May I also remind you,
in the love you bear both God and me,
about your Astralabe,
that you would find a prebend for him
either in Paris or another diocese.[4]

Farewell, and may the Lord keep you
and someday grant us your presence once again.

---

[2] In the Second Letter Abelard had expressed the wish to be buried at the Paraclete. For Peter to have had the body exhumed from its grave at St. Marcellus and to have personally accompanied it to the Paraclete was surely an extraordinary thing. To do so, he took the body "in secret," as he admits in his absolution of Abelard; see the note to his following letter.

[3] That is, a series of thirty commemorative masses, indeed a high distinction.

[4] Astralabe, son of Heloise and Abelard, would have been in his mid-twenties at the time of Abelard's death. By calling him "*your* Astralabe," Heloise seems simply to be commending his career to Peter's care; compare Peter's responding comment later.

# PETER TO HELOISE

*To Heloise, my revered and dearest sister, handmaid of God, and*
*teacher and captain of the handmaids of God*
*From her humble brother Peter, abbot of Cluny:*
*The fullness of God's salvation and of my own love in Christ.*

**I** am certainly delighted to discover from your letter that my visit to you was no transitory thing, that not only had I come to call but in fact I never left. My stay, I see, was not like the fleeting memory of a guest who spends a single night; I did not become "a stranger and sojourner among you"[1] but "a fellow-citizen of saintly women and a member of the household of God."[2] Your keen mind has held on to each detail. Everything I did or said on that whirlwind of a visit left an impression on your warm and generous heart—and I do not mean only what I said with careful consideration: not even what I might have said without giving it much thought has fallen to earth unnoticed. But *you* noticed it all and, with unbounded kindness, stored it away in your tenacious memory as if it were something great, something sent from heaven, something sacrosanct, like the words and deeds of Jesus Christ Himself. Possibly it struck you in this way because of what it says about guests in the monastic rule we both observe: "Let all who arrive be received like Christ."[3] Or possibly because of what is written about the holders of high positions, "He that heareth you, also heareth me,"[4] even though I hold no high position over you. I can only hope that I always remain in such high favor and that you remember me as faithfully in your prayers.

---

[1] Gen. 23:4.

[2] Eph. 2:19. Peter aptly feminizes the gender of the Vulgate's masculine "saints."

[3] *Rule of St. Benedict*, chapter 53.

[4] Luke 10:16.

But because long before I saw you, and even more now that I've met you, I have kept a special place of "charity unfeigned"[5] for you in the deepest recesses of my mind, I will reciprocate as I can. The gift of the trental of masses which I gave you while I was present, I am sending you in my absence, as you wanted, signed and sealed. I am also sending the absolution of Master Peter in a document likewise signed and sealed, just as you ordered.[6]

About your Astralabe, who for your sake is now my Astralabe, I will happily try to find him a prebend in some distinguished church or other as soon as I have the chance. It is not an easy matter, though, since, as I've often found, bishops usually make themselves very difficult when it comes to offering prebends in their own churches. But for your sake, I will do what I can as soon as I can.[7]

---

[5] 2 Cor. 6:6.

[6] The text of Peter's absolution survives:

> I, Peter abbot of Cluny, who received Peter Abelard as a monk of Cluny, and who took his body in secret and brought it to the abbess Heloise and the nuns of the Paraclete, by the authority of almighty God and all the saints, and in virtue of my office, absolve him of all his sins.

Peter also contributed (possibly to an obituary roll which circulated among religious houses) a verse epitaph for Abelard, which is among the most famous of the many composed for him:

> Socrates of Gaul, great Plato of the West,
> Our Aristotle, equal or superior in logic
> To anyone who has ever lived,
> Prince of learning, known throughout the world,
> Wide-ranging in his genius, subtle and acute,
> Mastering all things by reason and the art of speech—
> This was Abelard. But he came to greater mastery
> When, having professed himself a monk of Cluny,
> He came to the true philosophy of Christ.
> There he well completed the final tasks of his long life
> And, on the twenty-first day of April, gave hope
> Of being numbered among the good philosophers.

[7] Peter's actual efforts on behalf of Heloise's son are not known. Astralabe did, however, become a canon of the cathedral of Nantes.

SELECTED SONGS AND POEMS

OF

PETER ABELARD

Of all the love songs which Abelard wrote to Heloise, and of which he said in his *Calamities,* "Many . . . are still popular, as you know, and are sung throughout the country, especially by those who like the sort of life I was living then," none has been transmitted under his name. Among love lyrics transmitted anonymously, however, the most persistent case for Abelardian authorship has been made for the poem "Dull Is the Star" (*Hebet sidus laeti visus*), preserved in the collection of the *Carmina Burana,* partly—but not solely—on the basis of the pun on Heloise's name in the second stanza. For a discussion of the poem and the possibility of its attribution to Abelard, see Dronke (1968, 315 ff.) and Dronke and Orlandi (2005, 141).

## DULL IS THE STAR

Dull is the star once bright with grace
  In my heart's dark cloud.
Faded is the smile from my face,
  With no joy endowed.
    Justly I grieve,
For though it is near, hidden to me
Is the tender, blossoming tree
    To which I cleave.

In love this lovely girl outshines
  Every other one.                    10
Her name reflects the beaming lines
  Of Helios the Sun.
    She is the mirror
Of the sky. In her I rejoice.
She is my life, my only choice,
    Now and forever.

I rue the time, each day, each hour,
  Of my solitude,
I who nightly pulsed with power,
  With such aptitude               20
    For kissing lips
That breathe with spices when they part,
And from which, to bewitch the heart,
    Sweet cassia drips.

She wastes away and is without
  Hope of nourishment.
Her youth's flower withers with drought.
  May this banishment
    In reparation
Be annulled, and be it guaranteed                    30
That life together will succeed
  This separation.

*—translated by Stanley Lombardo*

Abelard was a prolific composer of liturgical songs, contributing over ninety hymns and several sequences for use at the Paraclete, text and melody alike. Of this great number, the music for only a few is recoverable in staff notation. The melody given below for the Hymn for Saturday Vespers, "*O Quanta Qualia*—How Great the Sabbath," follows Weinrich (1969, 302). For a sound recording of this and other melodies attributed to Abelard, see *Monastic Song: 12th Century Monophonic Chant,* performed by the Theatre of Voices; Paul Hillier, director.

# HYMN FOR SATURDAY VESPERS

O quan-ta    qua-li-a    sunt il-la Sab - - ba-ta
How great the Sab - - bath, how ho - ly is    the day,

quae sem-per ce - le - brat su-per-na cu - - ri-a.
Ob-served in hea-ven's court for all    e-ter - - ni-ty.

Quae fes-sis  re-qui-es,    quae mer-ces for-ti-bus
What rest for the wea-ry,   For the brave what  re-ward

cum    e-rit om-ni-a    De-us in    om-ni-bus
When at last our God will be  Ev'-ry-thing   in   all.

How great the Sabbath,
  How holy is the day
Observed in heaven's court
  For all eternity.
What rest for the weary,
  For the brave what reward
When at last our God will be
  Everything in all.

That will be the city
  Of the true Jerusalem,                              10
Where peace is perpetual,
  And happiness supreme.
Where neither does desire
  Outstrip its chosen prize,
Nor does the prize fall short
  Of all our desires.

What King is this, what court,
  What palace may this be,
What deep abiding peace,
  What sweet repose, what joy?                        20
They who share this glory
  Alone might ever tell,
Only if they could express
  Everything they feel.

Meanwhile it is our duty
  To lift on high our minds,
Seeking our fatherland
  With prayers of every kind;
And after our exile
  Come out of Babylon,                                30
And return to the city
  Of Jerusalem.

There will all our trials
  Be over at last and done,
And chant we then in peace
  The canticles of Zion.
Then will your blessed people
  For your grace bestowed

Render unto Thee, O Lord
  Continual gratitude.                                    40

Then Sabbath after Sabbath,
  Sabbath without cease,
Ever shall we celebrate
  In perpetual bliss.
Joy inexpressible,
  Everlasting jubilee,
Sing we with the angels
  For all eternity.

Glory be forever
  To the everlasting Lord,                                50
From whom, to whom, in whom
  Are all things that are.
All things are from the Father
  And come through the Son.
In the Father and Holy Spirit
  All things are one.

*—translated by Stanley Lombardo*

# HYMN FOR THE FEAST OF THE PRESENTATION OF JESUS IN THE TEMPLE

Adorn the chamber, Zion,
As you await the Lord,
Receive the bride and bridegroom
With the candles' light.

You virgins wise,[1]
Now trim your lamps,
Rise up, young girls,
And to your lady run.

---

[1] See the parable of the wise and foolish virgins, Matt. 25:1 ff., whose language pervades the first half of the hymn.

Let the household kindle torches
And to the world's true light                10
Run with all your lanterns lit,
All the household run.

Happy old man, hasten,[2]
Fulfill the promised joy,
A revelation to the gentiles,
Reveal the light to all.

The widow pledged to God[3]
And to his temple given,
Prophetess with equal joy
Profess unto the Lord.                        20

To the Father and the Son
With the Holy Paraclete
As there is one substance
So let one glory be.

—*translated by Stanley Lombardo*

## HYMN FOR THE NIGHT OFFICE AND VESPERS

After the Virgin's highest honor,
So high she is the mother of God,
With what virtue and what honor
Are the ranks of women endowed
In many ways and varied
Sacred history teaches us.

First to live in paradise, Adam
Was made outside, woman within,
So the very place betokens
How excelling their creation,             10

---

2 Simeon, who prophesied at the temple when Jesus was presented there; see Luke 2:25–35.

3 The prophetess Anna; see Luke 2:36–38.

Formed from the rib of a man,
Their strength the strength of bone.

This strength wells up in many women
When the courage of men runs dry,
Deborah the Judge is witness,
The widow who laid low Holofernes,
The woman worthy of solemn Mass,
The mother renowned of seven sons.

The daughter of victorious Jephtha
Livened his hand to her own throat,                    20
Choosing death so that her father
Would not defraud himself of grace.[4]

*—translated by Stanley Lombardo*

The laments for Jephtha's daughter and for Saul and Jonathan belong to a sequence of six laments Abelard composed for the Paraclete. The subject of the first, taken from Judges 11:30–40, is the ancient yearly ritual of mourning for a young woman who embraced her own death at her father's hands rather than see him violate a vow he had made to God. The image it presents of her determination to sacrifice herself in order to save the integrity of even a rash and foolish man seems to have been particularly compelling to Abelard, who returns to it in the Second and Sixth Letters and in the hymn, "After the Virgin's Highest Honor." As Mary Martin McLaughlin writes (1975, 313), "We are inevitably reminded of another vignette, the picture of the young Heloise taking the veil at Abelard's command." For an extended discussion of the form and the themes of the poem, see Dronke and Alexiou (Dronke 1992, especially 377–84).

## LAMENT OF THE VIRGINS OF ISRAEL FOR THE DAUGHTER OF JEPHTHA

To the festive choral dances
Come you virgins as accustomed.

---

[4] All part of Abelard's standard catalog of heroic women. For Deborah, see Judg. 4:4 ff.; for the widow Judith, slayer of Holofernes, see Jth. 8; for the mother of seven sons, "worthy of solemn Mass," see 2 Macc. 7; for Jephtha's daughter, see Judg. 11:30–40.

As accustomed sing now dirges
Mournful chants and melodies.
With your faces stained with tears now
Like mourners at a funeral,
Put away your gilded gowns,
All your finery and jewels.
Jephtha of Gilead's virgin daughter,
Pitiable sacrifice of her father                                    10
Demands her yearly threnody,
The virgin strains of melody
Owed to virtue of a virgin:
Every year her dirge is due.
O virgin more held in awe than mourned!
How rare the man who can compare to her!
That her father's vow not be vain
And he defraud our blessed Lord,
For him she comforted the people
And urges him to her own throat.                                    20
    When he returned victorious
    From the battle with his army
    She ran ahead of all to greet him,
    Rejoicing with her timbrel.

Seeing her the anxious father groans, aware
Of his vow, claps at first then beats his breast;
The people's triumph becomes lamentation.

    "You've cheated me, daughter,"
    The general says, "my only one,[5]
    And will destroy my joy                                   30
    When it is cheated of you.
    The victory the Lord gave
    Takes you away."

    His daughter replied,
    "Would that my ignorance
    Of such a great thing
    Befit a victim so placid.

---

[5] The Latin is *unica*, the term also used of Jephtha's daughter in the Second and Sixth Letters, despite the Vulgate's use of *unigenita*, "only daughter" (Judg. 11:34); otherwise, it is a term Abelard reserves for Heloise, as *unicus* is her term reserved for him.

Abraham willing
To sacrifice his son
Did not have from the Lord                          40
This grace: that God
Did not want the sacrifice
Of the man's own son.
As the Lord rejected a boy
So he now accepts a girl.

Please see my sex as something seemly
As you look upon the fruit of your loins,
And do that which will in fact bring you glory:

In spirit as well as in sex
Be a man, I beg of you.                             50
Do not, by preferring
Me to your soul, harm your soul or mine.
Do not let your choice
Injure others with a perverted example.
Prefer this girl to the Lord
And you will offend the Lord
As you harm your people.
Spare her, then, only
By displeasing the Lord.

This is cruelty here                                60
But piety for the Lord.
Had he not wanted sacrifice
He would not have made you victor.
So pay your debt
And please the Lord, Father.
If he is not pleased
It will not be right.
What a tender virgin
    Does not fear,
A man's strong right hand                           70
    Should bring to bear.
The promise that binds you
    Is what you yourself vowed.
But forbear for the space
Of two months' time,
And I will roam the valleys and hills
With my companions and give loud lament

That thus does the Lord deprive me of seed.
    Let the penalty of law
    Be all my punishment.                        80
    Let the remedy not be
    A victim pure in flesh
    Whom no defilement
    Nor stain has sullied."

This done, his only one returned to her father,
Entered the recesses of her chamber
And took off the veils and garments of mourning.
When she went into the bath
Surrounded by a circle of virgins
She slowly began to refresh herself,          90
Cleansing her body of all the dust,
Of all the weary toil of the road,
And then she rinsed herself off.

Cherished boxes containing
Oils of various scent
Weeping virgins brought her.
    Some anointed her
With these, while others
Did her hair, readying her for the Lord.
    A little later, coming out               100
    From the bath, the virgin, cleansed,
Sent to her father a messenger:
    Let him build an altar
    And light the fire
While she prepared the victim for sacrifice.
    What is meet for God
    Is fit for a prince.

O with how much wailing,
Universal lamentation,
    The lord receives the awful message.     110
    He urges on his people,
    They hasten to their work.
    The virgins do their
    Reverent tending,
    Readying as if for marriage
    Themselves for death.
One holds forth a silken robe

Dampened by her tears,
Another brings a purple veil
Moistened with her weeping.                    120

With gold, with gems, with pearls
Is her necklace intricate
That it may adorn her breast
And be adorned the more thereby.
Earrings and finger rings
With bracelets of solid gold
Weigh down the slender
Body of the tender virgin.

Impatient of ornate delay
She rises from her bed, rejects           130
The ponderous jewels,
And proclaims for what remained:
"What is sufficient for a bride
Is too much for one about to die."

The sword she soon brought to her father,
The naked sword she now snatched up.
Why should we go on to say more,
Why weep, lament, and beat our breasts?
Yet we will end what we've begun,
Weeping, mourning shall go on.            140
Gathering her vestments round her,
On the smoking altar's steps
She herself the sword delivered
And as she knelt the sword undid her.

O the mindless judge's mind,
O the prince's zeal insane,
O father hostile to your clan,
To destroy your only one!

Hebrew virgins tell the story
In memory of the virgin's glory,          150
O girls in Israel renowned,
With this virgin's splendor crowned.

*—translated by Stanley Lombardo*

The lament for Saul and Jonathan is based on the events of 1 Kings 31 and David's song in 2 Kings 1:17–27.

# LAMENT OF DAVID FOR SAUL AND JONATHAN

Solace of sorrows,
The cure for all woes
Is my lyre for me.
Now woes are more dire
And so my lyre
Is more sorely needed.

An army slaughtered,
A king and son dead,
Our enemy victorious,
The princes' desolation                              10
The people's desperation
Fills everything with grief.

Amalech gains strength
While Israel is forspent.
The Philistine infidel
Rejoices while
Judea laments
And torments itself.

An infidel people
Insults the faithful,                                20
The highest honor goes
To the aggressor,
Derision and scorn
Are heaped on the people.

Insulting us they say:
"The god of whom they speak
Has betrayed them—
Their own true god—
And has been cast down
By gods who are many.                                30

The king whom he appointed
Has been brought low.
Such is the selection
Of their own god,
Such the consecration
Of their great prophet."

Bravest of kings, O Saul,
Jonathan, most virtuous of all,
The enemy who could not conquer you
Has been allowed to cut you down.                    40

As if he were not consecrated,
Anointed of the Lord,
His throat has been cut in battle
By a sword in an impious hand.

More than a brother, Jonathan,
Your soul and mine were one,
What crimes, what sins
Have split our souls apart?

Mount Gilboa, may you thirst
For dew and rain.                                    50
May fruits from your fields
Never save your people.

Woe to you, woe to the soil
Soaked with royal blood,
The soil where an impious hand
Laid you low, my Jonathan,

Where the anointed of the Lord
And the glory of Israel
Lie in miserable death,
Destroyed with all their people.                     60

Jonathan, you above all
Are worthy of my grief.
Amid my every joy
Tears will fall perpetually.

O Zion's daughters, now begin
Your lamentation over Saul
In honor of whose great largesse
Purple shall adorn you.

Ah, why did I ever acquiesce
In the worst counsel                                    70
So that I was not there
To protect you in battle,

Or be run through with you
And so die happily?
For of all that love can do
Nothing is greater.

And to outlive you is for me
To perish constantly,
Nor is half a soul
Sufficient for life.                                    80

In return for friendship
I should have rendered to you
One of two services
In your desperate plight,

To share your triumph
Or be with you in defeat,
Come to your rescue
Or lie down with you in death,

And for your sake end my life
Which you so often saved                                90
So that death unite us
More than wrench us apart.

Meanwhile, having obtained
An inauspicious victory
I learned the joys that I had won
Were all too transitory.

How quickly came
The cruel messenger

Who in his pride
Had caused the death                                    100
That brought his own.
Sorrow's harbinger
Soon joined those
Whom he announced had died.

Now at last I still my lyre.
I wish my grief could rest as well.
My hands are worn from the strings.
My voice is hoarse from my lament,
And all my spirits fail.

*—translated by Stanley Lombardo*

The shaped or figurative poem had a long history in classical and medieval Latin verse. Often in such poems, the primary artifice of presenting form visually through the placement of letters on the page is supplemented by other devices—metrical, mathematical, aural, or visual—which lay stress on the materiality of language—the Word incarnate, in Christian terms—and which may rise to high levels of formal complexity and symbolic association. Such is the case in this poem, attributed to Abelard in the two manuscripts that preserve it. Its figure may derive from the mystic vision of Ezekiel 1:16: "And their appearance and their work were like a wheel in the midst of a wheel." Here, the outer wheel consists of two verses, each with the circular letter *O* at its beginning and end (and at the metrical caesura of the Latin original), so that they flow into each other, sharing a letter:

Open wide your eyes. See my body. Yes, look! To all, I show I am man, I
     wh(o),
On my throne hidden above, also command as God. This I d(o).

These *O*s (and some other *O*s spaced with rough regularity across the lines) also end ten other verses, which run outward like spokes from the center of the wheel, where their initial letters, all again *O*s, have combined into the large central *O* of the figure, the axle of the wheels. The verses together make a continuous poem:

Once by forbidden fruit the first man was so
Overcome; now my gift he's had to forgo,
Obeying woman's will, forsaking me, too.
Overwhelmed, man is imprisoned; his sobs echo.

# OPEN WIDE YOUR EYES

## A SHAPED POEM ON THE INCARNATION OF THE WORD

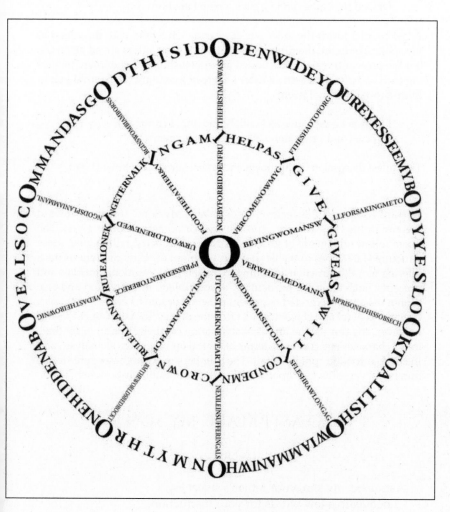

—*translated by Barbara Thorburn*

Owned by harsh toil, his flesh raw, long ago
Outcast, he knew earth in exile, in suffering also.
Openly I speak, I who firm the world's bedrock; to
Oppressed men to be received as their own I go.
Our world renewed in God's plan, I am made man. Lo!
Of God the Father and virgin's womb I am born so.

A last couplet forms the inner wheel, sharing ten letters with the verses of the spokes. In Latin, their initial, final, and caesural letters are all again Os, but the present translator has added an embellishment of her own, rendering each with the symmetrical letter I, thereby providing for an aural pun in this thoroughly visual poem:

I help as I give, I give as I will, I condemn, I crown, (I)!
I rule all and I rule alone. King, eternal king am (I).

The fullest discussion of this poem and its background is Ernst (1986).

Abelard composed the verses, "To Astralabe, My Son," sometime toward the end of his life—no more specific date or occasion can be given. The poem follows the genre of gnomic, or "advice," poetry, with a long, loose structure (1,042 lines in the latest critical edition) of many discrete sections offering moral instruction according to the terms of traditional maxims and precepts. Such a form is particularly susceptible to interpolation and also cannot usually be expected to present personal or idiosyncratic views apart from the general and conventional. Occasionally in "To Astralabe, My Son," however, one can see the unmistakable stamp of Abelard as an individual, in his characteristic concerns, terms of ethical and theological analysis, and in some autobiographical detail. The numbers in parentheses refer to the numbered verses as they appear in the edition of Rubingh-Bosscher (1987).

# TO ASTRALABE, MY SON

## (1–110)

Astralabe, my son, your father's sweet joy,
   I bequeath a few words for your instruction.
Strive hard to learn rather than to teach:
   One helps others, the other yourself.
Stop learning when there is no more for you to learn;
   Do not say or think you should stop before.
Attend to what is said, not to who says it:

Words well spoken give their author his name.
Neither should you swear by a beloved teacher's words,
  Nor be bound to him by your affection.                    10

It is the apple's fruit that nourishes, not its leaves.
  So too the sense must be preferred to the word.
Men's hearts are persuaded by elaborate language;
  Learning owes more to speech that is plain.
When words abound there is no abundance of sense:
  The wanderer must redouble his paths.
When you see that a teaching is not self-consistent
  There is nothing there that you can trust.
The unstable man changes like the face of the moon;
  The wise are always steady as the sun.                      20
A fool in his blindness wanders here and there;
  The prudent man's tread is everywhere firm.
He considers long how to be sound in his speech
  So that he is never untrue to himself.

Attend to the words of teachers, to good men's deeds;
  Let your heart be fervent with this desire.
Study long and hard but be slow to teach,
  And do not be too eager to write.
I would not have you learn from an upstart master
  Whose lessons must always be improvised.                     30
Beware above all any damage to your name
  And so remain useful to yourself and others.
Old accusations make new ones credible;
  Your earlier life vouches for your future.

Seek not your own glory but the Lord's, my son;
  Live not for yourself but for others and God.
Read Holy Scripture assiduously, I implore you,
  And other texts only for scripture's sake.
Your primary concern should be divine service;
  Let fear and love of God subdue you.                         40
No one will fear or love God as he should
  Without a proper understanding
Of how just he is, how powerful, how good in himself,
  How merciful to us, and how severe.
Let your will always be subject to God's;
  Dare to oppose it and you dare to be God.

Do not seek your own profit but what pleases him;
  The former is greed, the latter love.
It is enough that you seek only God's honor;
  He will remember to benefit you.                    50

Just as wisdom is worth more than any treasure,
  So nothing is worth less than its opposite.
No one becomes wise through native intelligence.
  A moral life is what makes a man wise.
Wisdom is nourished by deeds, not by words.
  This grace is granted to the good alone.
A wise son is a blessing and boon to his parents;
  A foolish son, their sorrow and disgrace.
What an elders bears should not be hard for one younger;
  No one should put himself above others.         60
Cato brought water and slaked the thirst of his people
  But would not allow his own thirst to be slaked.[6]
A foolish king is like a jackass sporting a crown,
  A bane to himself as well as to others.
Praise a prince's good sense rather than his army.
  Judgment, not power, is the highest regime.
When a ruler is good, it is a gift from heaven;
  Bad rulers appear when the people are bad.

Take care first to do, only later to teach, what is good
  And so remain in tune with yourself.          70
What you do not want done to others, do not to others;
  What you do want done, do also to them.
A simple man believes everyone is like himself.
  He is easy to deceive but unwilling to do so.
To be deceived is a fault, to deceive an offense.
  We cannot lack faults, but need not offend.
The wise cannot be deceived, and the good cannot deceive;
  To be deceived is a fault, deception an offense.
To think you are never deceived is the greatest deception;
  That is an attribute of God alone.              80
Do not liken yourself to God or seek the ether on high
  While confined to this shadowy earthly abode.

---

[6] See Lucan, *Pharsalia* 9.498 ff.

A just man renders to each whatever is his by right,
  The brave do not fear adversity.
A temperate man curbs his illicit impulses,
  Especially at times of prosperity.
As temperance protects us in adversity,
  So too prosperity calls for this virtue.
A virtue does not endure unless supported by others;
  Else in bad times it fails, or is lost in good.                    90
Examine well the nature of both virtue and vice:
  Lose this judgment and you lose what you are.
A philosopher discerns the hidden nature of things
  And seeks out their practical applications.

Whoever wants to be justified before the Lord
  Should never think of himself as just.
Accuse yourself, acknowledge your faults and correct them;
  Do not mouth remorse, but confess with your heart.
To avoid pride always look at your betters
  And see in them what you so far lack.                              100
Do not seek to be held great by one in power:
  You will be small if he sees you desire this.
Humble through sin and through religion proud:
  God makes us so or at some time will.
Work hard to avoid any scandal with men
  Lest you incur any scandal with God.
As much as God is better than all, so he should be more loved,
  And after him others according to degree.
Whom should we love except for the sake of God?
  In all that you do let this be the end.                           110


(247–56)


Rate reason higher than law, law higher than custom;
  Decide each case by its proper degree.
As a judge you should temper the law's rigor at times:
  This is what the lawmakers would want.                            250
Utility is the highest purpose for a law being written;
  Therefore nothing adverse should be done by law.
Believe not the greater but the better part of people:
  The number of fools is numberless.
No one adduces bad, but only good examples;
  If anyone does, he is held to be worthless.

(293–304)

A strange way of life should not make anyone proud:
   It is more seemly to live an ordinary life.
Do not seek a higher place in paradise;
   Whatever corner you have will be enough.[7]
Don't curry people's favor by wearing a habit;
   A sheepskin does not fool the wise.
They can tell the skin of sheep from the hide of a wolf;
   It is the common people who go wrong in this.      300
No opinion of the learned is more definite:
   The exterior does not commend us to God.
A habit will not make you holy; it can make you proud.
   This is truly loathsome to the best of men.

(363–84)

The world has so many religious sects
   That the path of life is hardly clear,
So many conflicting religious doctrines
   That each makes his own from his own tradition.
But in the end no one dares rely on reason
   Since his desire is just to live at peace.
A man can sin only through contempt for God
   And is not guilty except through this contempt.      370
Ignorance is not contempt for God
   Unless the ignorance is a man's own fault.
If you repent only when you can no longer offend,
   Sin abandons you, you do not abandon sin.
There are some whom their old sins still delight,
   So they never truly repent of them.
The sin's sweetness and pleasure may be so great
   That any amends are too much to bear.
This is our Heloise's constant complaint,
   Who often says to me and to herself:      380
"If, unless I repent of what I did in the past
   I cannot be saved, there is no hope for me.
The memory of what we did then, the exceeding joy,
   Is still too pleasurable and sweet for me."[8]

---

[7] Cf. the Third and Seventh Letters, p. 83 and p. 224.
[8] Cf. the Third Letter, pp. 78–9.

(637–48)

Philosophers and common people have never thought alike;
  For the latter, sensation overrules reason.
The corporeal alone holds their attention;
  They think that God has a body like theirs           640
And could not see or hear without physical organs,
  Or do anything if he did not have hands.
He is indeed all hand, eye, and ear, and from himself
  Creates all these for all his creatures.
He is in no place so that he may be everywhere at once
  And is himself the place for all places,
Nowhere confined, in potency everywhere,
  In whom all things have their subsistence.

(741–58)

There is no fault where the will is not depraved:
  It is the will alone that makes for guilt.
What we share with the wicked will not make us good;
  This has nothing at all to do with our merit.
When nature compels you to do good to someone,
  Do not count this among your good deeds.
When dumb animals' behavior is equal to humans',
  Do not think you are better but equal to them.
You should pay to Nature what is hers by right
  But still hold to God as the end in all things.      750
If you ever see anything cut off from this end,
  Know it is wholly devoid of merit.
We have been given reason for just this purpose:
  That our lives not be lacking in merit.
When you will what you do, even if under compulsion,
  Because you will it, count it to the good.
With a mind that is free foresee what must be done,
  So as not to be forced to live like a slave.

(845–58)

Although some say that everything happens by chance,
  The fact is that God arranges all things.
You may say that some things are not under our control,

But all is under the control of God.
You would be rash to thing that things happen by chance,
   When God's mind most high is present to all.     850
Nothing that happens provokes a just man's anger:
   He knows that all is well governed by God.
He is not perfect in his meditation on God
   Who even slightly doubts God's control.
I would not be surprised that those who believe in chance
   Do so only when misfortune befalls.
The just man consoles himself in every difficult strait
   That this, too, has been arranged by God.

(945–64)

Your writing and study should go on together;
   Only then can a man have a work of his own.
Nothing is more fleeting than words that you speak,
   But what you write remains when you are gone.
Poets who die live on in their writing.
   Life nature denied endures in their poems.     950
Learned men live on after death through their fame:
   Philosophy can do more than Nature.
Some who hardly had a name when they were alive
   Earned one afterward through their writings.
Socrates was poor, but is still rich in reputation
   Because he put writing above material goods.
So too Aristotle and his teacher Plato
   Are present to us in their own writings.
So too others who once in their own voices spoke
   Never stop speaking through what they have written.  960
Through writing a man, however distant, is present;
   There can be no faithful messenger.
A messenger can report only what you tell him;
   One may write much it would be awkward to speak.

(999–1006)

The perfection of supreme good set out by Christ
   Is signified in the persons of the Trinity:     1000
In God the Father divine power is expressed,
   Wherefore he is called Omnipotent.

The Holy Spirit is Goodness, the Word is Wisdom,
  One proceeding from the Father, one begotten.
A single substance unites these three persons,
  Who are distinct in their three properties.

*—translated by Stanley Lombardo*

# Appendix A

## From "The Letter to Philintus"

For most of their printed history, the letters of Abelard and Heloise have been known chiefly through a series of impostures, freewheeling and highly colored fantasias on their writings pretending to be faithful translations. Already in the fifteenth century, a forged manuscript purported to contain the French letters of "abbess Heloise of the Paraclete," which offered instruction in the art of love to a young disciple by the name of Gaultier, in the manner of one of the most famous medieval writers on love, Andreas Capellanus.[1] But the end of the seventeenth and beginning of the eighteenth century saw a vogue in such imposter texts that came to have a decisive role in how Abelard and Heloise were understood for well over a hundred years.

The scene for this vogue was set in 1675 when Jacques Alluis, a lawyer from Grenoble, published a fictionalized account of *Les amours d'Abailard et d' Héloïse* set in the form of a bourgeois romance, including many long passages of sentimental dialogue and such narrative innovations as romantic rendezvous set in gardens, a rival for Heloise's affections named Alberic (identified as "a native of Rheims"), and scenes of scandalous misbehavior among the nuns at Argenteuil. In a similar spirit twelve years later, Roger de Rabutin, count of Bussy, began privately circulating his own embellishments of the First, Second, and Third Letters composed as comic entertainments for his cousin Madame de Sévigné. These were not published until 1697, but even so they became the basis for further embellishments, written by Nicolas Rémond des Cours but published anonymously in 1693 and 1695 with the claim they were true translations from the Latin. A second edition in 1695 combined these with a reprint of Alluis' romance, anonymous versions of three additional

---

[1] See Dronke 1976, 29 ff. and 52 ff., and Brook 1993.

letters (which correspond to nothing in the Latin), and an anonymous version of the *Calamities*, which was offered under the title
*Lettre d'Abailard à Philinthe*. Different combinations of these texts
were published in the Netherlands, France, Germany, and Belgium
frequently over the next fifty years.[2]

The vogue for imposture became something more, however, in
1713, with the translation of the French texts into English by the
poet and musician John Hughes. Hughes could have had no access
to the Latin originals—the first Latin edition, published in 1616, was
unavailable to him and the second edition not published until
1718—yet his version became standard in the English-speaking
world with a position of authority that Joseph Berington's 1787
translation directly from the Latin did little to dislodge. Dozens of
editions were published through the 1940s. Even as late as the 1990s,
Hughes' words were quoted in published works as the actual words
of Abelard and Heloise,[3] and they remain the source of much misin-
formation reported on many Internet sites. But the effect of his
translations from the French went even deeper than this. It was on
Hughes' versions of the First and Third Letters that Alexander Pope
directly based his famous "Eloïsa to Abelard" of 1717, and through
the poem's own continual republication, imitation, and translation
into many European languages, the influence of the imposter texts
was considerably magnified and prolonged.

These early imposter texts were not unintelligently done, trans-
posing Abelard and Heloise into the sensibilities of the late seventeenth century. The narrative is given greater incident and color, a
wider cast of articulate characters, and a more specific psychological
background—standard devices for historical novels as well as many
screenplays made from literary sources—especially in places where
the Latin is conspicuously reticent. Abelard's correspondent in the
*Calamities*, for example, is supplied with a name (Philintus) and a
history (he also has suffered in love), and Abelard's silent sister
(here named Lucilla) now turns out to have a great deal to say. For

---

[2] The most complete account of these texts, with exhaustive publication data and fas-
cinating excerpts, is by Charrier 1933, 406 ff. In her bibliography, Charrier cites over
100 examples through 1916 of what she calls *traductions fantaisistes* into French alone
(1933, 602–13). For understandably briefer surveys, see McLeod 1971, 303 ff., and
Robertson 1972, 155–66.

[3] See, for example, Ackerman 1994, 65.

the most part, the interpretation strips away all but the erotic dimensions of the story and its characters. Abelard is cast as something of a gallant, and Heloise in her different letters vacillates between the roles of a flighty salon coquette and a Racinian Phèdre torn between reason and love.

It was Heloise in the latter role whom Pope chose to portray and whom nineteenth-century readers in particular chose to purify and elevate into "the great saint of love."[4] When her body was transported in 1800 for the collection of a Paris museum, scores of cultists made off with bits of bones and teeth to prize as relics.[5] During a rash of sentimental suicides in the 1830s, a professor at the University of Nancy proposed that a "hospice for the incurably heartsick" be founded on the site of the Paraclete.[6] The neo-Gothic tomb Heloise had shared with Abelard in the cemetery of Père-Lachaise since 1817 became a place of such constant pilgrimage that in 1869 Mark Twain could scoff, "Go when you will, you find somebody snuffling over that tomb."[7]

The imposter texts show traces of humor as well, a legacy of the work of Rabutin-Bussy, and occasionally an air of parody. But if it is parody, it is an exceptionally strong parody to have set its stamp on its material so deeply and for so long.

In the following excerpts from Hughes' "Letter to Philintus," I have modified the spelling and punctuation for a somewhat better fit with modern usage, and have silently corrected some obvious typographical errors. Otherwise, the passages are as they appear in *Letters of Abelard and Heloise, With a Particular Account of Their Lives and Misfortunes, to Which Are Added Poems by Pope, Madan, Cawthorne, etc. etc.*, printed for bookseller R. Scott by J. Hardcastle (New York 1808). No other author, translator, or editor is indicated.

---

[4] The phrase was first used by the nineteenth-century historian Henri Martin in his *Histoire de France*, cited by Charrier 1933, 499 n. 7. Charrier's account is by far the most complete for all periods of the reception of Heloise, but see also Robertson 1972, chapters 9–12.

[5] See Charrier 1933, 338 ff. and Plate 18, in particular, which depicts a reliquary in the shape of a young woman, designed to house these precious body parts; and McLeod 1971, 238 ff.

[6] Charrier 1933, 322, 501.

[7] Twain 1869, 141.

The last time we were together, Philintus, you gave me a melancholy account of your misfortunes. I was sensibly touched with the relation and, like a true friend, bore a share in your griefs. What did I not say to stop your tears? I laid before you all the reasons philosophy could furnish which I thought might any ways soften the strokes of fortune. Grief, I perceive, has wholly seized your spirits, and your prudence, far from assisting, seems quite to have forsaken you. But my skillful friendship has found out an expedient to relieve you. Attend to me a moment, hear but the story of my misfortunes, and yours, Philintus, will be nothing, if you compare them with those of the loving and unhappy Abelard. Observe, I beseech you, at what expense I endeavor to serve you, and think this no small mark of my affection, for I am going to present you with the relation of such particulars as it is impossible for me to recollect without piercing my heart with the most sensible affection. . . .

✌ ✳ ✌

There was in Paris a young creature (ah! Philintus) formed in a prodigality of nature to show mankind a finished composition—dear Heloise, the reputed niece of one Fulbert, a canon. Her wit and her beauty would have fired the most sensible heart, and her education was equally admirable. Heloise was a mistress of the most polite arts. You may easily imagine that this did not a little help to captivate me. I saw her, I loved her, I resolved to endeavor to engage her affections. The thirst of glory cooled immediately in my heart, and all my passions were lost in this new one. I thought of nothing but Heloise; everything brought her image to my mind. I was pensive, restless, and my passion was so violent as to admit of no restraint. I was always vain and presumptive; I flattered myself already with the most bewitching hopes. My reputation had spread itself everywhere, and could a virtuous lady resist a man that had confounded all the learning of the age? I was young: could she show an insensibility to those vows which my heart never formed for any but herself? My person was advantageous enough, and by my dress no one would have suspected me for a doctor; and dress, you know, is not a little engaging with women. Besides, I had wit enough to write a billet-doux and hoped, if ever she permitted my absent self to entertain her, she would read with pleasure those breathings of my heart.

Filled with these notions, I thought of nothing but the means to speak to her. Lovers either find or make all things easy. By the offices of common friends, I gained the acquaintance of Fulbert, and (can you believe it, Philintus?) he allowed me the privilege of his table and an apartment in his house. I paid him, indeed, a considerable sum, for persons of his character do nothing without money, but what would not I have given? You, my dear friend, know what love is. Imagine, then, what a pleasure it must have been to a heart so inflamed as mine to be always so near the dear object of desire! I would not have exchanged my happy condition for that of the greatest monarch on earth. I saw Heloise and spoke to her. Each action, each confused look, told her the trouble of my soul, and she on the other side gave me ground to hope for everything from her generosity. Fulbert desired me to instruct her in philosophy; by this means I found opportunities of being in private with her, and yet I was, sure, of all men the most timorous in declaring my passion.

As I was with her one day alone, "Charming Heloise," said I, blushing, "if you know yourself, you will not be surprised with what passion you have inspired me with. Uncommon as it is, I can express it but with the common terms—I love you, adorable Heloise! Till now I thought philosophy made us master of all our passions and that it was a refuge from the storms in which weak mortals are tossed and shipwrecked, but you have destroyed my security and broken this philosophic courage. I have despised riches, honor and its pageantries could never raise a weak thought in me, beauty alone has filled my soul. Happy, if she who raised this passion, kindly receives this declaration. But if it is an offense. . . ."

"No," replied Heloise, "she must be very ignorant of your merit, who can be offended at your passion. But for my own response, I wish either that you had not made this declaration or that I were at liberty not to suspect your sincerity."

"Ah! divine Heloise," said I, flinging myself at her feet, "I swear by yourself. . . ." I was going to convince her of the truth of my passion but heard a noise, and it was Fulbert. There was no avoiding it, but I must do violence to my desire and change the discourse to some other subject.

After this I found frequent opportunities to free Heloise from those suspicions which the general insincerity of men had raised in her, and she too much desired what I said were truth not to believe it. Thus there was a most happy understanding between us. The same house, the same love, united our persons and our desires. How many soft moments did we pass together? We took all opportunities to express to each other our mutual affections and were ingenious in contriving incidents which might give us a plausible occasion of meeting. Pyramis and Thisbe's discovery of a crack in the wall was but a slight representation of our love and its sagacity.[8] In the dead of the night, when Fulbert and his domestics were in a sound sleep, we improved

---

[8] Pyramis and Thisbe were the lovers of Ovid's *Metamorphoses* 4.55 ff., who were able to converse only through a small chink in the wall dividing their houses. When a lion interrupted a planned rendezvous outside the city, their affair ended dismally.

the time proper to the sweet thefts of love. Not contenting ourselves, like those unfortunate lovers, with giving insipid kisses to a wall, we made use of all the moments of our charming interviews. In the place where we met we had no lions to fear, and the study of philosophy served us for a blind. But I was so far from making my advances in the sciences that I lost all my taste of them, and when I was obliged to go from the sight of my dear mistress to my philosophical exercises, it was with the utmost regret and melancholy. Love is incapable of being concealed: a word, a look, nay silence speaks it. My scholars discovered it first; they saw I had no longer that vivacity of thought to which all things were easy. I could now do nothing but write verses to soothe my passion; I quitted Aristotle and his dry maxims to practice the precepts of the more ingenious Ovid. No day passed in which I did not compose amorous verses. Love was my aspiring Apollo. My songs were spread abroad and gained me frequent applauses. Those who were in love, as I was, took a pride in learning them, and by luckily applying my thoughts and verses, have obtained favors which, perhaps, they could not otherwise have gained. This gave our amours such an eclat that the loves of Heloise and Abelard were the subject of all conversations.

The town-talk at last reached Fulbert's ears. It was with great difficulty he gave credit to what he heard, for he loved his niece and was prejudiced in my favor; but, upon closer examination, he began to be less incredulous. He surprised us in one of our more soft conversations. How fatal sometimes are the consequences of curiosity! The anger of Fulbert seemed to moderate on this occasion, and I feared in the end some more heavy revenge. It is impossible to express the grief and regret which filled my soul when I was obliged to leave the canon's house and my dear Heloise. But this separation of our persons more firmly united our minds, and the desperate situation we were reduced to made us capable of attempting any thing.

My intrigues gave me but little shame, so lovingly did I esteem the occasion. Think what the gay young divinities said when Vulcan caught Mars and the goddess of beauty in his net, and impute it all to me. Fulbert surprised me with Heloise, and what man that had a soul in him would not have borne any ignominy on the same conditions? The next day I provided myself with a private lodging near the loved house, being resolved not to abandon my prey. I continued some time without appearing publicly. Ah! how long did these few moments seem to me! When we fall from a state of happiness, with what impatience do we bear our misfortunes.

It being impossible that I could live without seeing Heloise, I endeavored to engage her servant, whose name was Agaton, in my interest. She was brown, well-shaped, of a person superior to the ordinary rank, her features regular, and her eyes sparkling, fit to raise love in any man whose heart was not prepossessed by another passion. I met her alone and entreated her to have pity on a distressed lover. She answered, she would undertake anything to serve me, but there was a reward. At these words I opened my purse and showed the shining metal which lays asleep guards, forces a way though rocks, and softens the heart of the most obdurate fair.

"You are mistaken," said she, smiling and shaking her head, "you do not know me. Could gold tempt me? A rich abbot takes his nightly station and sings under my window; he offers to send me to his abbey, which, he says, is situated in the most pleasant country in the world. A courtier offers me a considerable sum and assures me I need have no apprehensions, for if our amours have consequences, he will marry me to his gentleman and give him a handsome employment. To say nothing of a young officer, who patrols about here every night and makes his attacks after all imaginable forms. It must be love only which could oblige him to follow me, for I have not, like your great ladies, any rings of jewels to tempt him; yet during all his siege of love, his feather and his embroidered coat have not made any breach in my heart. I shall not quickly be brought to capitulate; I am too faithful to my first conqueror," and then she looked earnestly on me.

I answered, I did not understand her discourse. She replied, "For a man of sense and gallantry, you have a slow apprehension. I am in love with you, Abelard. I know you adore Heloise; I do not blame you. I desire only to enjoy the second place in your affections. I have a tender heart, as well as my mistress; you may without difficulty make returns of my passion. Do not perplex yourself with unfashionable scruples. A prudent man ought to love several at the same time; if one should fail, he is not then left unprovided."

You cannot imagine, Philintus, how much I was surprised at these words. So entirely did I love Heloise that, without reflecting whether Agaton spoke anything reasonable or not, I immediately left her. When I had gone a little way from her, I looked back and saw her biting her nails in the rage of disappointment, which made me fear some fatal consequences. She hastened to Fulbert and told him the offer I had made her but, I suppose, concealed the other part of the story. The canon never forgave this affront. I afterwards perceived he was more deeply concerned for his niece than I at first imagined. Let no lover hereafter follow my example; a woman rejected is an outrageous creature. Agaton was day and night at her window on purpose to keep me at a distance from her mistress, and so gave her own gallants opportunity enough to display their several abilities.

I was infinitely perplexed what course to take. At last I applied myself to Heloise's singing master, the shining metal, which had no affect on Agaton, charming him. He was excellently qualified for conveying a billet with the greatest dexterity and secrecy. He conveyed one of mine to Heloise, who, according to my appointment, was ready at the end of a garden, the wall of which I scaled by a ladder of ropes. I confess to you all my feelings, Philintus. How would my enemies, Champeaux and Anselm, have triumphed, had they seen the redoubted philosopher in such a wretched condition? Well, I met my soul's joy, my Heloise. I shall not describe our transports; they were not long, for the first news Heloise acquainted me with plunged me in a thousand distractions. A floating Delos was to be sought for, where she might be safely delivered of a burden she began already to feel.[9] Without losing much time in debating, I made her presently quit the canon's house and at break of day depart for Bretagne, where she, like another goddess, gave the world another Apollo, which my sisters took care of.

This carrying off Heloise was sufficient revenge upon Fulbert. It filled him with the deepest concern and had like to have deprived him of all that little share of wit which Heaven had allowed him. His sorrow and lamentation gave the censorious an occasion of suspecting him for something more than the uncle of Heloise. In short, I began to pity his misfortunes and to think this robbery, which love had made me commit, was a sort of treason. I endeavored to appease his anger by hearty engagements to marry Heloise secretly. He gave me his consent, and with many protestations and embraces confirmed our reconciliation. But what dependences can be placed on the word of an ignorant devotee? He was only plotting a cruel revenge, as you will perceive by the sequel.

I took a journey into Bretagne in order to bring back my dear Heloise, whom I now considered as my wife. When I had acquainted her with what had passed between the canon and me, I found her opinion contrary to mine. She urged all that was possible to divert me from marriage: that it was a bond always fatal to a philosopher, that the cries of children and the cares of a family were utterly inconsistent with the tranquility and application which the study of philosophy required. She quoted to me all that was written on the subject by Theophrastus, Cicero, and, above all, insisted on the unfortunate Socrates, who quitted life with joy, because by that means he left Xanthippe. "Will it not be more agreeable to me," said she, "to see myself your mistress than your wife? And will not love have more power than marriage to keep our hearts more firmly united? Pleasures tasted sparingly and with difficulty have always a higher relish, while every thing by being easy and common grow flat and insipid."

I was unmoved by all this reasoning. Heloise prevailed upon my sister to engage me. Lucilla (for that was her name) taking me aside

---

[9] Pregnant with Apollo and Diana but harried by her rival, Juno, the goddess Latona found refuge on the island of Delos, then floating on the Aegean Sea. As a reward for its service to her, the island was subsequently fixed in place.

one day, said, "What do you intend, brother? Is it possible that Abelard should in earnest think of marrying Heloise? She seems, indeed, to deserve a perpetual affection. Beauty, youth, and learning, all that can make a person valuable, meet in her. You may adore all this, if you please, but, not to flatter you, what is beauty but a flower, which may be blasted by the least fit of sickness? When those features with which you have been so captivated shall be sunk and those graces lost, you will too late repent that you have entangled yourself in a chain from which death only can free you. I shall see you reduced to the married man's only hope of survivorship. Do you think learning ought to make Heloise more amiable? I know she is not one of those affected females who are continually oppressing you with fine speeches, criticizing books, and deciding on the merit of authors. When such an one is in the fury of her discourse, husband, friends, servants, all fly before her. Heloise has not this fault, yet 'tis troublesome not to be at liberty to use the least improper expression before a wife, which you bear with pleasure from a mistress.

"But you say you are sure of the affection of Heloise. I believe it; she has given you no ordinary proofs. But can you be sure marriage will not be the tomb of her love? The names of husband and master are always harsh, and Heloise will not be the phoenix you think her. Will she not be a woman? Come, come, the head of a philosopher is less secure than those of other men." My sister grew warm in the argument and was going on to give me a hundred more reasons of this kind, but I angrily interrupted her, telling her only that she did not know Heloise.

A few days after, we departed together from Bretagne and came to Paris, where I completed my project. It was my intent my marriage should be kept secret, and thereafter Heloise retired among the nuns of Argenteuil.

I now thought Fulbert's anger disarmed; I lived in peace. But, alas! our marriage proved but a weak defense against his revenge. Observe, Philintus, to what a barbarity he pursued it! He bribed my servants; an assassin came into my bedchamber by night with a razor in his hand and found me in a deep sleep. I suffered the most shameful punishment that the revenge of an enemy could invent, in short, without losing my life: I lost my manhood. I was punished indeed in the offending part: the desire was left me but not the possibility of satisfying the passion. So cruel an action escaped not unpunished; the villain had the same inflicted on him, poor comfort for so irretrievable an evil! I confess to you, shame, more than sincere repentance, made me resolve to hide myself from the sight of men, yet I could not separate myself from my Heloise. Jealousy took possession of my mind, and at the very expense of her happiness, I decreed to disappoint all rivals. Before I put myself in a cloister, I obliged her to take the habit, and retire into the nunnery at Argenteuil. I remember somebody would have opposed her making such a cruel sacrifice of herself, but she answered, in the words of Cornelia after the death of Pompey the Great—

> Ah! my once greatest lord! Ah! cruel hour!
> Is thy victorious head in Fortune's pow'r?
> Since miseries my baneful love pursue,
> Why did I wed thee only to undo?
> But see, to death my willing neck I bow;
> Atone the angry gods by one kind blow.

—Rowe's Lucan

Speaking these verses, she marched up to the altar and took the veil with a constancy which I could not have expected in a woman who had so high a taste of pleasures which she might still enjoy. I blushed at my own weakness, and, without deliberating a moment longer, I hurried myself in a cloister, resolved to vanquish a fruitless passion. . . .

❧ ✳ ❧

I live in a barbarous country, the language of which I do not understand; I have no conversation but with the rudest people. My walks are on the inaccessible shores of a sea which is perpetually stormy. My monks are only known by their dissoluteness and living without any rule or order. Could you see the abbey, Philintus, you would not call it one. The doors and walls are without any ornament, except the heads of wild boars and hinds' feet with the hides of frightful animals, which are nailed up against them. The cells are hung with the skins of deer. The monks have not so much as a bell to wake them, the cocks and dogs supply that defect. In short, they pass their whole days in hunting. Would to Heaven that were their greatest fault! or that their pleasures terminated there! I endeavored in vain to recall them to their duty. They all combined against me, and I only expose myself to continual vexations and dangers. I imagine I see every moment a naked sword hang over my head. Sometimes they surround me and load me with infinite abuses; sometimes they abandon me and I am left alone to my own tormenting thoughts. I make it my endeavor to merit by my sufferings and to appease an angry God. Sometimes I grieve for the loss of the house of the Paraclete and wish to see it again. Ah! Philintus, does not the love of Heloise still burn in my heart? I have not yet triumphed over that unhappy passion. In the midst of my retirement I sigh, I weep, I pine, I speak the dear name Heloise and am pleased to hear the sound. I complain of the severity of Heaven. But, oh! let us not deceive ourselves; I have not made a right use of grace. I am thoroughly wretched. I have not yet torn from my heart the deep roots which vice has planted in it; for if my conversion was sincere, how could I take a pleasure to relate my past follies?

Could I not more easily comfort myself in my afflictions? Could I not turn to my advantage those words of God himself, "If they have persecuted me, they will also persecute you; if the world hate you, ye know that it hated me also"? Come, Philintus, let us make a strong effort, turn our misfortunes to our advantage, make them meritorious, or at least wipe out our offenses. Let us receive without murmuring what comes from the hand of God, and let us not oppose our will to his. Adieu, I give you advice which could I myself follow, I should be happy.

# APPENDIX B

## FROM *THE LETTERS OF TWO LOVERS*

The text known as *The Letters of Two Lovers* (*Epistolae Duorum Amantium*) contains the fragments of 113 letters preserved in a late fifteenth-century manuscript between individuals, identified only as "the Woman" and "the Man," who represent themselves as an enthusiastic student and her teacher, both in love. The manuscript's first editor, Ewald Könsgen, very cautiously suggested that the fragments might be remnants of the letters exchanged between Abelard and Heloise in the early days of their affair and fondly remembered by them both.[1] The suggestion naturally focused attention on the fragments, and several scholars have supported it with arguments stressing the similarity of the situations and the fragments' use of what are taken to be characteristically Abelardian turns of phrase. The most notable and extensive set of arguments has been offered by Constant J. Mews, who confidently dubbed the fragments "the lost love letters of Heloise and Abelard" (1999). Others scholars have been decidedly more skeptical, however, pointing to the existence of other medieval letter collections that proceed from similar premises, to what are at least apparent inconsistencies between the circumstances described in *The Letters of Two Lovers* and Abelard's *Calamities*, to difficulties of preserving and transmitting such a collection, and to wide stylistic differences in the literary habits of the fragments and the accepted letters of Abelard and Heloise, differences that are unlikely to be accounted for by the passage of time alone.[2] In the face of these counterarguments, it becomes very difficult to ascribe the fragments to Abelard and Heloise, though, no doubt, the debate will continue for some time.

---

[1] Könsgen 1974. For Abelard and Heloise's recollections of their early correspondence, see pp. 11 and 62.

[2] See, e.g., the very different arguments of Dronke 1976, 24–26; von Moos 2003; Ziolkowski 2004; Constable 2005; and Dronke and Orlandi 2005.

One conspicuous feature of the fragments calls for a brief explanatory comment here, their frequent elaboration of the standard formula of salutation, "To A, from B: greetings." Each element of the formula may be extended until the salutation comes to resemble a self-conscious artifact on its own. At times the salutation is virtually all that has been preserved; at other times it can be seen introducing a specific trope, verbal device, or set of bookish references that the body of the letter will develop. Hence, Letter 22 begins

*To his jewel, fairer and brighter than the present day*
*From him who is wrapped in deep shadow:*
   *What else but that you glory in your natural radiance without cease?*

and goes on to expand the conceit into a small essay on sunlight, moonlight, and the passage of time; and Letter 45 begins

*To her house of cedar, the ivory column on which the whole house rests:*
   *The white of snow, the bright of moon, the light of sun, the height of stars, the*
   *delight of roses, the sight of lilies, the sweet of balsam, the might of earth, the*
   *respite of sky—and whatever else is sweet within their realm*

before turning its catalog of rhymes into a catalog of lovers from Terence and Ovid. Such a procedure—though not often carried out to this length—was not uncommon in medieval letters, either in genuine letters or in the numerous fictional letter collections composed as rhetorical exercises or as learned *jeux d'ésprit,* to which category *The Letters of Two Lovers* may well belong.

The selection of the fragments presented here follows the text and numbering of Könsgen's edition; ellipses [. . .] indicate omissions by the original manuscript's copyist.

## 1: The Woman to the Man

*To her heart's own love, scented sweeter than any spice*
*From her who is his in body and heart:*
   *As the flowers of your youth may fade, the bloom of happiness forever.*

. . . Farewell, my life's deliverance.

## 2: The Man to the Woman

*To the matchless joy and only solace of a weary mind*
*From him whose life is death without you:*
   *What more than himself, as he has strength in body and in soul?*

. . . Farewell, my light, for whom I would gladly die.

## 5: The Woman to the Man

*To my joyful hope:*
   *My faith and myself with every devotion, so long as I live.*

May he who bestows all arts and gives the gift of human intelligence fill my breast with the art of philosophy that I may greet you in writing, my beloved, as I would wish.
   Farewell, farewell, hope of my youth.

## 9: The Woman to the Man

*To a burning lamp, a city set on a hill:*
   *May he fight to win and race to gain the prize.*

. . . It is my deepest wish that by the exchange of letters you have proposed we may strengthen the warm friendship between us, until that happy day dawns when I will see your face—I have longed for it with all my prayers. As the weary long for shade and the thirsty long for water, so I long to see you. . . . Nothing will ever be so difficult for my body or so dangerous for my soul that I would not pay its price out of devotion to you. . . .
   Farewell in God, who is most well.

## 12: The Man to the Woman

*To one who is loved with passion and will be loved with greater passion*
*From one who is faithful beyond all others and truly is the only faithful one:*
   *Whatever the rule of sincerest love requires.*

There is no need, my sweetest, to show me in words the faith you show in your actions. If I should spend all my strength in your service, I would count it nothing, a paltry labor next to what you deserve. If every earthly good could be gathered together and placed in one heap for me to choose between that and your friendship, I would think it all worthless, out of the faith that I owe to you. . . . Yes, I am glad to have done that.

Farewell, my beauty, incomparably sweeter than every sweet thing. May you always live as happy as I wish you to be: for anything better, there is no need.

## 13: The Woman to the Man

. . . My mind is always bound in gratitude to you by a duty freely chosen. But since it could not send all the many greetings it wished, it now is silent: I did not want to list only some and then seem to slight them all. I cannot think you find it hard for me to write so often, repeating the same things over and over again, and it is easy for me, since I love you as myself and do not fail to love you with all the strength of my heart. . . .

Farewell, you who are dearer than life. Know that my life is in you, my death in you.

## 17: The Man to the Woman

*To the bottomless vessel of his every sweetness*
*From her most beloved:*
   *Let me turn from the light of the sky and gaze without end at you alone.*

As day was turning into night, I could no longer hold back from the duty I choose freely of sending you a greeting—but you dawdle and put it off.

Farewell, and know that without your welfare, no welcome and no life exist for me.

## 18: The Woman to the Man

*From an equal to an equal*
*To a reddening rose under the spotless white of lilies:*
   *Whatever lover gives to lover.*

It is deep winter, yet my breast grows warm with the heat of love. What else should I say? I would write you many more words, but a few are enough for the wise man.

Farewell, my body and heart, and all that I love.

## 19: The Man to the Woman

Yes, your words are few, but I have made them many by reading them over and over. I do not care how much you say but how giving is the heart from which it comes.

Farewell, my sweetest.

### 20: The Man to the Woman

Stars turn in the sky, the moon reddens the night,
And dull is the star which ought to be my guide.[3]
But if my star should rise and turn back the dark,
My mind will no longer know the darkness of grief.
You are my day star, my Lucifer:[4]
Without you even light is night to me,
And with you even night is splendid light.

Farewell, my star, whose splendor never wanes. Farewell, my highest hope, in whom alone I am well pleased, whom I never need bring back to mind since you never fade from mind. Farewell.

### 21: The Woman to the Man

*To her beloved, both in species and from experience of the thing itself:*
    *The being that she is.*

My mind is busy with many questions about "things,"[5] but it fails me, run through as it is by the sharp hook of love. . . . As fire cannot be mastered by any material thing but water, which nature makes its effective remedy, so my love cannot be healed by anything but you, who are its only remedy. What can I give you in return? My mind is troubled, I do not know. Glory of our young men, peer of our poets,[6] how beautiful you are to see, yet how much nobler you are to love. Being with you is my joy, being apart my sorrow. With equal force and in either case, I love you.
    Farewell.

### 22: The Man to the Woman

*To his jewel, fairer and brighter than the present day*
*From him who is wrapped in deep shadow:*
    *What else but that you glory in your natural radiance without cease?*

---

3 Cf. the poem "Dull Is the Star."

4 Lucifer, the day star, as in Job 11:17 and 2 Pet. 1:19. Cf. Letter 22 below.

5 The salutation of this letter uses the formal terminology of dialectic. It is possible that *res* in the first line of the body of the letter also should be understood in a technical way as "entities which have real being"; or the word may have its ordinary, non-technical meaning of, simply, "things." Double quotes have been set around the word in the translation at least to allow for the first possibility.

6 Perhaps in direct response to Letter 20.

Naturalists tell us that the moon takes its light from the sun. Deprived of this light, without benefit of heat or luster of its own, it shows to mortals only a dim and pallid sphere. And so it is with you and me. You are my sun, and with the happy splendor of your face you shine and give me light. I have no light but yours; without you I am faded, dark, dull, dead. But, to tell the truth, you give me more than the sun gives the moon. For the moon grows dim as it nears the sun, but the nearer I move to you, the closer I come to you, the more I burn and grow so inflamed that when I am right by you—as you have often seen—I become all fire, ablaze to the marrow of my bones.

What can I do to answer all your kindness? Nothing, I think, since in your deeds you transcend even the sweetest of your words and exceed them all in the proof of your love, so that you seem poorer in words than in deeds. Among the countless things that set you above any others, you now have this as well—that, rich in deeds but poor in words, you do more for a lover than you say. It is as much to your glory as deeds are more difficult than words. . . .

You are buried forever in my breast, and from this tomb you will never arise so long as I live. There you lie and there you rest. You are with me when I fall asleep, and while I sleep you never leave me, and after sleep I wake to see you before I see the sun itself. Others have my words, you have my thoughts. I often stumble over words because my thoughts are else-where. Who can then deny you are buried within me? . . . Time presses upon us, jealous of our love, but still you delay as if we had all the time in the world.

Farewell.

## 24: The Man to the Woman

*To a soul brighter and dearer than anything the earth has brought forth*
*From the flesh which that soul causes to breathe and move:*
    *All I owe to her through whom I breathe and move.*

The richness of your letters—and yet their insufficiency—brings me the clearest evidence of two things, your overflowing faith and your love: as it is written, "Out of the abundance of the heart the mouth doth speak."[7] . . . I receive your letters so eagerly that they always seem brief to me, both sating and inflaming my desire. I am like a man who is suffering from a fever: the more he drinks and is refreshed, the hotter he becomes. As God is my wit-ness, I am moved in a strange way the closer I look at your letters, a strange way, yes, because my heart is then struck with a joyful shudder and my

---

[7] Matt. 12:34.

body takes on a new habit and posture. Your letters are worthy of every praise, directing my attention as I read them wherever they wish.

You have often asked me, my sweet soul, what love is. I cannot excuse myself by claiming ignorance, as if I had been asked about something I have not known. For love has brought me under its command, not as some strange, external thing, but something familiar and close, even something within myself. Love is then a force of the soul, not existing through itself nor content in itself, but always pouring itself out into another with a certain appetite and desire, wanting to become one with the other and making from two diverse wills a single one in their non-difference.[8] . . .

Love may be a universal thing, but it has been contracted into such a narrow space that I would boldly claim that it reigns only in us, that it has made its home in you and me. In us it is whole, protected, and sincere, for nothing is sweet or without care for one of us if it does not bring some benefit to us both: we affirm the same things, we deny the same things, we feel the same about everything. The way you anticipate my thoughts easily proves this; what I think about writing, you write to me first, and if I remember correctly, you have said the same about yourself.

Farewell, and think of me with steadfast love, the way I think of you.

## 25: The Woman to the Man

*To her treasure beyond compare, her delight beyond all delights of this world:*
*Blessedness without end, well-being without weakness.*

I also have been thinking about love, what it is and what it can be, seeing how it derives from the likeness of our characters and interests, which most creates the bond of friendship, and how, once that is seen, it leads me to repay you with the exchange of love and also to obey you in all things. . . . If our own love could disappear on such a light impulse, it never was true love; and the sweet, smooth words that before now passed between us also were not true, but only pretended love. For love does not easily forsake whoever has once been pierced by its dart. You know, my heart's own love, that the duties of true love are performed well only when we owe them without pause, when we act for a friend as all our strength permits and never stop wishing to do more.

I will try, then, to repay this debt of love I owe to you but, to my sorrow, I cannot do so in full. But if my poor intelligence is not enough to wish you well as you deserve, then at least let my constant wish be of some benefit to you. For you should know, my love, and know it truly, that ever since your

---

[8] The formal language of dialectic, known to everyone in the schools, is evident here, as it is in the following sentence, but used in a playful and parodic way. Cf. the *Calamities*, p. 4, n. 6.

love claimed my heart for its refuge—or I should say, its crude shack—it always has been a welcome guest, more beloved every day, and—unlike the usual course of things—its constant presence has not led to familiarity, and familiarity to trust, and trust to negligence, and negligence at last to loathing.

You desired me from the beginning of our friendship, but with a greater desire you have tried to make our love last and grow. Our heart, then, varies as your circumstances change: your joy becomes my gain, your adversity my bitter loss. But for you to fulfill what you began and to increase what you completed seem two separate things to me; in the first case, something is added that was lacking, in the second, something added that was complete. We may show perfect charity to everyone, but we do not love everyone the same: what is general for all becomes specific to a few. It is one thing to sit at the table of a prince, another to be a member of his council, a greater thing to be brought there out of love than simply invited to sit down. I owe you less for not driving me away than I do for welcoming me in your arms.

I will speak plainly to your brilliant mind and to your spotless heart. It is not a great thing if I love you, no, but a dreadful thing if I ever forget you. And so, my dear, do not be away so often from your faithful friend who loves you. So far I have been able to bear it somehow, but now, hearing the song of birds, sensing the green of the forests, without your presence I languish for your love. I would have rejoiced in all these things if I also could enjoy being with you and speaking with you according to my wish. May God do for me all I desire for you.

Farewell.

## 33: The Man to the Woman

We must shake off this sloth and take up a new heat for writing along with the heat of the season. Will you go first, or shall I?

Farewell, you who are brighter than the present moon, more welcome than tomorrow's sun.

## 34: The Woman to the Man

Farewell, and think: prudent delay is better than reckless haste. Choose a time for our meeting and let me know. Farewell.

## 45: The Woman to the Man

*To her house of cedar, the ivory column on which the whole house rests:*

*The white of snow, the bright of moon, the light of sun, the height of stars, the*
*delight of roses, the sight of lilies, the sweet of balsam, the might of earth, the*
*respite of sky—and whatever else is sweet within their realm.*

Let my lyre be at your service with my sweetly sounding drum. If all would
happen as I wish, my most beloved, everything I send to you by letter I
would say to you in person. . . . When you left, I went along with you in
spirit and in mind, nothing was left at home except a useless, stolid body,
and the pain your absence causes is known only to him who sees the secrets
of each and every heart. As a desert land in summer hopes for rain from the
sky, so my mind longs for you in grief and care. But glory to God in heaven
and joy to me on earth now that I know that you are alive and well, whom I
love before all others. As often as Fortune casts me down, the consolation of
your sweetness restores me. You ride now on the wheels of your virtues,
and so are more precious to me than topaz or gold.[9] And I cannot deny you
any more than Byblis could deny Caunus, or Oenone could deny Paris, or
Briseis could deny Achilles.[10] . . . What more do I need to say? I send you all
the joys that Antiphila had when Clinia came back to her.[11] Do not be slow
in coming, for the quicker you return, the quicker you will have reason to be
glad. Now, live and be well, so you may see the time of Elijah.[12]

## 55: The Woman to the Man

*To the dearest of all things alive, who will be loved more than life itself*
*From a lover deeply devoted:*
  *Whatever is best from my whole heart and soul.*

I am sure you know, my sweet light, that ashes placed on a sleeping fire
never put it out, and though they cut off its light, they will not keep it from
smoldering forever. Even so, nothing can ever happen to quench the memory of you, which I have bound to my heart with a chain of gold. Is there
something more? As God is my witness, I love you with a true and sincere
love.

  My greatest sweetness, farewell.

---

[9] Cf. Ps. 118:127.

[10] Lovers out of Ovid, all of whom communicated by letter. For Byblis and Caunus,
see *Metamorphoses* 9.454–665; for Oenone and Paris, *Heroides* 5; for Briseis and Achilles, *Heroides* 3.

[11] Antiphila and Clinia are lovers in Terence's *Heautontimorumenos*.

[12] In Mal. 4:5, Elijah is to come before the coming of the Lord; in Ecclus. 48:11, those
who see Elijah are called blessed.

### 58: The Woman to the Man[13]

*To a friend, as I once thought*
*From the one who once was loved above all others with your words, but who now*
*    has lost love's privilege wrongfully:*
*        What the eye hath not seen and what hath not entered the heart.*[14]

Farewell. I hope you are quick to lighten my burden.

### 59: The Man to the Woman

*To his most beloved, who will be loved beyond everything that is or can be:*
*    Well-being forever and the richest success in all good things.*

Something unavoidable has come up and put its left foot against my desire.
I am the guilty one, who forced you to sin.

### 60: The Woman to the Man

*To him who up to now has been faithfully loved, who will not be loved from this*
*    time forward with a bond of weak devotion:*
*        The firm promise of love and faith, nonetheless.*

While your true love was seated firmly on its foundation, I had opened
myself to you with a great pledge of charity and had placed all my hope in
you, my tower of strength. You also know, if you can only grant it, that I
have never been deceitful toward you and that I do not wish to be. Now,
think and think again on this: I have borne many things for your sake fully
and completely. I can never write with what strength, with what intensity, I
first began to love you. If it was necessary for the ties between us to be severed, even though it may entail much bitterness, nonetheless they will not
be broken again. No more of your outcries; I will not hear your words any
more. Where I had only hoped for good, I have found tearful laments
instead.

   May almighty God, who wants no one to perish, who loves sinners with
a love beyond a father's, brighten your heart with the splendor of his grace.
May he call you back to the road of salvation. And may you understand that
his will is well-disposed and perfect.

---

[13] Letter 58 begins a sequence in which the Woman and the Man appear to quarrel. As
Letters 62 and 63 indicate, however, it has been a rhetorical exercise.
[14] Cf. 1 Cor. 2.9.

Farewell. Your wisdom and your knowledge have deceived me. From this point forward, let all our writing cease.

## 61: The Man to the Woman

*To his lady who is loved and who always will be loved*
*From her most unhappy lover and friend, whose life and death now can scarcely be*
   *distinguished from each other:*
      *That the road of the friendship we began might never come to an end,*
      *whether it is your will or not.*

I do not know what sin I have committed that in such a short time you could wish to discard every feeling of compassion and closeness for me. There can be only two possibilities: either I have sinned against you in some most serious way, or your earlier love had only been slight, that you can discard it so easily and carelessly now. If you do not explain to me more fully what you meant, I cannot see my guilty conduct toward you, unless you call it guilt to lament unhappiness and misfortunes to the one from whom some remedy is sought, some consolation expected. . . . These are not the words of a friend, not the words of someone whose heart was always kind, but of someone looking for a pretext, someone who has waited for a reason to break off love. What did I do, what did I say, I beg of you, to provoke such unforgiving words? You have thrown me half dead into the middle of the sea, have inflicted new wounds on my wounds, have heaped only pain on my pain. . . . If you had loved me, you would not have said all this. Now, choose anyone you like to judge between us, and I will clearly prove that you have sinned more against me than I have sinned against you. If anyone looked more closely at your words, he would see that they are not the words of a lover but of someone seeking a breech: nowhere in them is there a tender heart, but only a cruel breast, impervious to love. . . . But dry your tears, my soul, though I cannot dry mine.

Farewell. I received your letter with your tears, I return my letter with my own.

## 62: The Woman to the Man

*To a beloved*
*From a beloved:*
      *Whatever can be most honorable and most joyful among men.*

If I had the wit and ease of expression to respond intelligently to your words, I would happily reply with the proper decorum. As it is, I will answer as best I can within the narrow limits of my learning, although I cannot do so to your satisfaction.

Let the matter between us be resolved so that you may face no danger and I no scandal. O the hard-heartedness of man! The often-cited proverb is true, that a man's devotion is tied to the throw of the dice. If you had had to suffer shackles or chains, iron or a prison, if you had had to face the sword, I would have hoped you could not have stopped yourself from coming to me by any means you could and discussing with me those things you wrote about in your letter. I do not want any further tears to flow forth from your eyes. It is not proper for a man to cry. A man of firmness and of honor ought to conduct himself with gravity.

But it is time, my dearest, to stop these bitter and tearful disquisitions. Let us put our hands to writing happier and more cheerful things. So, write me something happy, my beloved, sing me a happy song, live in good hope and good cheer. I think you have almost forgotten me, my sweetness—when will I see you? Save at least one happy hour for me.

## 63: The Man to the Woman

*To his most beloved:*
  *Whatever sincere devotion demands uniquely of lovers.*

. . . Your letter displayed well-formed sentences and an orderly and logical arrangement. I've never seen one more appropriately set out. And, God willing, my sweetest, I will put aside for you many hours, all of them sweet and full of joy.
  Farewell, my heart.

## 66: The Woman to the Man

Clio, be with me now.[15] Give me a sign
That you will grace my tablets with your song.
Let my sleepy mind awake, for it is now
Enriched by her most glorious patronage.
And let every instrument of music play,
Inspired by the breath of Jupiter.

Look! The day advances, night retreats.
Look! The day has come and night is routed.
Look! The troop of clerics begins to shine

---

[15] Clio, presented as the chief of the Muses, all of whom make their appearances in this rather mechanical poem.

In the reflected light of their own master,
And the brilliance of their teacher puts to flight
The darkness of the one that came before him.
So, sing, you Muses, sing his praises now.

First, Clio, you: "O flower of clerics, hail!"
And then Euterpe: "May you reap all joys!"
Next Thalia: "Prosper in the waxing moon!"
Melpomene adds: "In winter storms as well!"
Terpsichore: "May you be blest forever!"
Blend your sweet song, Calliope, with theirs,
You, too, Urania: "May he grow in virtue!"
Grant him honor and moral worth, Polymnia.
And you, Erato, speak your blessing now:
"Live long and be happy through the life of this world!
Live long and rejoice in the life to come
When the blessed rejoice in each other forever!"
Let all the Muses sing: "Live long, live well,
And may your joys outnumber the fish in the sea,
The grass in the field, the drops of water in ocean!"

What more is there to say? "Have peace!"

> Amen.

Farewell, my breath, my inspiration.

## 74: The Man to the Woman

Finally I understand, my sweetest, that you are mine in all your heart and soul since you can forget all the wrongs I have done—stupidly and heedlessly, with a mind too reckless and too weak to stand up to all my sorrows—to you, my most beloved, without thought. What I said was empty, weightless, meaning nothing; and if you, my heart, will compare my words with my actions, you will see they were only words, unconfirmed by any action. You ask about my health? If you are well, then I am well; if you are glad, then I am glad: I want only to tie myself to you in every fortune.

My heart, farewell.

## 101: The Man to the Woman

*To his starry eye:*
   *Always to see what gives joy, never to feel what gives pain.*

I am who I have been. Nothing about my love for you has changed, except that the flame of love grows greater each day. This one change I confess and concede, that my love increases every moment. I speak with more caution now, you will note, approach with more caution. Shame tempers love, modesty keeps it in check—it must not rush out in full flood—so we may have all our sweet desires and little by little put this rumor about us to rest.

Farewell.

## 102: The Woman to the Man

*To him who flows with milk and honey*
*From the whiteness of milk and the sweetness of honey:*
*The liquid of every sweetness, the increase of saving joy.*

As you are the most cherished, the most beloved in my heart, as you are the most fitting for my love, as you are most auspicious, the complete answer to my prayer, may you always be well, may you always live in sweetness— this I wish you with all of my heart. The most precious thing I have I give to you—myself, firm in love and faith, fixed in my desire, forever without change.

Farewell, be happy, may nothing offend you; and may nothing hurt me through you.

# WORKS CITED AND SELECT BIBLIOGRAPHY

Ackerman, Diane. 1994. *The Natural History of Love.* New York: Vintage.

Adams, Henry. 1986 (c. 1905). *Mont Saint Michel and Chartres.* Harmondsworth and New York: Penguin.

Auerbach, Erich. 1959. *"Figura."* In *Scenes from the Drama of European Literature,* 11–76. Trans. R. Mannheim. New York: Meridian.

Bautier, R.-H. 1981. "Paris au temps d'Abélard." In *Abélard en son temps,* 21–77. Ed. J. Jolivet. Paris: Belles Lettres.

Benton, John F. 1975. "Fraud, Fiction, and Borrowing in the Correspondence of Abelard and Heloise." In Louis, Jolivet, and Châtillon 1975, 467–511.

———. 1980. "A Reconsideration of the Authenticity of the Correspondence of Abelard and Heloise." In Thomas et al. 1980, 41–52.

Blamires, Alcuin. 1997. *The Case for Women in Medieval Culture.* Oxford: Clarendon Press.

Brook, L. C. 1993. *Two Late Medieval Love-Treatises.* Oxford: Clarendon Press.

Brooke, Christopher. 1989. *The Medieval Idea of Marriage.* Oxford: Clarendon Press.

Brower, Jeffrey E., and Kevin Guilfoy, eds. 2004. *The Cambridge Companion to Abelard.* Cambridge: Cambridge University Press.

Buytaert, E. M., and C. J. Mews, eds. 1987. *Petri Abaelardi Opera Theologica. Corpus Christianorum Continuatio Mediaevalis* 13. Turnholt: Brepols.

Charrier, Charlotte. 1933. *Héloïse dans l'histoire et dans la légende.* Paris: Librarie ancienne Honoré Champion.

Chase, Wayland Johnson, ed. 1922. "Distichs of Cato." *University of Wisconsin Studies in the Social Sciences and History* 7.

Clanchy, Michael T. 1997. *Abelard: A Medieval Life.* Oxford and Malden, MA: Blackwell.

Constable, Giles. 1967. *The Letters of Peter the Venerable.* 2 vols. Cambridge, MA: Harvard University Press.

————. 2005. "The Authorship of the *Epistolae Duorum Amantium:* A Reconsideration." In *Voices in Dialogue: Reading Women in the Middle Ages,* 167–78. Ed. Linda Olson and Kathryn Kerby-Fulton. Notre Dame, IN: University of Notre Dame Press.

Dronke, Peter. 1968. *Medieval Latin and the Rise of the European Love-Lyric.* 2nd ed. Oxford: Clarendon Press.

————. 1970. *Poetic Individuality in the Middle Ages.* Oxford: Clarendon Press.

————. 1975. "Francesa and Heloise." *Comparative Literature* 26, 113–35. Reprinted in Dronke 1984a, 359–85.

————. 1976. *Abelard and Heloise in Medieval Testimony.* Glasgow: University of Glasgow. Reprinted in Dronke 1992, 247–94.

————. 1980. "Heloise's *Problemata* and *Letters:* Some Questions of Form and Content." In Thomas et al. 1980, 53–73. Reprinted in Dronke 1992, 295–322.

————. 1984a. *The Medieval Poet and His World.* Rome: Edizioni di storia e letteratura.

————. 1984b. *Women Writers of the Middle Ages: A Critical Study of Texts from Perpetua (†203) to Marguerite Porete (†1310).* Cambridge: Cambridge University Press, 107–43.

————. 1988a. "Heloise, Abelard, and Some Recent Discussions." *Proceedings of the British Academy* 74, 247–83. Reprinted in Dronke 1992, 323–42.

————. ed. 1988b. *A History of Twelfth-Century Western Philosophy.* Cambridge: Cambridge University Press.

————. 1992. *Intellectuals and Poets in Medieval Europe.* Rome: Edizioni di storia e letteratura.

Dronke, Peter, and Margaret Alexiou. 1971. "The Lament of Jephtha's Daughter: Themes, Traditions, Originality." *Studi Medievali* 3rd series 12, 819–63. Reprinted in Dronke 1992, 346–88.

Dronke, Peter, and G. Orlandi. 2005. "New Works by Abelard and Heloise." *Filologia mediolatina* 12, 123–77.

Ebbesen, Sten. 2004. "Where Were the Stoics in the Late Middle Ages?" In Strange and Zupko 2004, 108–31.

Ernst, Ulrich. 1986. "Ein unbeachtetes 'Carmen figuratum' des Petrus Abaelardus." *Mittellateinishes Jahrbuch* 21, 125–46.

Gass, William H. 1985. "The Soul inside the Sentence." In *Habitations of the Word,* 113–40. New York: Simon and Schuster.

Georgianna, Linda. 1987. "Any Corner of Heaven: Heloise's Critique of Monasticism." *Mediaeval Studies* 49, 221–53.

Gilson, Étienne. 1960 (c. 1938). *Heloise and Abelard*. Trans. L. K. Shook. Ann Arbor: University of Michigan Press.

Kauffman, Linda S. 1986. *Discourses of Desire: Gender, Genre, and Epistolary Fictions*. Ithaca, NY: Cornell University Press, 63–89.

King, Peter. 2004. "Metaphysics." In Brower and Guilfoy 2004, 65–125.

Könsgen, Ewald. 1974. *Epistolae duorum amantium. Briefe Abaelards und Heloises? Mittellateinisches Studien und Texte* 8. Leiden: E. J. Brill.

Louis, R., J. Jolivet, and J. Châtillon, eds. 1975. *Pierre Abélard—Pierre le Vénérable*. Paris: Éditions du Centre national de la recherche scientifique.

Luscombe, David E. 1969. *The School of Peter Abelard: The Influence of Abelard's Thought in the Early Scholastic Period*. Cambridge: Cambridge University Press.

———, ed. and trans. 1971. *Peter Abelard's Ethics*. Oxford: Clarendon Press.

———. 1980. *Peter Abelard*. London: Historical Association.

———. 1988a. "From Paris to the Paraclete: The Correspondence of Abelard and Heloise." *Proceedings of the British Academy* 74, 247–83.

———. 1988b. "Peter Abelard." In Dronke 1988b, 279–307.

Marenbon, John. 1997. *The Philosophy of Peter Abelard*. Cambridge: Cambridge University Press.

———. 2006. "The Rediscovery of Peter Abelard's Philosophy." *Journal of the History of Philosophy* 44, 331–51.

McLaughlin, Mary Martin. 1967. "Abelard as Autobiographer: The Motives and Meaning of His 'Story of Calamities.'" *Speculum* 42, 463–88.

———. 1975. "Abelard and the Dignity of Women." In Louis, Jolivet, and Châtillon 1975, 287–334.

———. 2000. "Heloise the Abbess: The Expansion of the Paraclete." In Wheeler 2000, 1–17.

McLaughlin, T. P. 1941. "The Prohibition against Marriage of Canons in the Early Twelfth Century." *Mediaeval Studies* 3, 94–100.

———, ed. 1956. "Abelard's Rule for Religious Women." *Mediaeval Studies* 18, 241–92.

McLeod, Enid. 1971. *Héloïse: A Biography*. 2nd ed. London: Chatto and Windus.

McLeod, Glenda. 1993. "Wholly Guilty, Wholly Innocent: Self-Definition in Héloïse's Letters to Abélard." In *Dear Sister: Medieval Women and the Epistolary Genre*, 64–86. Ed. K. Cherewatuk and U. Wiethaus. Philadelphia: University of Pennsylvania Press.

Mews, Constant J. 1988. "In Search of a Name and Its Significance: A Twelfth-Century Anecdote about Thierry and Peter Abelard." *Traditio* 44, 171–200.

———. 1999. *The Lost Love Letters of Heloise and Abelard: Perceptions of Dialogue in Twelfth-Century France*. Trans. with N. Chiavaroli. New York: St. Martin's.

———. 2005. *Abelard and Heloise*. Oxford: Oxford University Press.

Moncrieff, C. K. Scott, trans. 1926. *The Letters of Abelard and Heloise*. New York: Knopf.

Monfrin, J., ed. 1959. *Historia Calamitatum*. Paris: J. Vrin.

Moore, George, 1926. "Prefatory Letter." In Moncrieff 1926, xv–xxiii.

Muckle, J. T., ed. 1950. "Abelard's Letter of Consolation to a Friend (*Historia Calamitatum*)." *Mediaeval Studies* 12, 163–213.

———. ed. 1953. "The Personal Letters between Abelard and Heloise." *Mediaeval Studies* 15, 47–94.

———. ed. 1955. "The Letter of Heloise on the Religious Life and Abelard's First Reply." *Mediaeval Studies* 17, 240–81.

———. 1964. *The Story of Abelard's Adversities*. Toronto: Pontifical Institute of Mediaeval Studies.

Newman, Barbara. 1992. "Authority, Authenticity, and the Repression of Heloise." *Journal of Medieval and Renaissance Studies* 22, 121–57. Reprinted in *From Virile Woman to WomanChrist: Studies in Medieval Religion and Literature*. Philadelphia: University of Pennsylvania Press, 1995.

Normore, Calvin. 2004. "Abelard's Stoicism and Its Consequences." In Strange and Zupko 2004, 132–47.

Orlandi, G. 1980. "*Minima Abaelardinana:* Note sul testo dell' *Historia Calamitatum*." *Res Publica Litterarum* 3, 131–38.

Pernoud, Régine. 1973. *Heloise and Abelard*. Trans. P. Wiles. New York: Stein and Day.

Radice, Betty, trans. 1974. *The Letters of Abelard and Heloise*. Revised ed. by Michael Clanchy. London: Penguin, 2003.

Robertson, D. W., Jr. 1972. *Abelard and Heloise*. New York: Dial Press.

Rubingh-Bosscher, J. M. A., ed. 1987. *Peter Abelard. Carmen ad Astralabium. A Critical Edition.* Groningen: Rijksuniversiteit.

Southern, R. W. 1970. "The Letters of Abelard and Heloise." In *Medieval Humanism and Other Studies*, 95–104. Oxford: Blackwell.

Spade, Paul Vincent, trans. 1995. *Peter Abelard: Ethical Writings.* Indianapolis and Cambridge, MA: Hackett Publishing.

Stewart, Marc, and David Wulstan, eds. 2003. *The Poetic and Musical Legacy of Heloise and Abelard.* Ottawa: Institute of Mediaeval Music.

Strange, Steven K., and Jack Zupko, eds. 2004. *Stoicism: Traditions and Transformations.* Cambridge: Cambridge University Press.

Thomas, R., J. Jolivet, D. E. Luscombe, and L. M. de Rijk, eds. 1980. *Petrus Abaelardus (1079–1142): Person, Werke und Wirkung.* Trier: Paulinus Verlag.

Twain, Mark. 1869. *The Innocents Abroad.* Hartford, CT: American Publishing Company.

Von Moos, Peter. 2003. "Die *Epistolae duorum amantium* und die säkulare Religion der Liebe." *Studi Medievali* 3rd series 1, 1–115.

Waddell, Chrysogonus. 1980. "Peter Abelard as Creator of Liturgical Texts." In Thomas et al. 1980, 267–80.

———. 1987. *The Paraclete Statutes: Institutiones Nostrae.* Trappist, KY: Gethsemani Abbey.

Weinrich, Lorenz. 1969. "Peter Abaelard as Musician." *The Musical Quarterly* 55, 464–86.

Wheeler, Bonnie, ed. 2000. *Listening to Heloise: The Voice of a Twelfth-Century Woman.* London: Macmillan.

Ziolkowski, Jan. 2004. "Lost and Not Yet Found: Heloise, Abelard, and the *Epistolae duorum amantium.*" *Journal of Medieval Latin* 14, 171–202.

———, trans. Forthcoming. *Letters of Peter Abelard, Beyond the Personal.* Washington, DC: Catholic University of America Press.

# INDEX OF PASSAGES
## QUOTED, CITED, AND DISCUSSED

# General Index

Aaron, 130, 139, 141–42, 192
abbess. *See* deaconess or abbess
Abel, 122
Abelard, Peter, abbot, as, xiii, 36–
    37, 43–45, 50, 53–54, 98; affair
    with Heloise of, xi, xiii–xvii,
    xl, 10–20, 306–12; *Calamities*
    of, xii–xvii, xx–xxiii, xxvi–
    xxix, xxxiv, xli, 279, 304, 315;
    castration of, xi, xiii, xv–xvii,
    xxiii, xxv, xl, 18–20, 39–40, 54,
    58n13, 75–76, 93–94, 95–98,
    100–102, 311; *Confession of
    Faith* of, xvii; conflict with
    church of, xiii, xvii–xviii, xli,
    22–27, 35–36, 260–61; death of,
    xvii–xviii, xxiv, xli, 69–70, 72–
    74, 91–92, 269–71, 272–73,
    275n6; *De Trinitate* or *Theologia
    "Summi Boni"* of, xl, 21–24, 50;
    ethical writings of, xxiii–xxiv;
    fame of, xi, xv, 3, 5–6, 9, 21, 25,
    33, 35–36, 57–58, 269, 271,
    275n6; *Logica "Ingredientibus"*
    of, 4n6; marriage to Heloise,
    xiii, xl, 18, 78, 97, 310–11; Para-
    clete and, xiii, xviii, xxiii, xxv,
    xl, 21, 33–35, 38–43, 50, 52–54,
    65n7, 68–70, 106–7, 126, 127,
    272n1, 273n2; poet, as, 12, 58,
    62, 279–301; teacher, as, xi–
    xiii, xvi–xvii, 5–6, 8–9, 12, 20–
    23, 31–33, 52–53, 106–7, 259;
    *Theologia Christiana* of, 22n48;
    *Theologia "Scholarium"* of,
    22n48; writer, as, xi–xii, xxvi–
    xxix; youth of, 1–3. *See also*
    Index of Passages

Abigail, 65
Abraham, 111, 121, 206, 227, 286
Abraham, disciple of Sisoi, 117,
    220
Academy, Plato's, 32, 266
Achilles, 323
Ackerman, Diane, 304n3
Adam, 151, 283
Adam, abbot, 20–21, 26, 29–30
Adams, Henry, xix
Aegean Sea, 310n9
Aeschines the Socratic, 56
Agatha, Saint, 160
Agatho, abbot, 176
Agaton, 308–9
Agnes, 161
Ahasuerus, King, 40
Ajax, 6
Alberic of Rheims, 9, 22–24, 26,
    50, 303
Albula. *See* Tiber River
Alexander the Great, 183
Alexandria, 21n46, 36n83, 137,
    139, 195
Alexiou, Margaret, 284
Alluis, Jacques, 303
Amalech, 289
Amazons, 267–68
Ambrose, Saint, 166. *See also*
    Index of Passages
Ananias, 203, 239
Andreas Capellanus, 303
Andrew, 158
angels, 40, 70, 77, 102, 135, 184,
    195, 207, 218, 230, 266, 270–71,
    282
Anna, prophetess, 128, 143, 151,
    154–55, 283n3

347

cellaress, 185, 201, 202–3
Cenchrae, 146
Cephas. *See* Peter, apostle
Challoner, Richard, xxxv
Châlons-sur-Marne, 2n3
Chalon-sur-Saône, xviii, xli, 270
Champagne, 21n46, 30n66
chantress, 185, 200
Charrier, Charlotte, 304n2, 305nn4–6
Charybdis, 17, 95, 261
Chase, Wayland Johnson, 249n261
chastity, 138, 149, 151, 160–65, 168–69, 171–72, 181, 237, 254
Chaucer, Geoffrey: *The Canterbury Tales* of, 14n28
Christ (Bridegroom, Lamb, Lord, Son, etc.). *See* Trinity
Christian Bible. *See* Index of Passages
Christmas or Nativity, 34, 211
Chrysostom, John. *See* Index of Passages
Cicero, xix, 15, 57n10, 170–71, 310. *See also* Index of Passages
Clanchy, Michael T., xiin1, xviin2, xixn7, xxivn11, 1n1, 8n16, 9n18, 10n21, 14n27, 23n51
Claudia, vestal virgin, 162–63
Claudius, 146
Clinia, 323
Clotilda of Burgundy, 67n18
Clovis, 67
Cluny, xviii, 265, 268–70, 272–75
Cono of Palestrina, bishop, 22–24, 26–28
consent, doctrine of, xxiii, 78, 122–23, 300
Constable, Giles, xxxv, 265n1, 270n18, 272n1, 315n2
convent chapter meetings, 206, 208–11
convent diet, 118, 202–3, 211–35. *See also* fasting; meat; wine

convent discipline, 200, 206–8
convent officials, 183–204. *See also* deaconess or abbess
convents, presence of men in, 107–8, 126, 195–99, 200–1, 204, 211
convents, reading in, 125, 200, 205–6, 211–12, 243–55, 258–59
Corbeil (town), xl, 3
Cornelia, xx, 20, 101, 311
Cours, Nicolas Rémond des, 303
Crispinus, 164
Croton, 170
Cupid, 108
Cyprian, council of (*Concilio Cypriani*), 209n119
Cyprian, saint, 209

Dagobert (Abelard's brother), 2n2
Dalila, 77
Damocles, sword of, 45n111
Daniel, 27, 129
Dante Alighieri: *Paradiso* of, 164n138
David, xxxv, 65, 111, 130, 152, 206, 289. *See also* Index of Passages *under* Hebrew Bible: Psalms
deaconess or abbess, 141, 145–48, 185–99, 201, 202, 203–4, 207, 210–11, 230, 234
deacons, seven, 124–25, 136–37, 195
Deborah, judge, 140, 151–52, 267–68, 284
Delos, 310
Demetrias, 167
Denis/Dionysius, Saint, 20n43, 29n65
Denise/Dionysia (Abelard's sister), 2n2, 13
dialectic, 2, 4–5, 87n6, 260, 319n5, 321n8
Diana, 310n9
Dido, xx